# La Corda d'Oro

**8**
**Story & Art by Yuki Kure**

# La Corda d'Oro

## CONTENTS
### Volume 8

## Kahoko Hino
### (General Education School, 2nd year)

The heroine. She knows nothing about music, but she still finds herself participating in the music competition equipped with a magic violin.

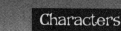

## Ryotaro Tsuchiura
### (General Education, 2nd year)

A member of the soccer team who seems to be looking after Kahoko as a fellow Gen Ed student.

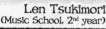

## Len Tsukimori
### (Music School, 2nd year)

A violin major and a cold perfectionist from a musical family of unquestionable talent.

## Kazuki Hihara
### (Music school, 3rd year)

An energetic and friendly trumpet major and a fan of anything fun.

## Keiichi Shimizu
### (Music school, 1st year)

A cello major who walks to the beat of his own drum and is often lost in the world of music. He is also often asleep.

## Azuma Yunoki
### (Music school, 3rd year)

A flute major and the son of a graceful and kind traditional flower arrangement master. He has a dedicated fan club called the "Yunoki Guard."

## Hiroto Kanazawa
### (Music teacher)

The contest coordinator whose lazy demeanor suggests he is avoiding any hassle.

The music fairy Lili, who got Kahoko caught up in this affair. ↓

## Story

Our story is set at Seiso Academy, which is split into the General Education School and the Music School. Kahoko, a Gen Ed student, encounters a music fairy named Lili, who gives her a magic violin that anyone can play. Suddenly, Kahoko finds herself in the school's music competition, with good-looking, quirky Music School students as her fellow contestants! Kahoko comes to accept her daunting task and finds herself enjoying music. But on the day of the Third Selection, Lili gives Kahoko some ominous news: the magic of the violin is fading, and this may be her last performance. Refusing to forfeit, Kahoko takes the stage...

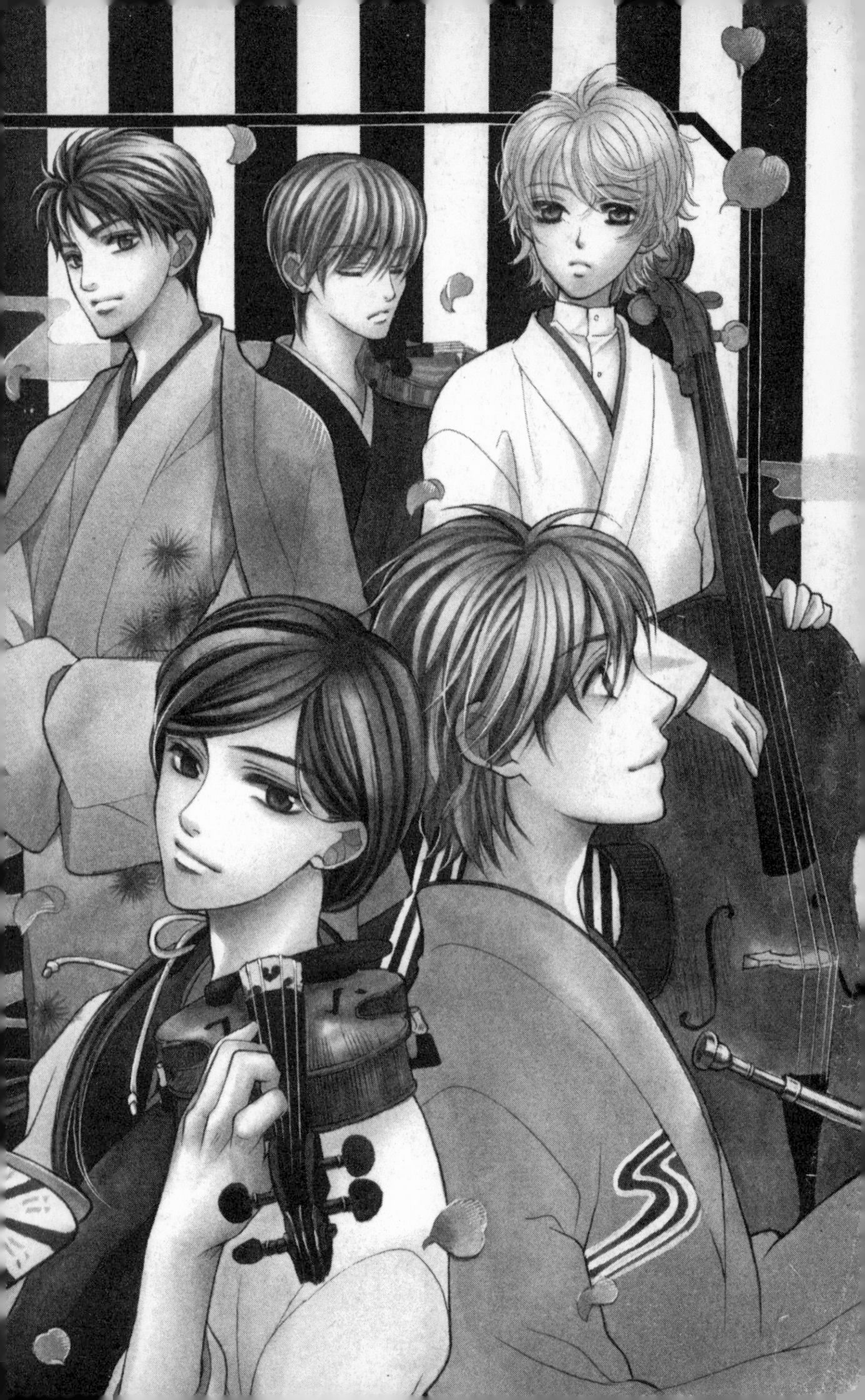

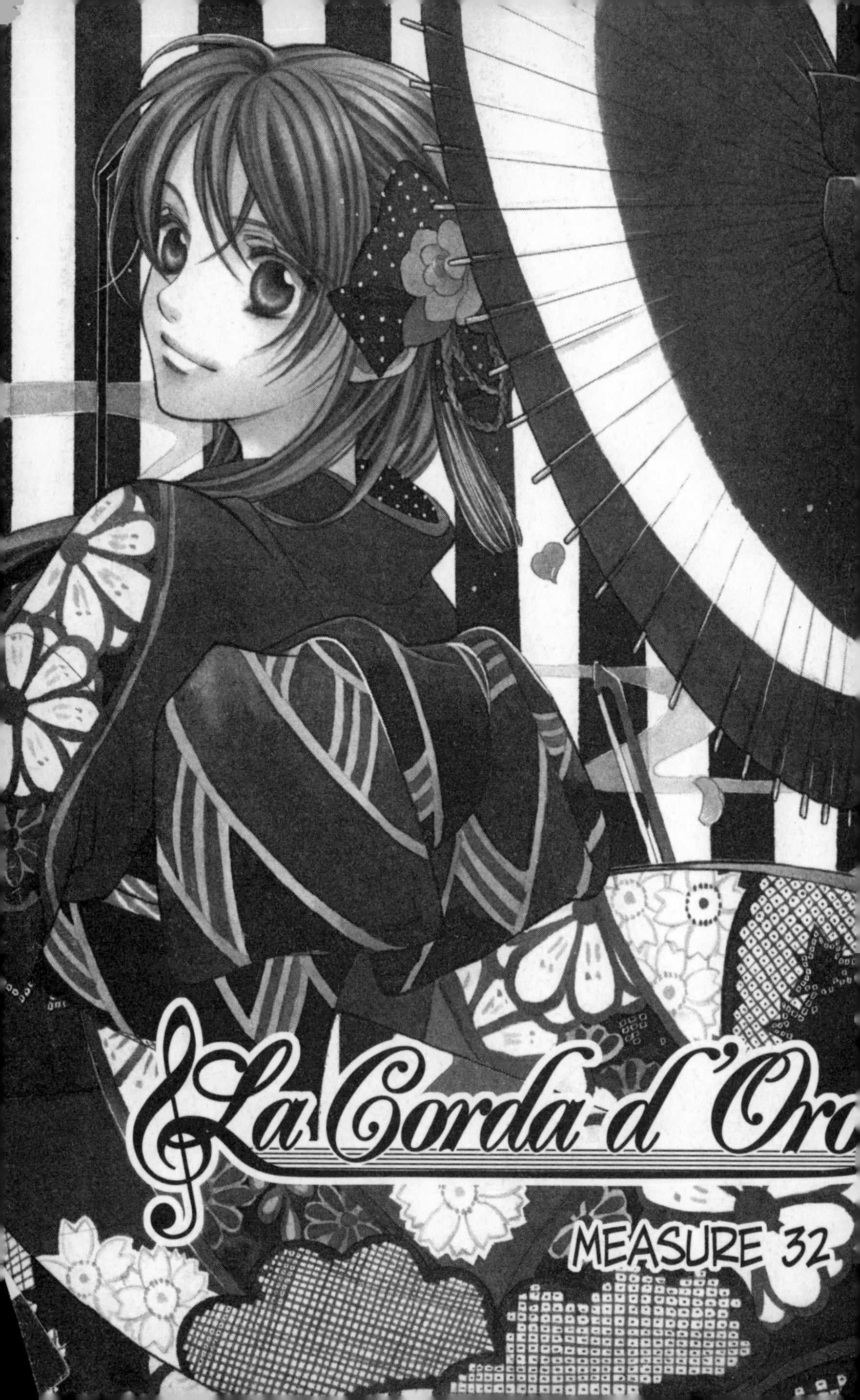
La Corda d'Oro
MEASURE 32

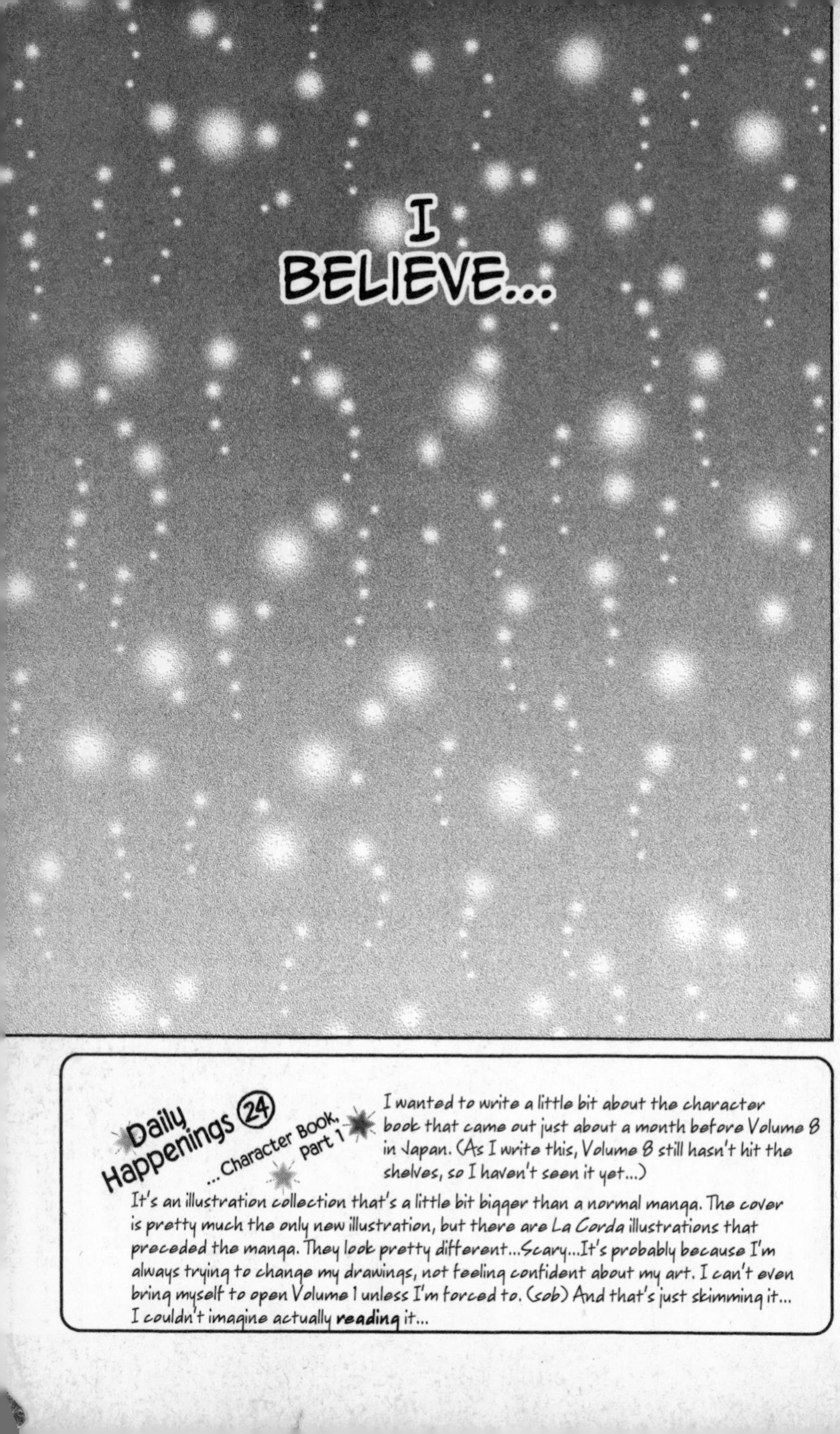
I BELIEVE...

Daily Happenings 24 ...Character Book, Part 1

I wanted to write a little bit about the character book that came out just about a month before Volume 8 in Japan. (As I write this, Volume 8 still hasn't hit the shelves, so I haven't seen it yet...)

It's an illustration collection that's a little bit bigger than a normal manga. The cover is pretty much the only new illustration, but there are *La Corda* illustrations that preceded the manga. They look pretty different...Scary...It's probably because I'm always trying to change my drawings, not feeling confident about my art. I can't even bring myself to open Volume 1 unless I'm forced to. (sob) And that's just skimming it... I couldn't imagine actually **reading** it...

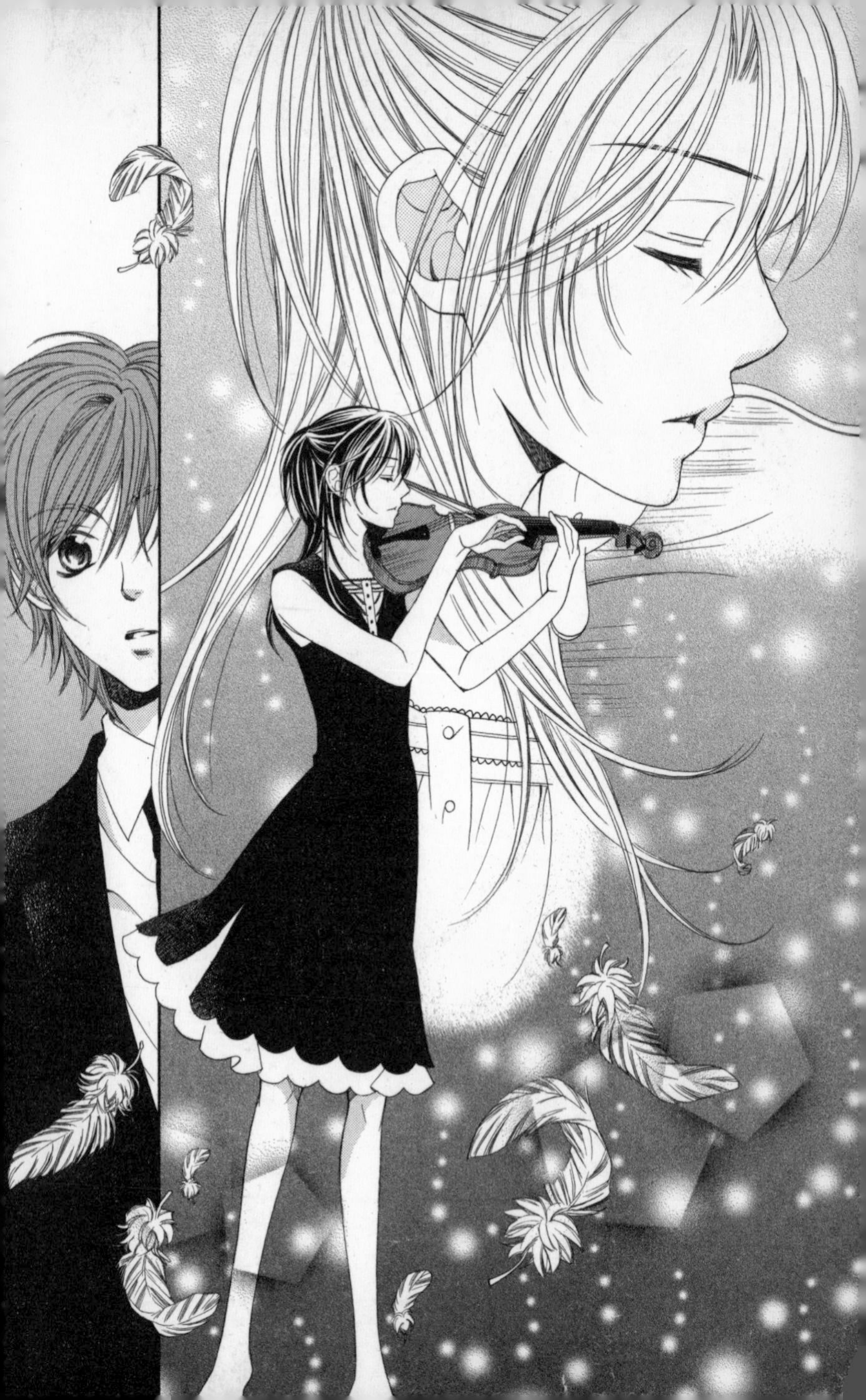

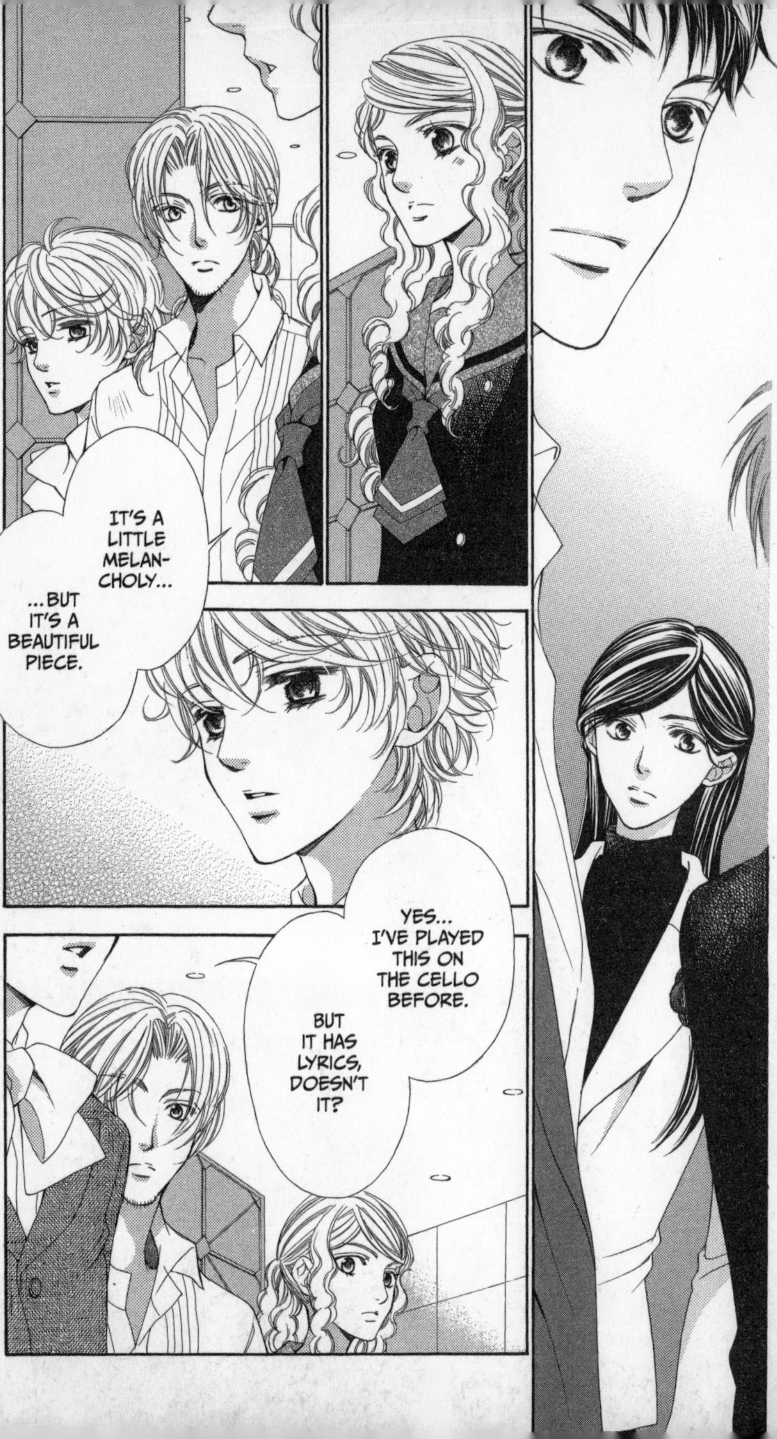
IT'S A LITTLE MELAN-CHOLY...
...BUT IT'S A BEAUTIFUL PIECE.
YES... I'VE PLAYED THIS ON THE CELLO BEFORE.
BUT IT HAS LYRICS, DOESN'T IT?

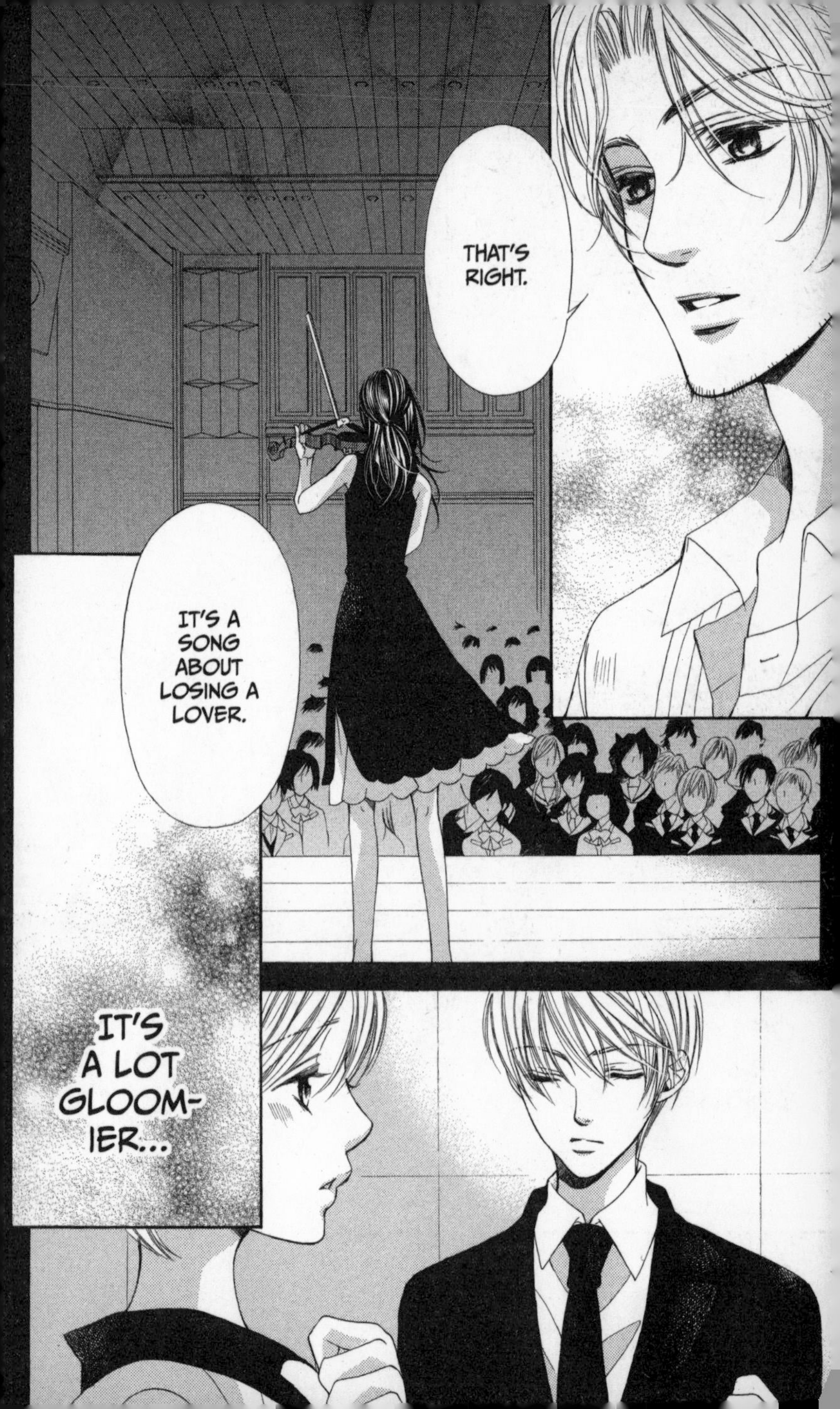
THAT'S RIGHT.
IT'S A SONG ABOUT LOSING A LOVER.
IT'S A LOT GLOOM-IER...

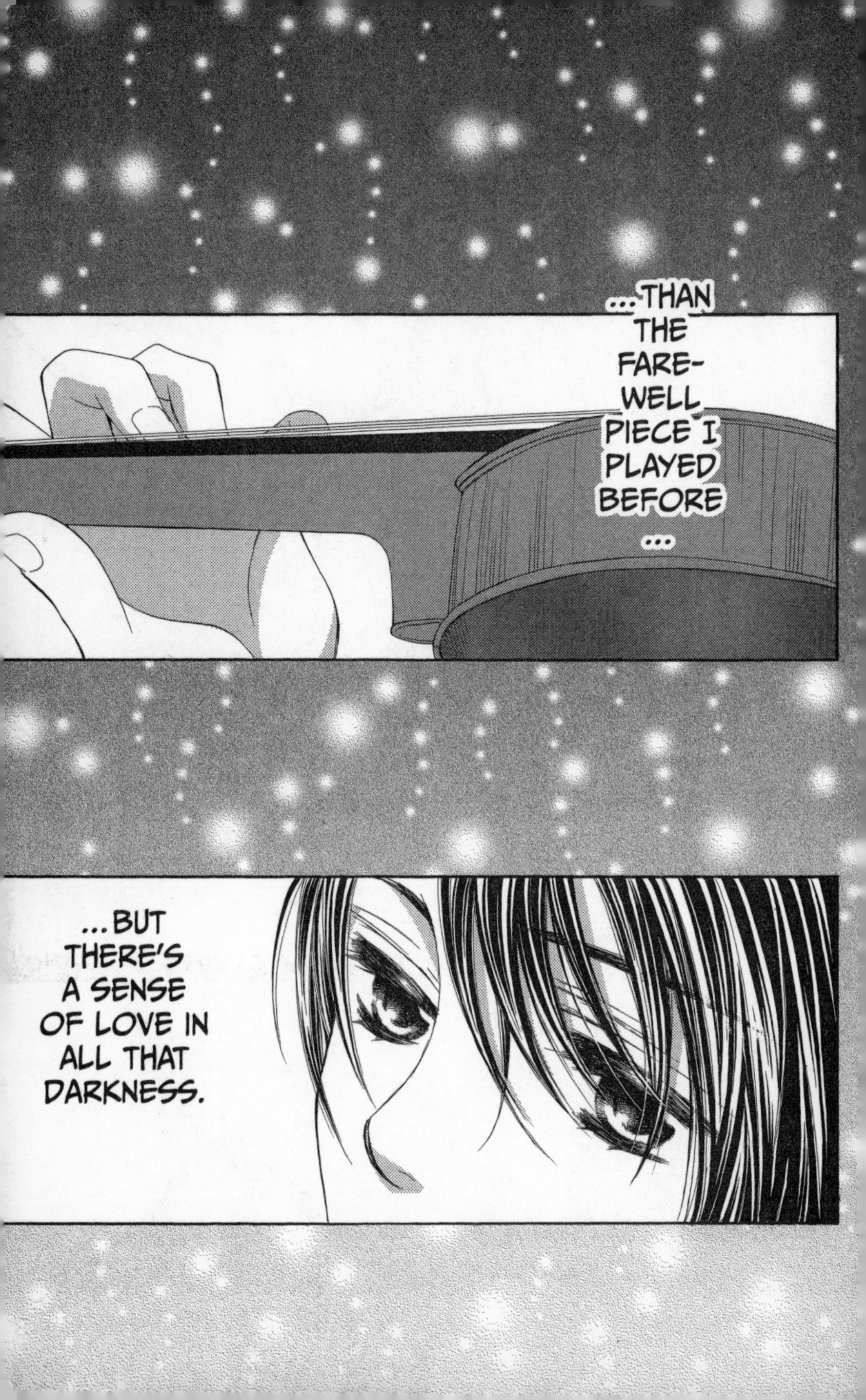
...THAN THE FARE-WELL PIECE I PLAYED BEFORE...
...BUT THERE'S A SENSE OF LOVE IN ALL THAT DARKNESS.

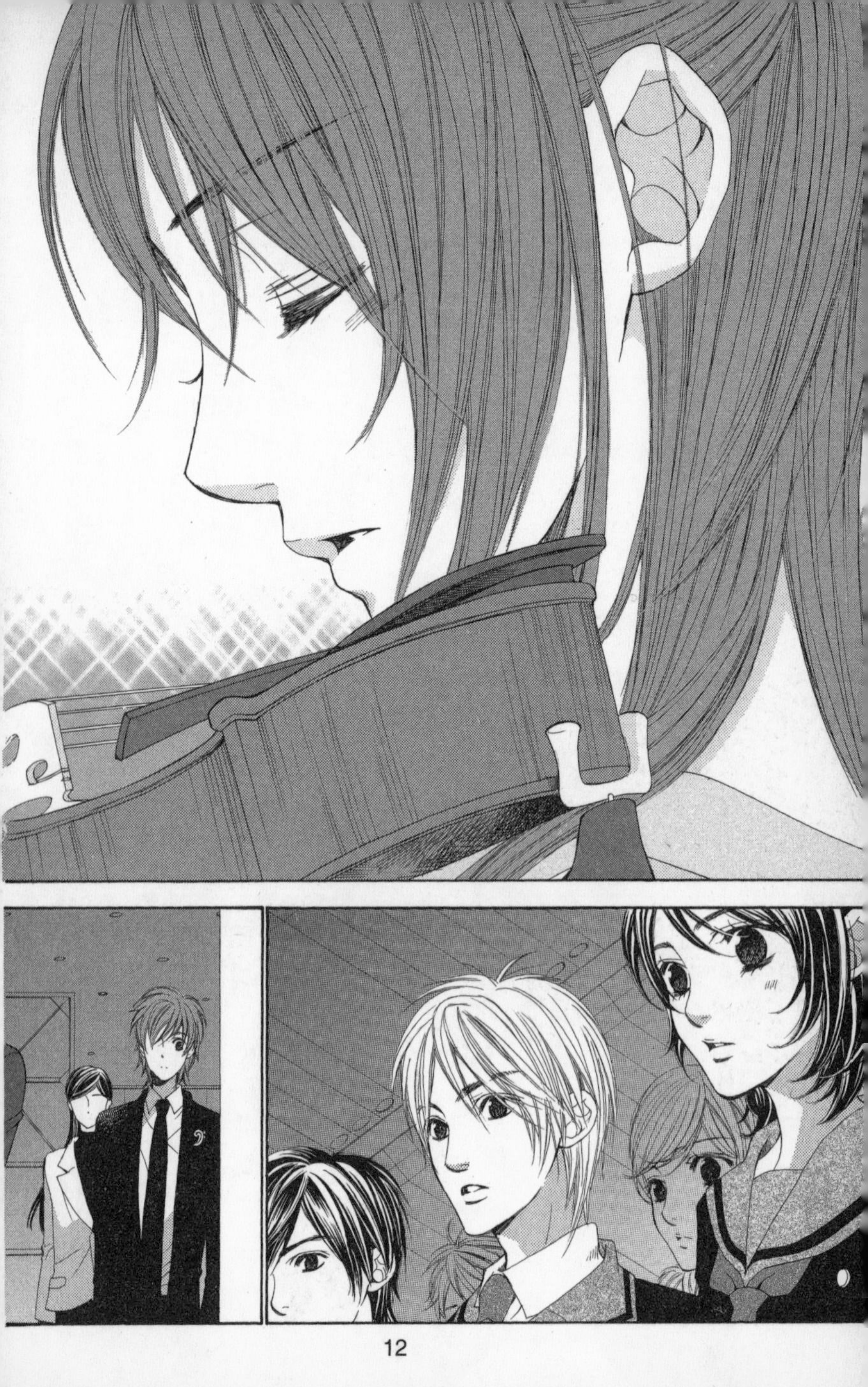

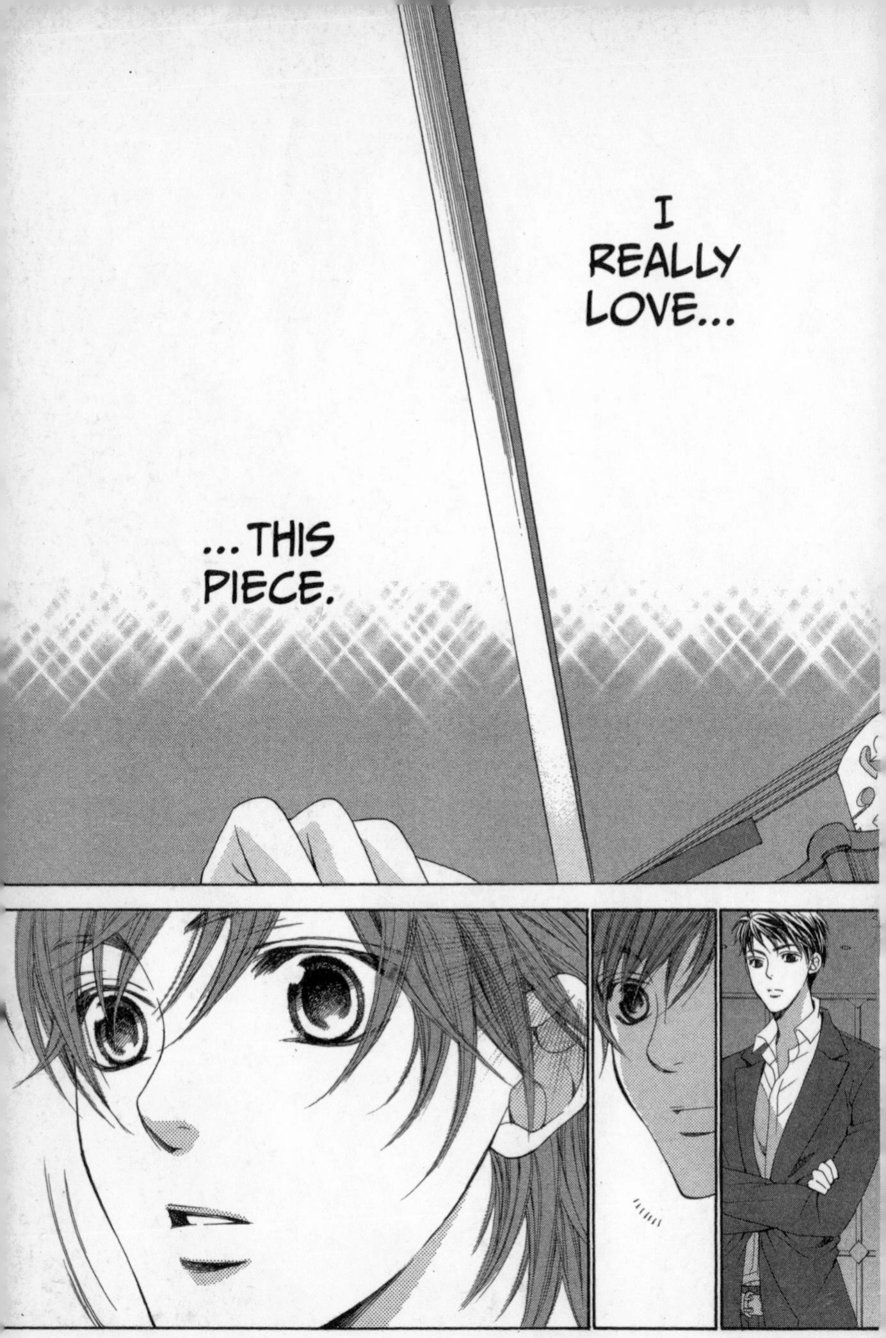
I REALLY LOVE...
...THIS PIECE.

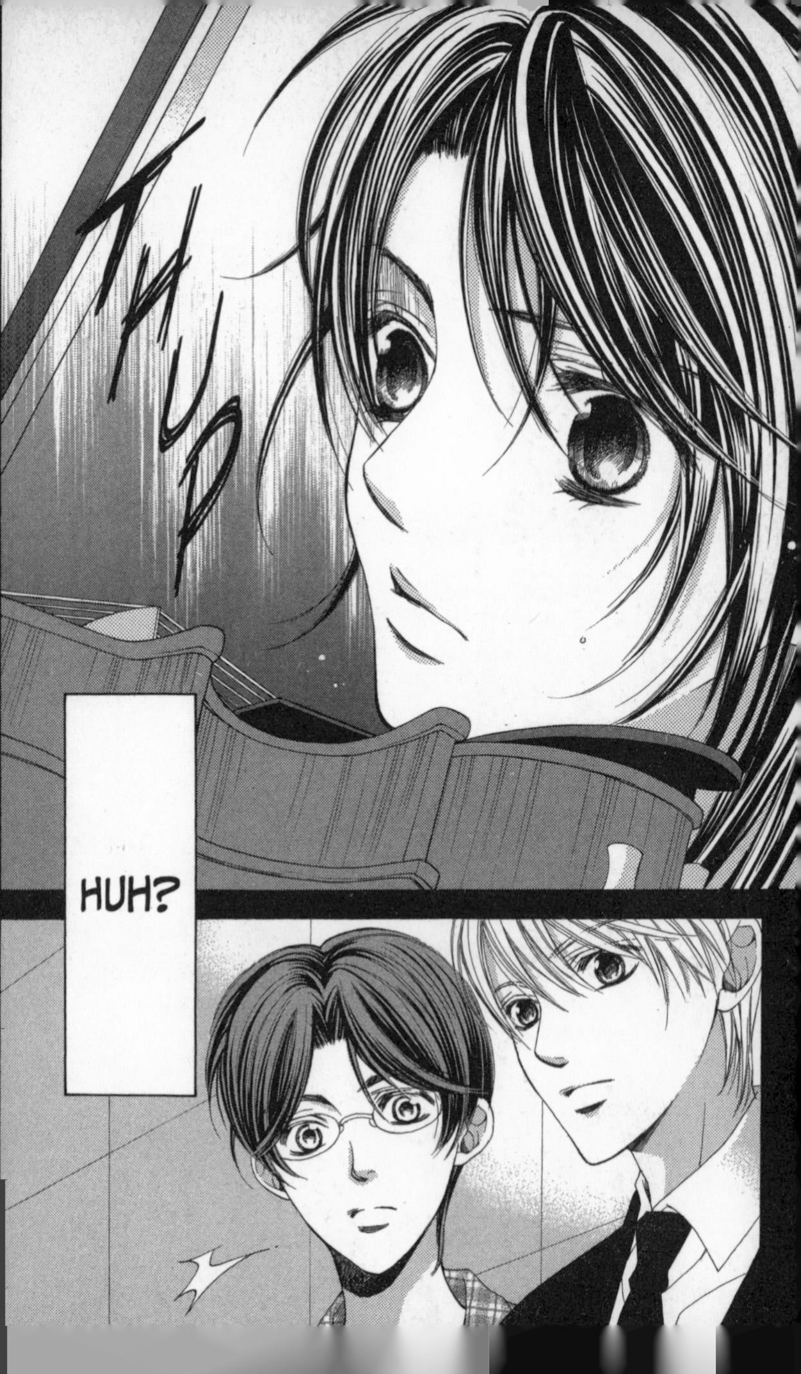
THUD
HUH?

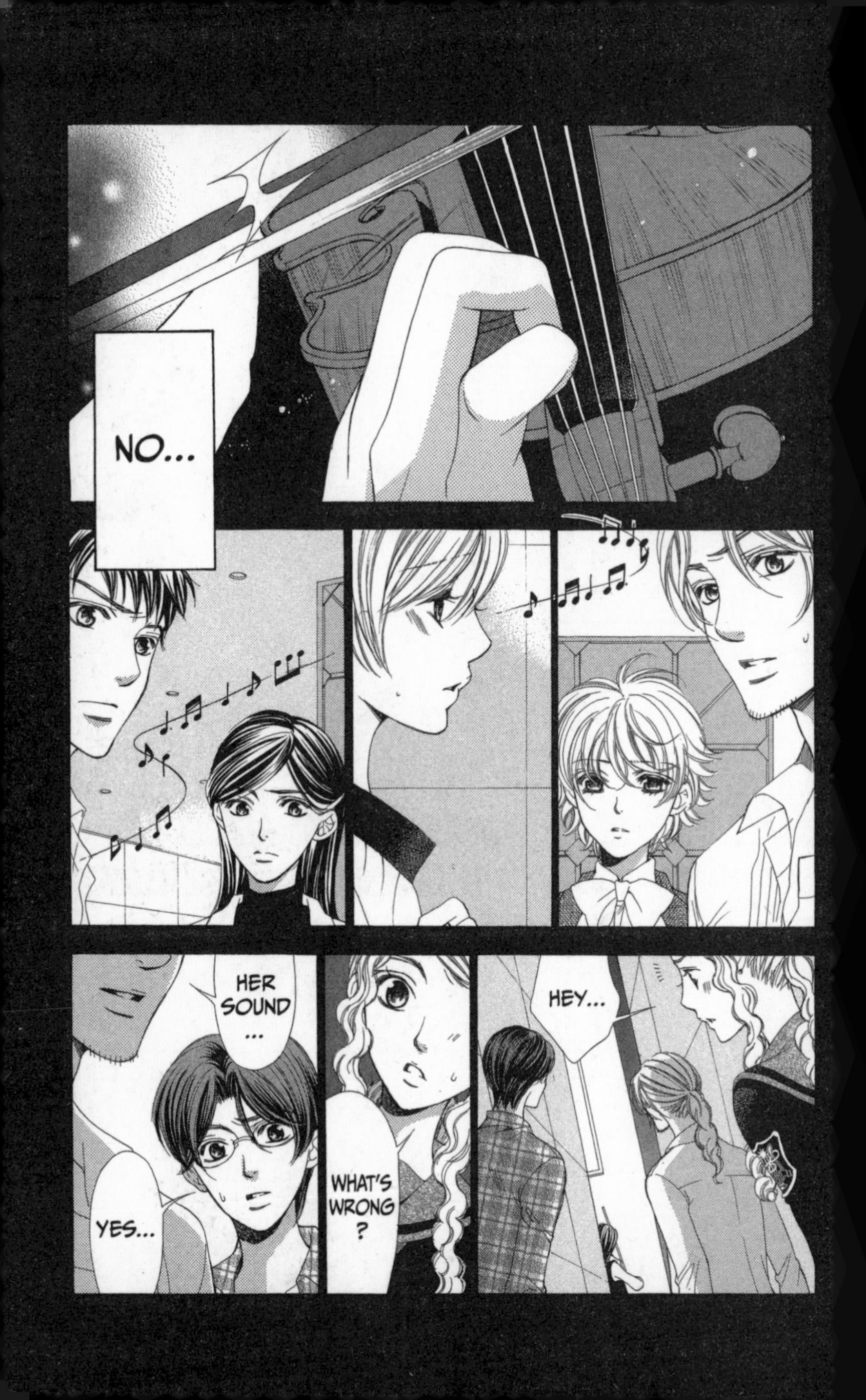
NO...
HEY...
WHAT'S WRONG?
HER SOUND ...
YES...

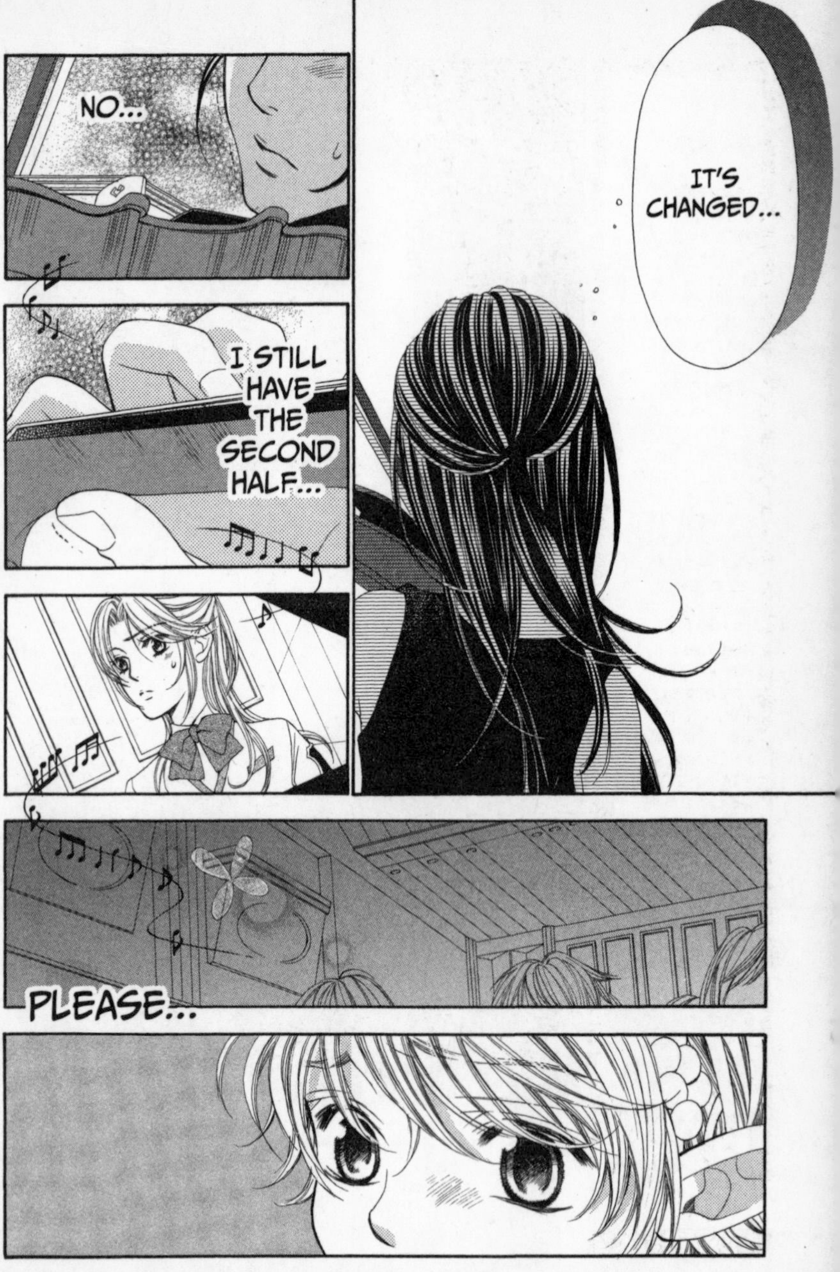
IT'S CHANGED...
NO...
I STILL HAVE THE SECOND HALF...
PLEASE...

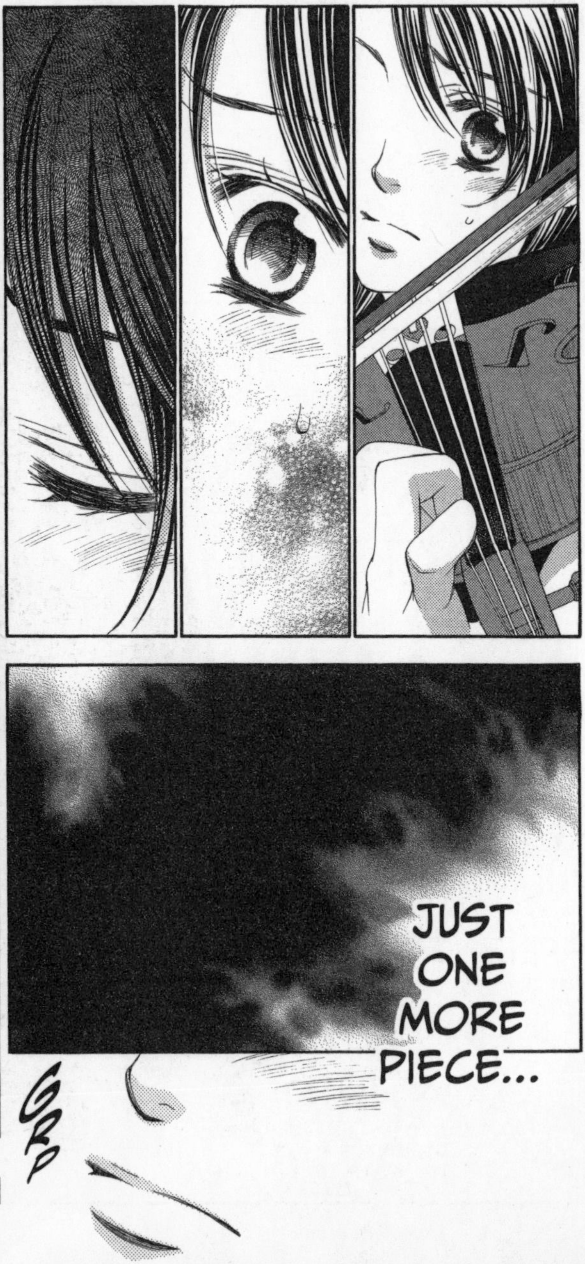
JUST ONE MORE PIECE...
GRP

## ONE

Hello. ✷
Thank you so much for purchasing Volume 8 of *La Corda*. The cover for this volume is an illustration of the three girls, because the last volume was the five boys. I think this was the first time I'd ever drawn just girls on a cover, so it was very refreshing. Although their hair kind of resembles a traffic light... I'd be grateful if you could let that slide. (lol) Kahoko really seems like a jeans person to me, so I dress her in denim a lot. I always want to dress her up in something not too sweet, like shorts. In contrast, I always want to dress Shoko in something elegant that falls below her knees... ↘

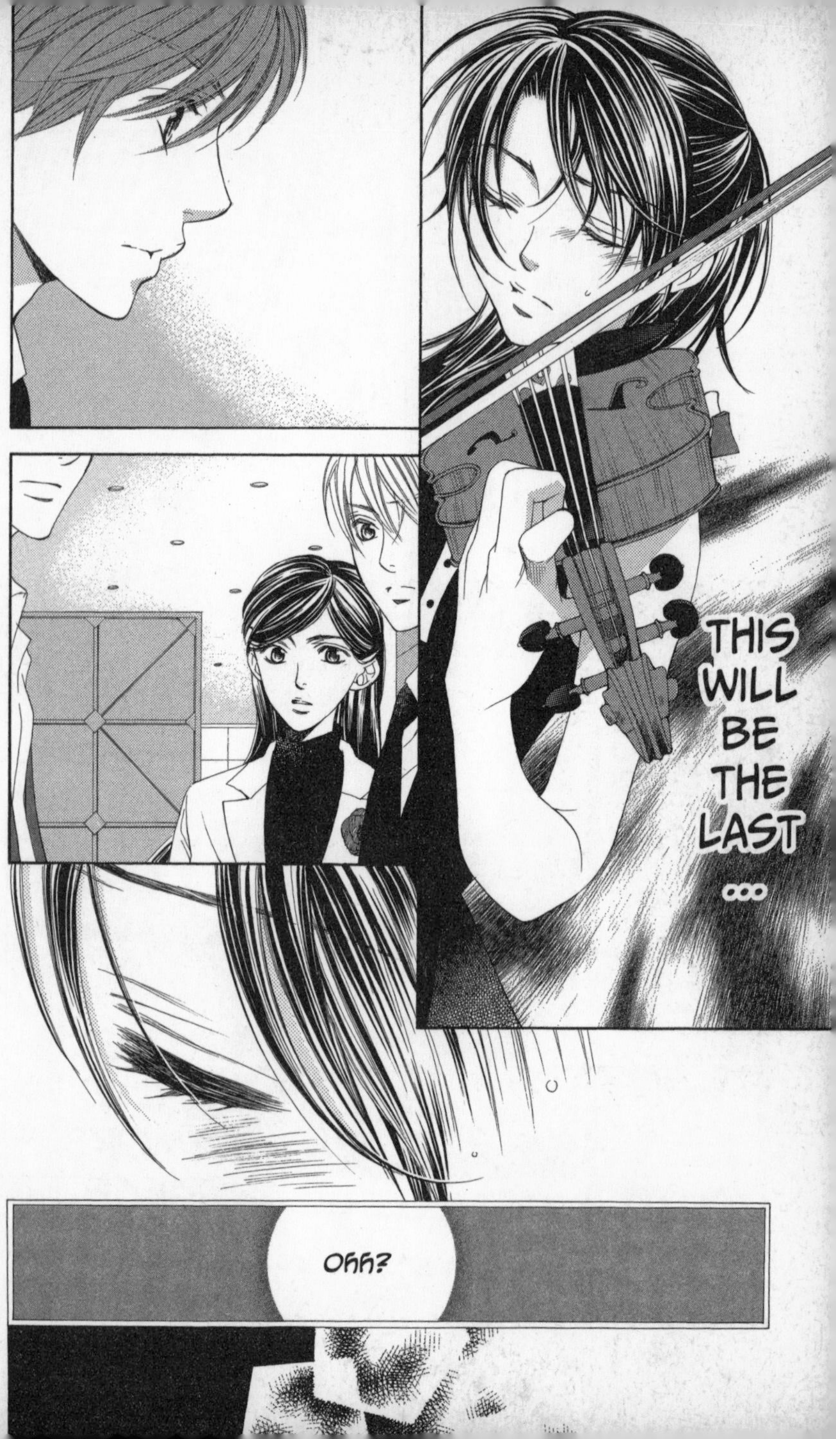
THIS WILL BE THE LAST...
Ohh?

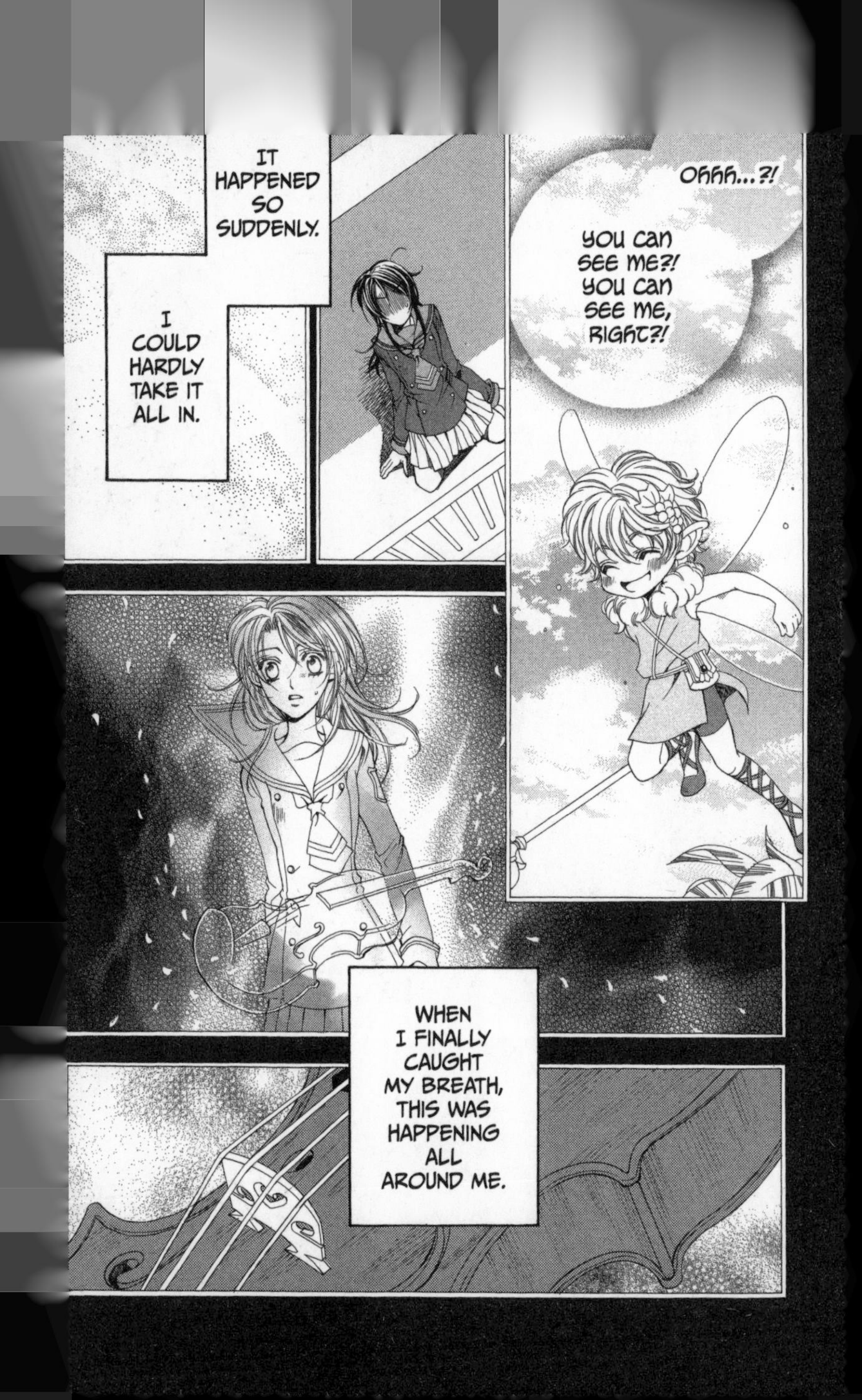
OHHH...?!
YOU CAN SEE ME?! YOU CAN SEE ME, RIGHT?!
IT HAPPENED SO SUDDENLY.
I COULD HARDLY TAKE IT ALL IN.
WHEN I FINALLY CAUGHT MY BREATH, THIS WAS HAPPENING ALL AROUND ME.

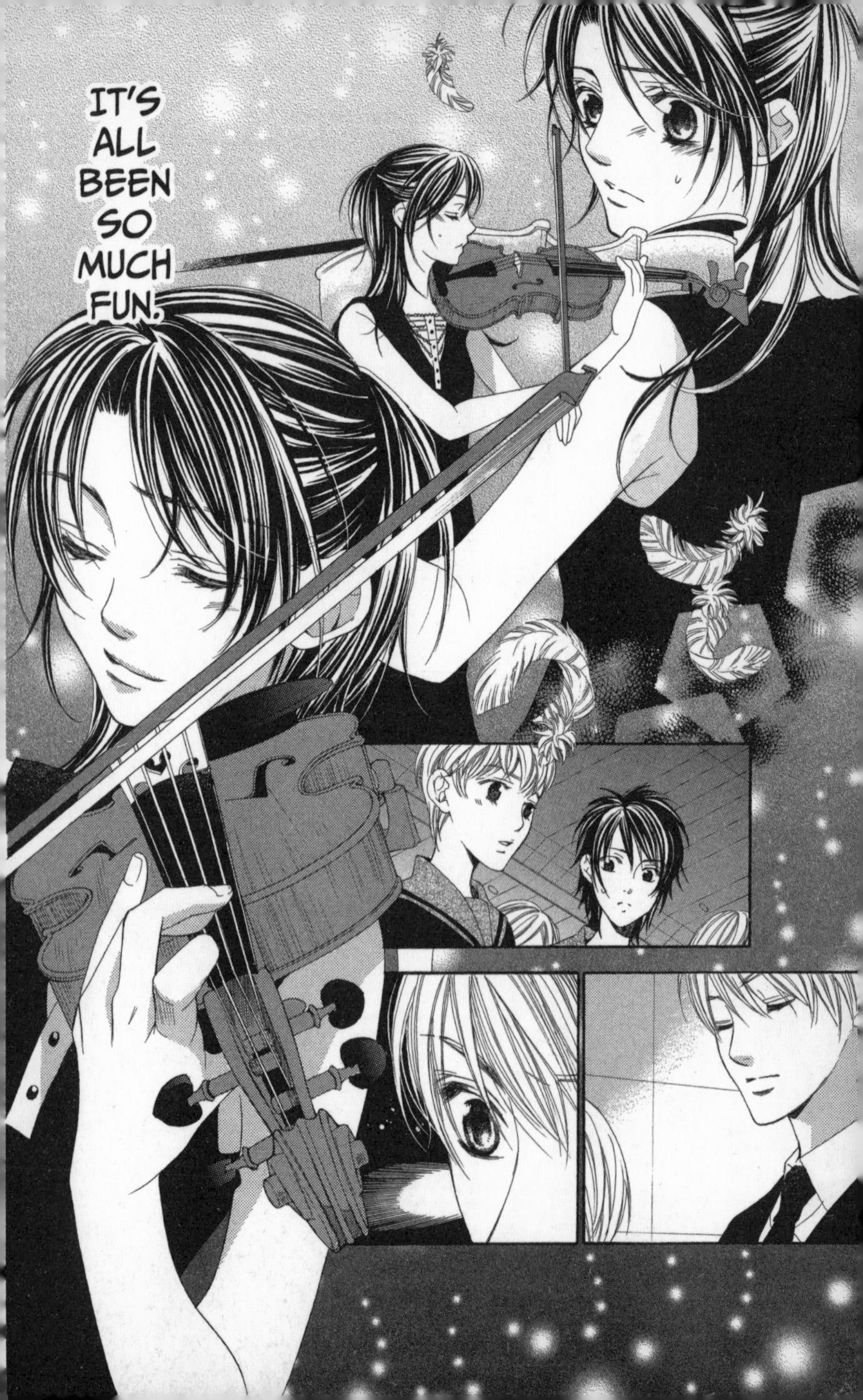
IT'S ALL BEEN SO MUCH FUN.

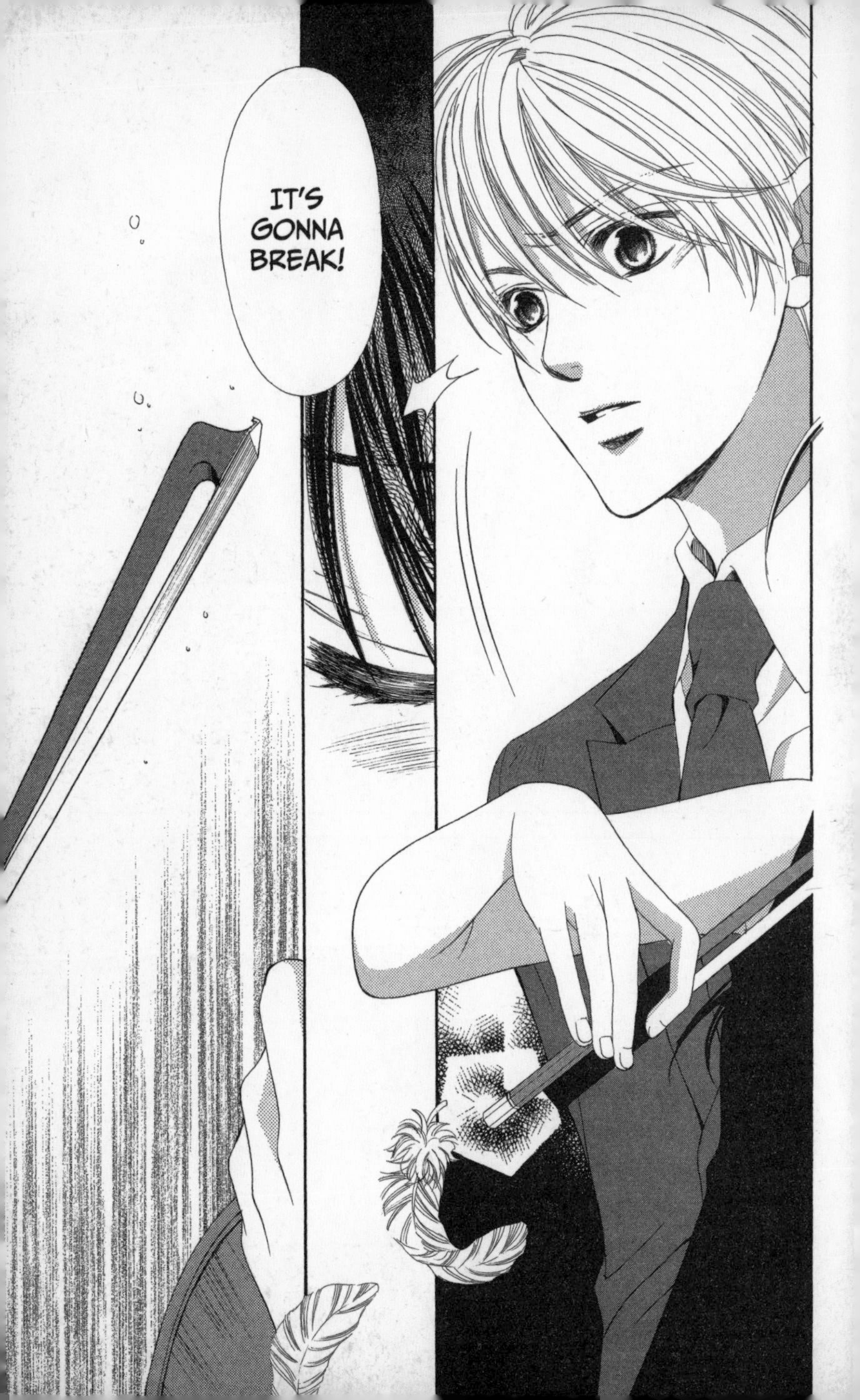
IT'S GONNA BREAK!

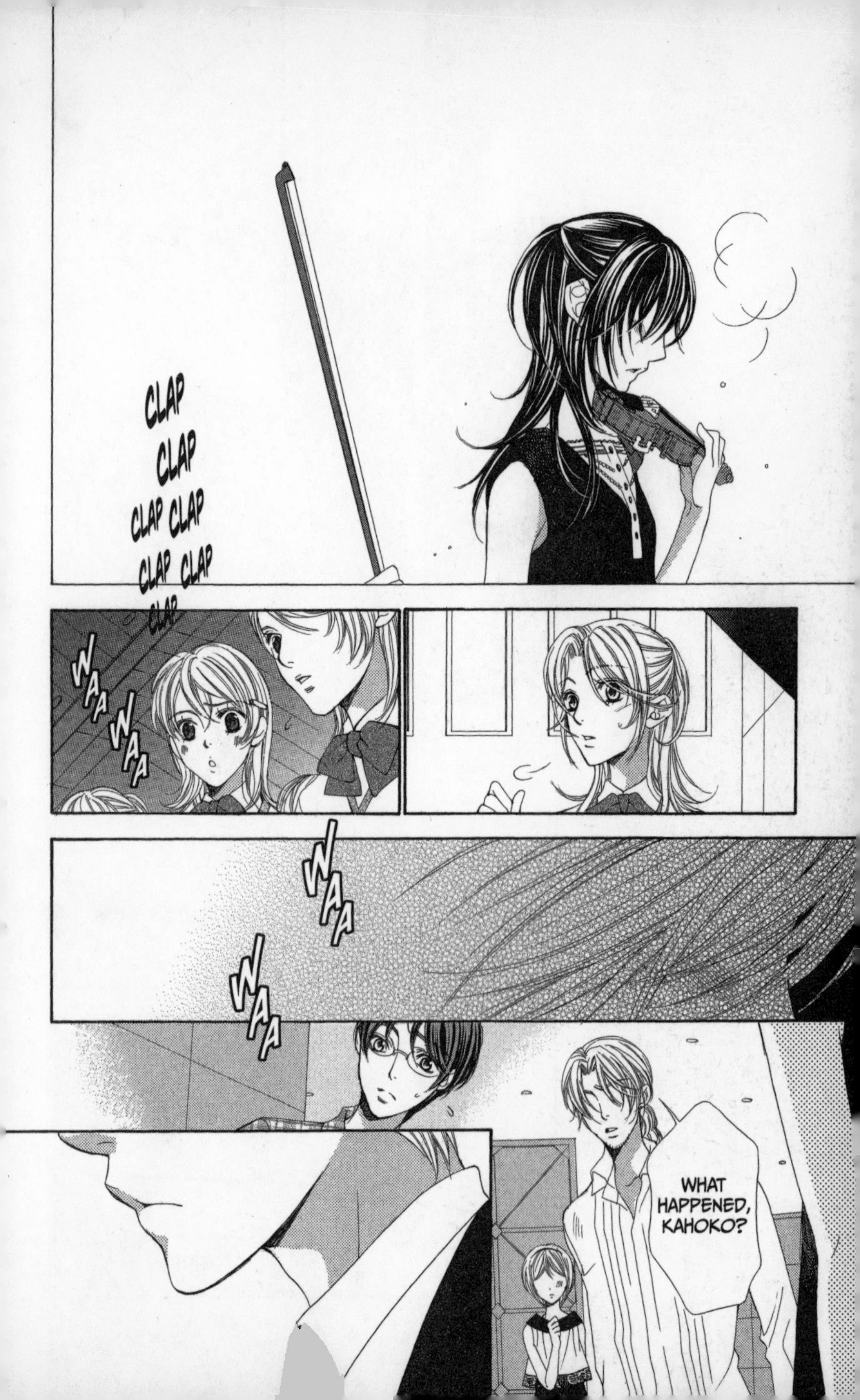
CLAP
CLAP
CLAP CLAP
CLAP CLAP
CLAP
WAA WAA WAA
WAA
WAA
WHAT HAPPENED, KAHOKO?

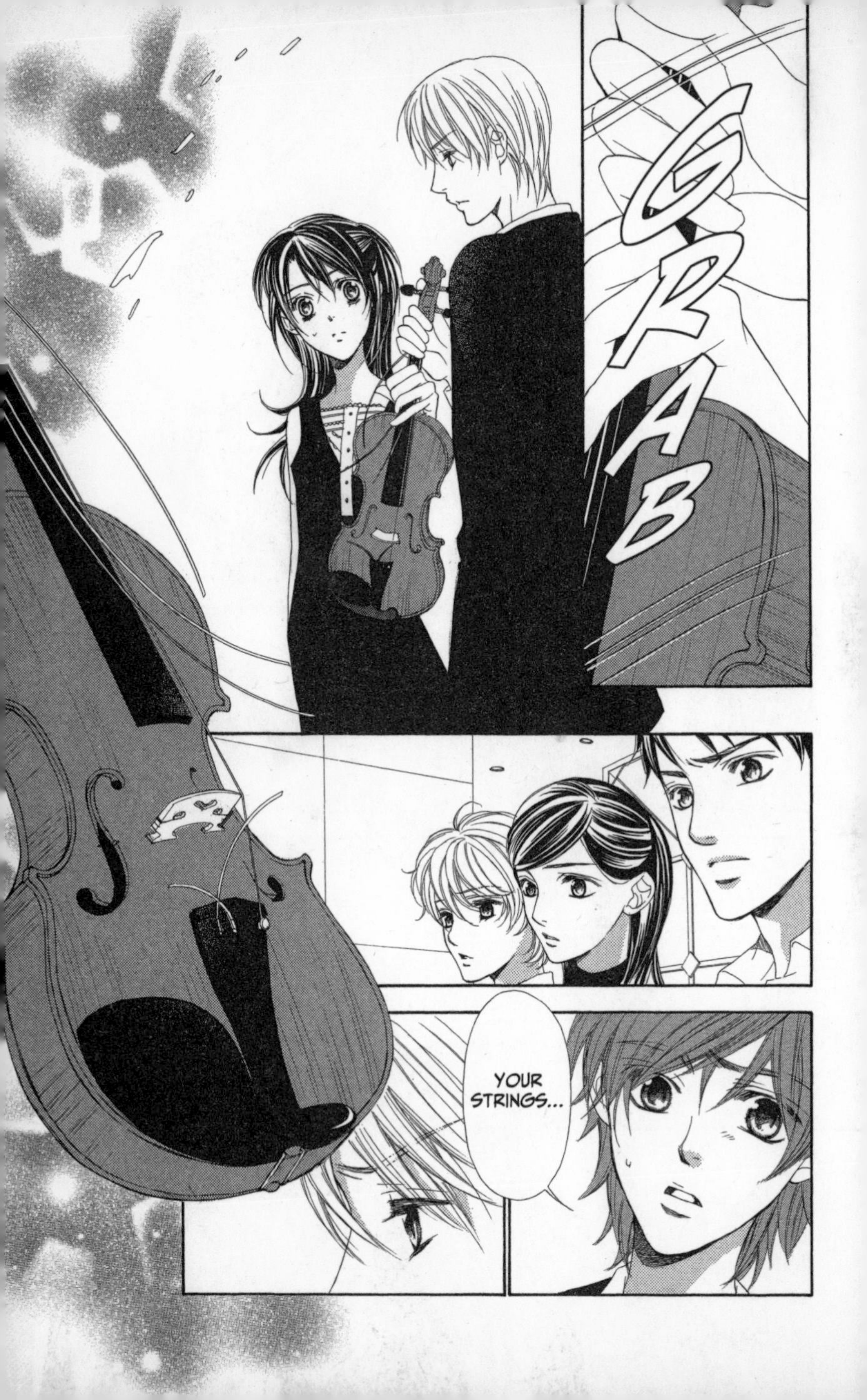
GRAB
YOUR STRINGS...

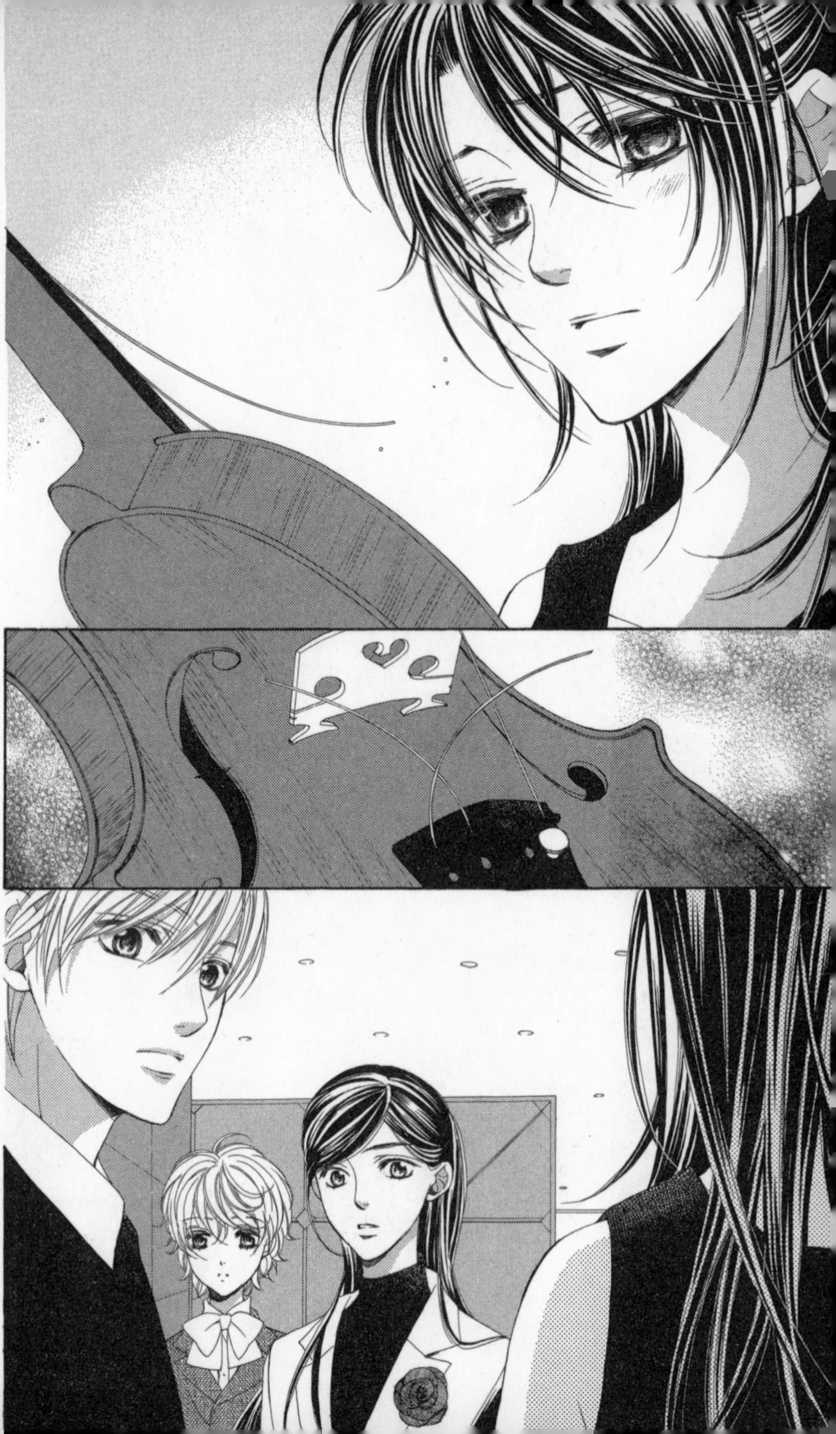

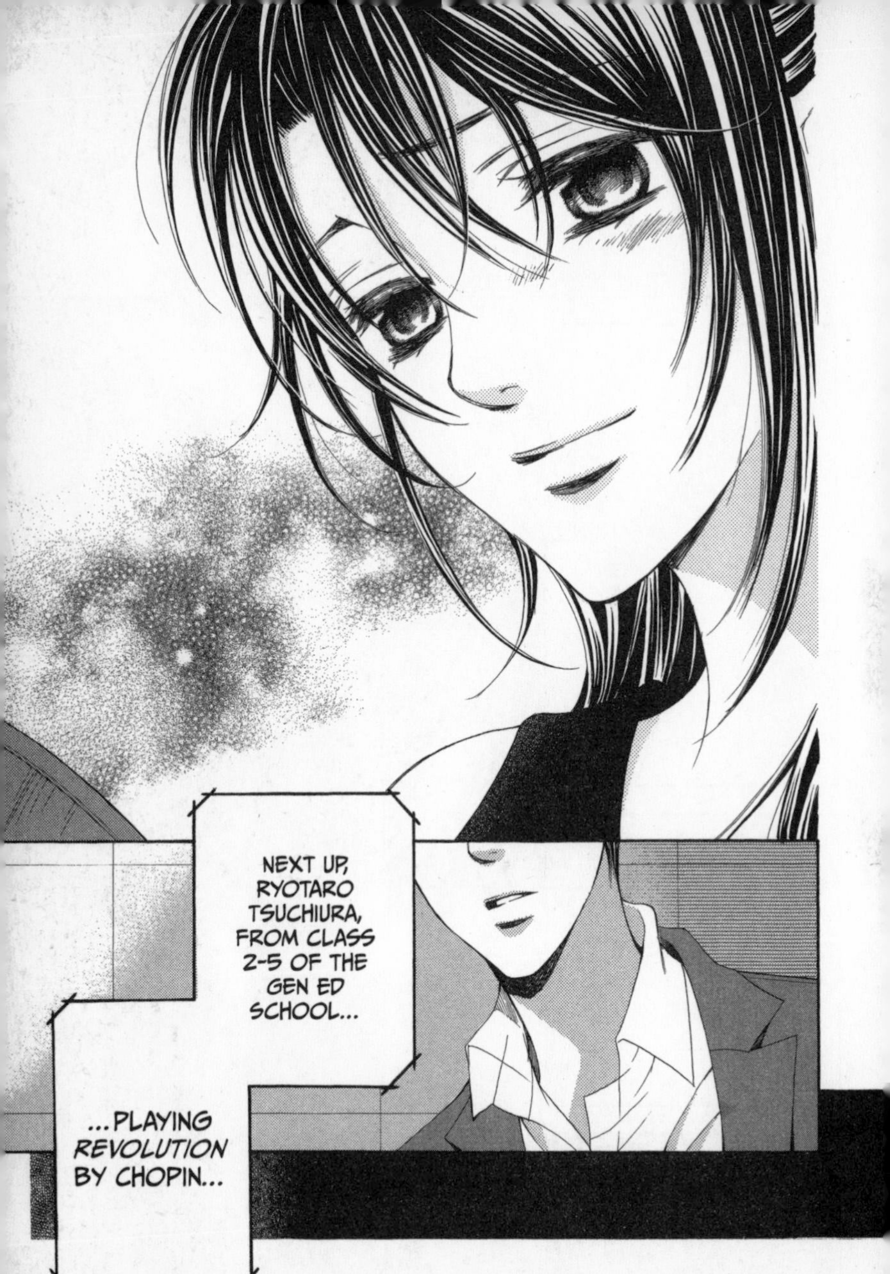
NEXT UP, RYOTARO TSUCHIURA, FROM CLASS 2-5 OF THE GEN ED SCHOOL...
...PLAYING *REVOLUTION* BY CHOPIN...

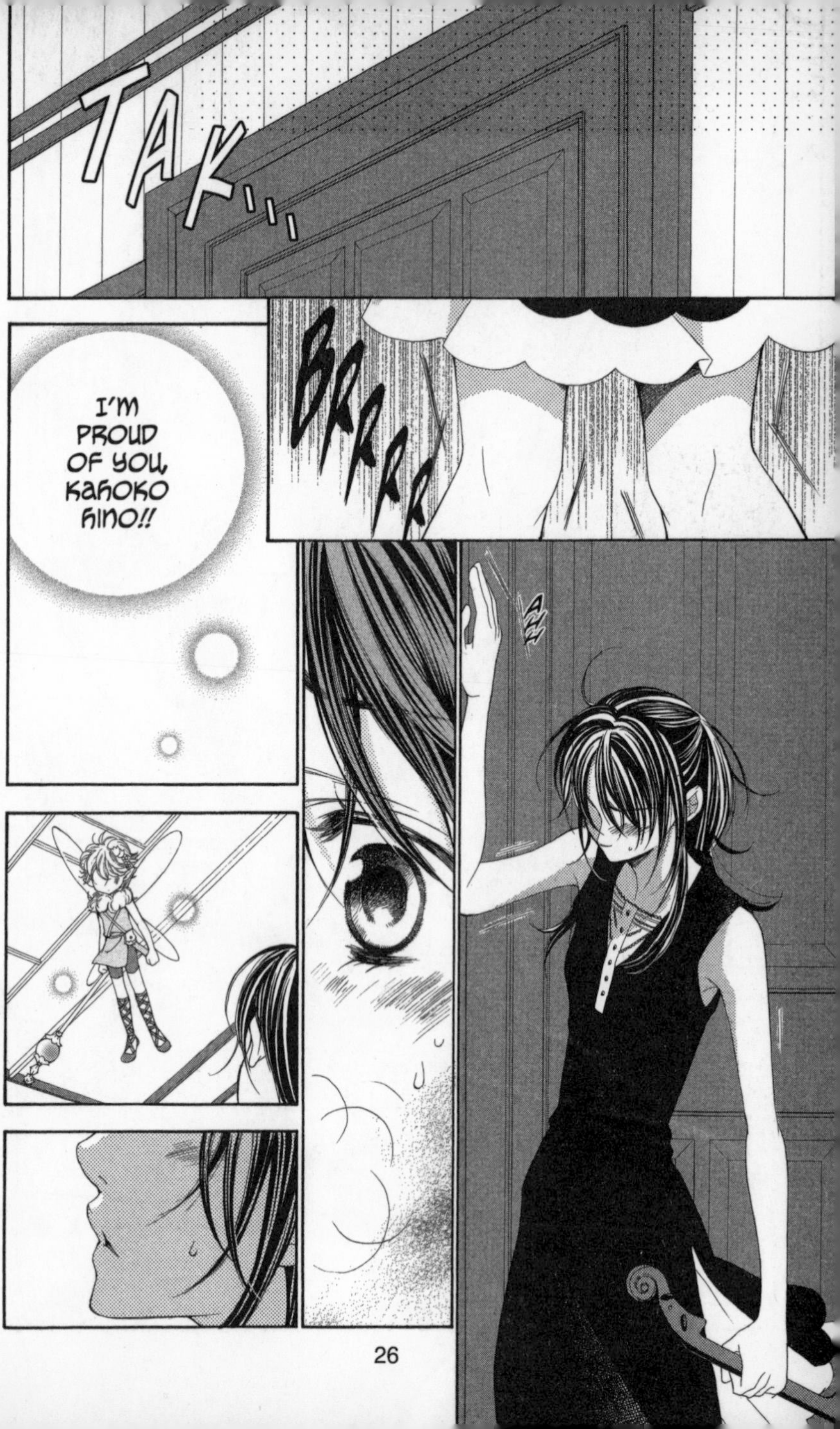
TAK...
BRRRR
I'M PROUD OF YOU, KAHOKO HINO!!
AHH

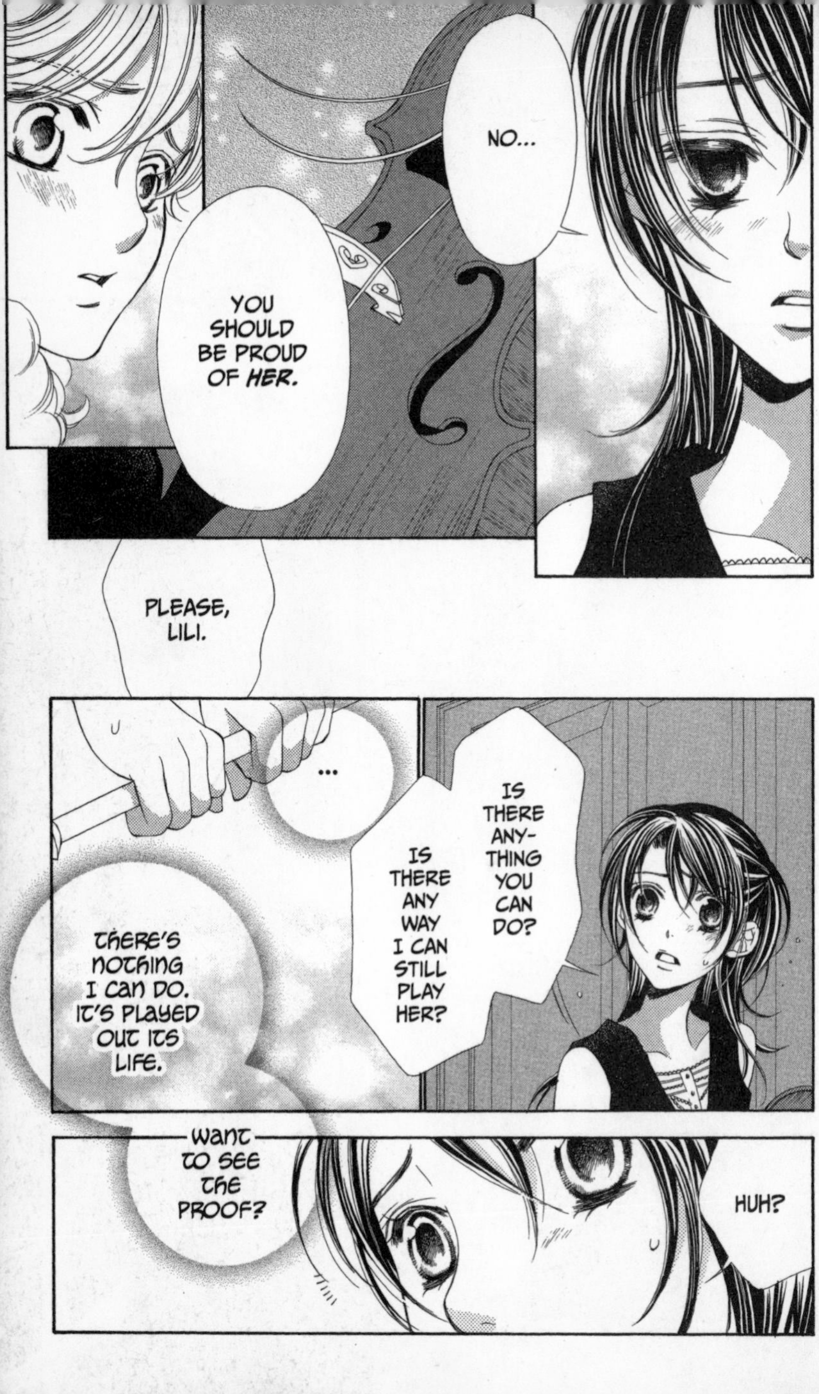
NO...
YOU SHOULD BE PROUD OF HER.
PLEASE, LILI.
IS THERE ANY-THING YOU CAN DO?
IS THERE ANY WAY I CAN STILL PLAY HER?
...
THERE'S NOTHING I CAN DO. IT'S PLAYED OUT ITS LIFE.
WANT TO SEE THE PROOF?
HUH?

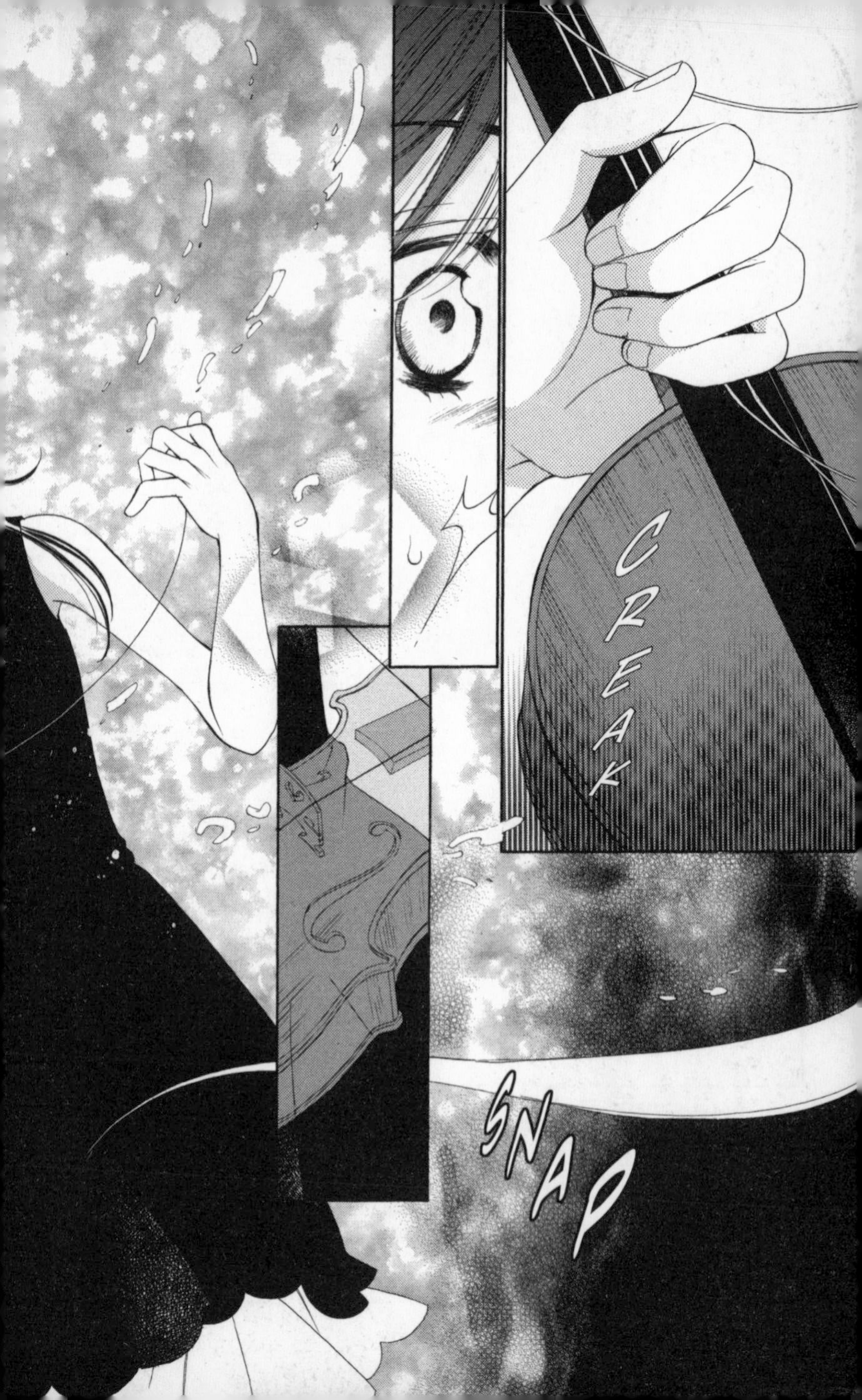
CREAK
SNAP

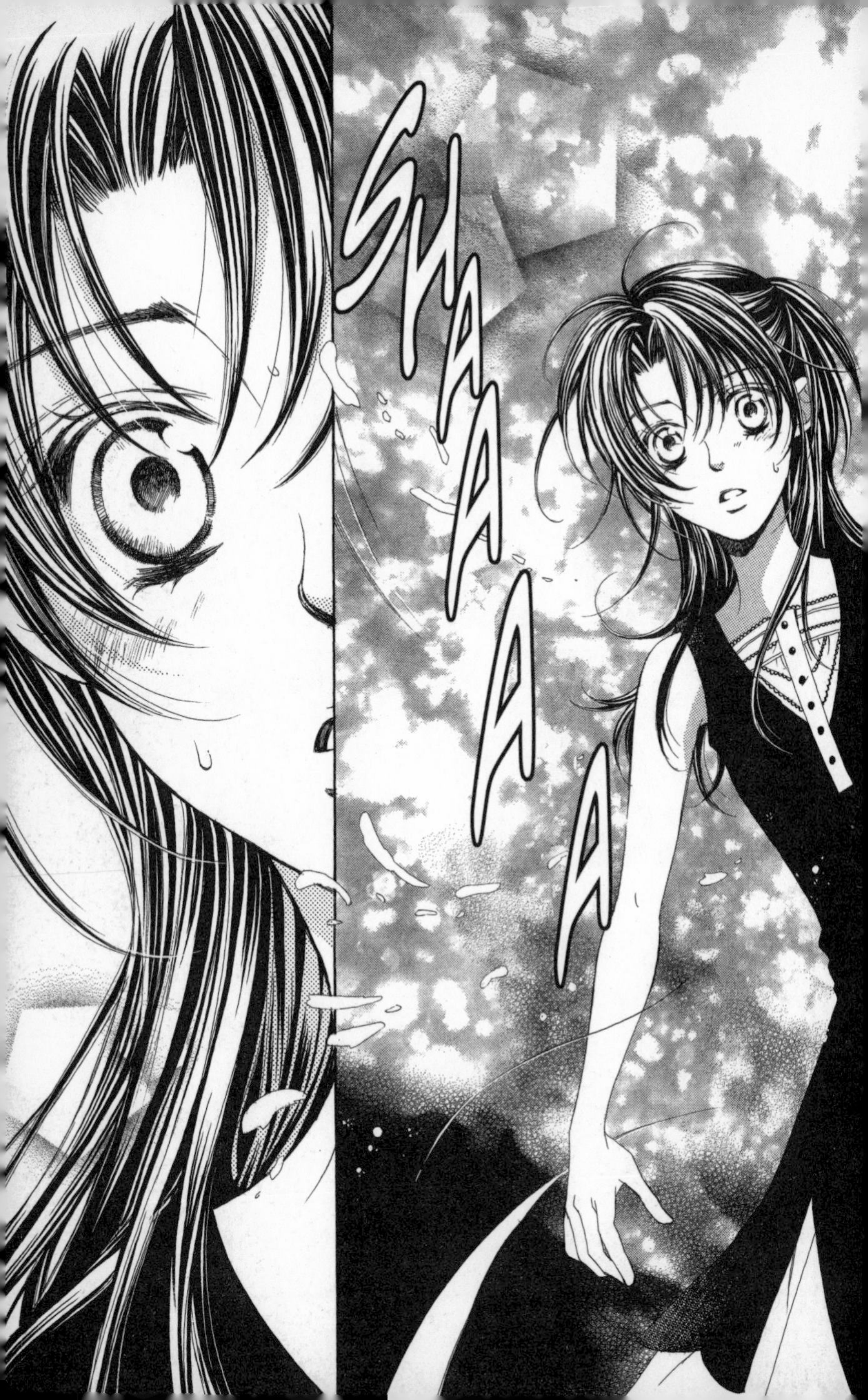
SHAAAAAA

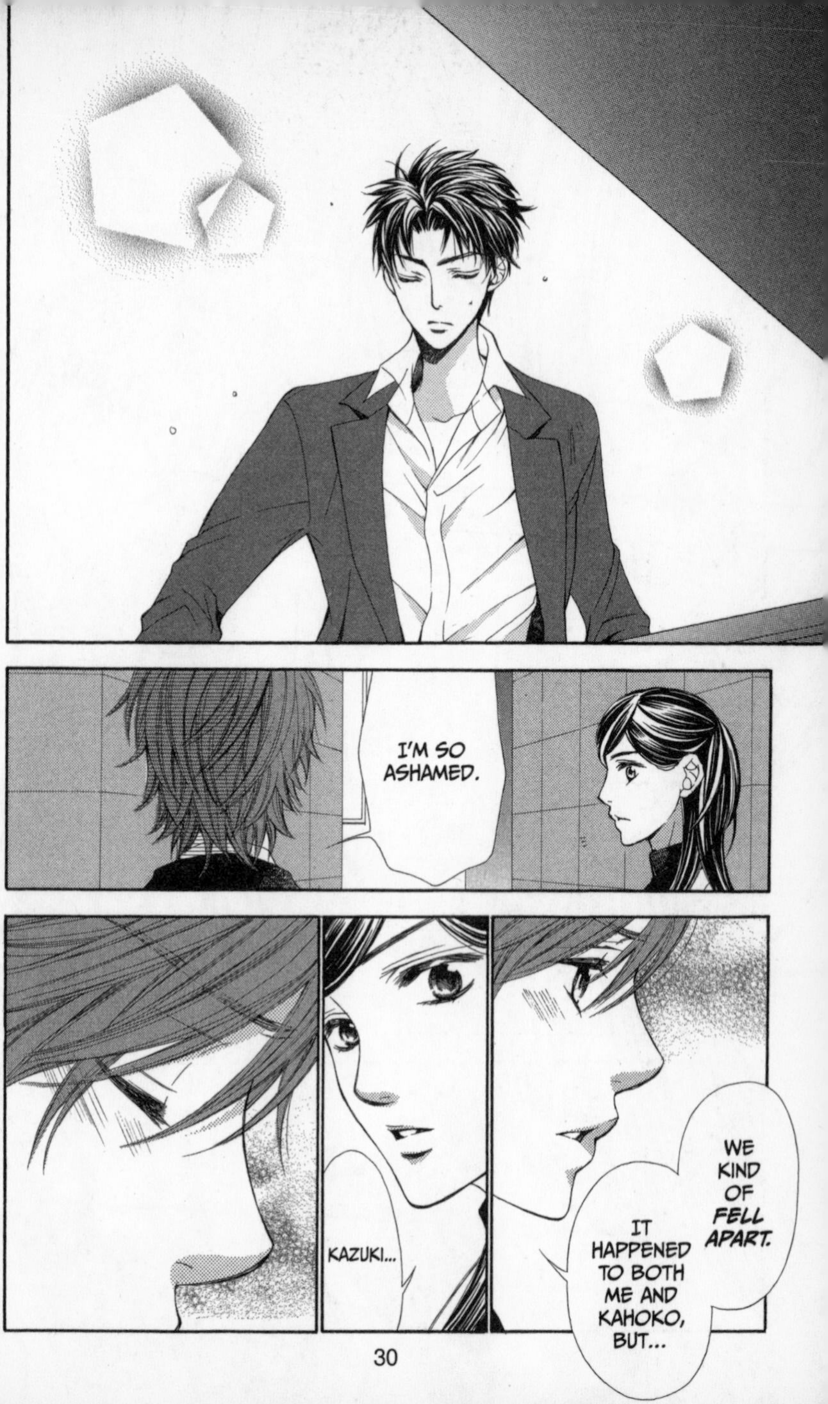
I'M SO ASHAMED.
WE KIND OF *FELL APART.*
IT HAPPENED TO BOTH ME AND KAHOKO, BUT...
KAZUKI...

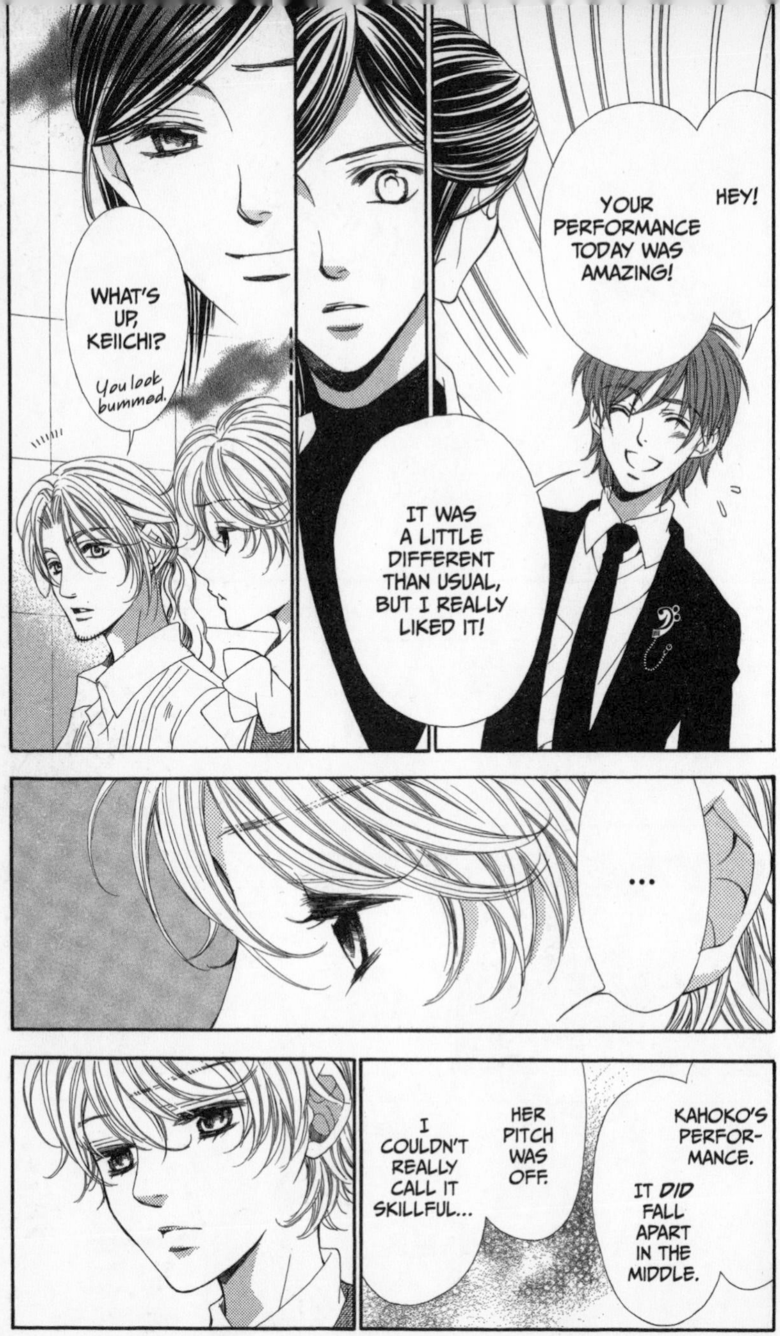
HEY!
YOUR PERFORMANCE TODAY WAS AMAZING!
IT WAS A LITTLE DIFFERENT THAN USUAL, BUT I REALLY LIKED IT!
WHAT'S UP, KEIICHI?
You look bummed.
...
KAHOKO'S PERFORMANCE.
IT *DID* FALL APART IN THE MIDDLE.
HER PITCH WAS OFF.
I COULDN'T REALLY CALL IT SKILLFUL...

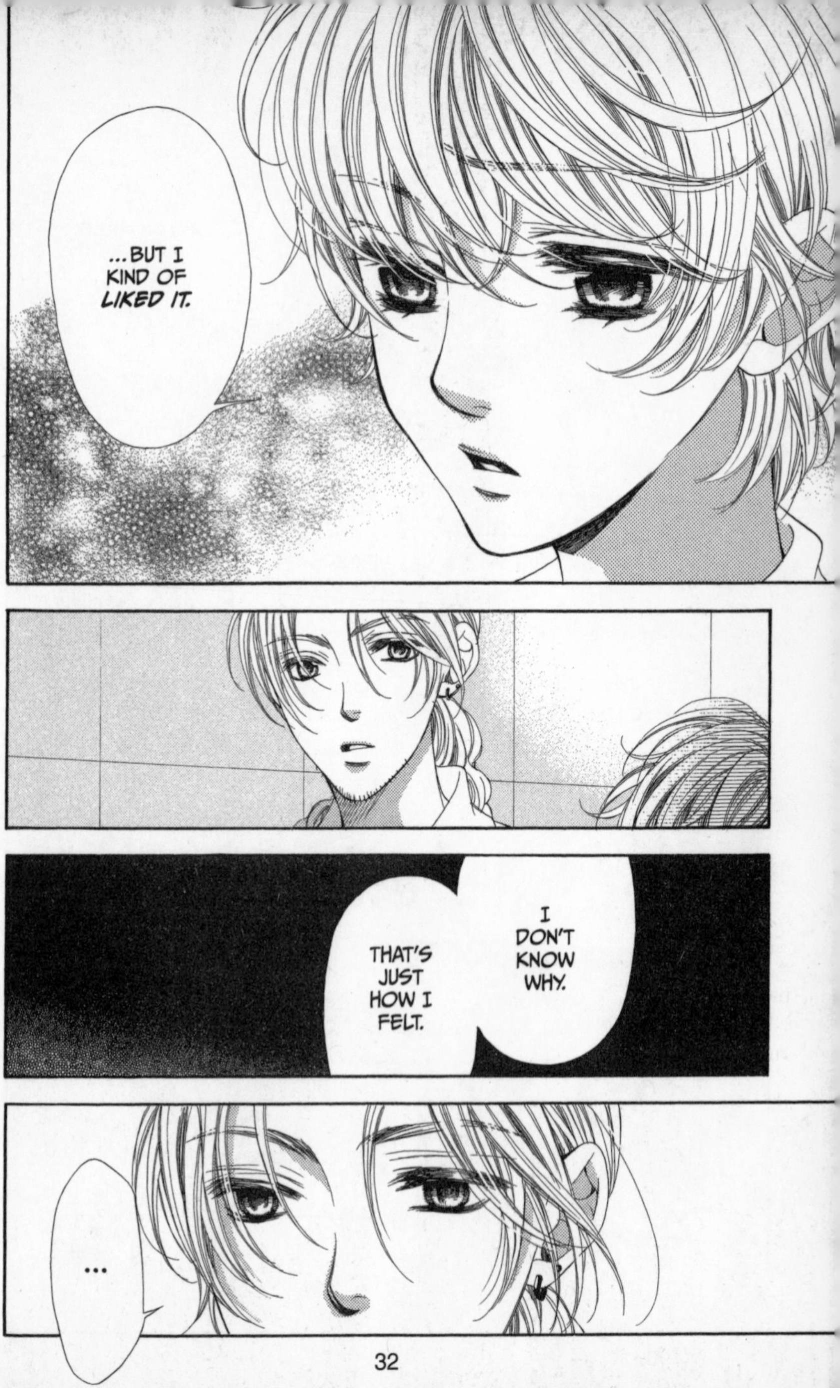
...BUT I KIND OF LIKED IT.
I DON'T KNOW WHY.
THAT'S JUST HOW I FELT.
...

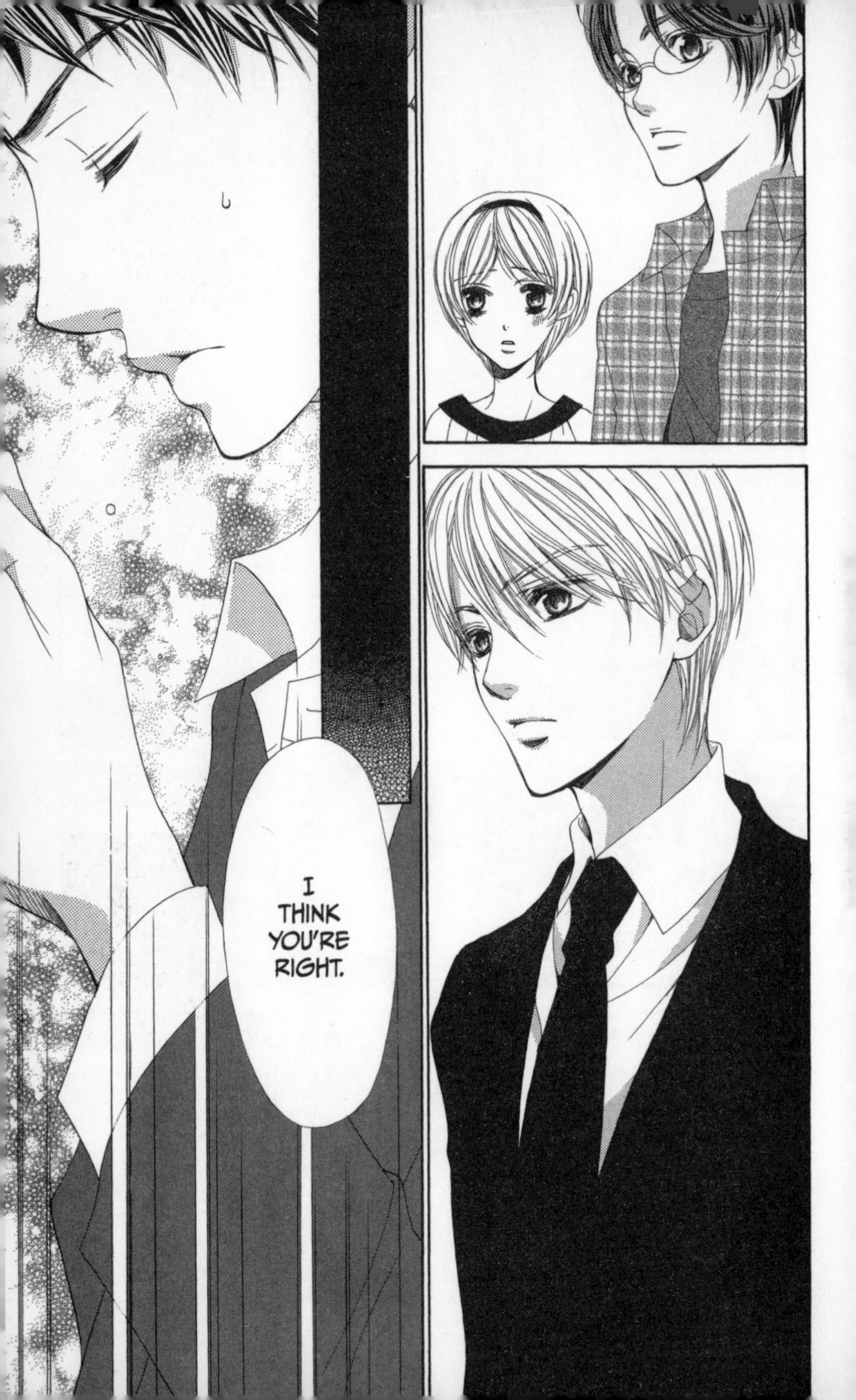
I THINK YOU'RE RIGHT.

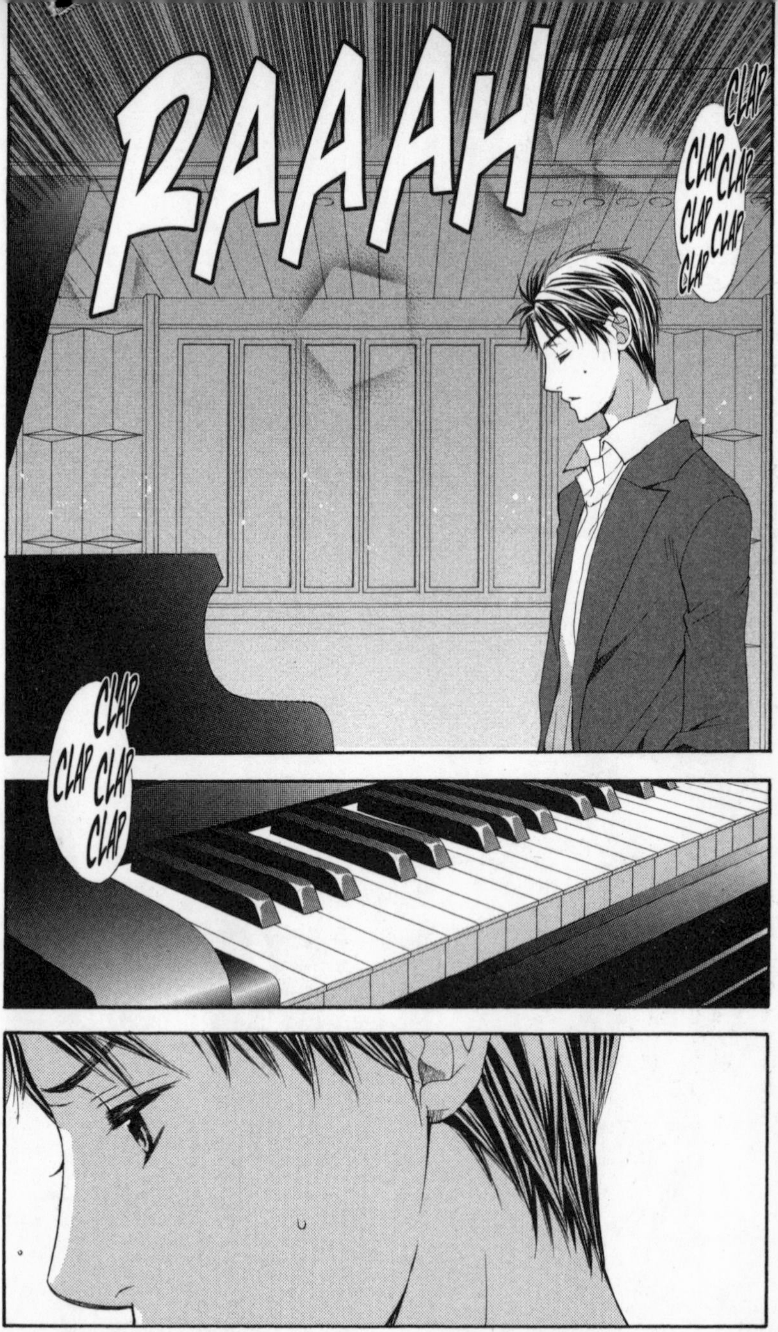
CLAP CLAP CLAP CLAP CLAP CLAP
RAAAH
CLAP CLAP CLAP CLAP

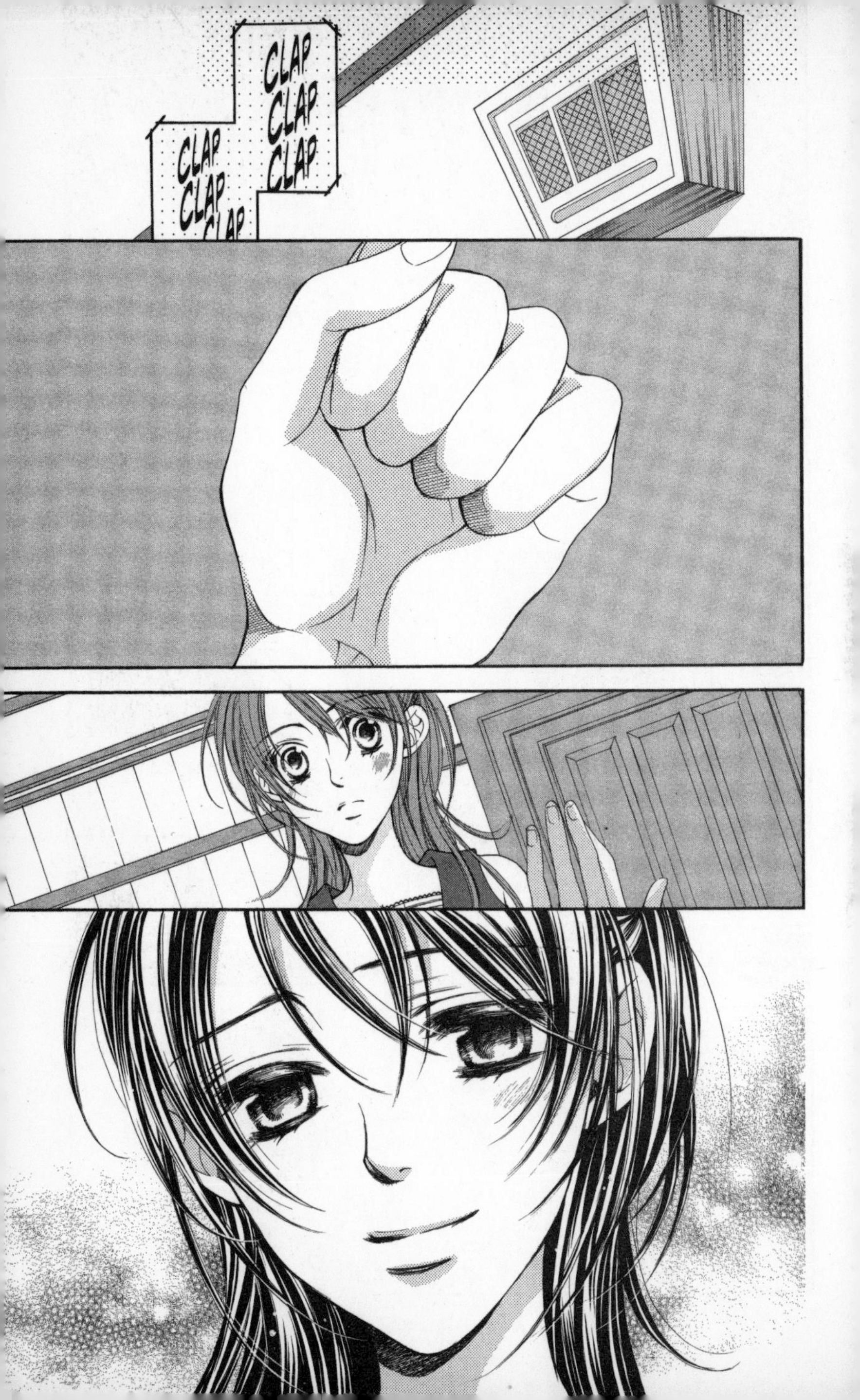
CLAP CLAP CLAP
CLAP CLAP

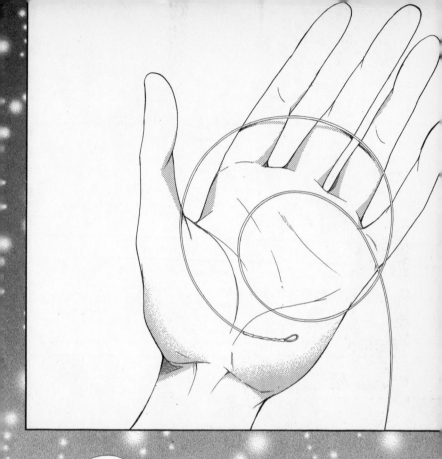

THANK
YOU...

END OF MEASURE 32

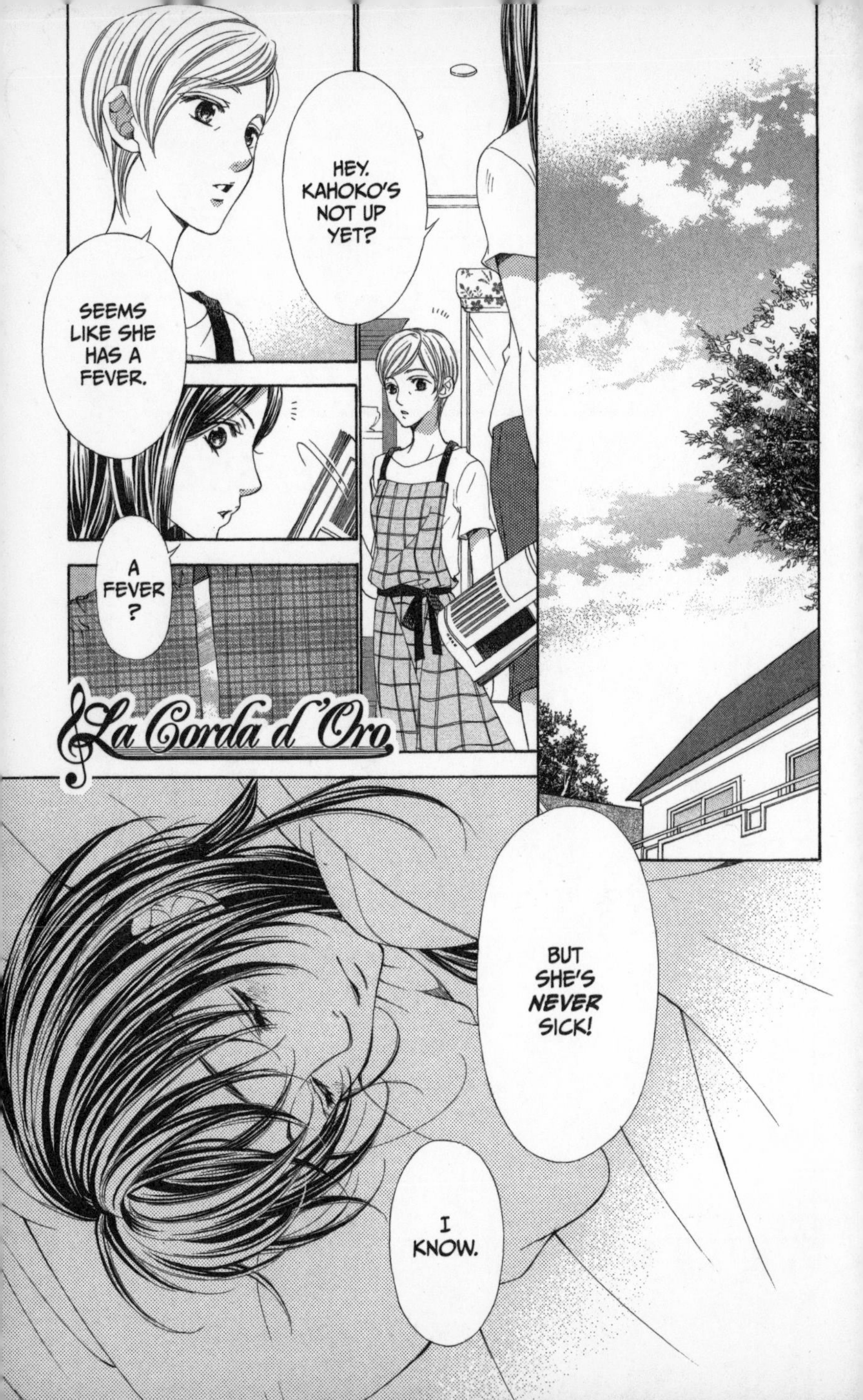
HEY. KAHOKO'S NOT UP YET?
SEEMS LIKE SHE HAS A FEVER.
A FEVER?
La Corda d'Oro
BUT SHE'S **NEVER** SICK!
I KNOW.

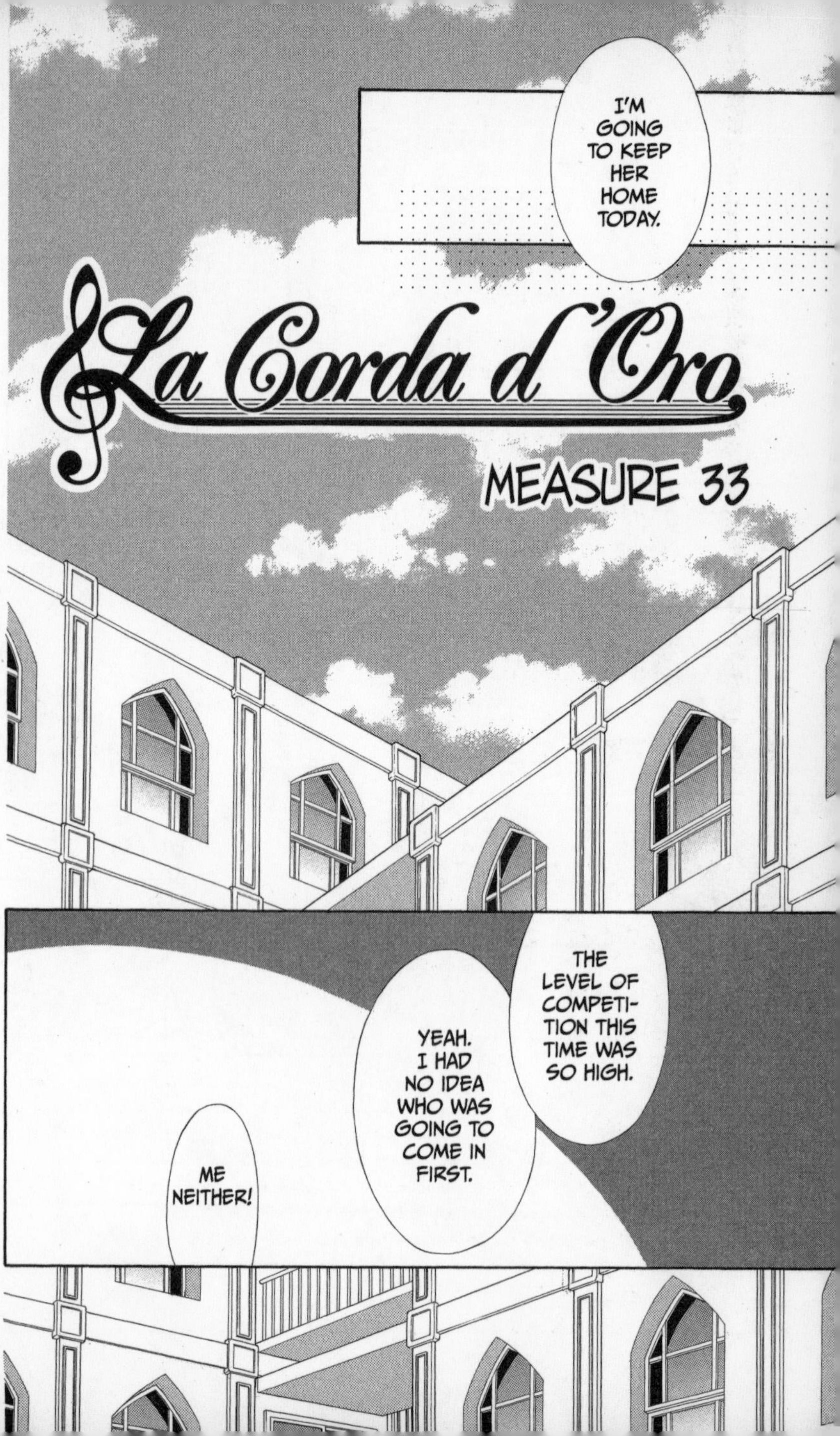
I'M GOING TO KEEP HER HOME TODAY.
La Corda d'Oro
MEASURE 33
THE LEVEL OF COMPETITION THIS TIME WAS SO HIGH.
YEAH. I HAD NO IDEA WHO WAS GOING TO COME IN FIRST.
ME NEITHER!

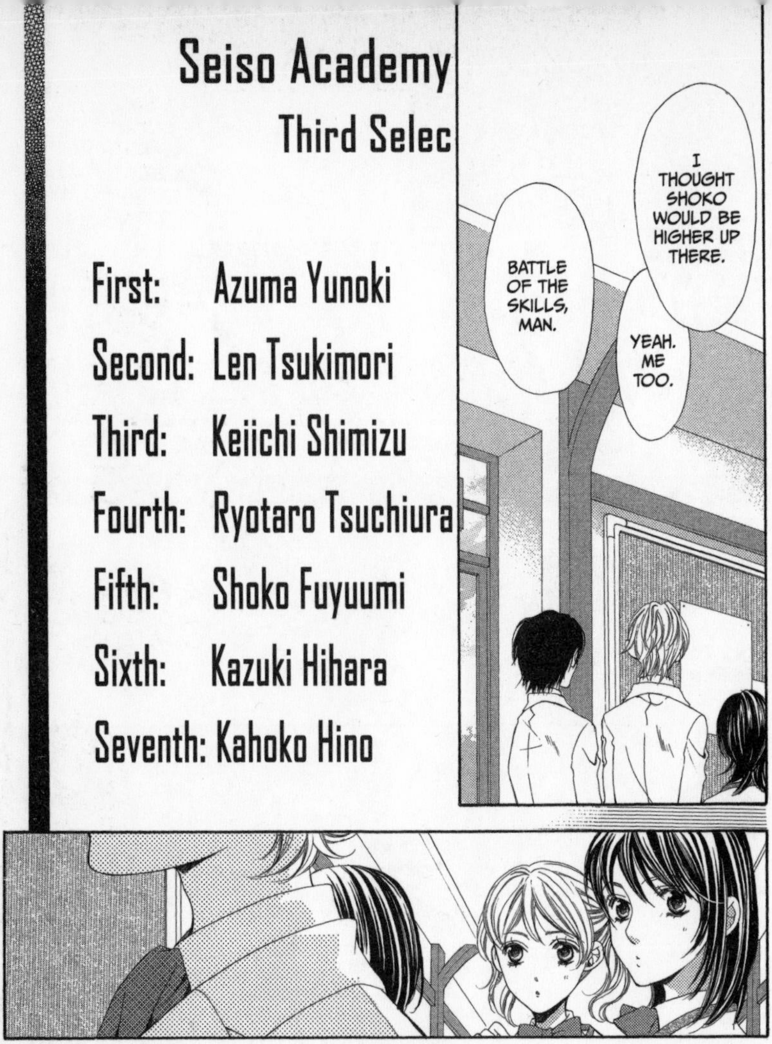
I THOUGHT SHOKO WOULD BE HIGHER UP THERE.
BATTLE OF THE SKILLS, MAN.
YEAH. ME TOO.
Seiso Academy
Third Selec
First: Azuma Yunoki
Second: Len Tsukimori
Third: Keiichi Shimizu
Fourth: Ryotaro Tsuchiura
Fifth: Shoko Fuyuumi
Sixth: Kazuki Hihara
Seventh: Kahoko Hino

**Daily Happenings 25 ...Character Book, Part 2**

I wonder who makes the most appearances in my color illustrations...Kazuki, maybe? He's definitely the most requested for the cover of LaLa. I think the fact that he's always smiling makes him good cover material. I get lots of requests for the other boys, too. Kazuki and Ryotaro...Len and Azuma...Ryotaro and Azuma...Well, that's never happened...Also Keiichi and Azuma...maybe it's just an Azuma thing.

I guess I can't blame people. Sorry to have babbled on, but if you have the time, please check out the book.

I swear that's it for my PR!

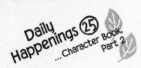

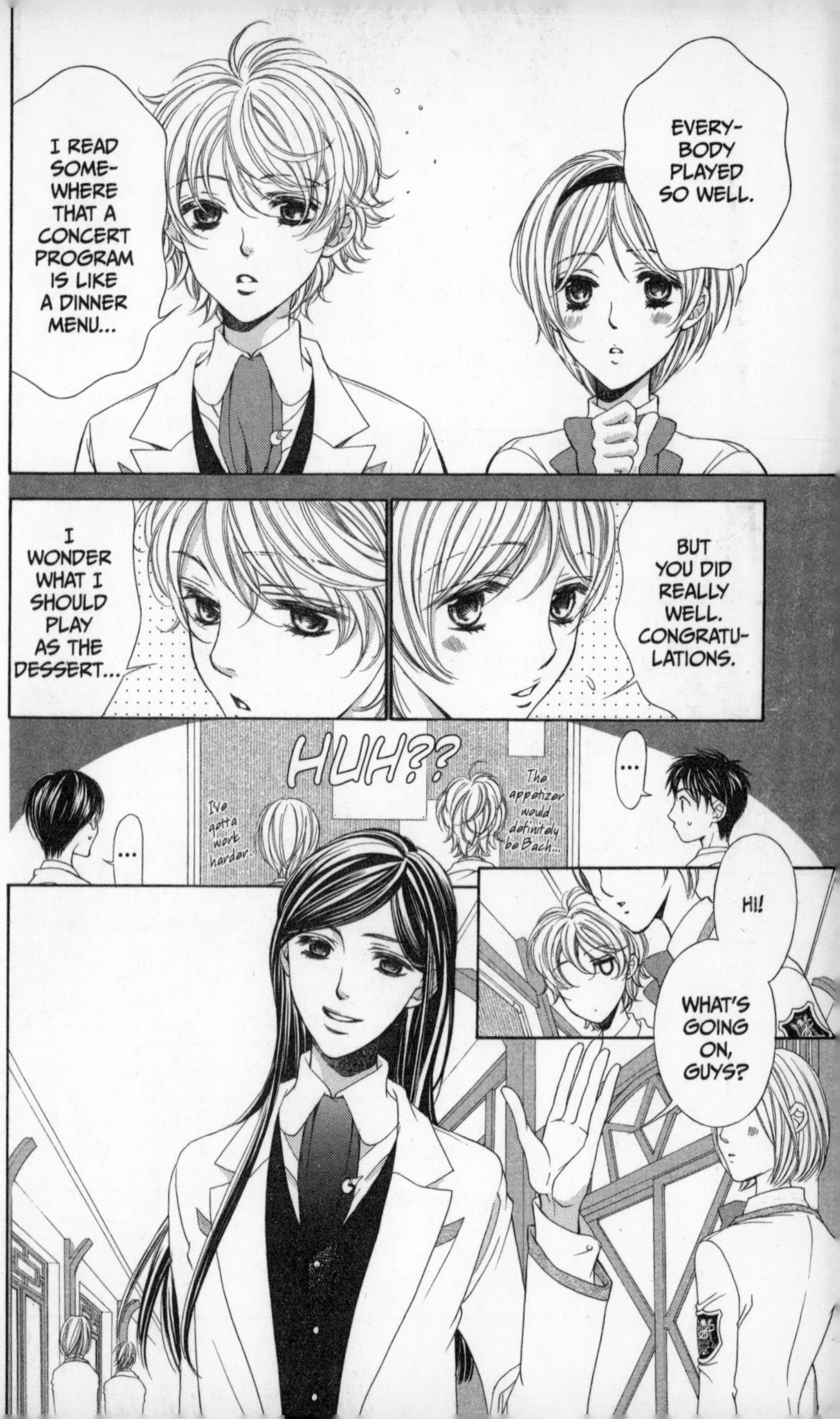
EVERY-BODY PLAYED SO WELL.
I READ SOME-WHERE THAT A CONCERT PROGRAM IS LIKE A DINNER MENU...
BUT YOU DID REALLY WELL. CONGRATU-LATIONS.
I WONDER WHAT I SHOULD PLAY AS THE DESSERT...
...
The appetizer would definitely be Bach...
HUH??
I've gotta work harder.
...
HI!
WHAT'S GOING ON, GUYS?

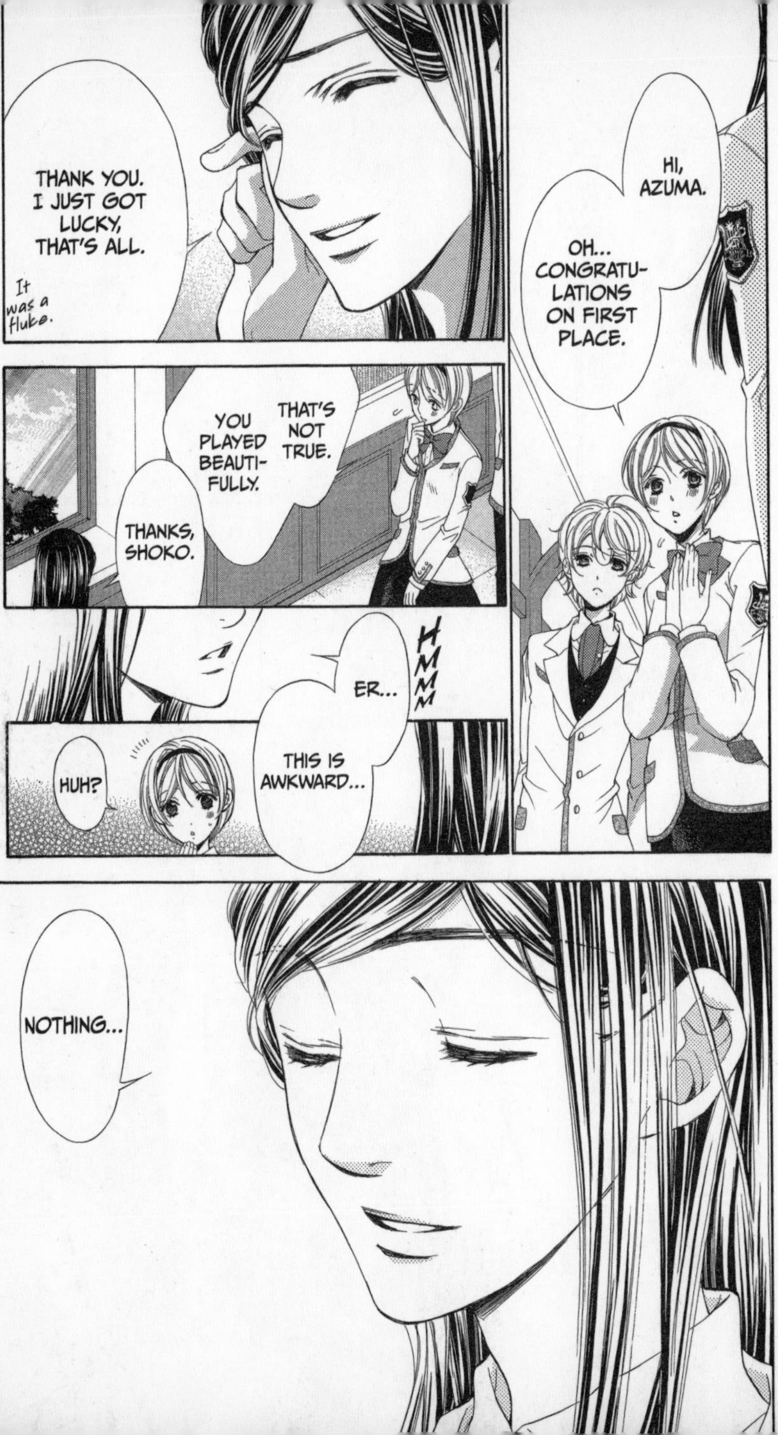
HI, AZUMA.
OH... CONGRATULATIONS ON FIRST PLACE.
THANK YOU. I JUST GOT LUCKY, THAT'S ALL.
It was a fluke.
THAT'S NOT TRUE.
YOU PLAYED BEAUTIFULLY.
THANKS, SHOKO.
HMMM
ER...
THIS IS AWKWARD...
HUH?
NOTHING...

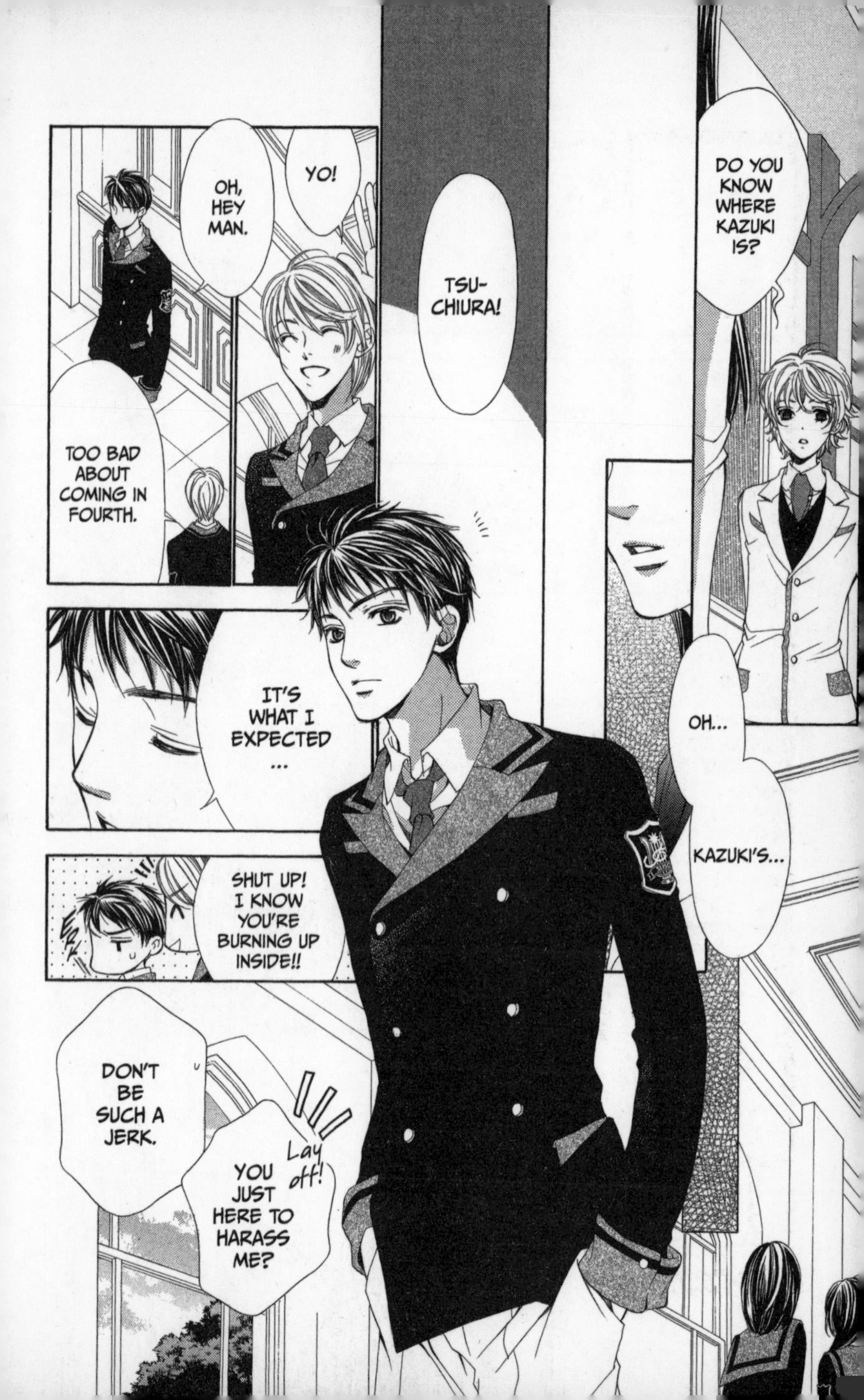
DO YOU KNOW WHERE KAZUKI IS?
OH...
KAZUKI'S...
TSU-CHIURA!
YO!
OH, HEY MAN.
TOO BAD ABOUT COMING IN FOURTH.
IT'S WHAT I EXPECTED...
SHUT UP! I KNOW YOU'RE BURNING UP INSIDE!!
DON'T BE SUCH A JERK.
YOU JUST HERE TO HARASS ME?
Lay off!

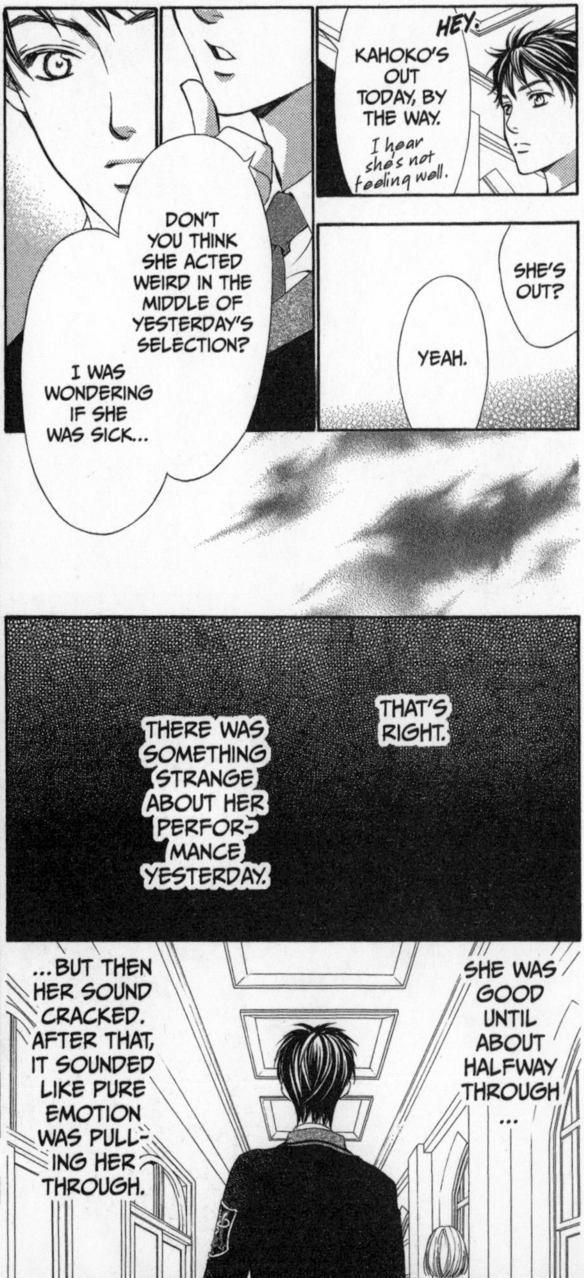
HEY.
KAHOKO'S OUT TODAY, BY THE WAY.
I hear she's not feeling well.
SHE'S OUT?
YEAH.
DON'T YOU THINK SHE ACTED WEIRD IN THE MIDDLE OF YESTERDAY'S SELECTION?
I WAS WONDERING IF SHE WAS SICK...
THAT'S RIGHT.
THERE WAS SOMETHING STRANGE ABOUT HER PERFOR-MANCE YESTERDAY.
SHE WAS GOOD UNTIL ABOUT HALFWAY THROUGH...
...BUT THEN HER SOUND CRACKED. AFTER THAT, IT SOUNDED LIKE PURE EMOTION WAS PULL-ING HER THROUGH.

## TWO

Shoko ought to wear a skirt or a dress. I think some-where between teenage and adult clothes. Nami, on the other hand, would do well in a pair of slacks. She's got great style, so she can wear some-thing mature and casual.

Speaking of clothes, the spread for Measure 32 is a kimono shot. I wanted it to have a retro look, but it didn't come out quite as I planned. I wanted Keiichi to look more old-school, but I couldn't balance him well with the rest and just gave up. I wanted it to have a feel of the Meiji/Taisho era.

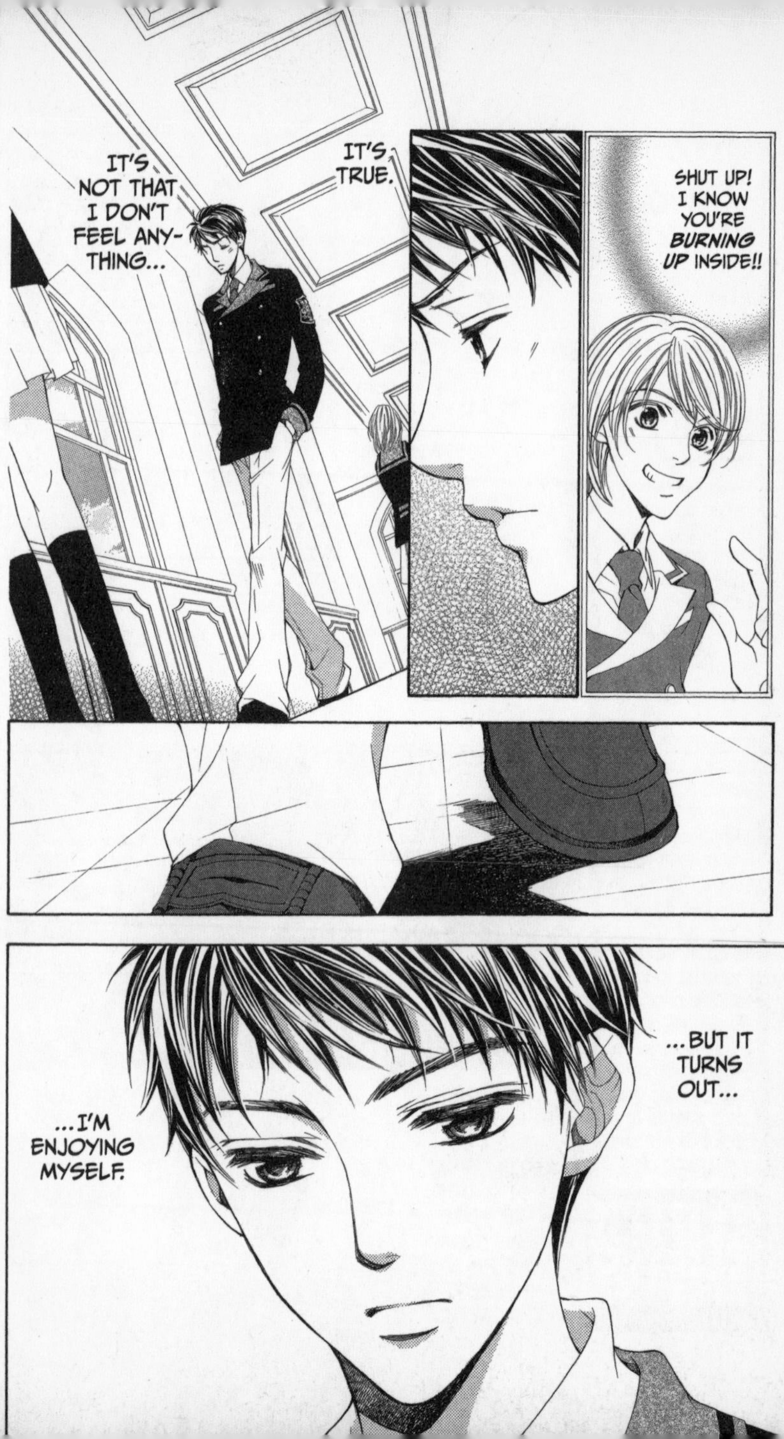
SHUT UP! I KNOW YOU'RE *BURNING UP* INSIDE!!
IT'S TRUE.
IT'S NOT THAT I DON'T FEEL ANY-THING...
...BUT IT TURNS OUT...
...I'M ENJOYING MYSELF.

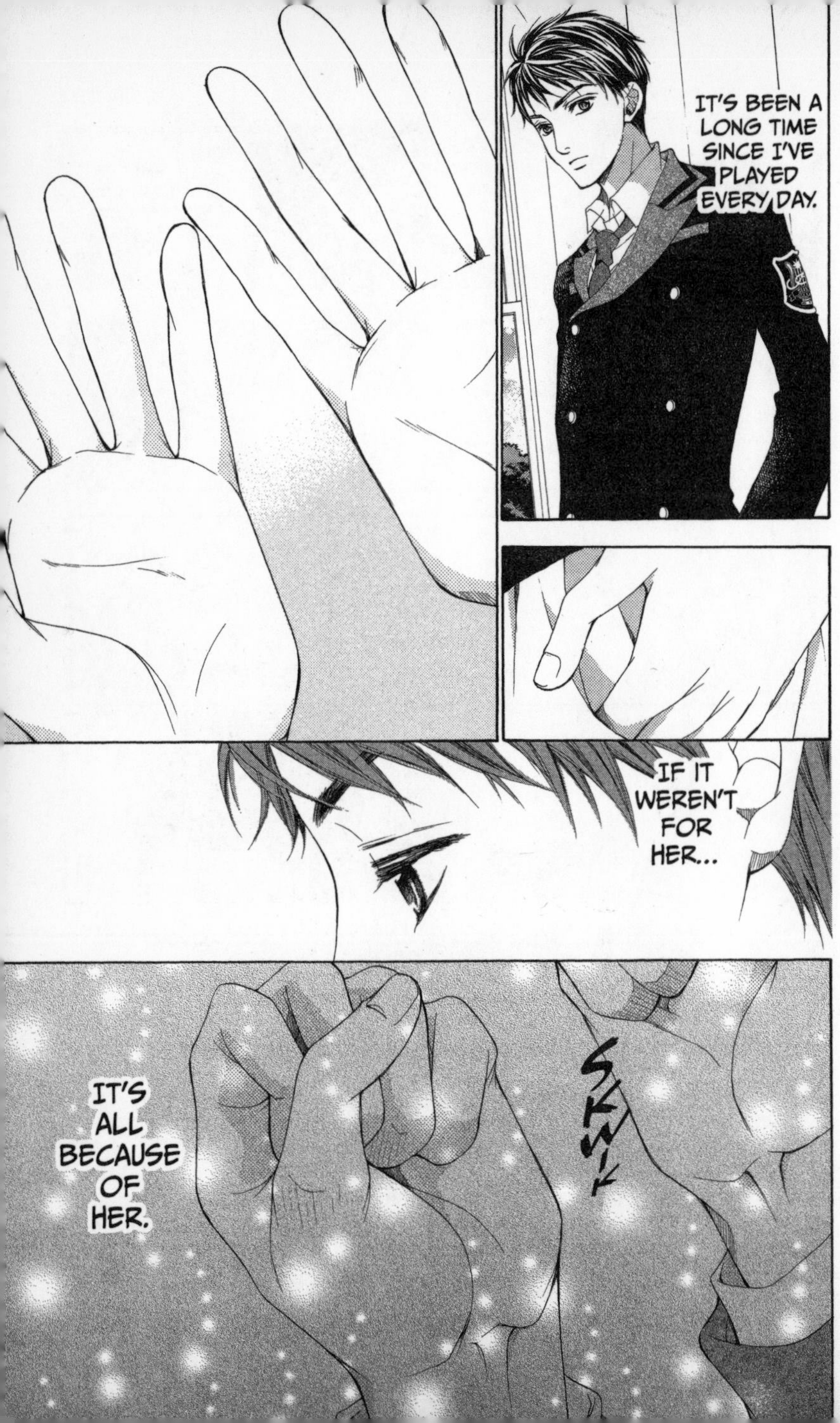
IT'S BEEN A LONG TIME SINCE I'VE PLAYED EVERY DAY.
IF IT WEREN'T FOR HER...
SKWIK
IT'S ALL BECAUSE OF HER.

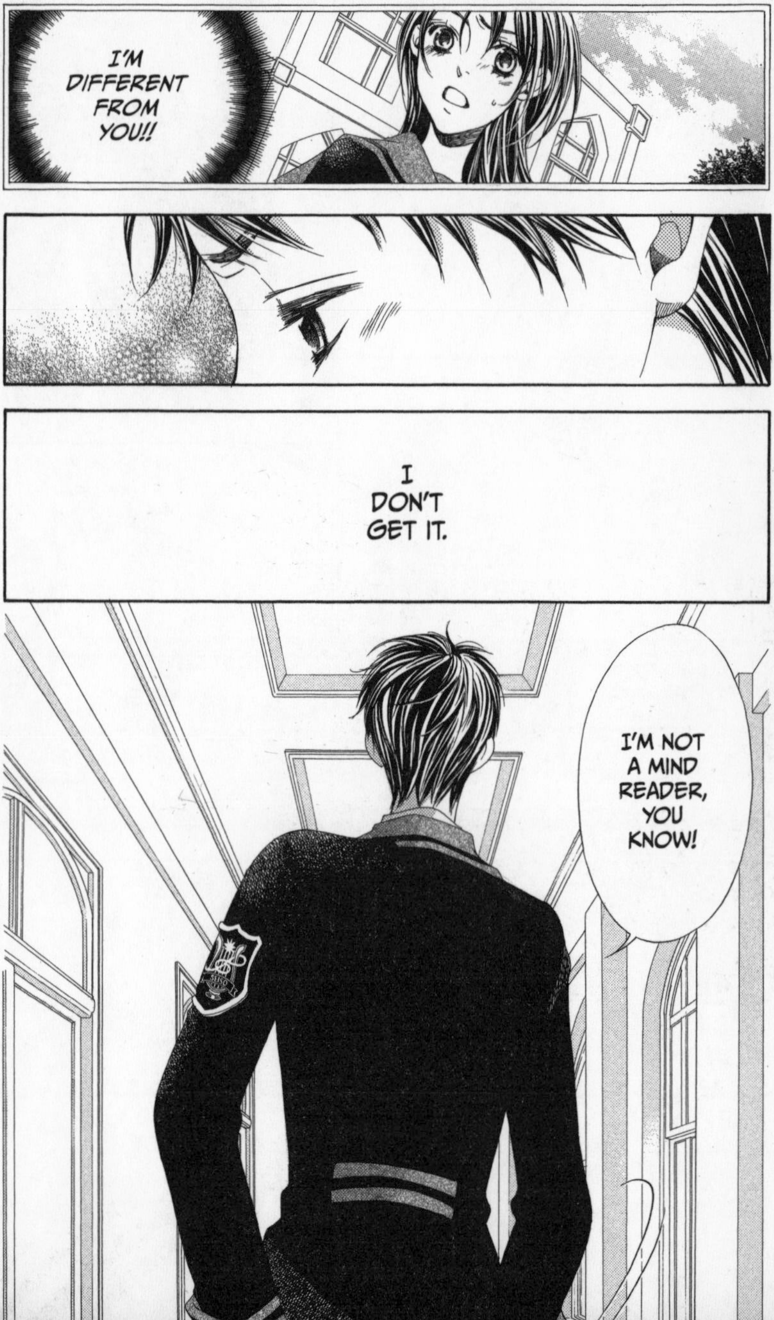
I'M DIFFERENT FROM YOU!!
I DON'T GET IT.
I'M NOT A MIND READER, YOU KNOW!

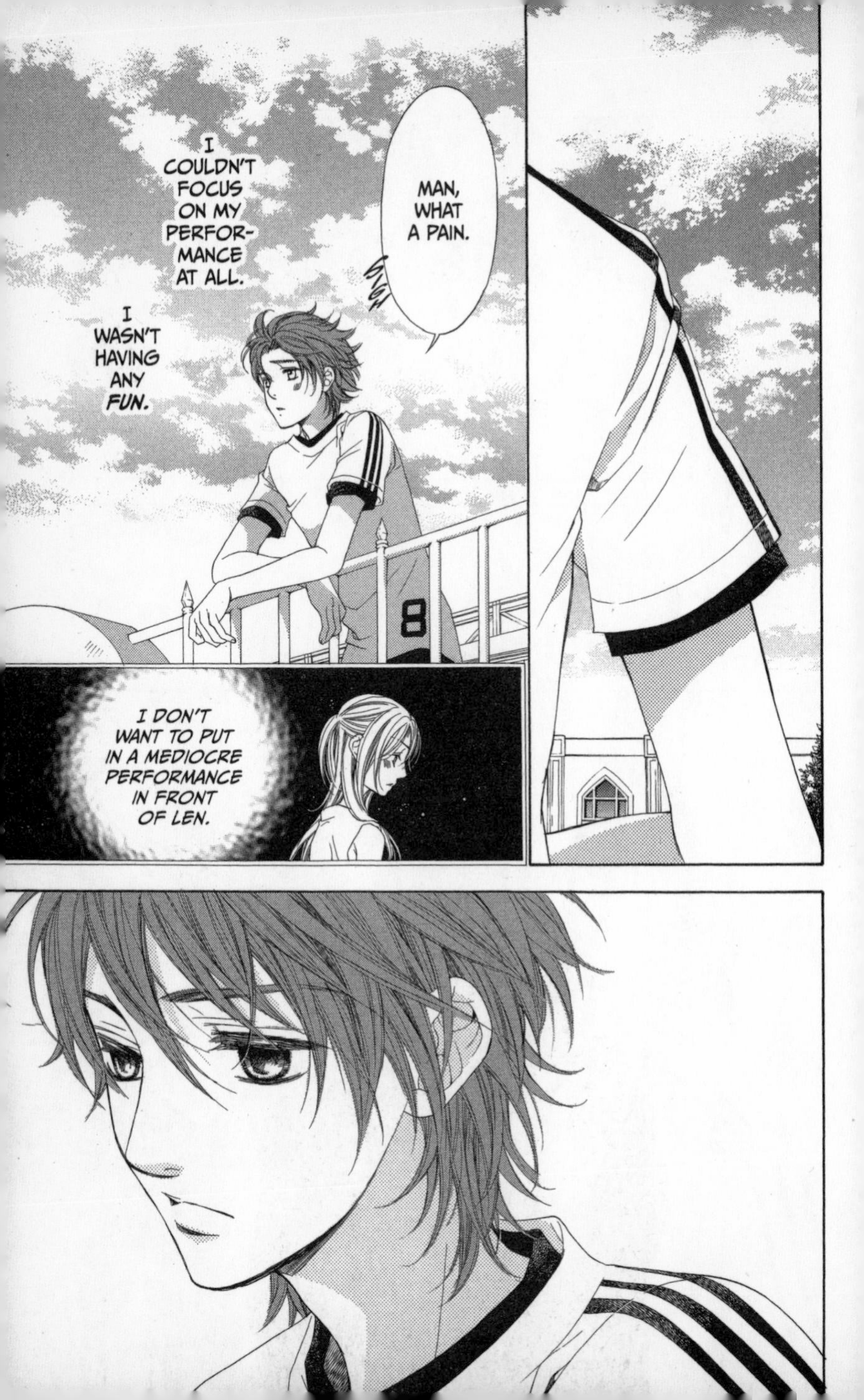

MAN, WHAT A PAIN.
SIGH
I COULDN'T FOCUS ON MY PERFORMANCE AT ALL.
I WASN'T HAVING ANY *FUN.*
I DON'T WANT TO PUT IN A MEDIOCRE PERFORMANCE IN FRONT OF LEN.

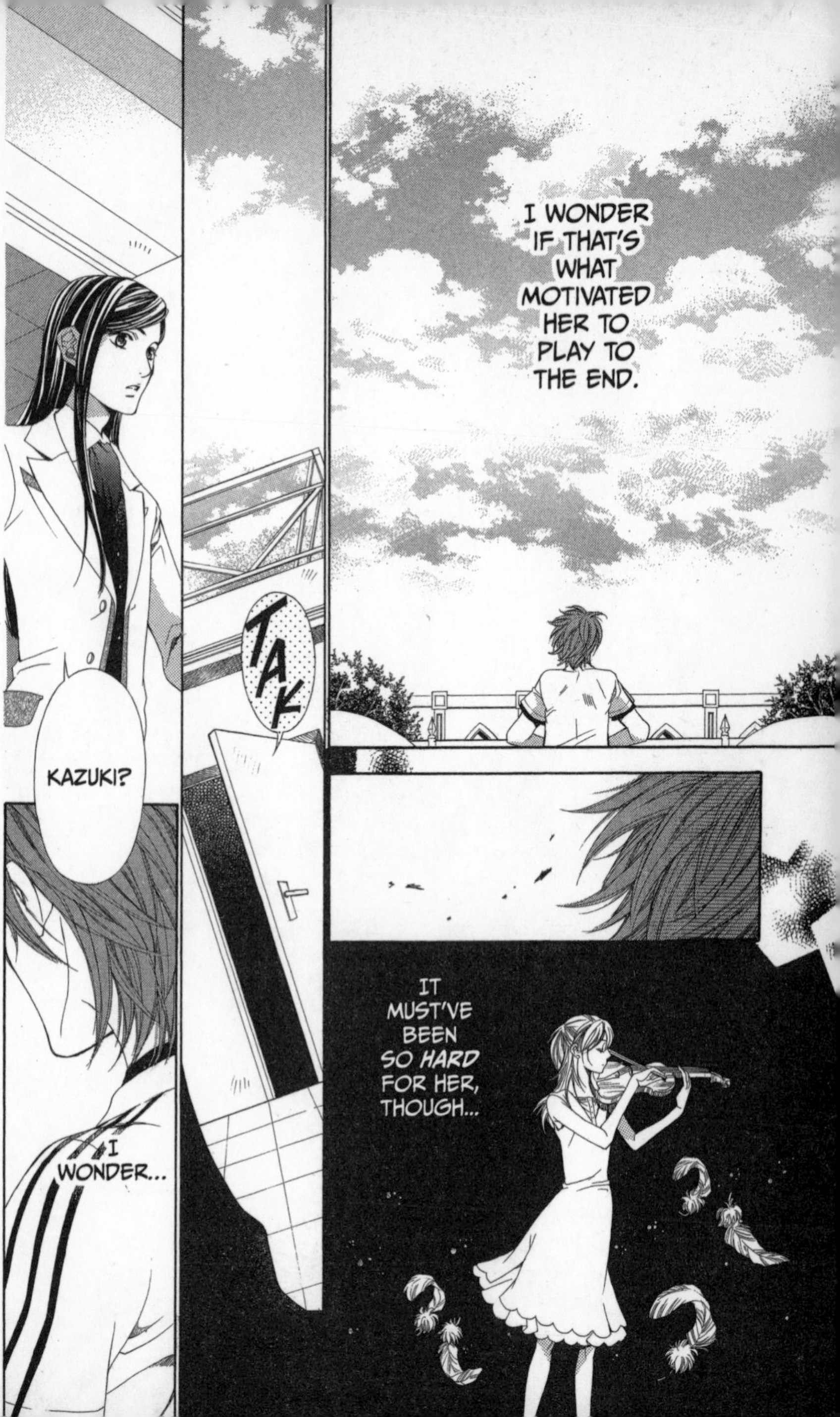
I WONDER IF THAT'S WHAT MOTIVATED HER TO PLAY TO THE END.
IT MUST'VE BEEN SO *HARD* FOR HER, THOUGH...
TAK
KAZUKI?
I WONDER...

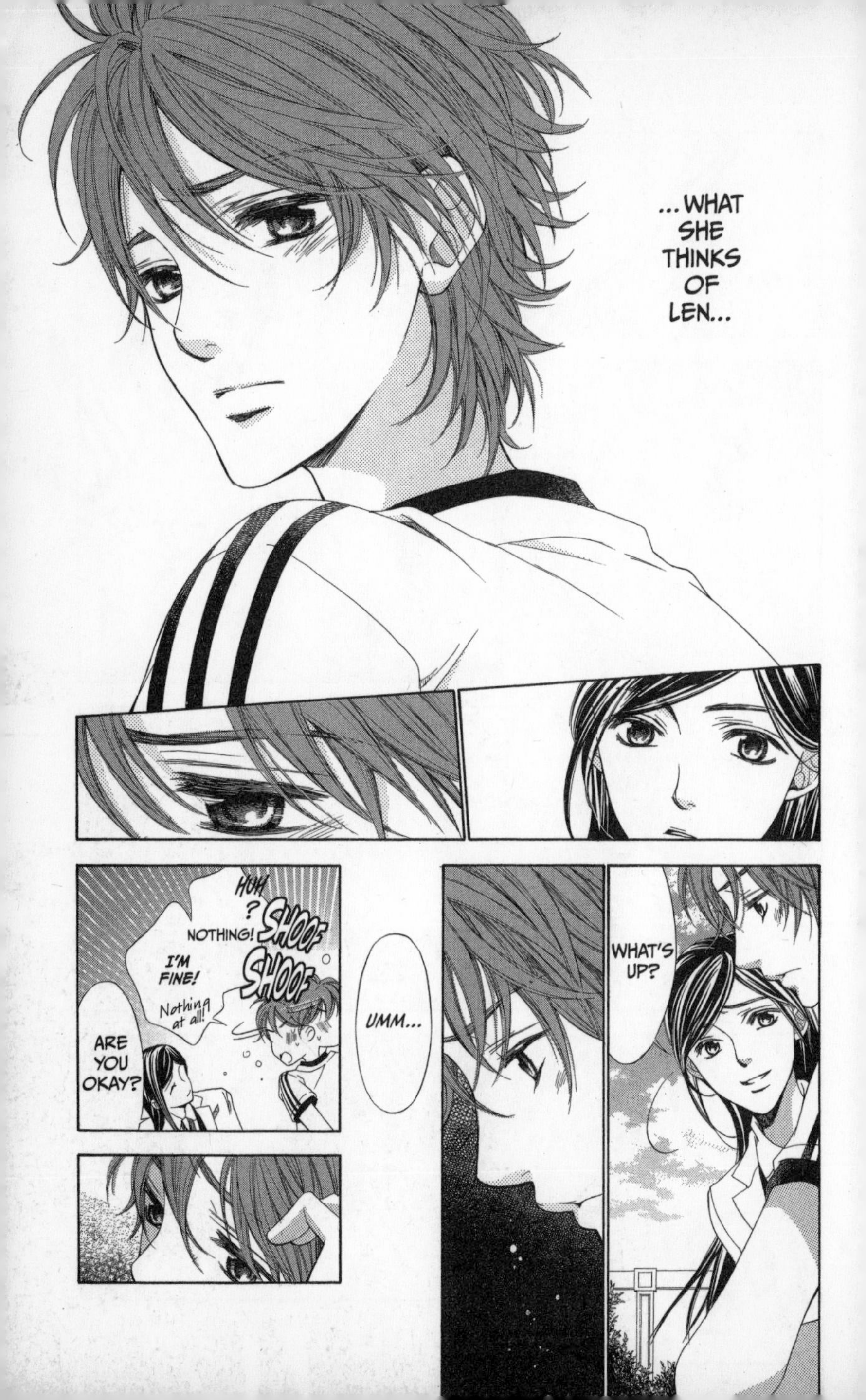
...WHAT SHE THINKS OF LEN...
WHAT'S UP?
UMM...
HUH?
SHOOF
SHOOF
NOTHING!
I'M FINE!
Nothing at all!
ARE YOU OKAY?

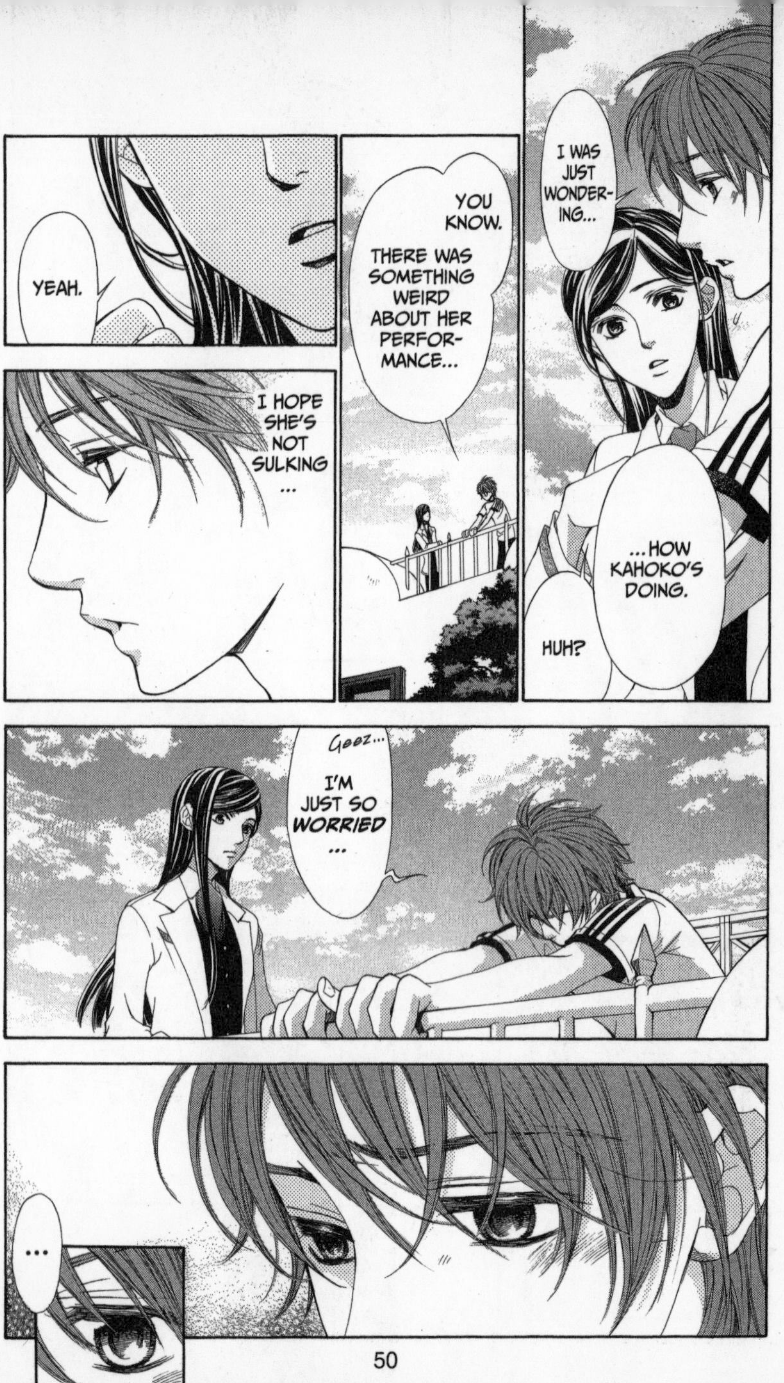
I WAS JUST WONDER-ING...
...HOW KAHOKO'S DOING.
HUH?
YOU KNOW.
THERE WAS SOMETHING WEIRD ABOUT HER PERFORMANCE...
YEAH.
I HOPE SHE'S NOT SULKING...
Geez...
I'M JUST SO *WORRIED*...
...

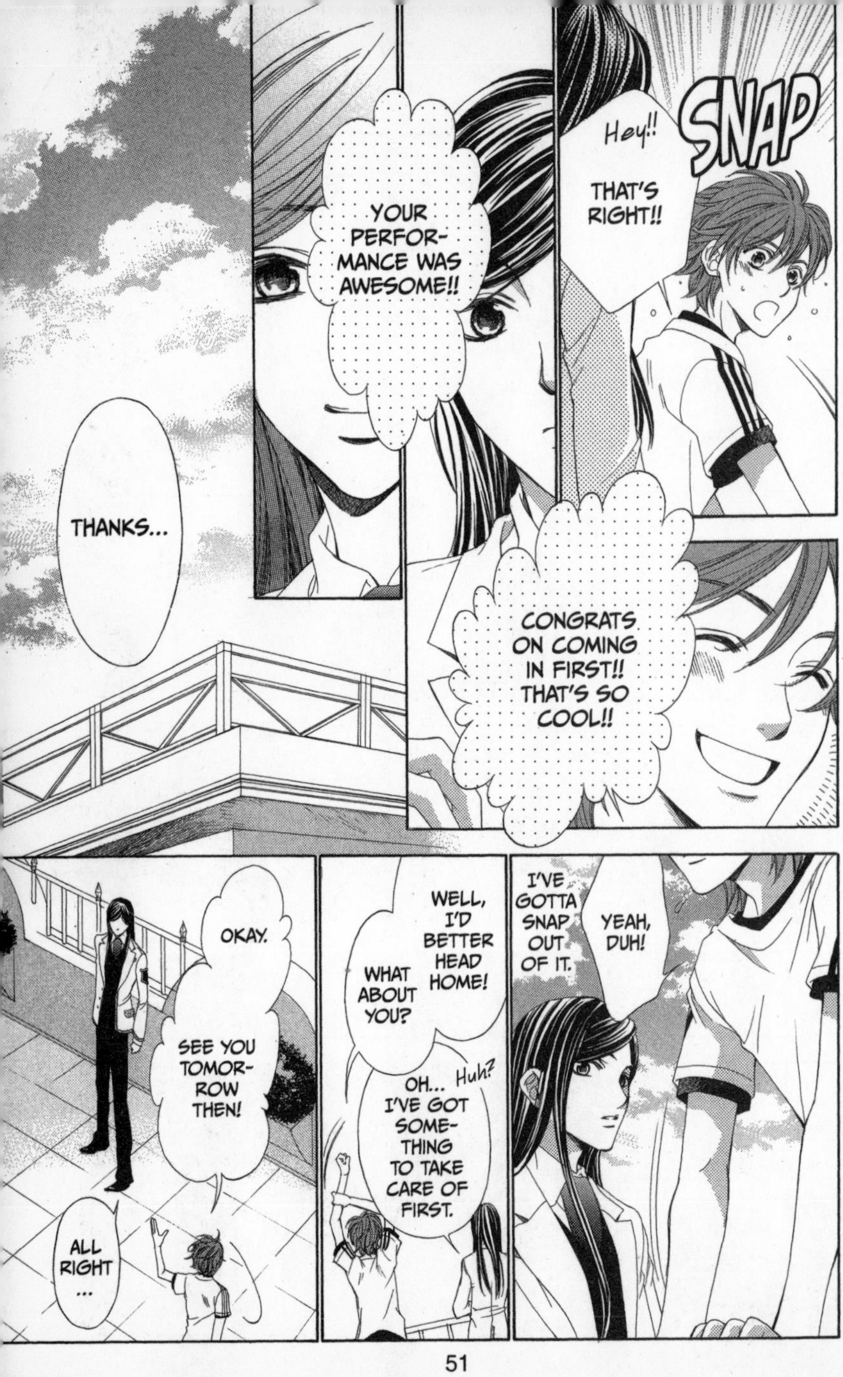
SNAP
Hey!!
THAT'S RIGHT!!
YOUR PERFOR-MANCE WAS AWESOME!!
CONGRATS ON COMING IN FIRST!! THAT'S SO COOL!!
THANKS...
YEAH, DUH!
I'VE GOTTA SNAP OUT OF IT.
WELL, I'D BETTER HEAD HOME!
WHAT ABOUT YOU?
Huh?
OH... I'VE GOT SOME-THING TO TAKE CARE OF FIRST.
OKAY.
SEE YOU TOMOR-ROW THEN!
ALL RIGHT ...

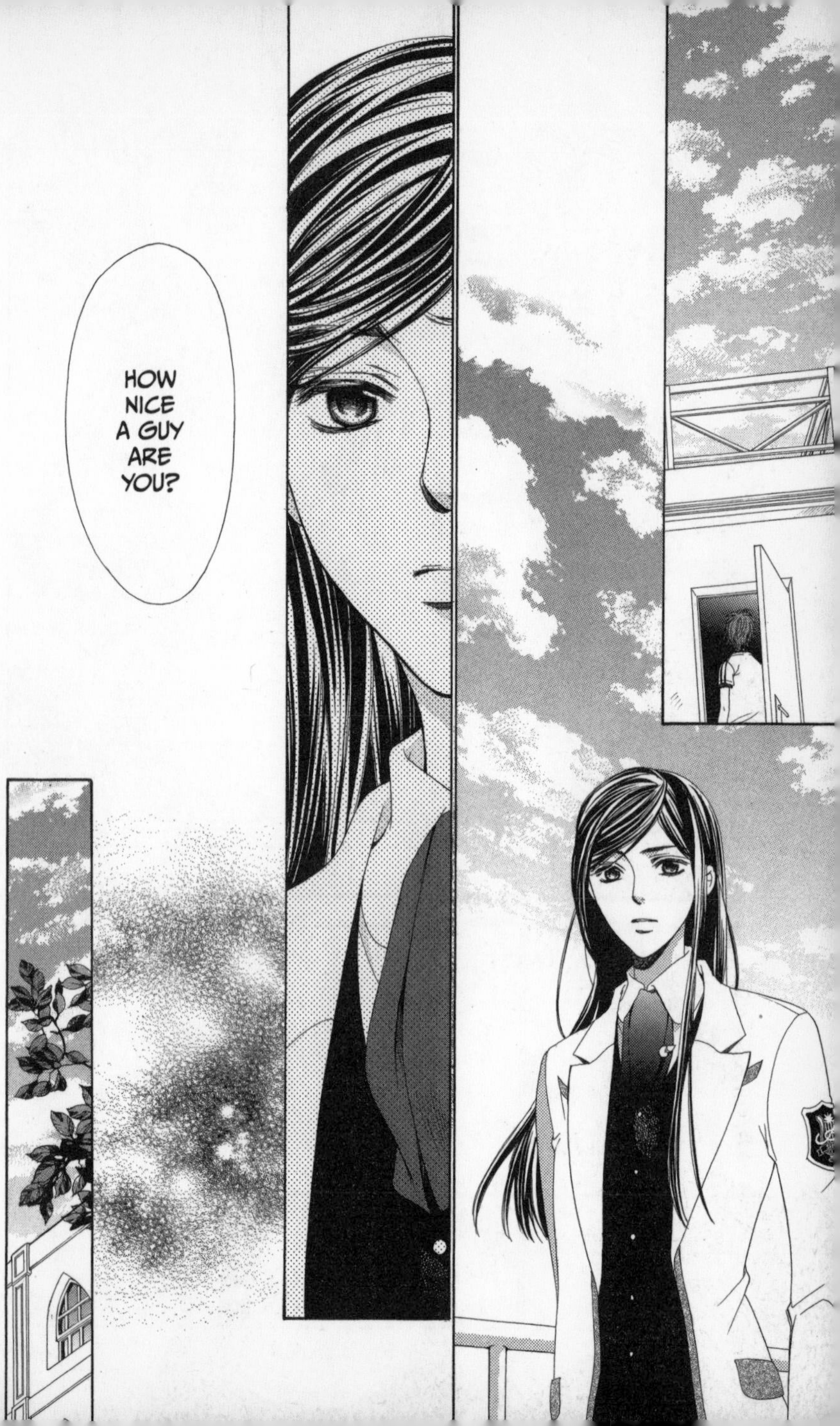
HOW NICE A GUY ARE YOU?

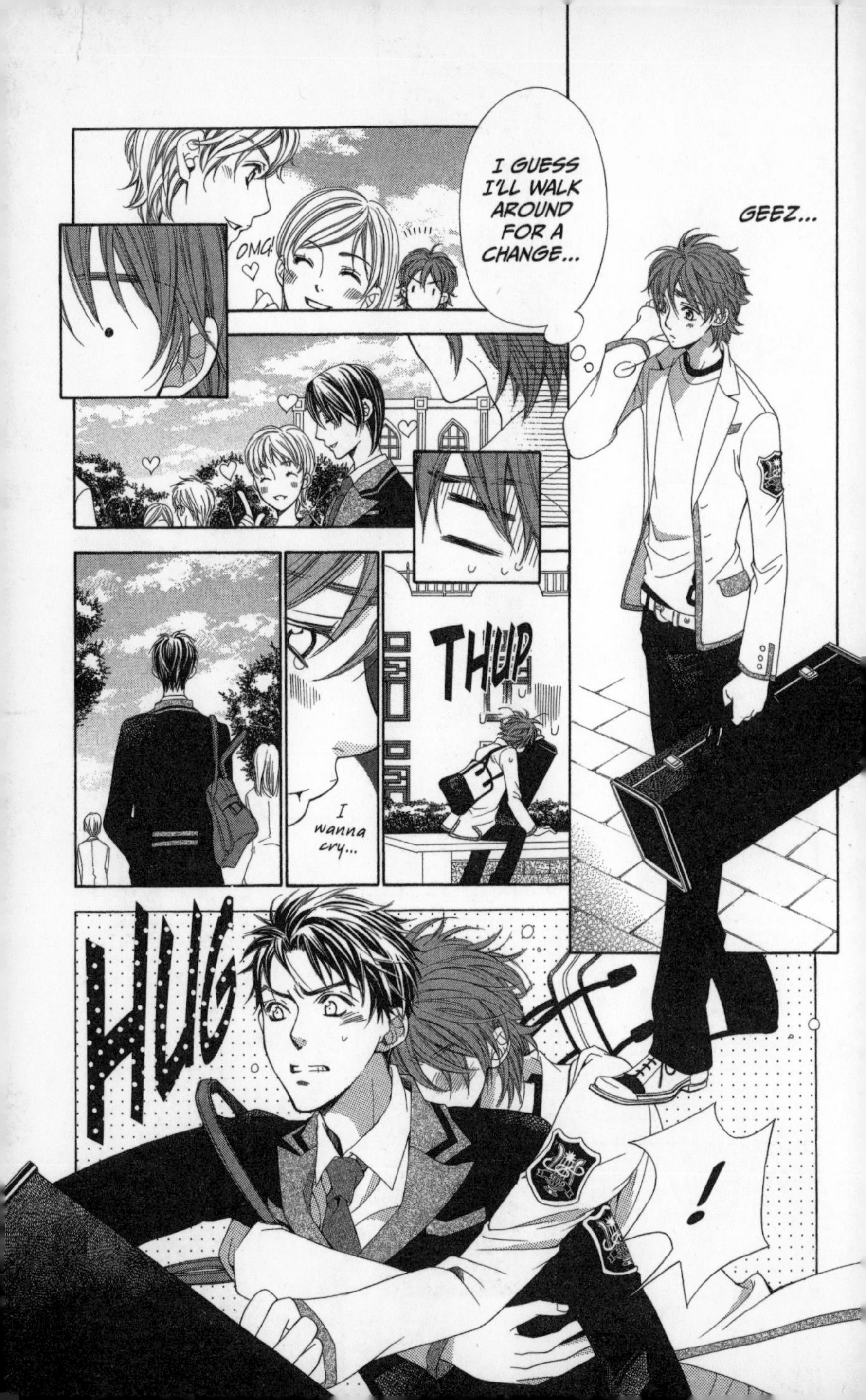
GEEZ...
I GUESS I'LL WALK AROUND FOR A CHANGE...
OMG!
THUP
I wanna cry...
HUG
!

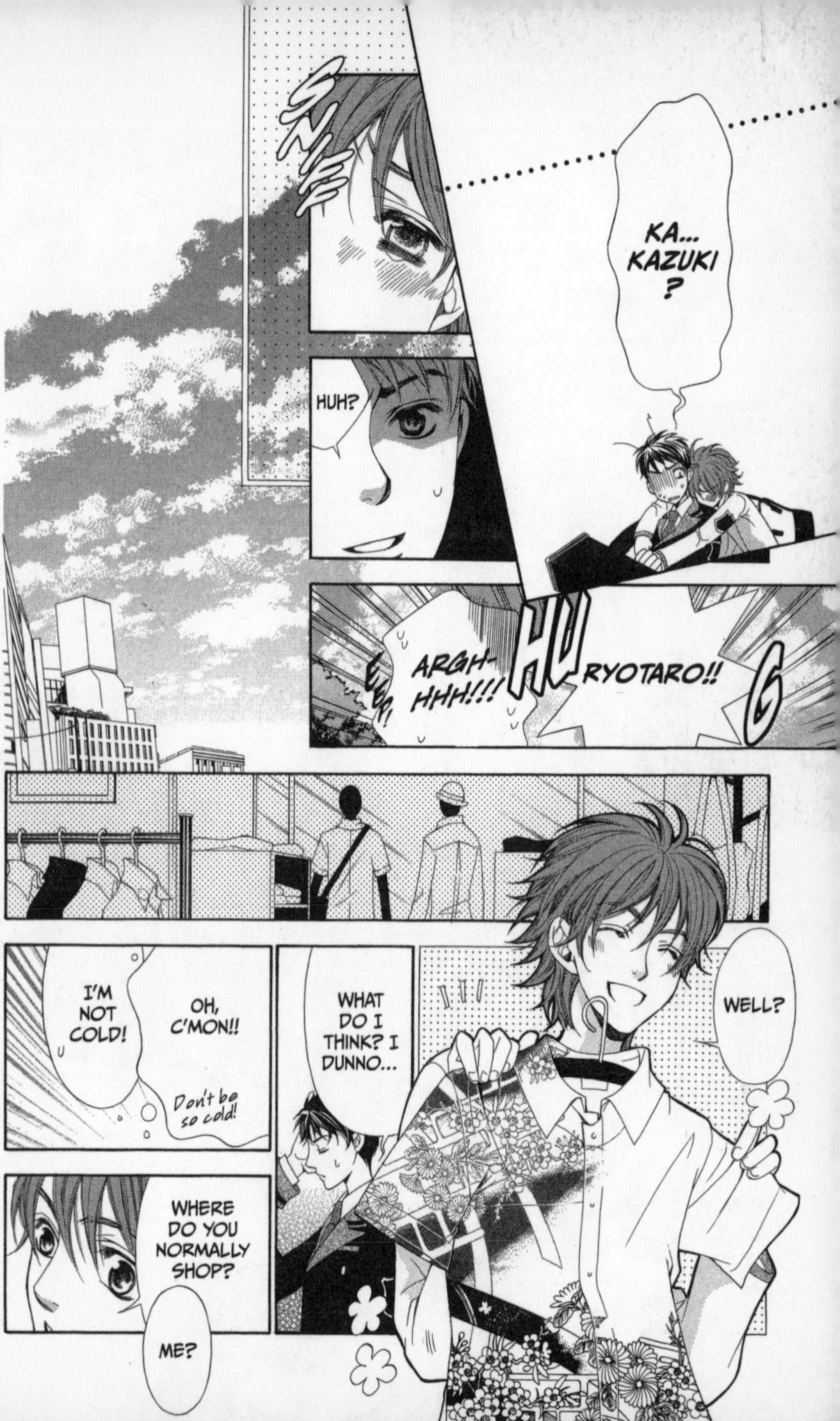
KA... KAZUKI?
HUH?
RYOTARO!!
ARGH-HHH!!!
WELL?
WHAT DO I THINK? I DUNNO...
OH, C'MON!!
Don't be so cold!
I'M NOT COLD!
WHERE DO YOU NORMALLY SHOP?
ME?

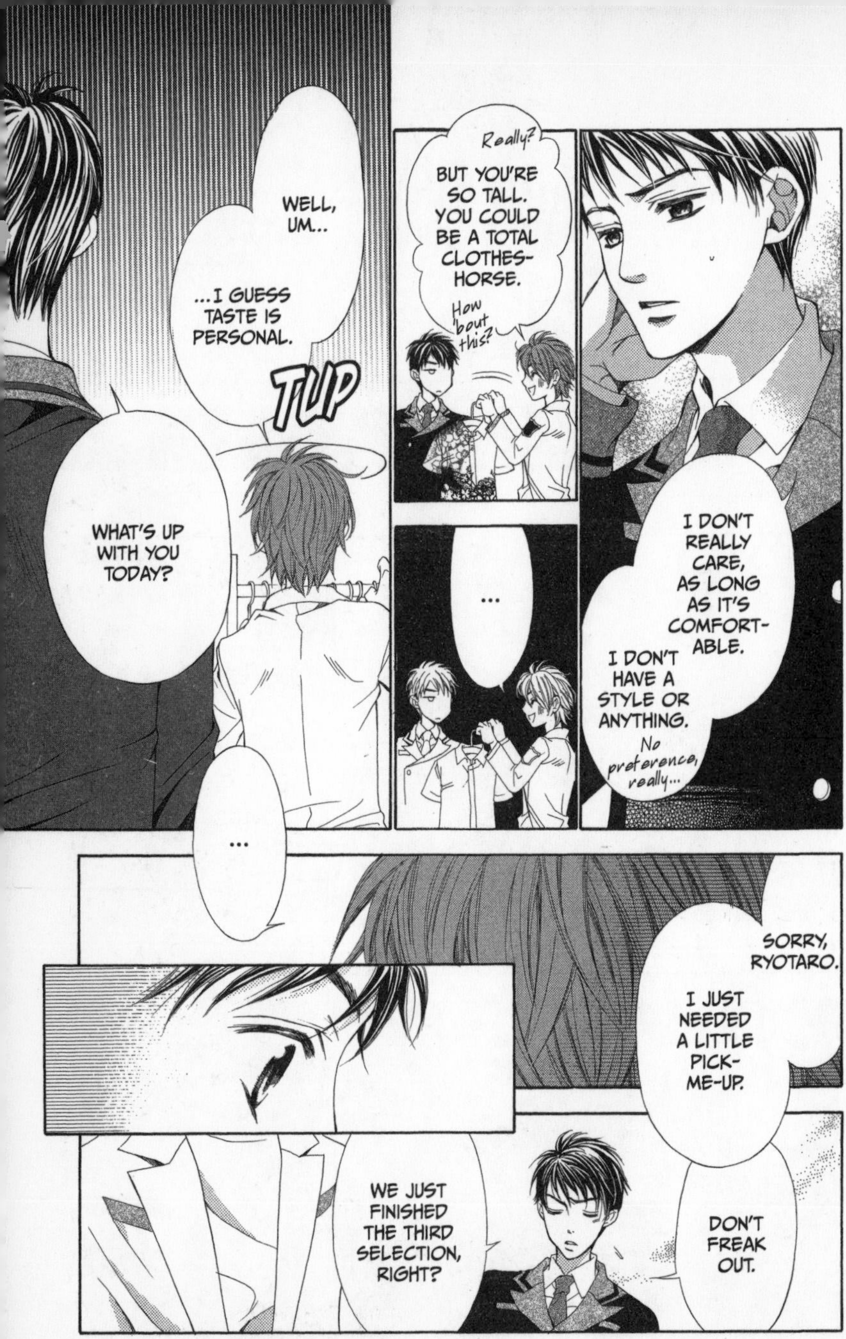
I DON'T REALLY CARE, AS LONG AS IT'S COMFORTABLE.
I DON'T HAVE A STYLE OR ANYTHING.
No preference, really...
Really?
BUT YOU'RE SO TALL. YOU COULD BE A TOTAL CLOTHES-HORSE.
How 'bout this?
...
WELL, UM...
...I GUESS TASTE IS PERSONAL.
TUP
WHAT'S UP WITH YOU TODAY?
...
SORRY, RYOTARO.
I JUST NEEDED A LITTLE PICK-ME-UP.
DON'T FREAK OUT.
WE JUST FINISHED THE THIRD SELECTION, RIGHT?

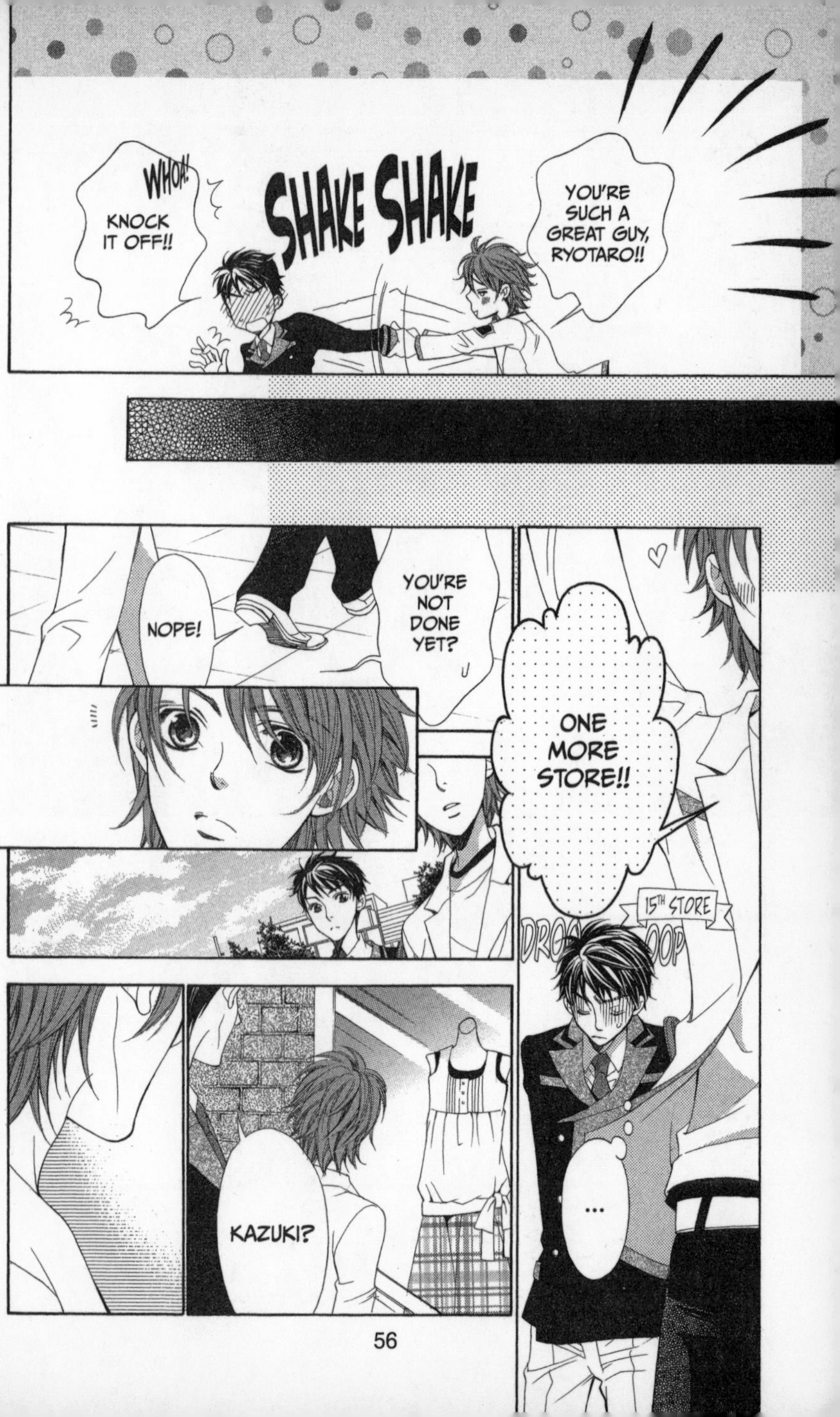
YOU'RE SUCH A GREAT GUY, RYOTARO!!
SHAKE SHAKE
WHOA!
KNOCK IT OFF!!
ONE MORE STORE!!
15TH STORE
...
YOU'RE NOT DONE YET?
NOPE!
KAZUKI?

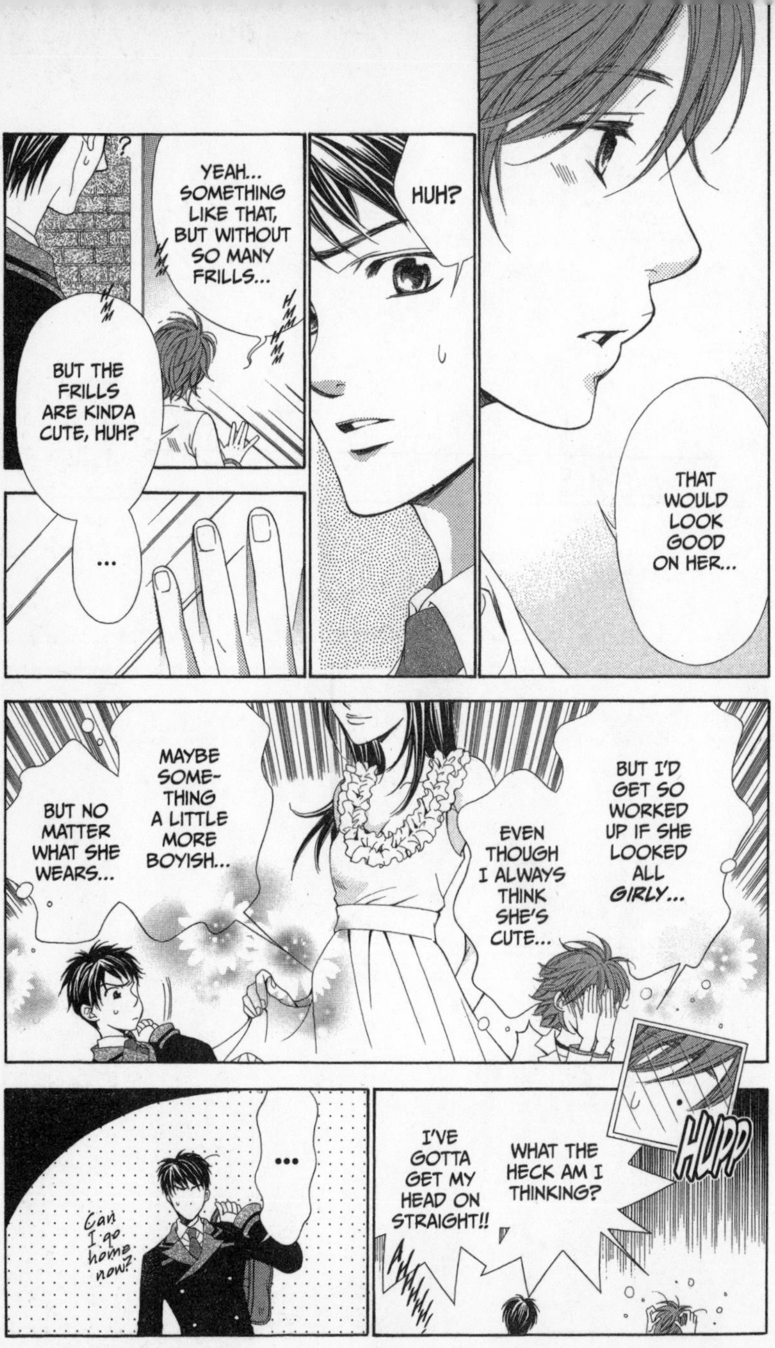
THAT WOULD LOOK GOOD ON HER...
HUH?
YEAH... SOMETHING LIKE THAT, BUT WITHOUT SO MANY FRILLS...
?
BUT THE FRILLS ARE KINDA CUTE, HUH?
...
BUT I'D GET SO WORKED UP IF SHE LOOKED ALL *GIRLY*...
EVEN THOUGH I ALWAYS THINK SHE'S CUTE...
MAYBE SOME-THING A LITTLE MORE BOYISH...
BUT NO MATTER WHAT SHE WEARS...
HUPP
WHAT THE HECK AM I THINKING?
I'VE GOTTA GET MY HEAD ON STRAIGHT!!
...
Can I go home now?

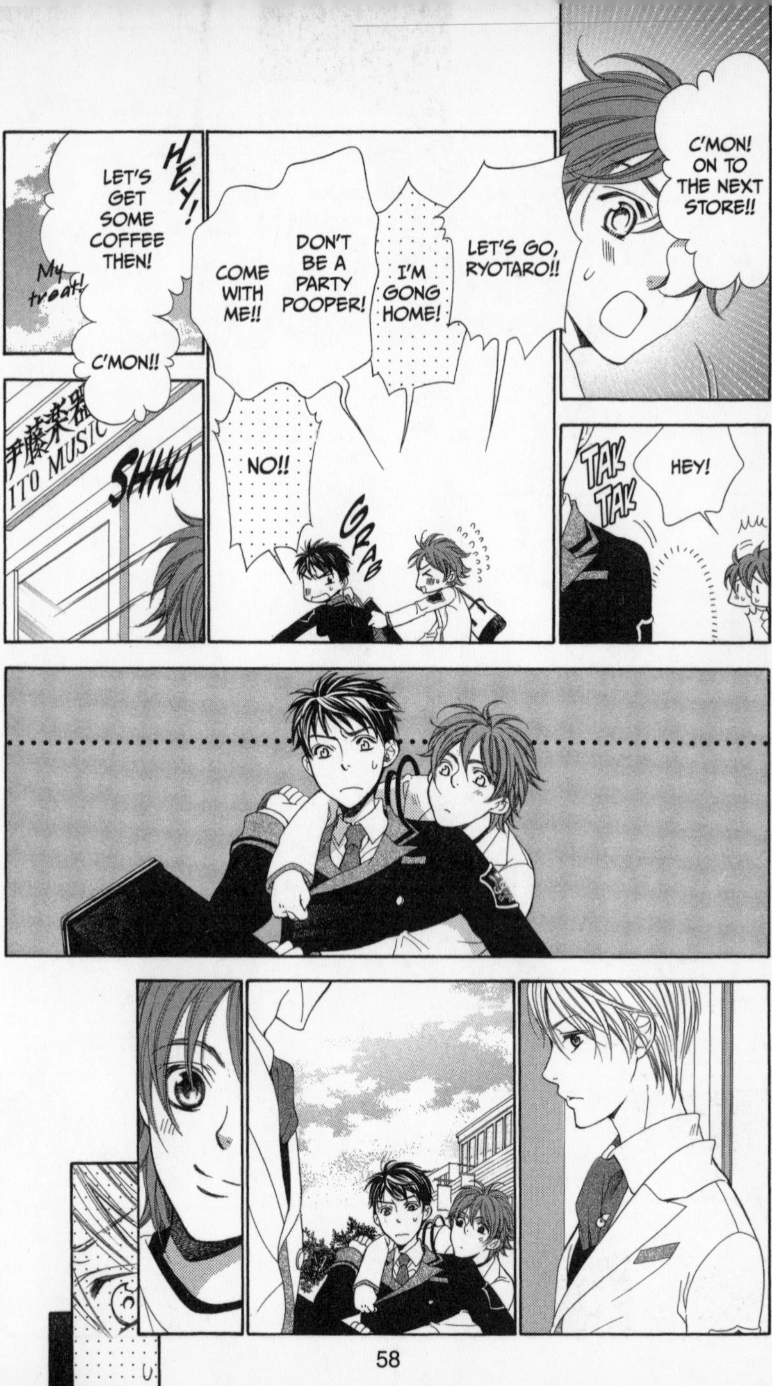
C'MON! ON TO THE NEXT STORE!!
TAK TAK
HEY!
MU
LET'S GO, RYOTARO!!
I'M GONG HOME!
DON'T BE A PARTY POOPER!
COME WITH ME!!
NO!!
GRAB
HEY!!
LET'S GET SOME COFFEE THEN!
My treat!
C'MON!!
伊藤楽器
ITO MUSIC
SHHU

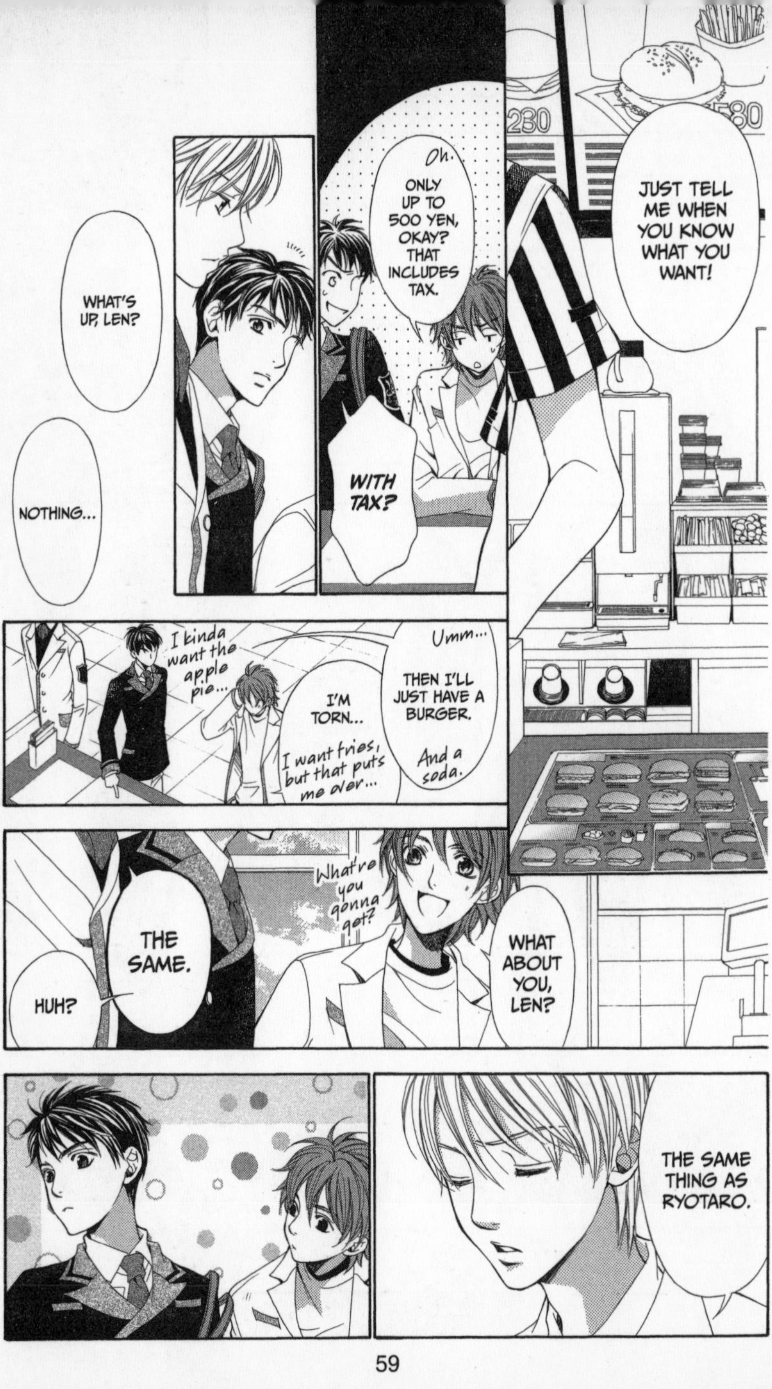
JUST TELL ME WHEN YOU KNOW WHAT YOU WANT!
Oh.
ONLY UP TO 500 YEN, OKAY? THAT INCLUDES TAX.
WITH TAX?
WHAT'S UP, LEN?
NOTHING...
Umm...
THEN I'LL JUST HAVE A BURGER.
And a soda.
I'M TORN...
I want fries, but that puts me over...
I kinda want the apple pie...
WHAT ABOUT YOU, LEN?
What're you gonna get?
THE SAME.
HUH?
THE SAME THING AS RYOTARO.

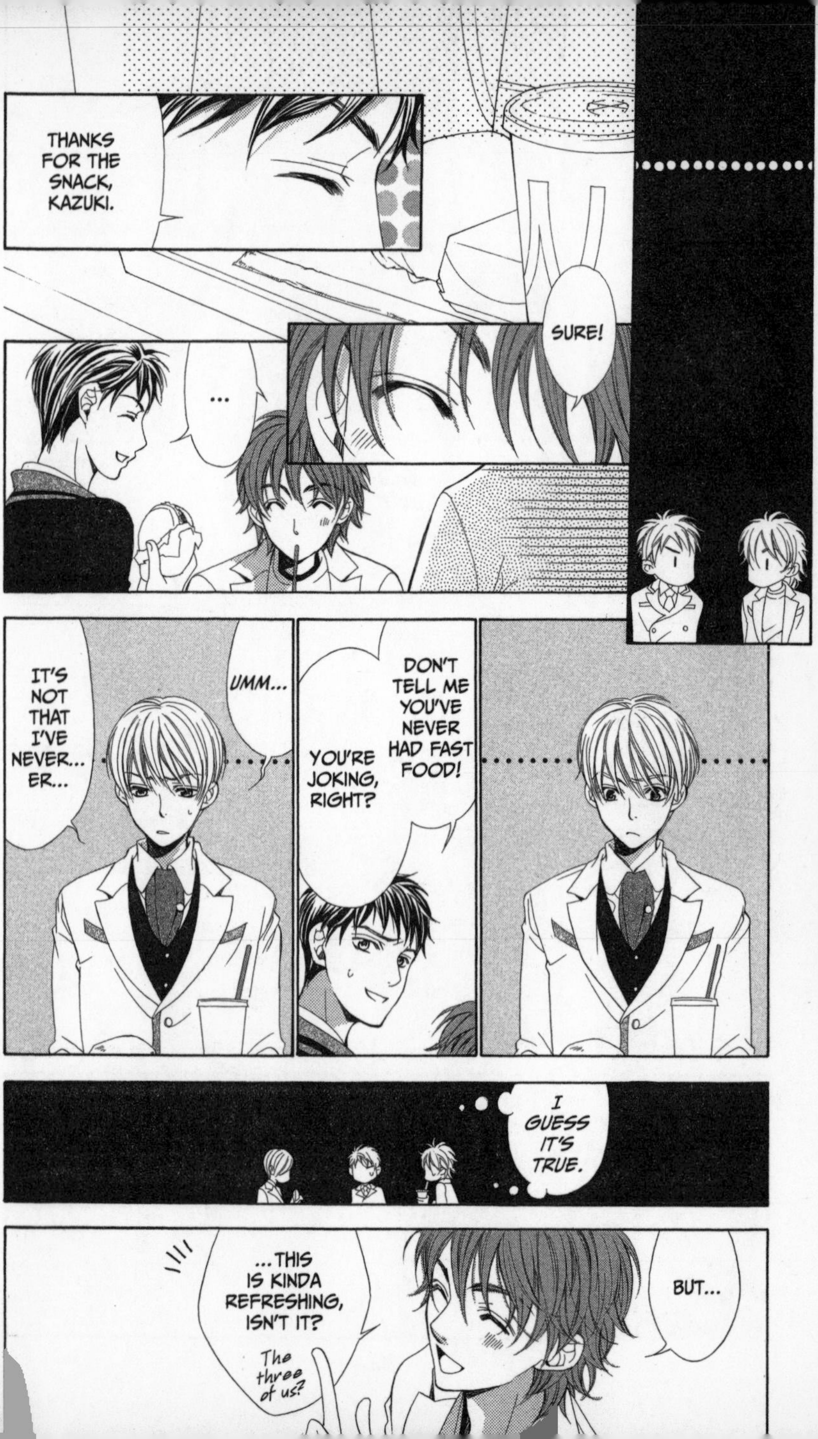
THANKS FOR THE SNACK, KAZUKI.
SURE!
...
DON'T TELL ME YOU'VE NEVER HAD FAST FOOD!
YOU'RE JOKING, RIGHT?
UMM...
IT'S NOT THAT I'VE NEVER... ER...
I GUESS IT'S TRUE.
BUT...
...THIS IS KINDA REFRESHING, ISN'T IT?
The three of us?

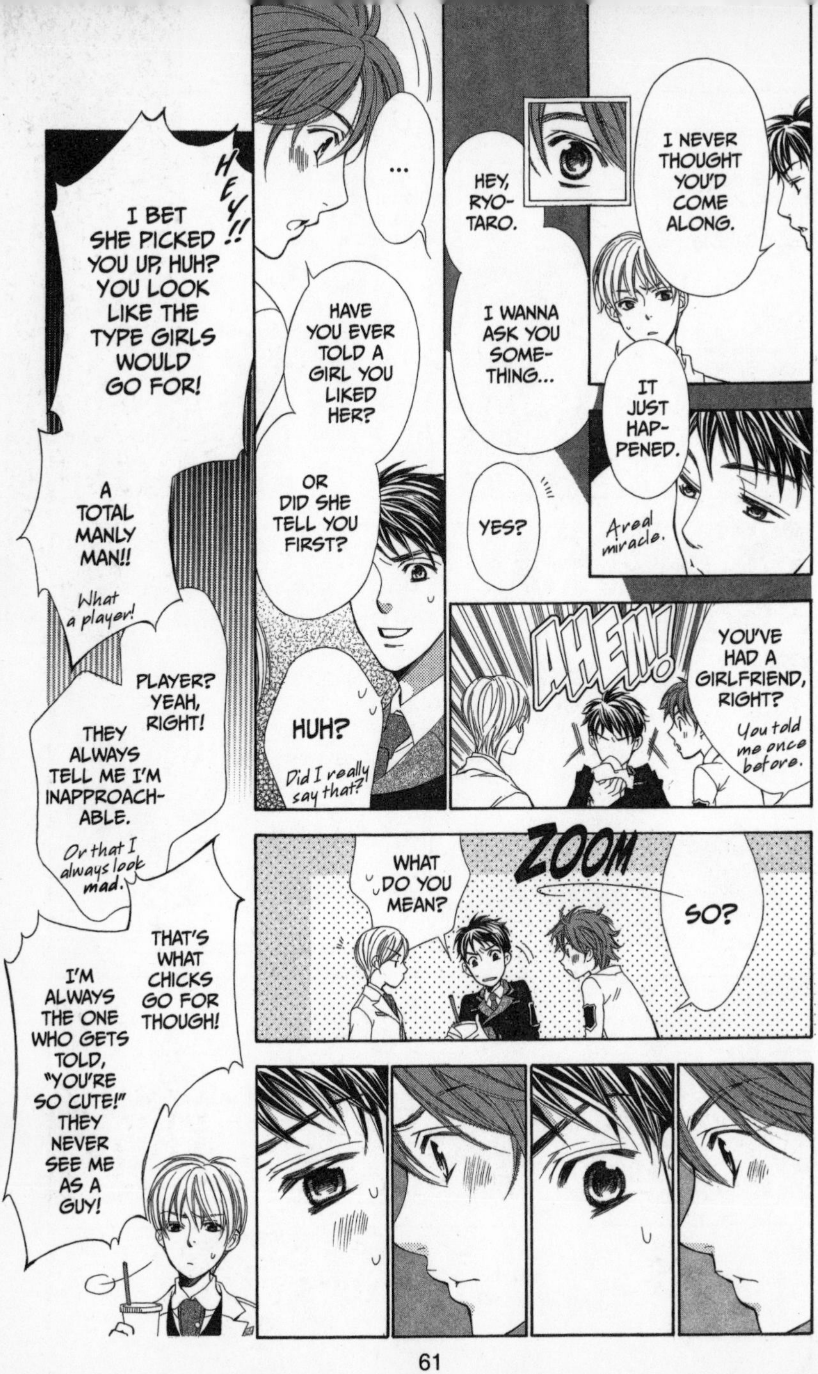
I NEVER THOUGHT YOU'D COME ALONG.
IT JUST HAPPENED.
A real miracle.
HEY, RYO-TARO.
I WANNA ASK YOU SOME-THING...
YES?
YOU'VE HAD A GIRLFRIEND, RIGHT?
You told me once before.
AHEM!
...
HAVE YOU EVER TOLD A GIRL YOU LIKED HER?
OR DID SHE TELL YOU FIRST?
HUH?
Did I really say that?
HEY!!
I BET SHE PICKED YOU UP, HUH? YOU LOOK LIKE THE TYPE GIRLS WOULD GO FOR!
A TOTAL MANLY MAN!!
What a player!
PLAYER? YEAH, RIGHT!
THEY ALWAYS TELL ME I'M INAPPROACH-ABLE.
Or that I always look mad.
THAT'S WHAT CHICKS GO FOR THOUGH!
I'M ALWAYS THE ONE WHO GETS TOLD, "YOU'RE SO CUTE!" THEY NEVER SEE ME AS A GUY!
SO?
ZOOM
WHAT DO YOU MEAN?

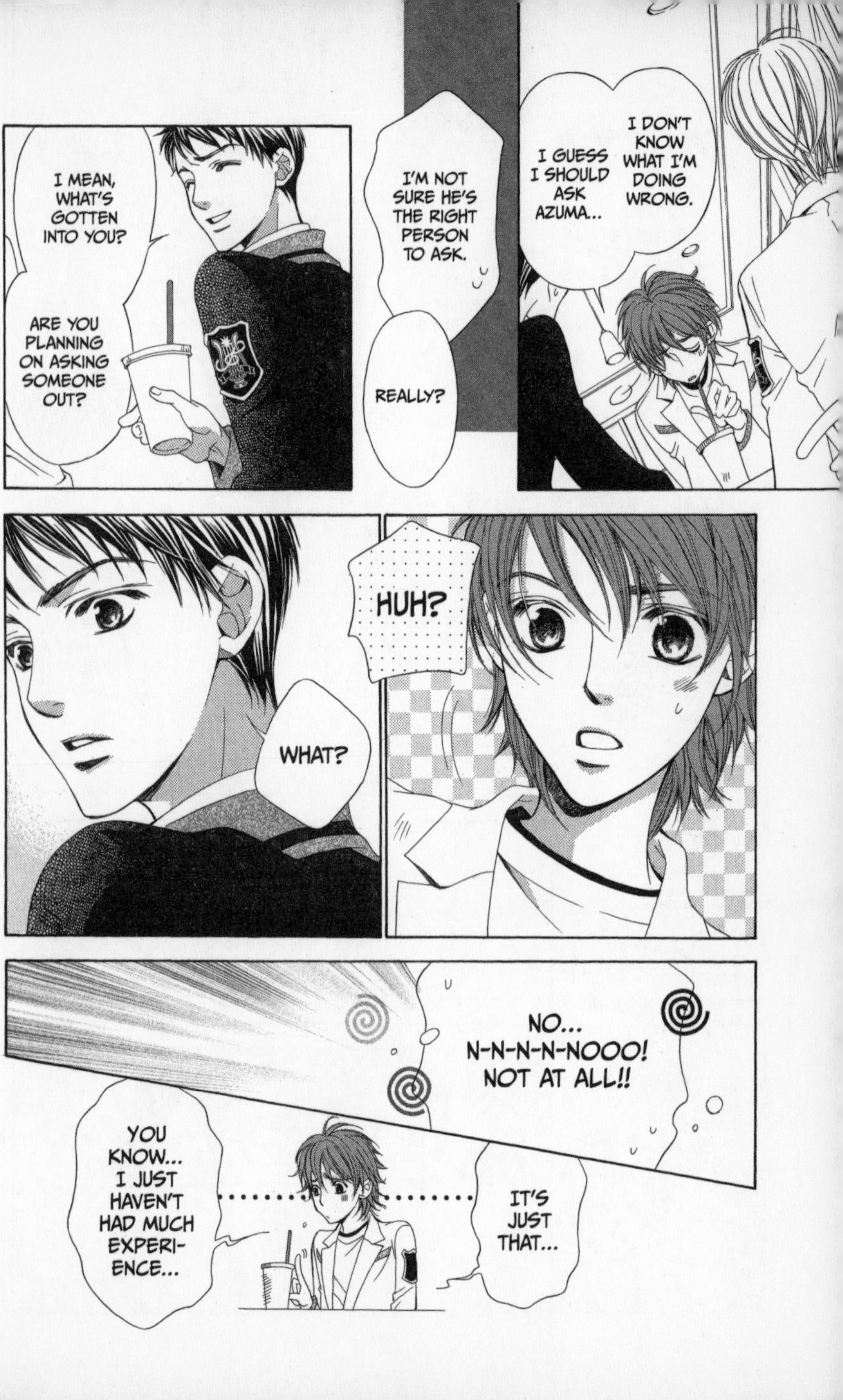
I DON'T KNOW WHAT I'M DOING WRONG.
I GUESS I SHOULD ASK AZUMA...
I'M NOT SURE HE'S THE RIGHT PERSON TO ASK.
REALLY?
I MEAN, WHAT'S GOTTEN INTO YOU?
ARE YOU PLANNING ON ASKING SOMEONE OUT?
HUH?
WHAT?
NO... N-N-N-N-NOOO! NOT AT ALL!!
IT'S JUST THAT...
YOU KNOW... I JUST HAVEN'T HAD MUCH EXPERI-ENCE...

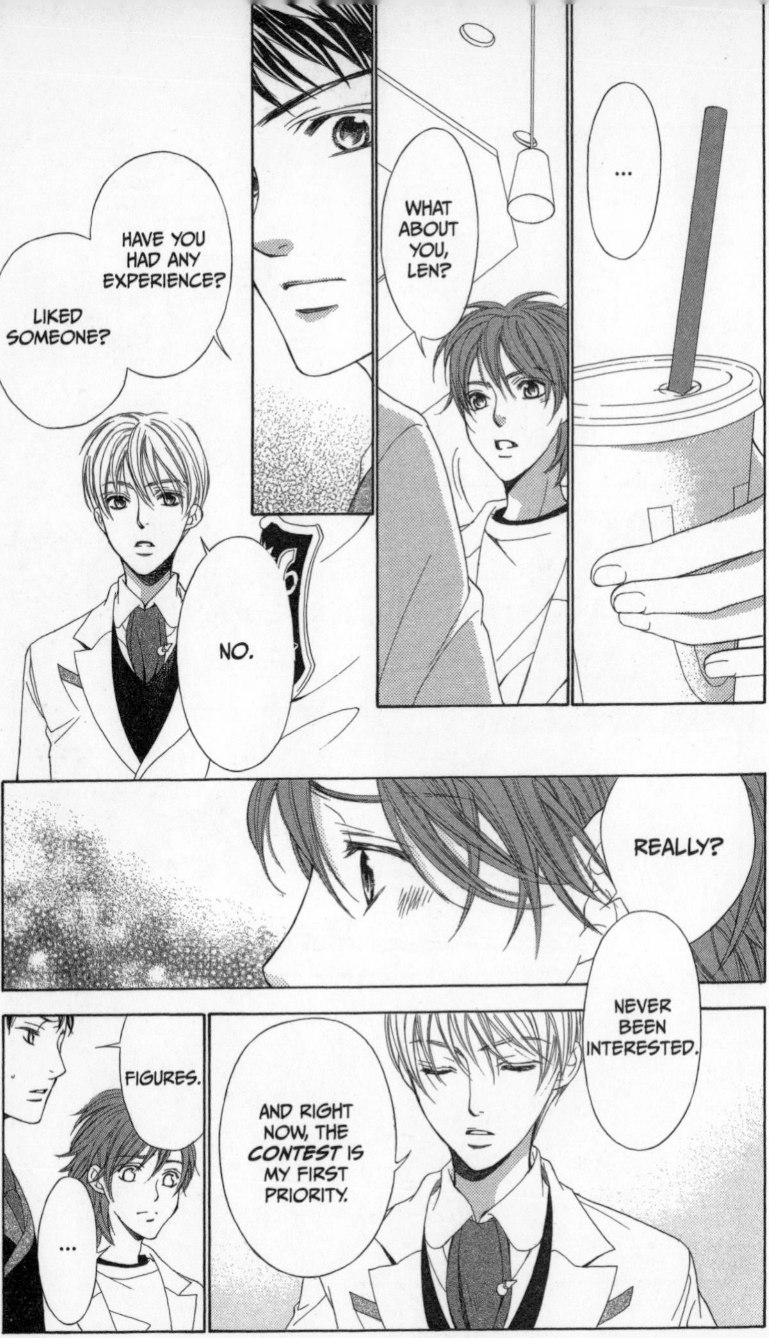
...
WHAT ABOUT YOU, LEN?
HAVE YOU HAD ANY EXPERIENCE?
LIKED SOMEONE?
NO.
REALLY?
NEVER BEEN INTERESTED.
AND RIGHT NOW, THE *CONTEST* IS MY FIRST PRIORITY.
FIGURES.
...

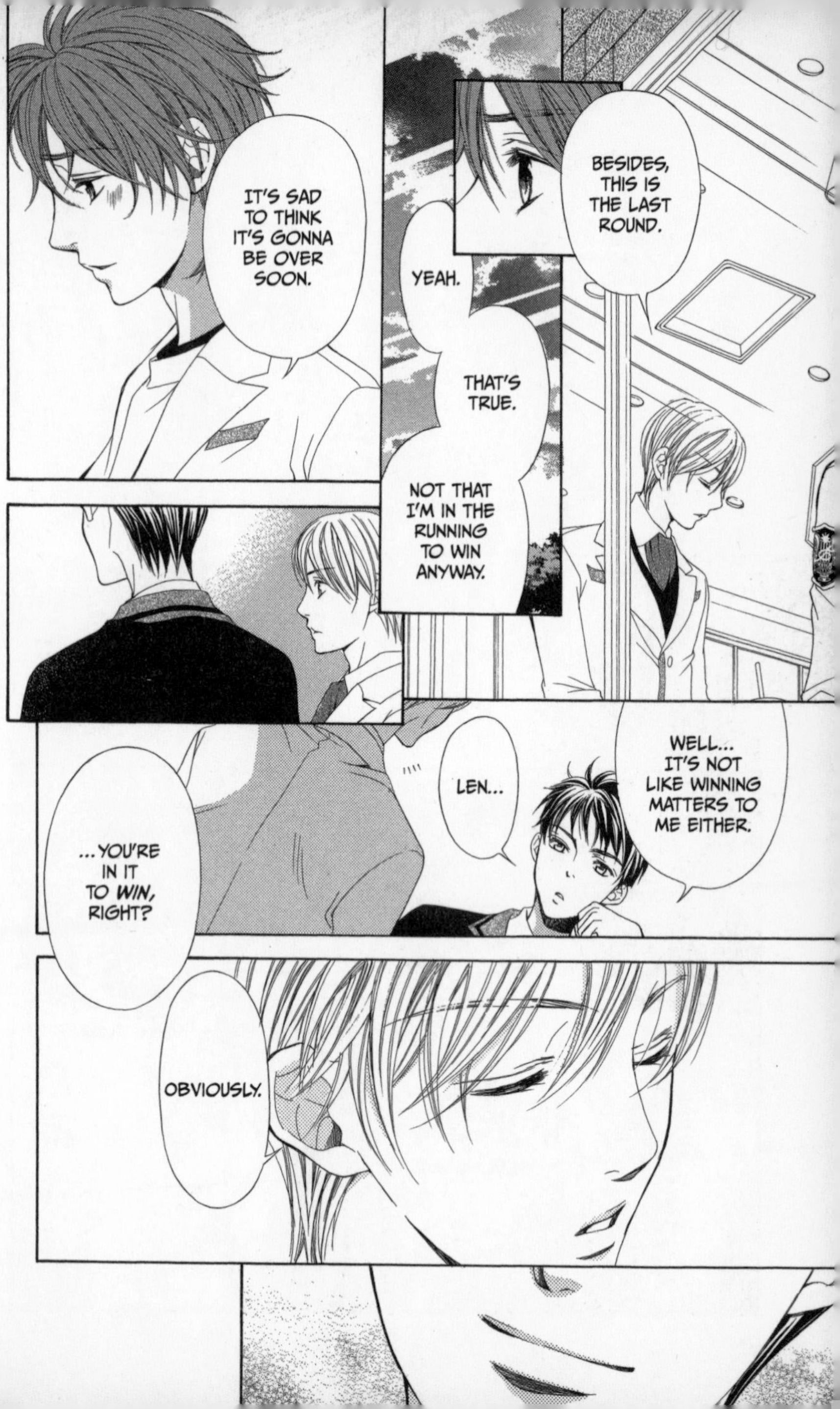
BESIDES, THIS IS THE LAST ROUND.
YEAH.
THAT'S TRUE.
NOT THAT I'M IN THE RUNNING TO WIN ANYWAY.
IT'S SAD TO THINK IT'S GONNA BE OVER SOON.
WELL... IT'S NOT LIKE WINNING MATTERS TO ME EITHER.
LEN...
...YOU'RE IN IT TO *WIN*, RIGHT?
OBVIOUSLY.

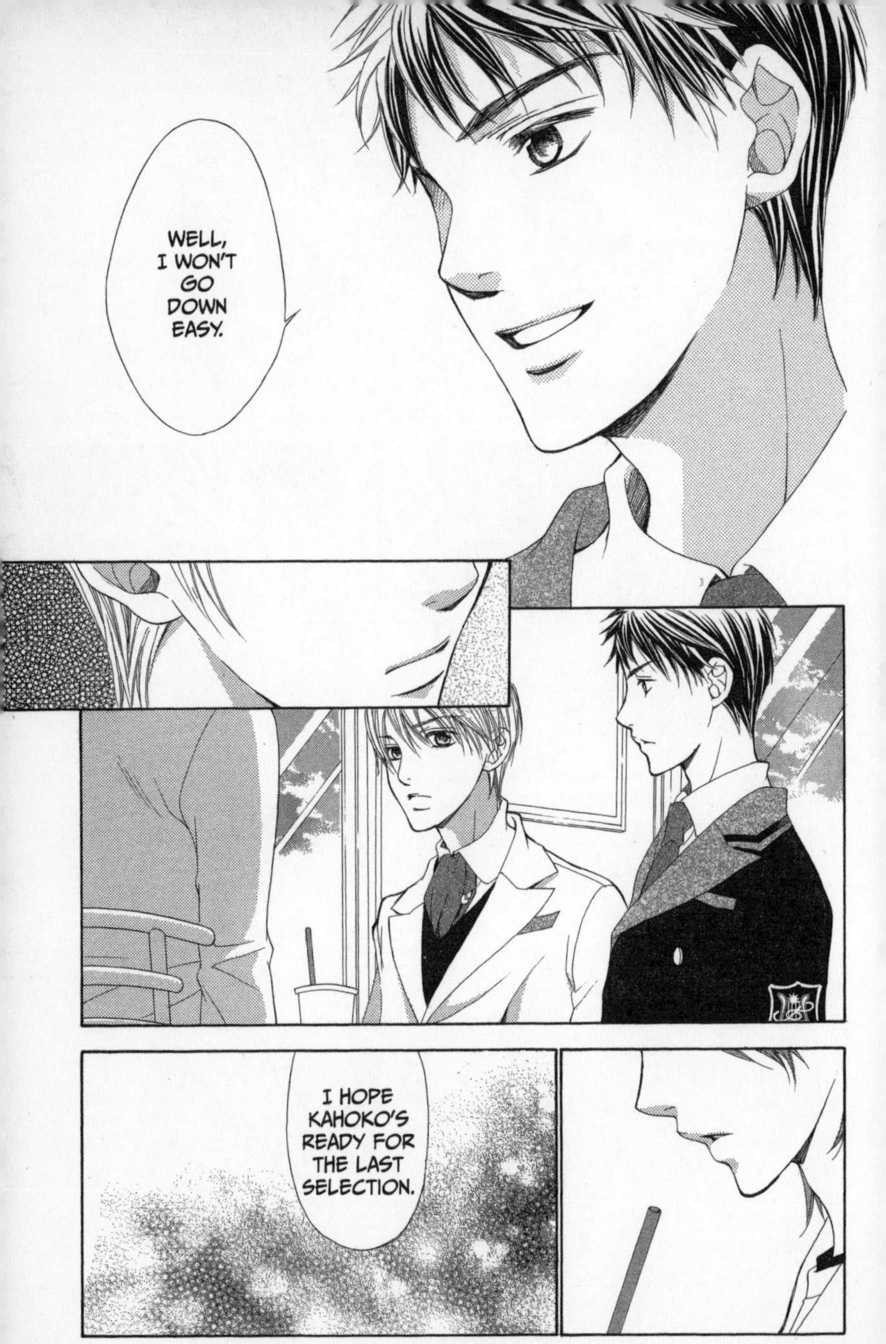
WELL, I WON'T GO DOWN EASY.
I HOPE KAHOKO'S READY FOR THE LAST SELECTION.

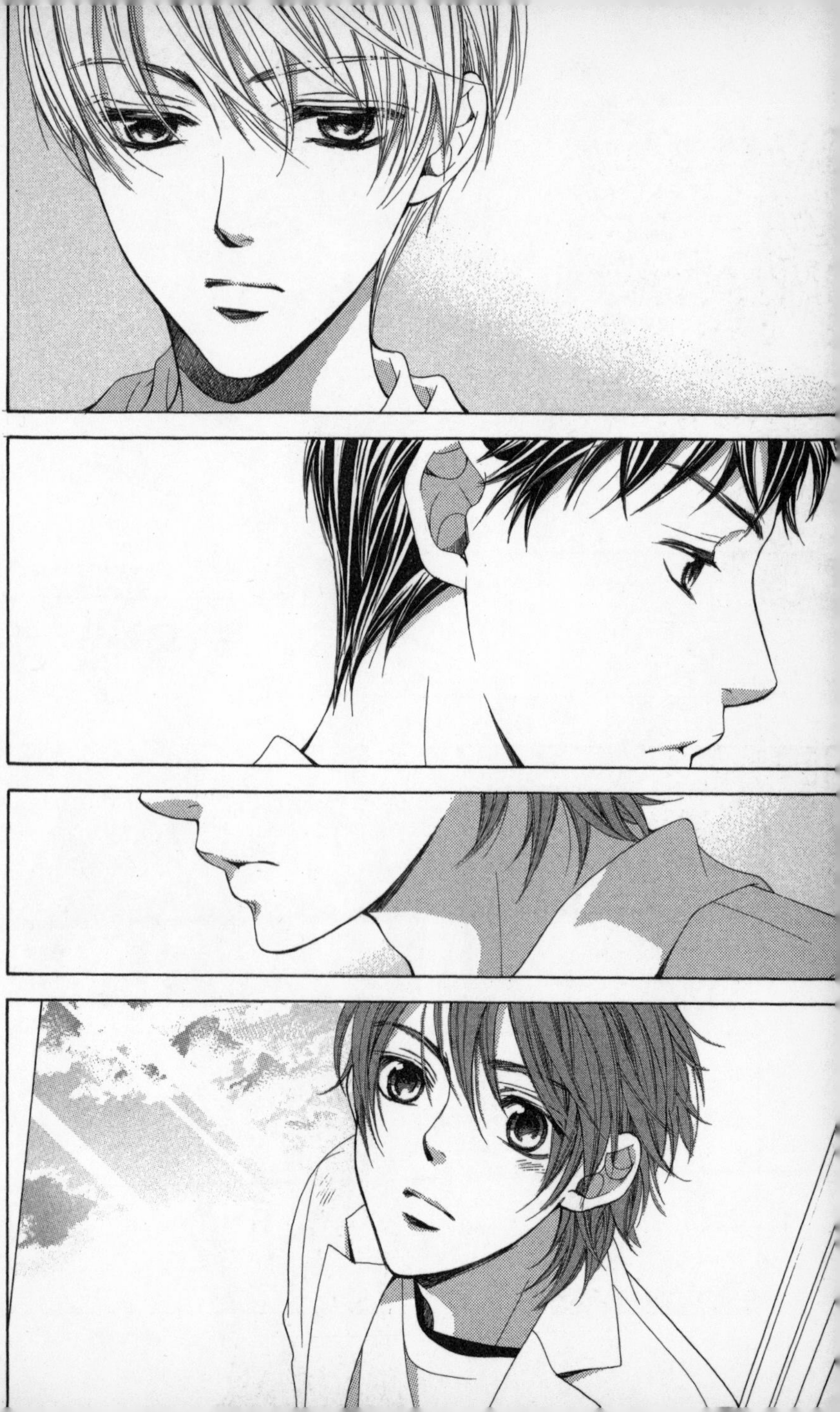

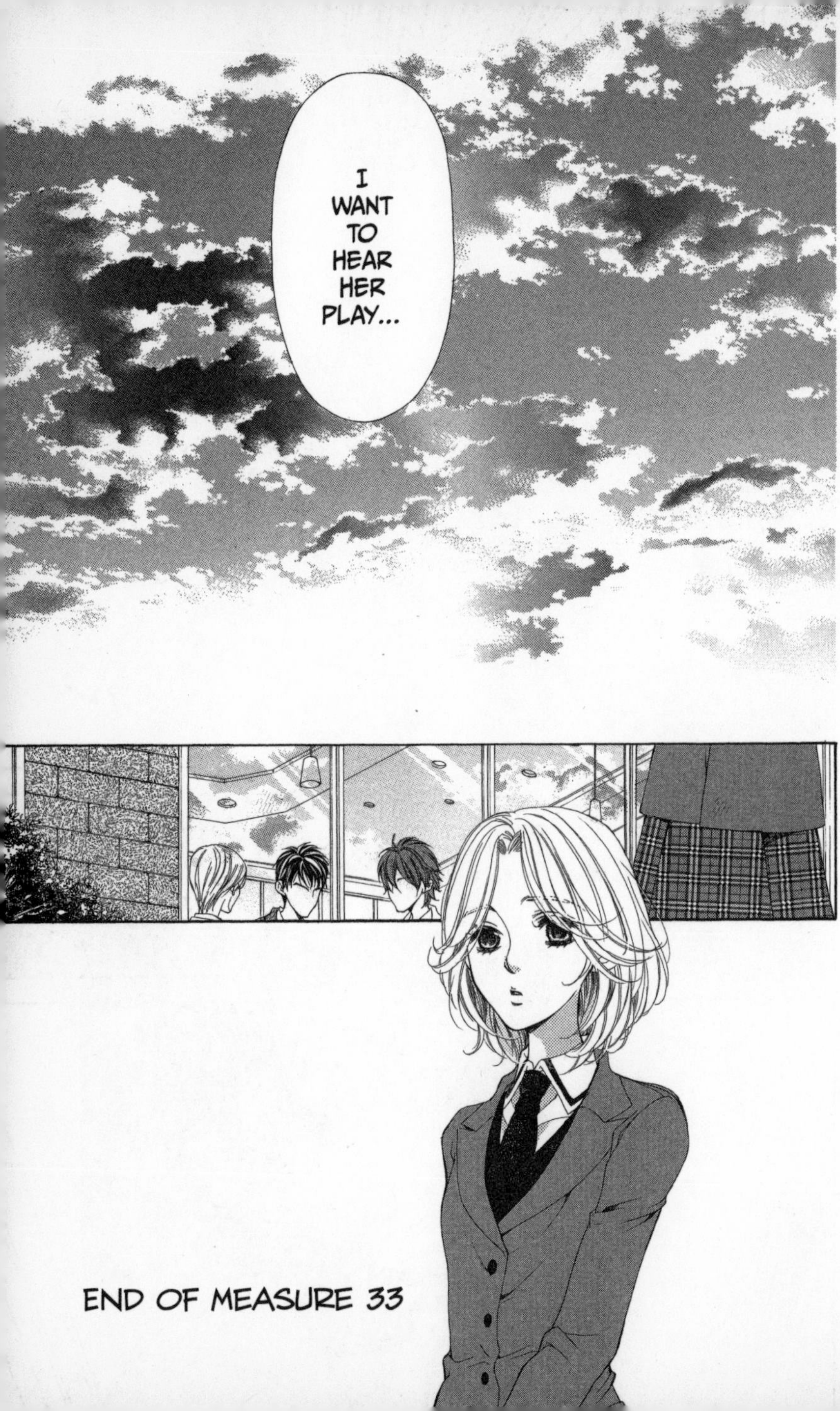
I WANT TO HEAR HER PLAY...
END OF MEASURE 33

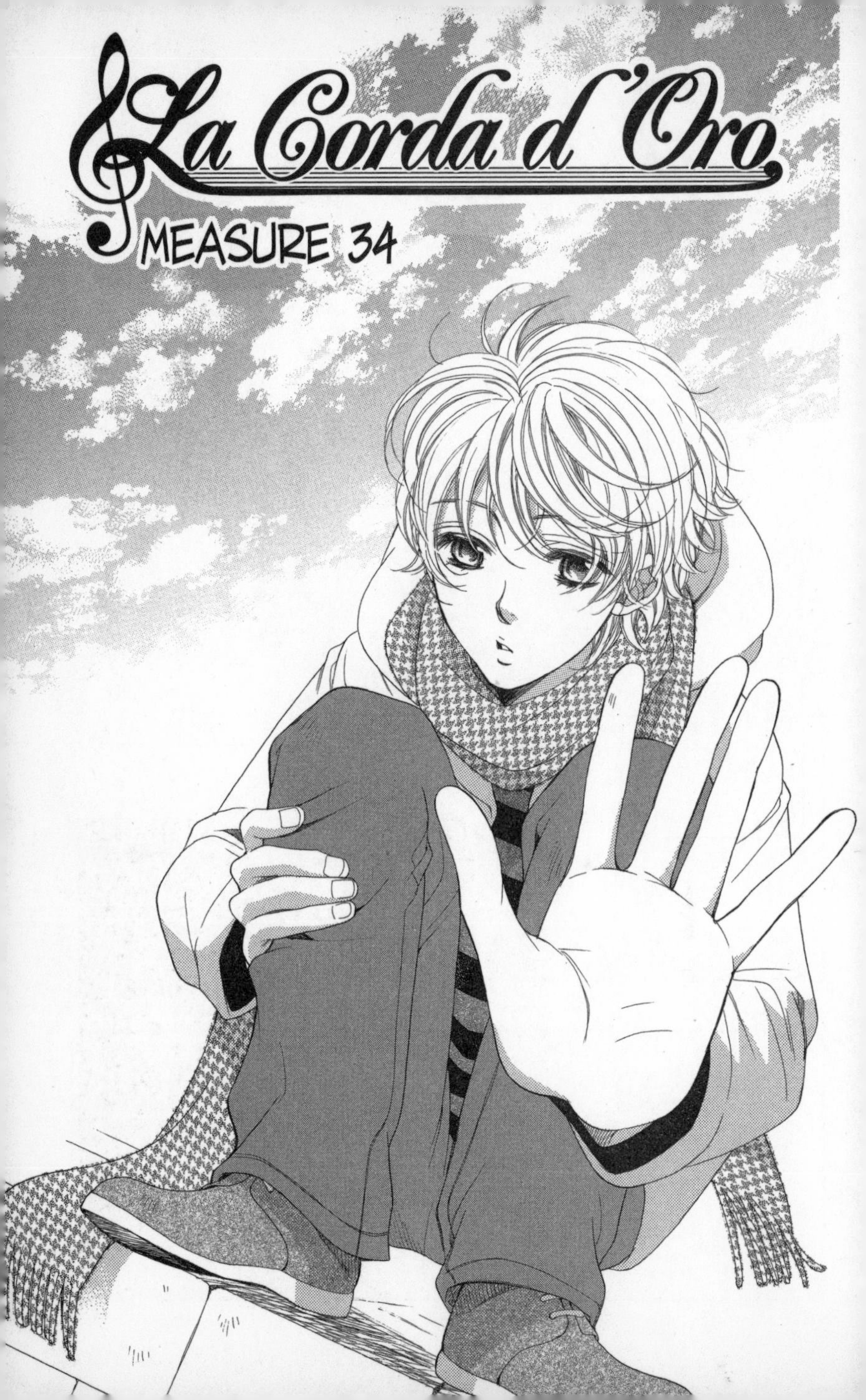
La Corda d'Oro
MEASURE 34

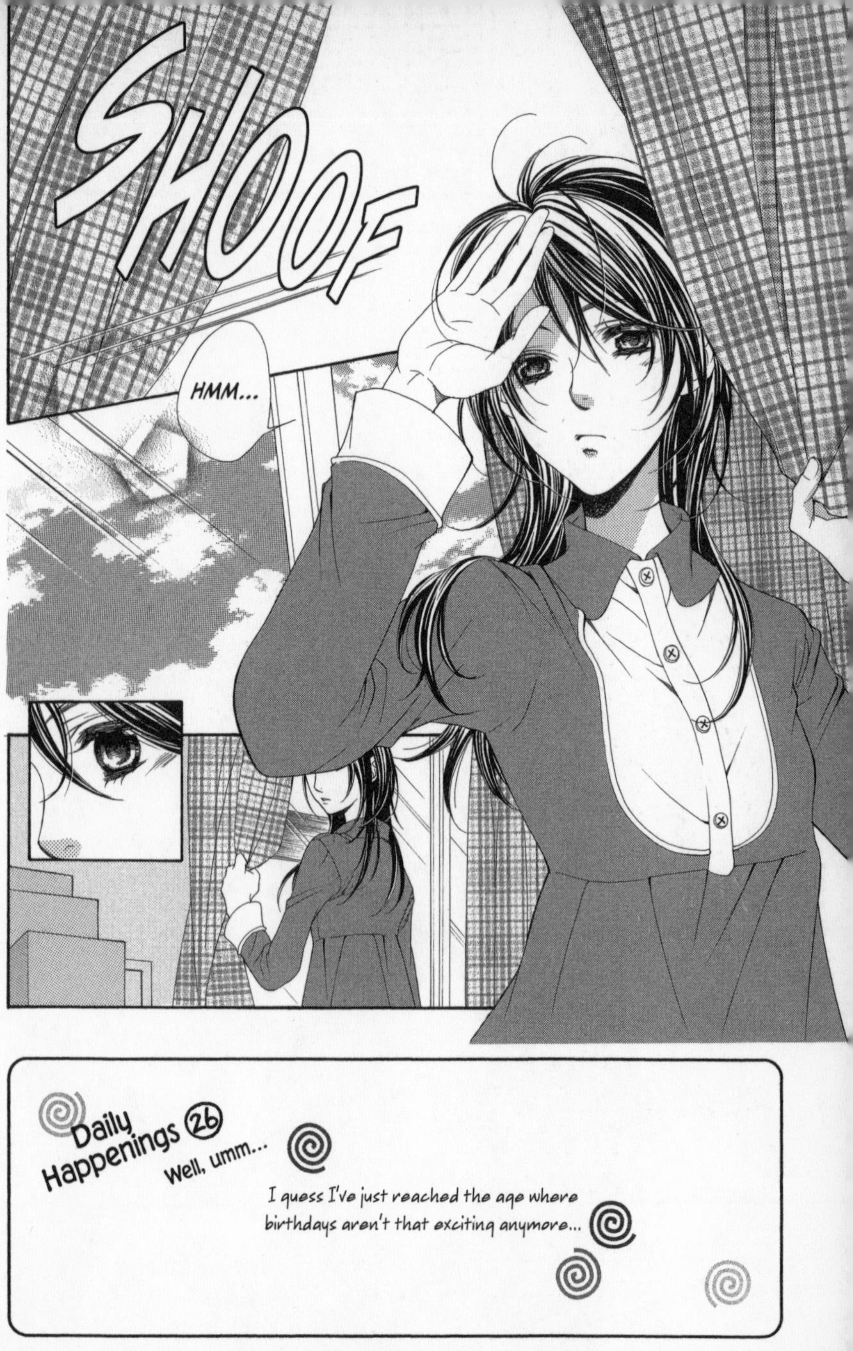
SHOOF
HMM...

Daily Happenings 26

Well, umm...

I guess I've just reached the age where birthdays aren't that exciting anymore...

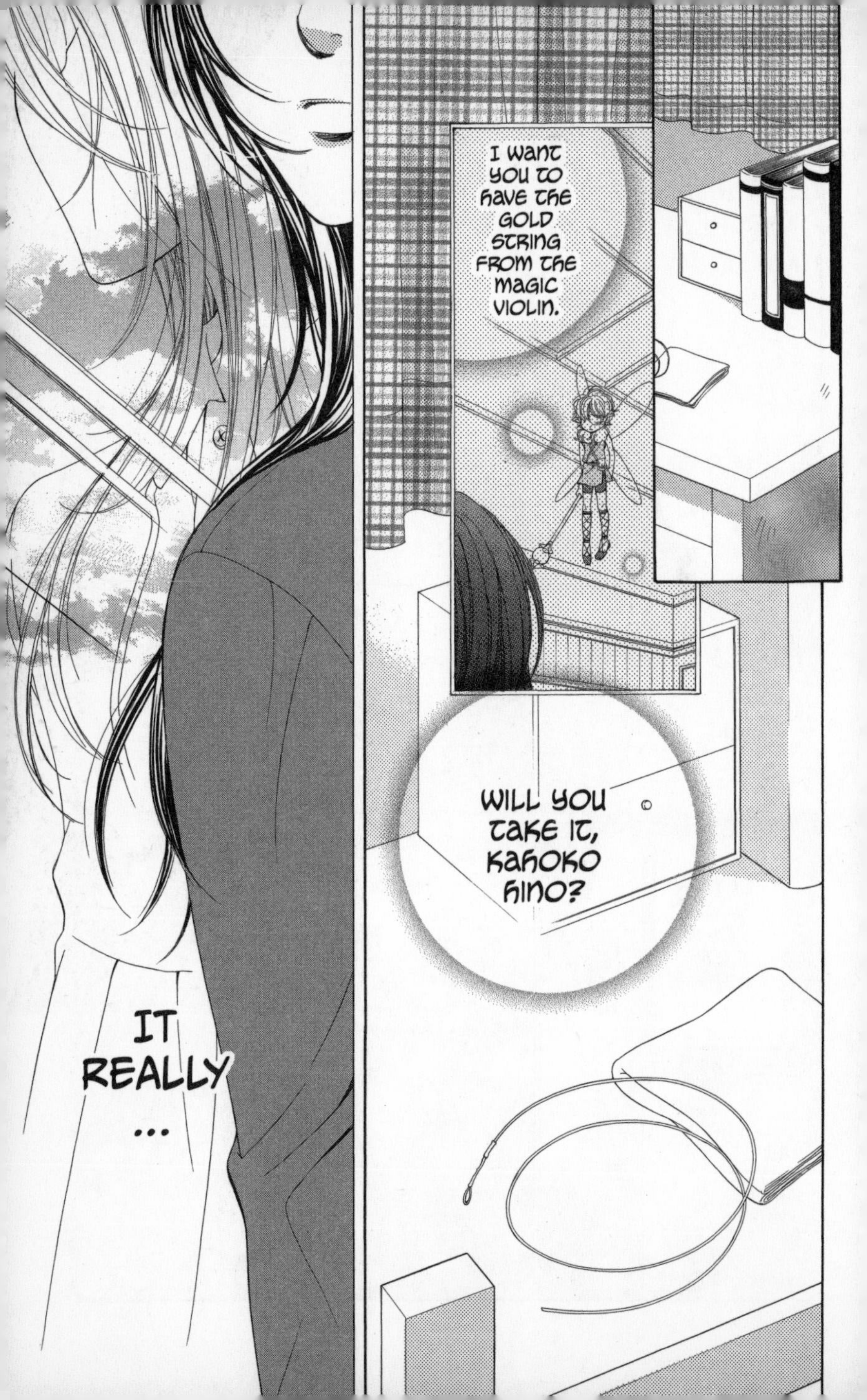
I WANT YOU TO HAVE THE GOLD STRING FROM THE MAGIC VIOLIN.
WILL YOU TAKE IT, KAHOKO HINO?
IT REALLY ...

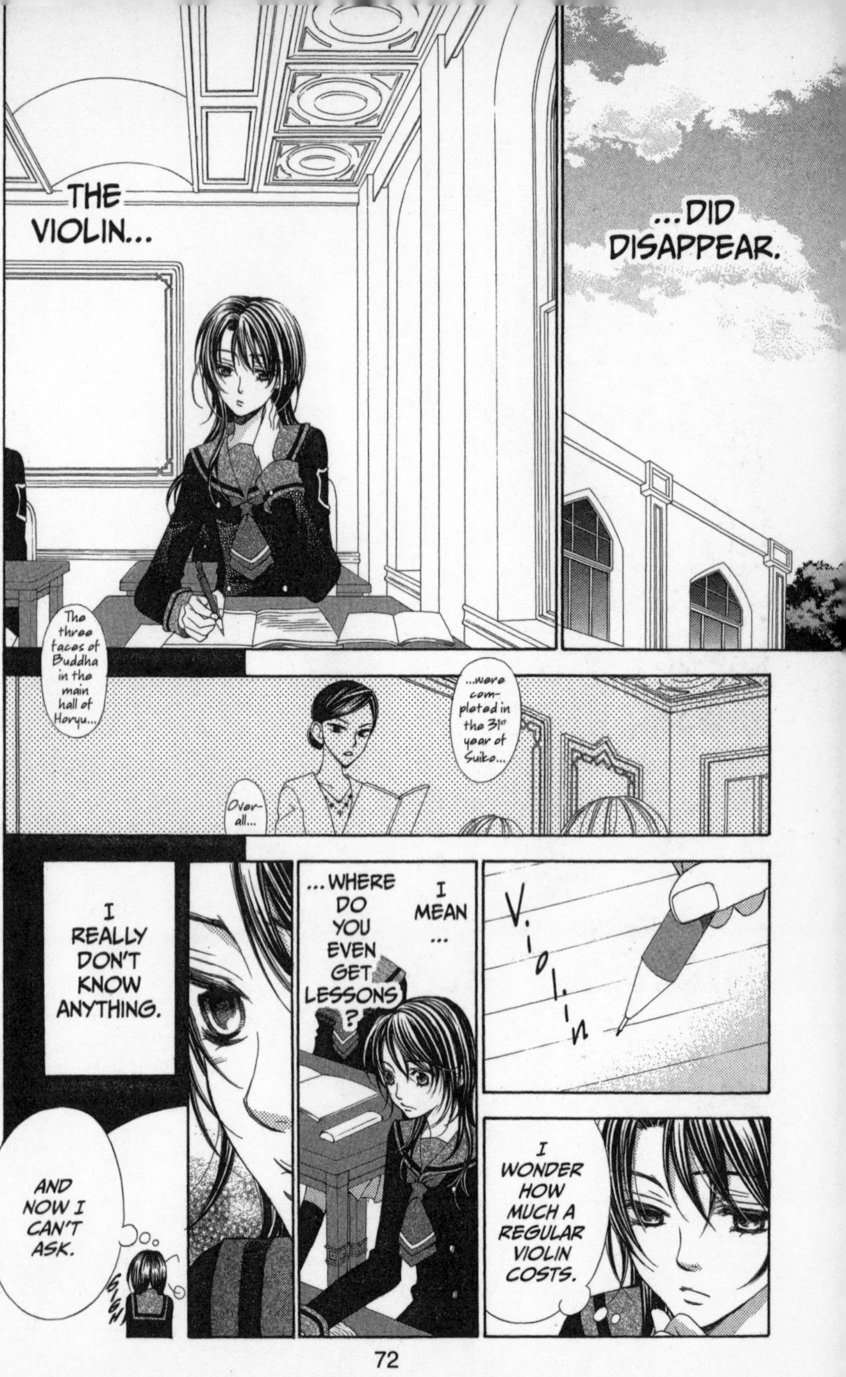
...DID DISAPPEAR.
THE VIOLIN...
The three faces of Buddha in the main hall of Horyu...
...were completed in the 31st year of Suiko...
Overall...
Violin
I WONDER HOW MUCH A REGULAR VIOLIN COSTS.
I MEAN ...
...WHERE DO YOU EVEN GET LESSONS?
I REALLY DON'T KNOW ANYTHING.
AND NOW I CAN'T ASK.
SIGH

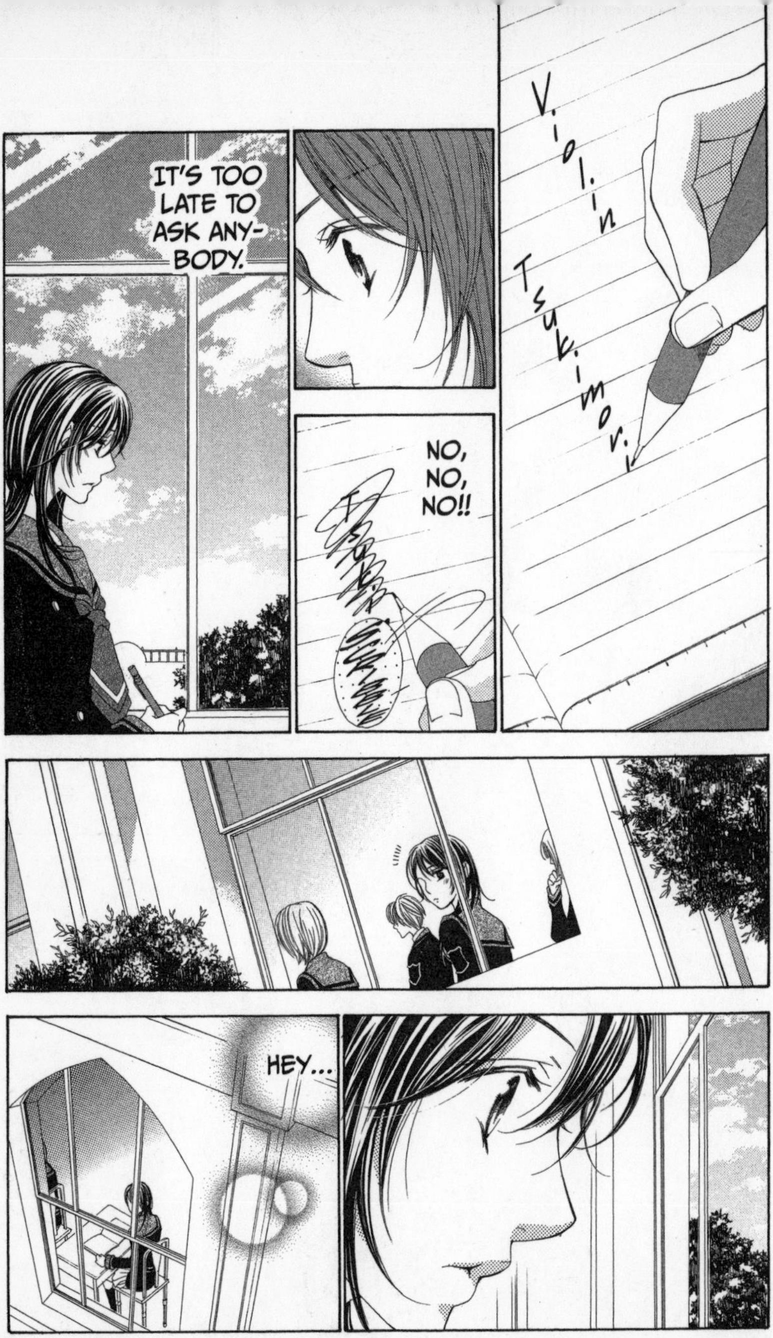
Violin Tsukimori
NO, NO, NO!!
IT'S TOO LATE TO ASK ANYBODY.
HEY...

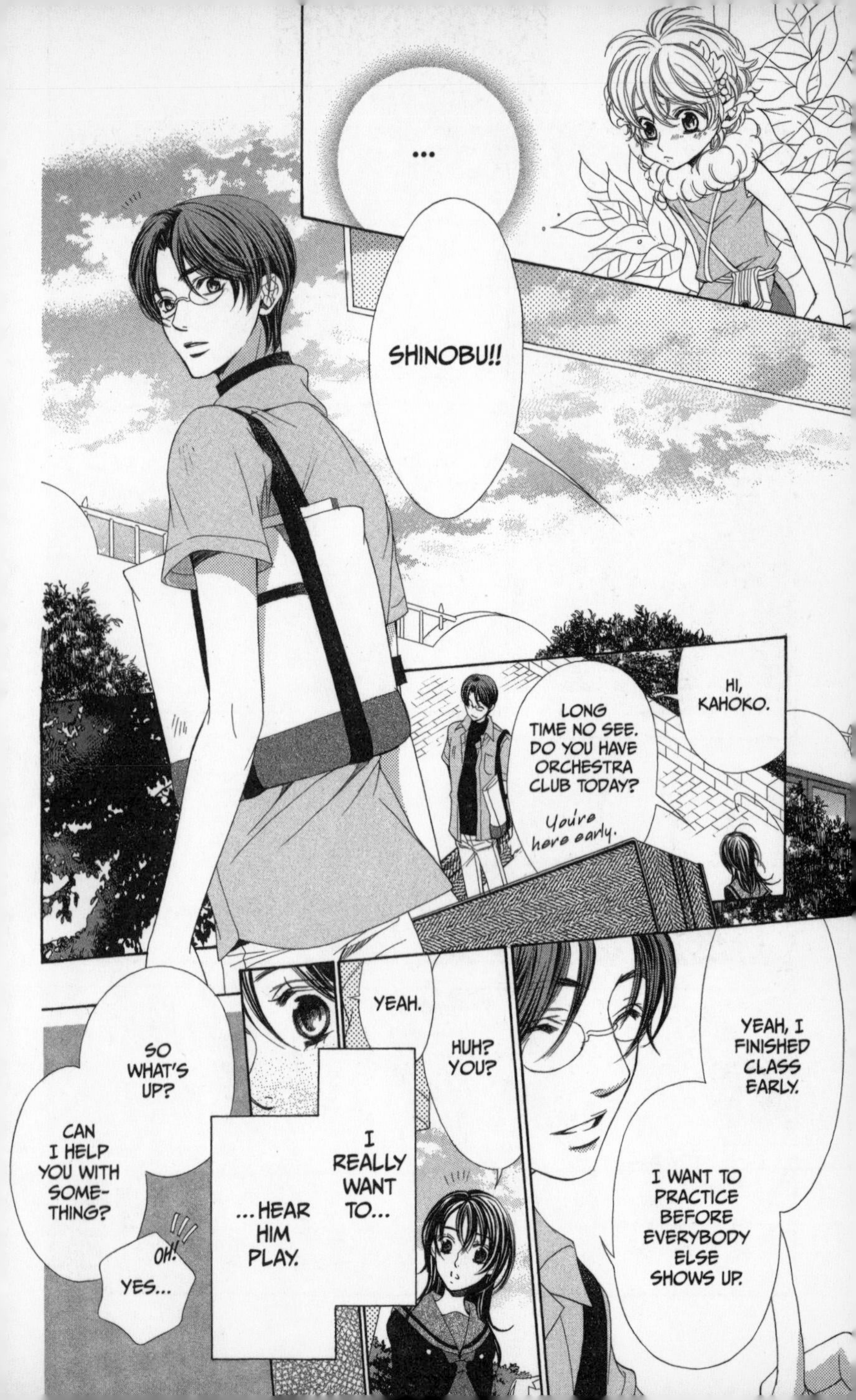
...
SHINOBU!!
HI, KAHOKO.
LONG TIME NO SEE. DO YOU HAVE ORCHESTRA CLUB TODAY?
You're here early.
YEAH, I FINISHED CLASS EARLY.
I WANT TO PRACTICE BEFORE EVERYBODY ELSE SHOWS UP.
HUH? YOU?
YEAH.
I REALLY WANT TO...
...HEAR HIM PLAY.
SO WHAT'S UP?
CAN I HELP YOU WITH SOMETHING?
OH!
YES...

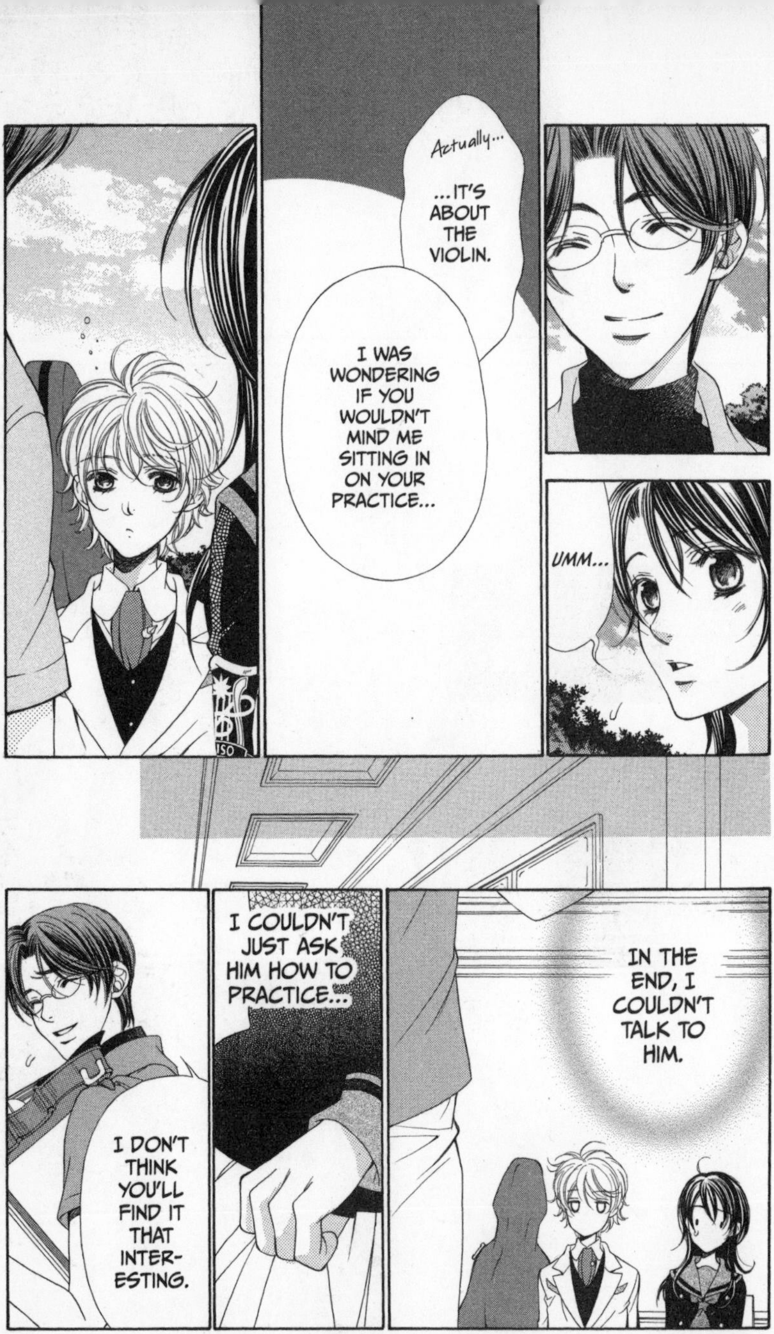
UMM...
Actually...
...IT'S ABOUT THE VIOLIN.
I WAS WONDERING IF YOU WOULDN'T MIND ME SITTING IN ON YOUR PRACTICE...
IN THE END, I COULDN'T TALK TO HIM.
I COULDN'T JUST ASK HIM HOW TO PRACTICE...
I DON'T THINK YOU'LL FIND IT THAT INTER-ESTING.

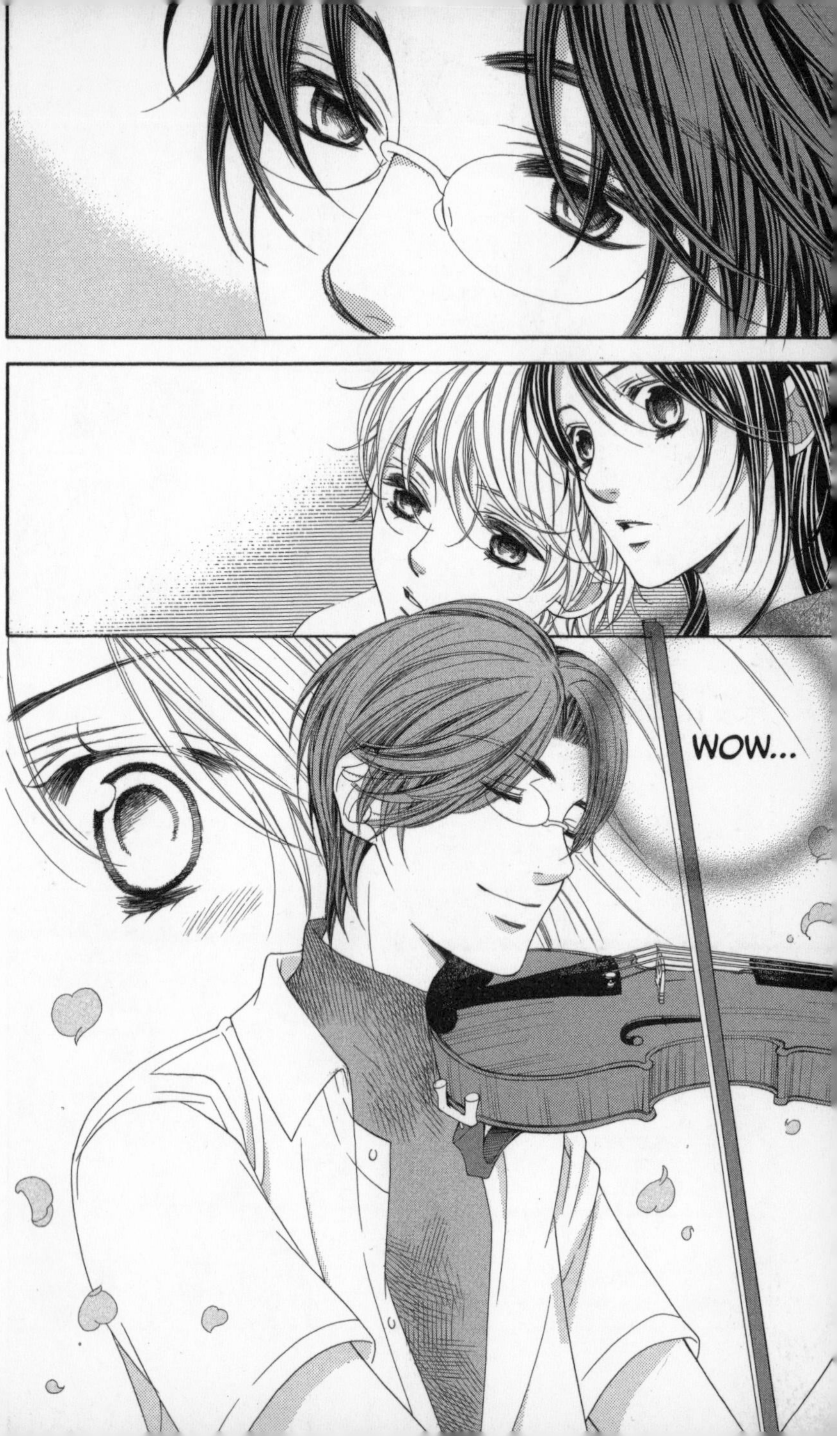
WOW...

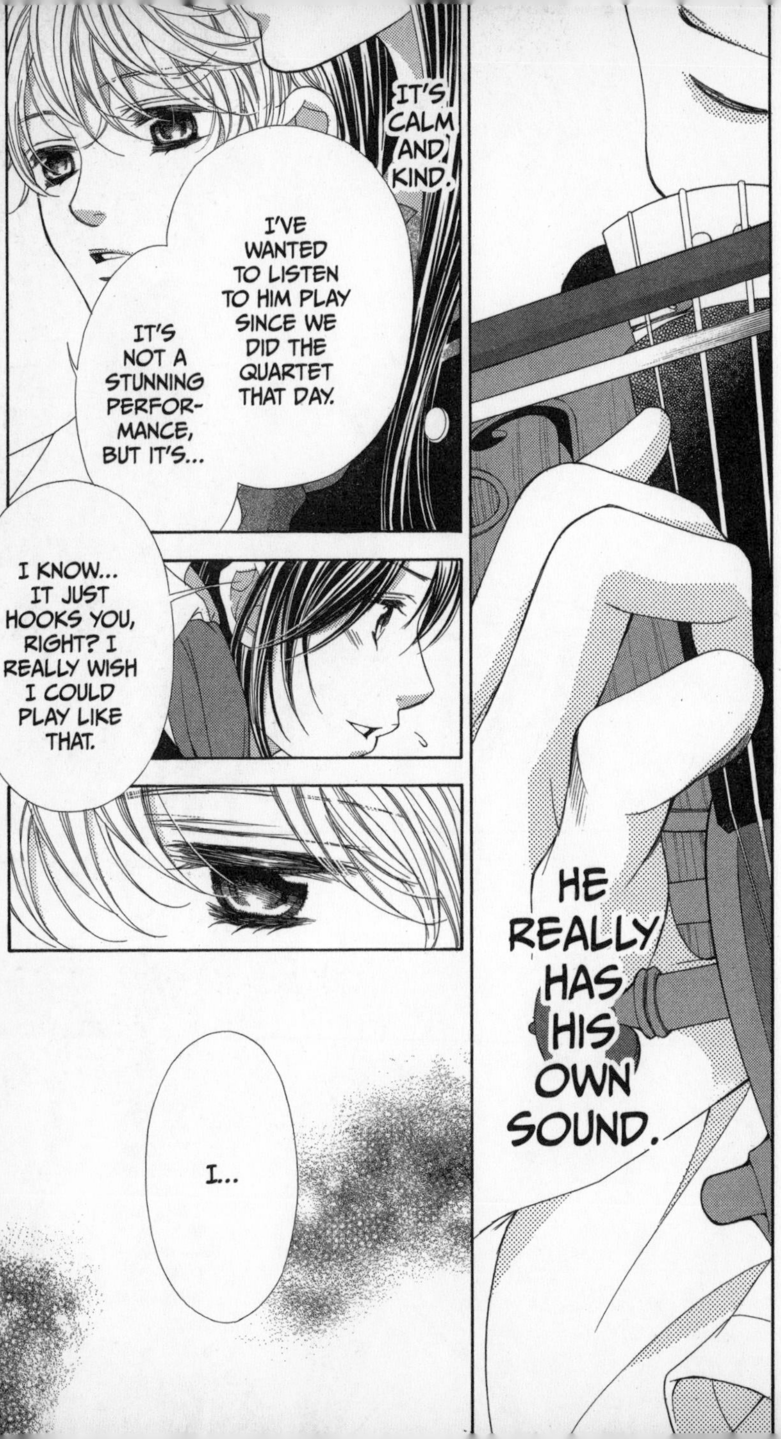
HE REALLY HAS HIS OWN SOUND.
IT'S CALM AND KIND.
I'VE WANTED TO LISTEN TO HIM PLAY SINCE WE DID THE QUARTET THAT DAY.
IT'S NOT A STUNNING PERFORMANCE, BUT IT'S...
I KNOW... IT JUST HOOKS YOU, RIGHT? I REALLY WISH I COULD PLAY LIKE THAT.
I...

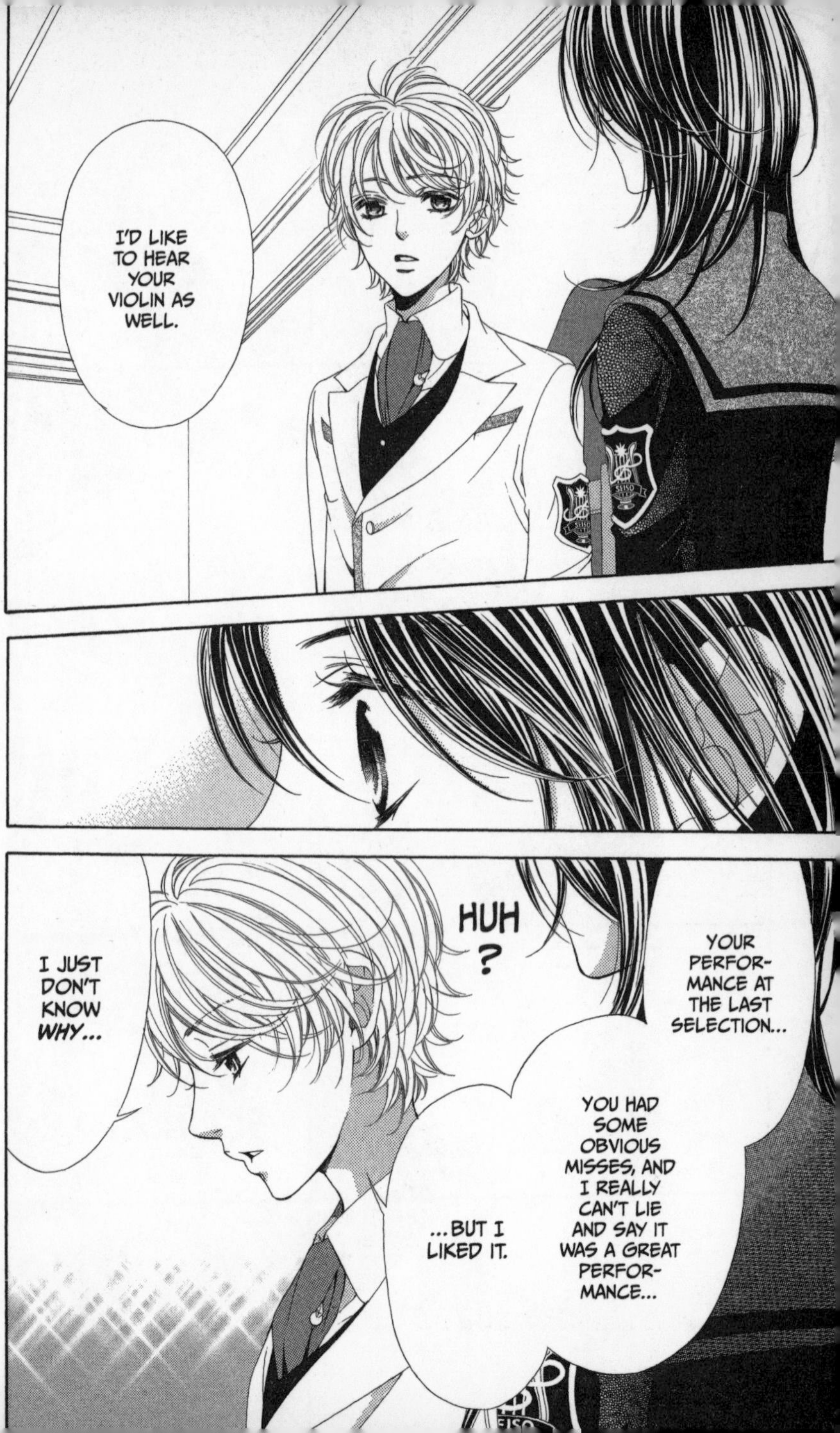

I'D LIKE TO HEAR YOUR VIOLIN AS WELL.
YOUR PERFORMANCE AT THE LAST SELECTION...
HUH?
YOU HAD SOME OBVIOUS MISSES, AND I REALLY CAN'T LIE AND SAY IT WAS A GREAT PERFORMANCE...
...BUT I LIKED IT.
I JUST DON'T KNOW *WHY*...

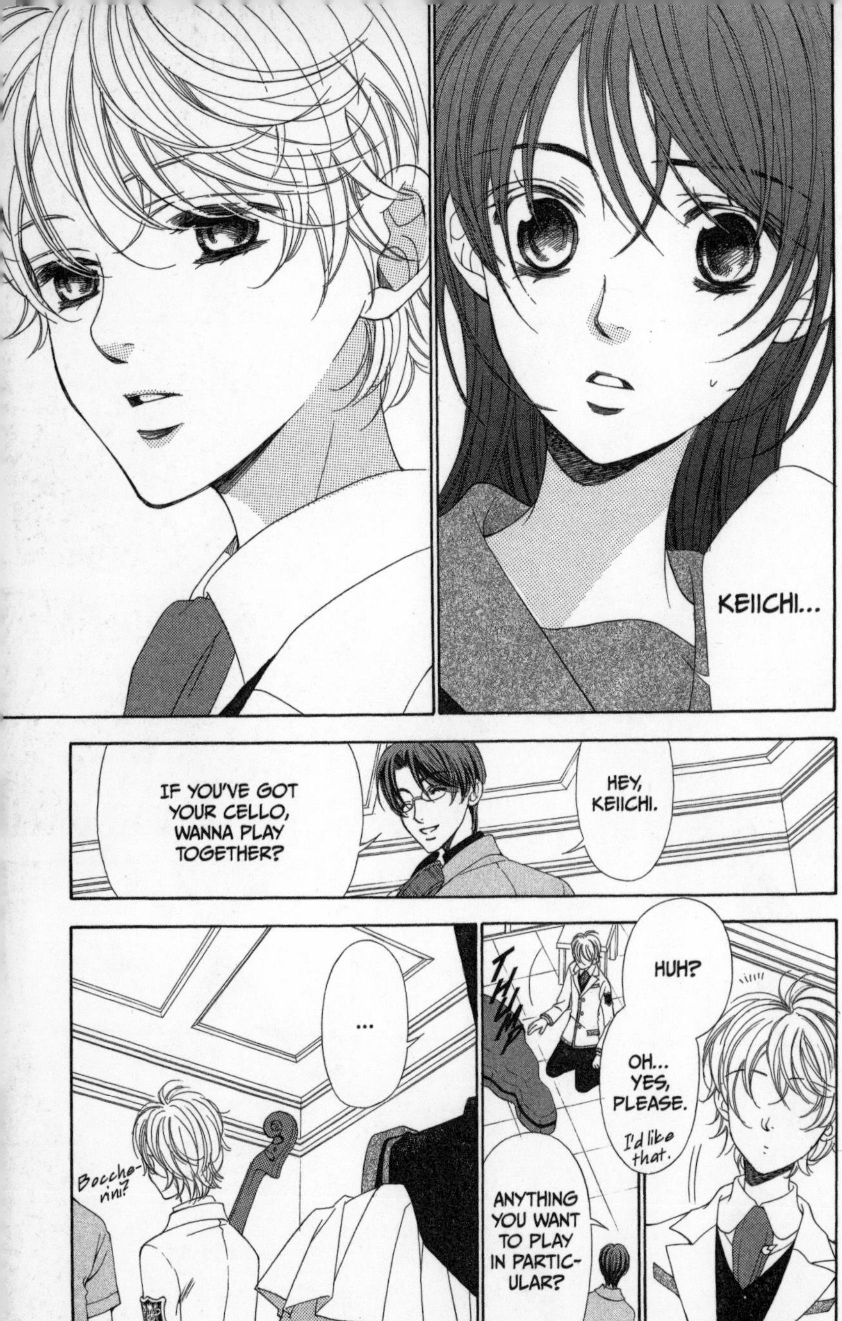
KEIICHI...
HEY, KEIICHI.
IF YOU'VE GOT YOUR CELLO, WANNA PLAY TOGETHER?
HUH?
OH... YES, PLEASE.
I'd like that.
THUMP
ANYTHING YOU WANT TO PLAY IN PARTICULAR?
...
Boccherini?

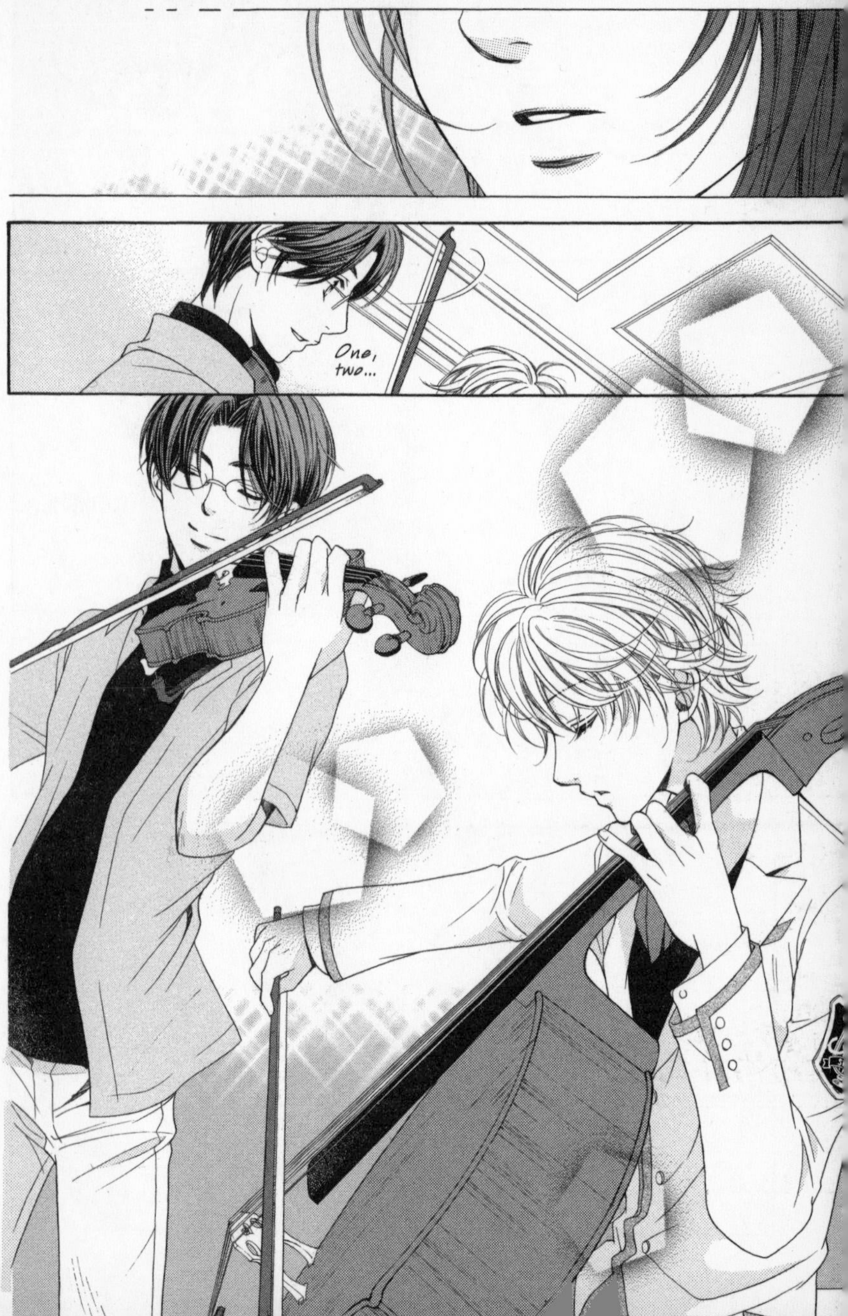
One, two...

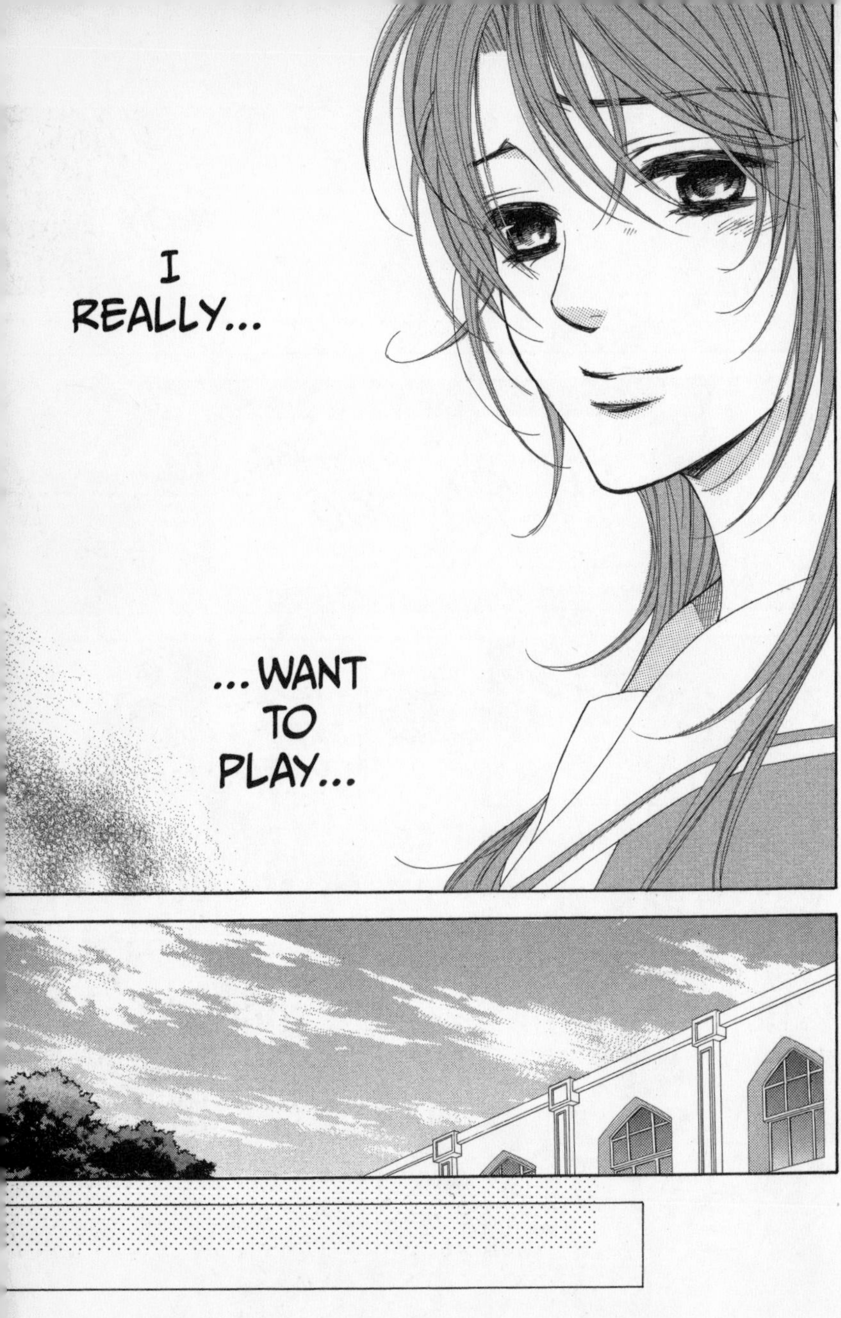
I REALLY...
...WANT TO PLAY...

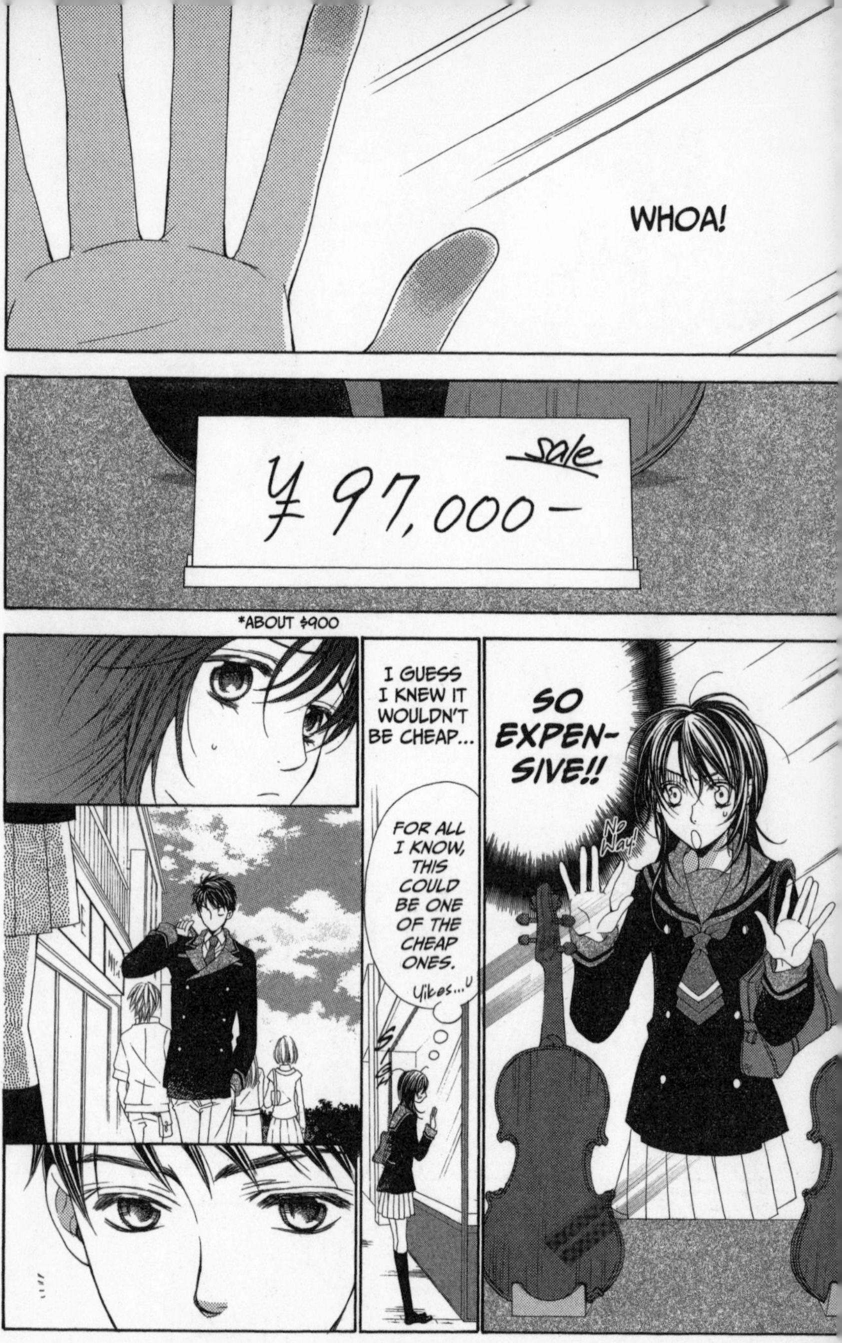
WHOA!
sale
¥97,000-
*ABOUT $900
SO EXPEN-SIVE!!
No Way!
I GUESS I KNEW IT WOULDN'T BE CHEAP...
FOR ALL I KNOW, THIS COULD BE ONE OF THE CHEAP ONES.
Yikes...

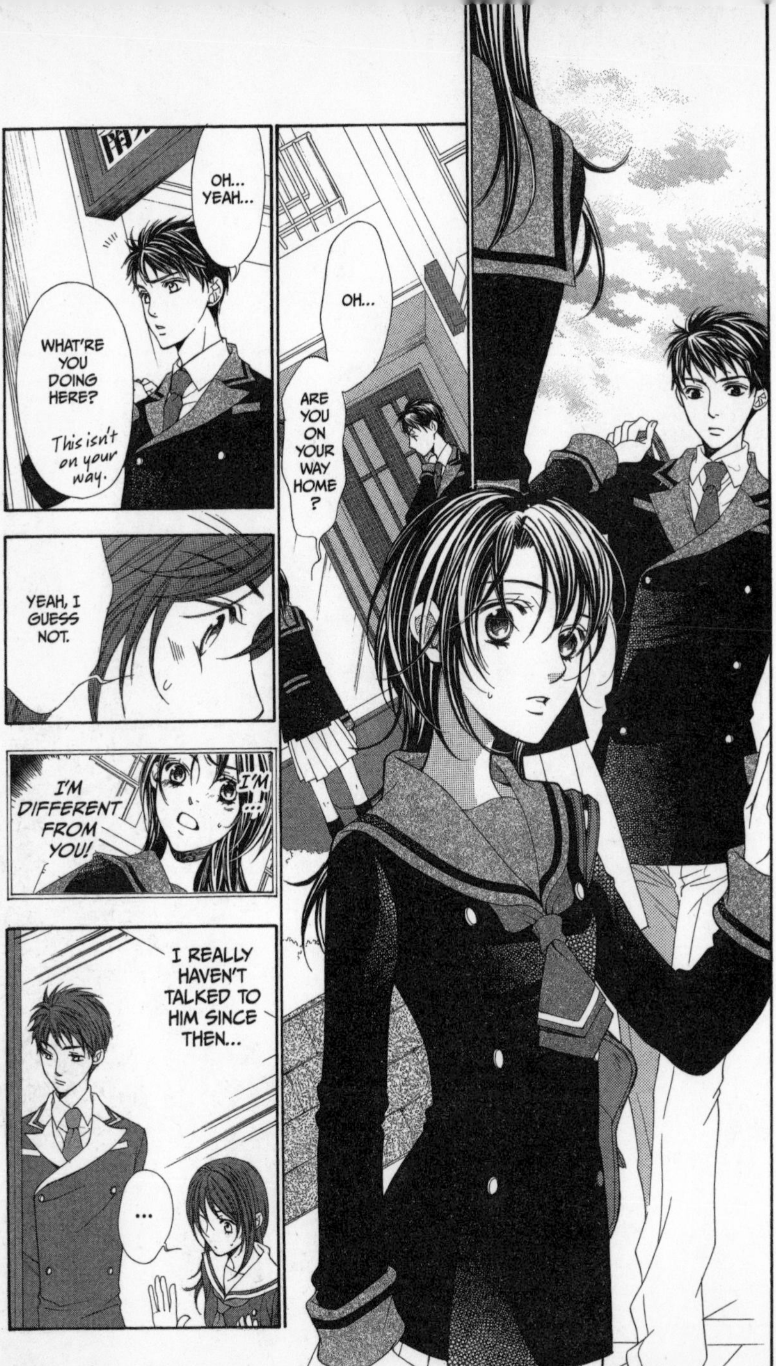
OH...
ARE YOU ON YOUR WAY HOME?
OH... YEAH...
WHAT'RE YOU DOING HERE?
This isn't on your way.
YEAH, I GUESS NOT.
I'M...
I'M DIFFERENT FROM YOU!
I REALLY HAVEN'T TALKED TO HIM SINCE THEN...
...

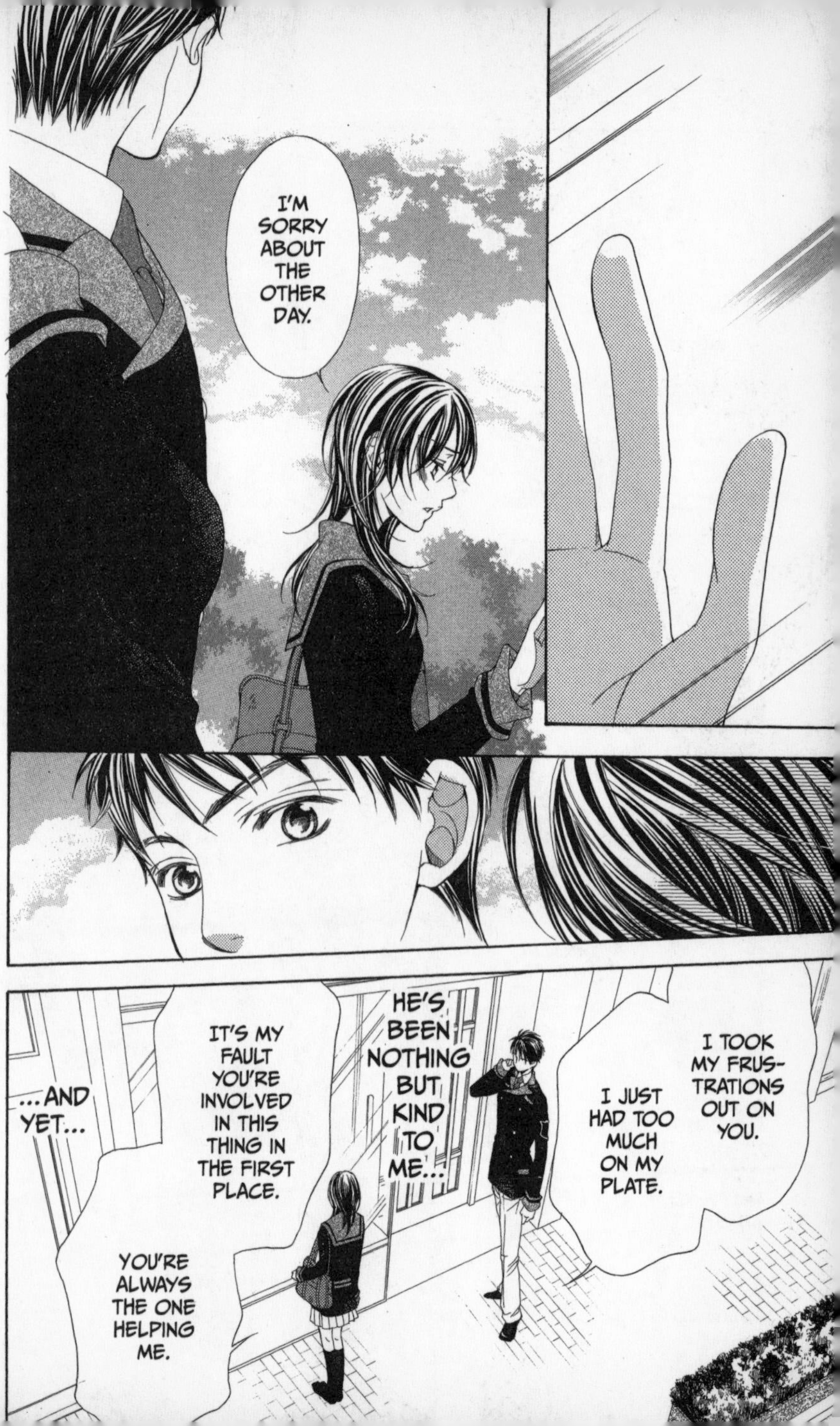
I'M SORRY ABOUT THE OTHER DAY.
I TOOK MY FRUS-TRATIONS OUT ON YOU.
I JUST HAD TOO MUCH ON MY PLATE.
HE'S BEEN NOTHING BUT KIND TO ME...
IT'S MY FAULT YOU'RE INVOLVED IN THIS THING IN THE FIRST PLACE.
YOU'RE ALWAYS THE ONE HELPING ME.
...AND YET...

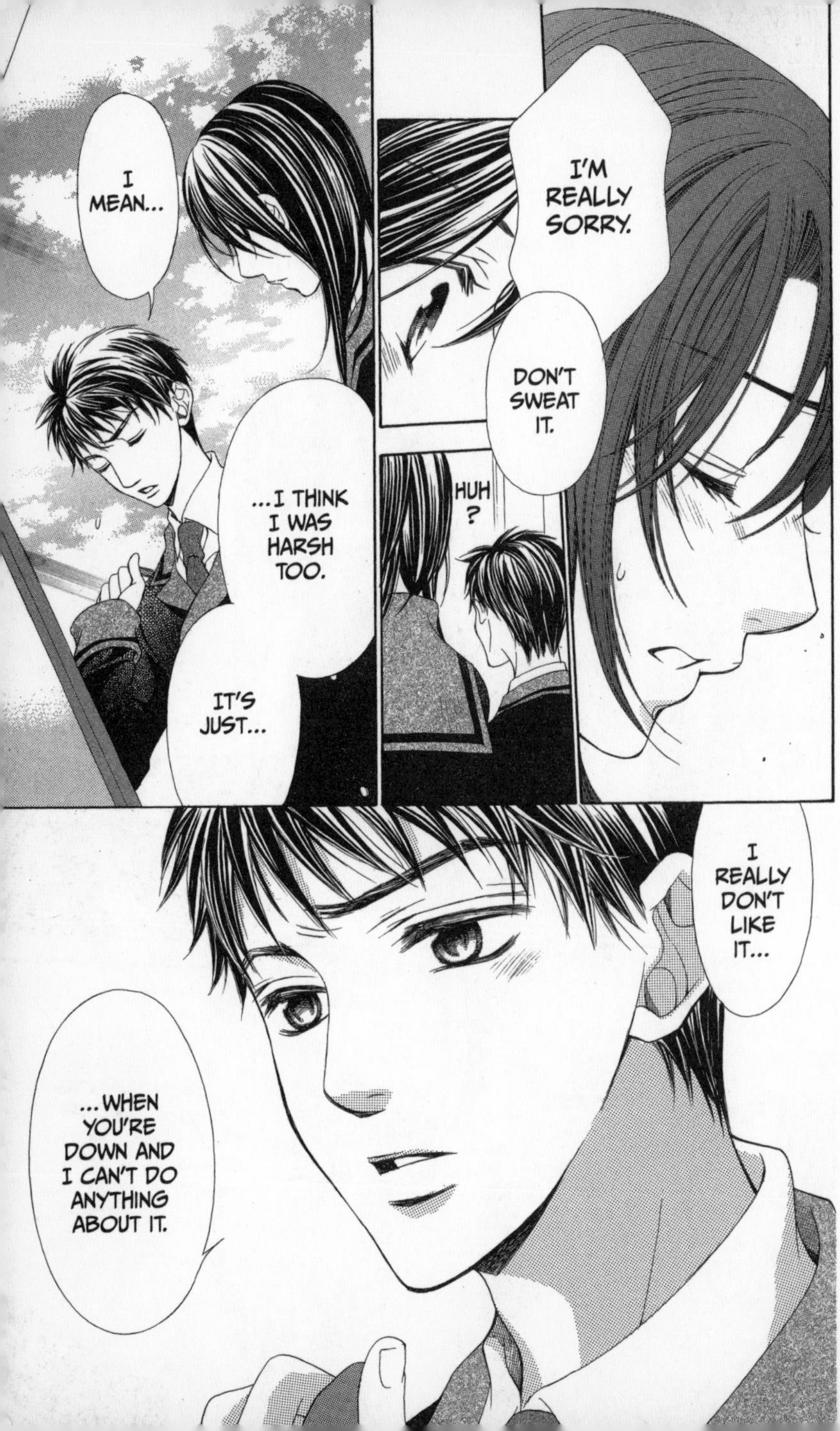
I'M REALLY SORRY.
DON'T SWEAT IT.
HUH?
I MEAN...
...I THINK I WAS HARSH TOO.
IT'S JUST...
I REALLY DON'T LIKE IT...
...WHEN YOU'RE DOWN AND I CAN'T DO ANYTHING ABOUT IT.

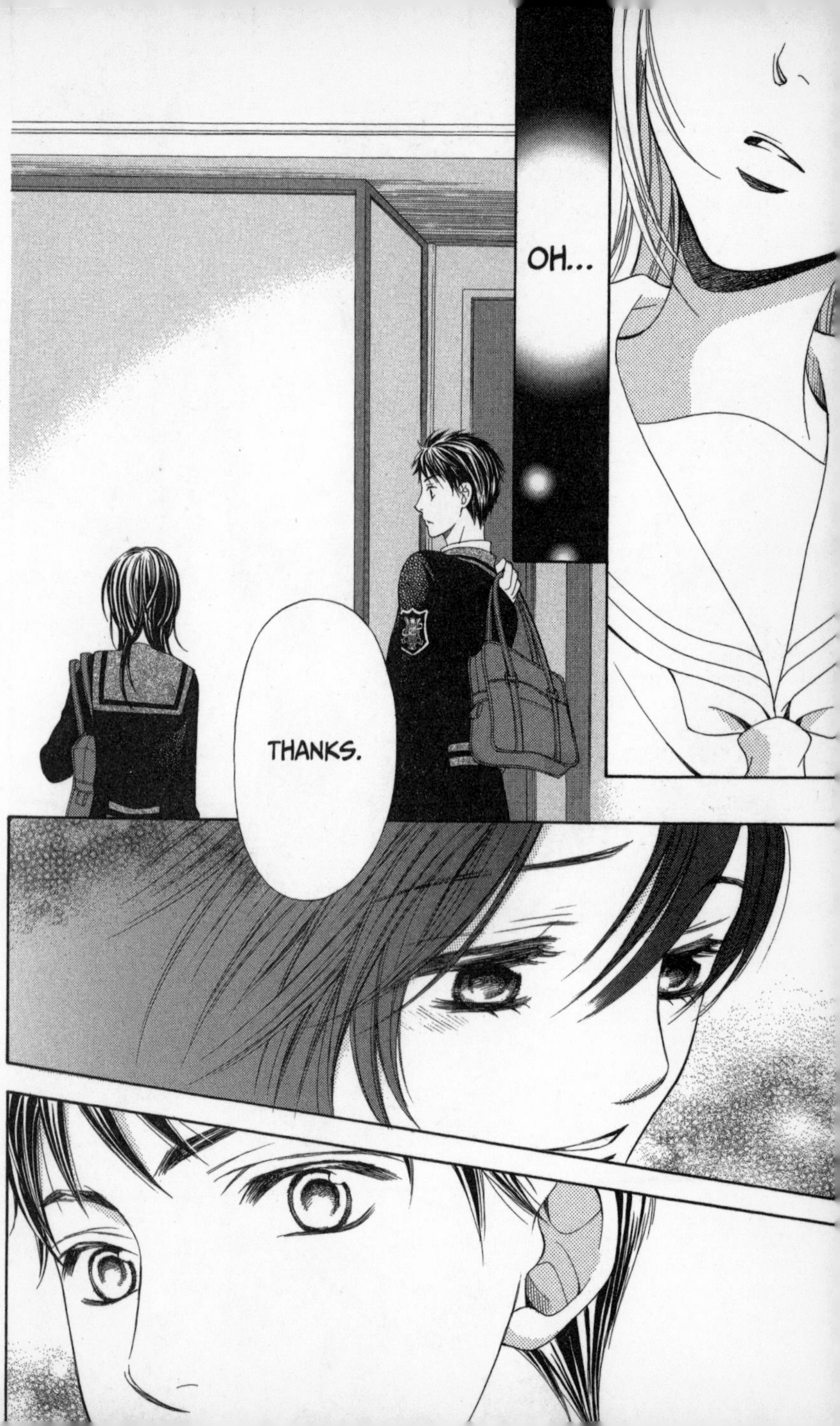
OH...
THANKS.

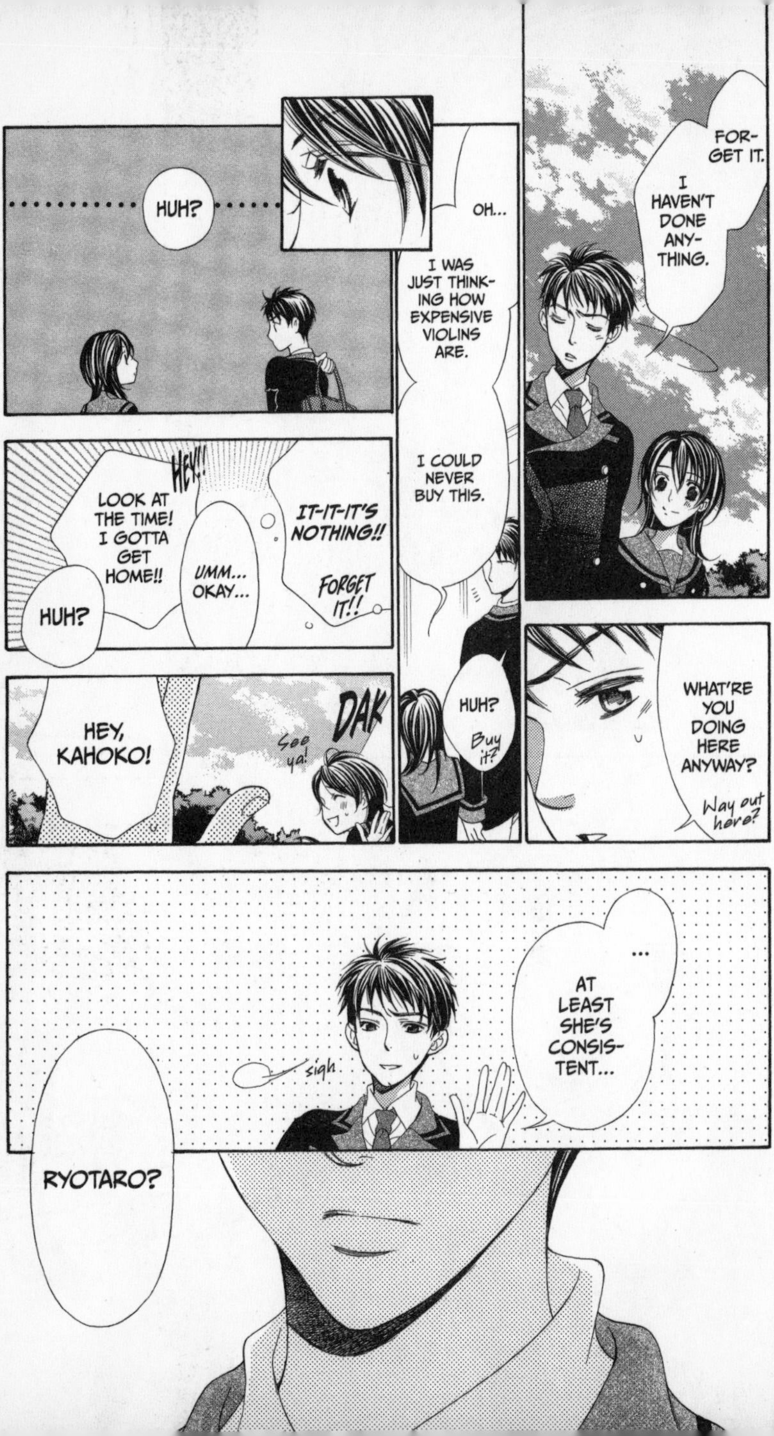
FORGET IT.
I HAVEN'T DONE ANYTHING.
WHAT'RE YOU DOING HERE ANYWAY?
Way out here?
OH...
I WAS JUST THINKING HOW EXPENSIVE VIOLINS ARE.
I COULD NEVER BUY THIS.
HUH?
Buy it?
HUH?
IT-IT-IT'S NOTHING!!
FORGET IT!!
UMM... OKAY...
HEY!!
LOOK AT THE TIME! I GOTTA GET HOME!!
HUH?
DAK
See ya!
HEY, KAHOKO!
...
AT LEAST SHE'S CONSISTENT...
sigh
RYOTARO?

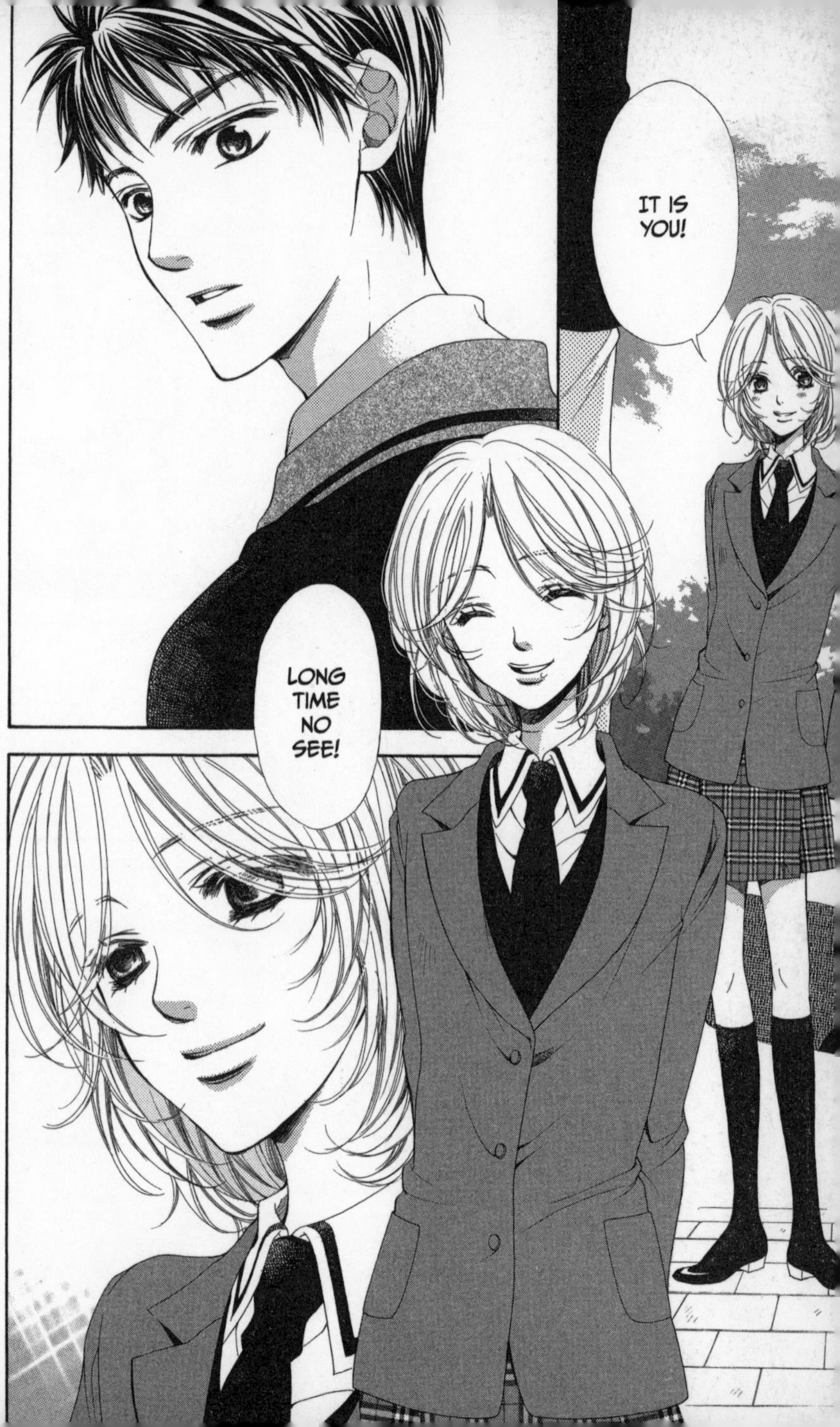
IT IS YOU!
LONG TIME NO SEE!

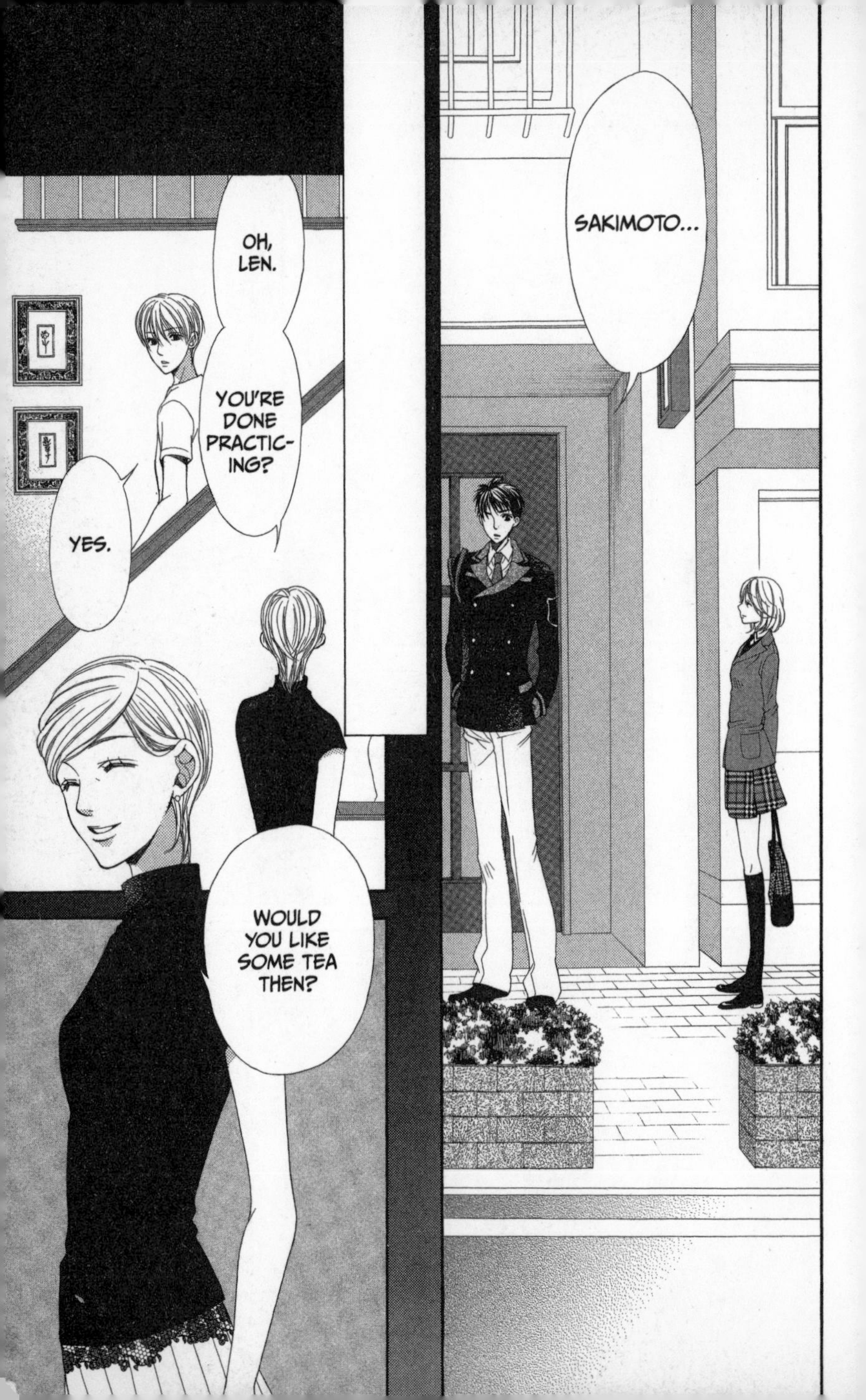
SAKIMOTO...
OH, LEN.
YOU'RE DONE PRACTIC-ING?
YES.
WOULD YOU LIKE SOME TEA THEN?

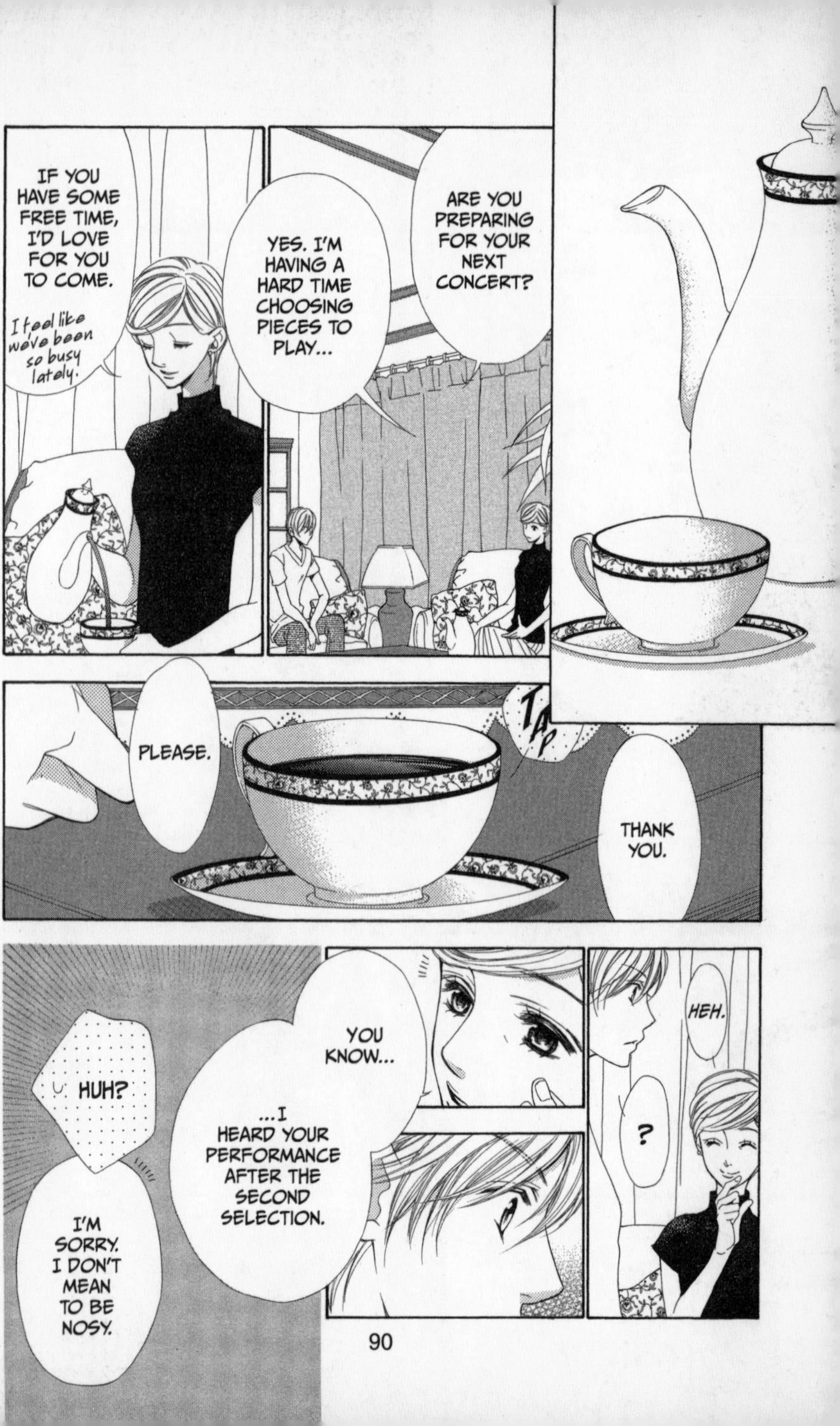
ARE YOU PREPARING FOR YOUR NEXT CONCERT?
YES. I'M HAVING A HARD TIME CHOOSING PIECES TO PLAY...
IF YOU HAVE SOME FREE TIME, I'D LOVE FOR YOU TO COME.
I feel like we've been so busy lately.
TAP
THANK YOU.
PLEASE.
HEH.
?
YOU KNOW...
...I HEARD YOUR PERFORMANCE AFTER THE SECOND SELECTION.
HUH?
I'M SORRY. I DON'T MEAN TO BE NOSY.

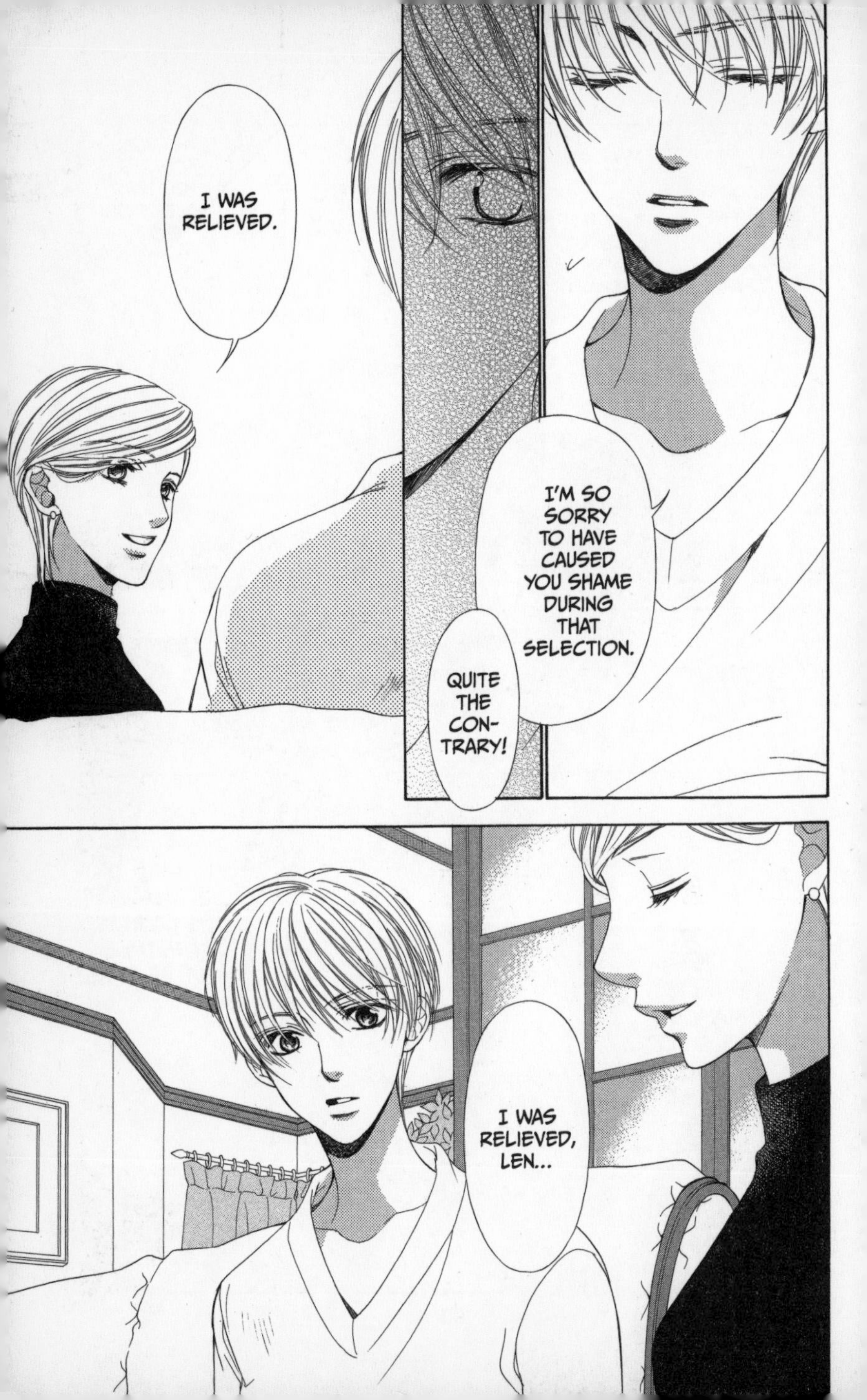
I'M SO SORRY TO HAVE CAUSED YOU SHAME DURING THAT SELECTION.
QUITE THE CON-TRARY!
I WAS RELIEVED.
I WAS RELIEVED, LEN...

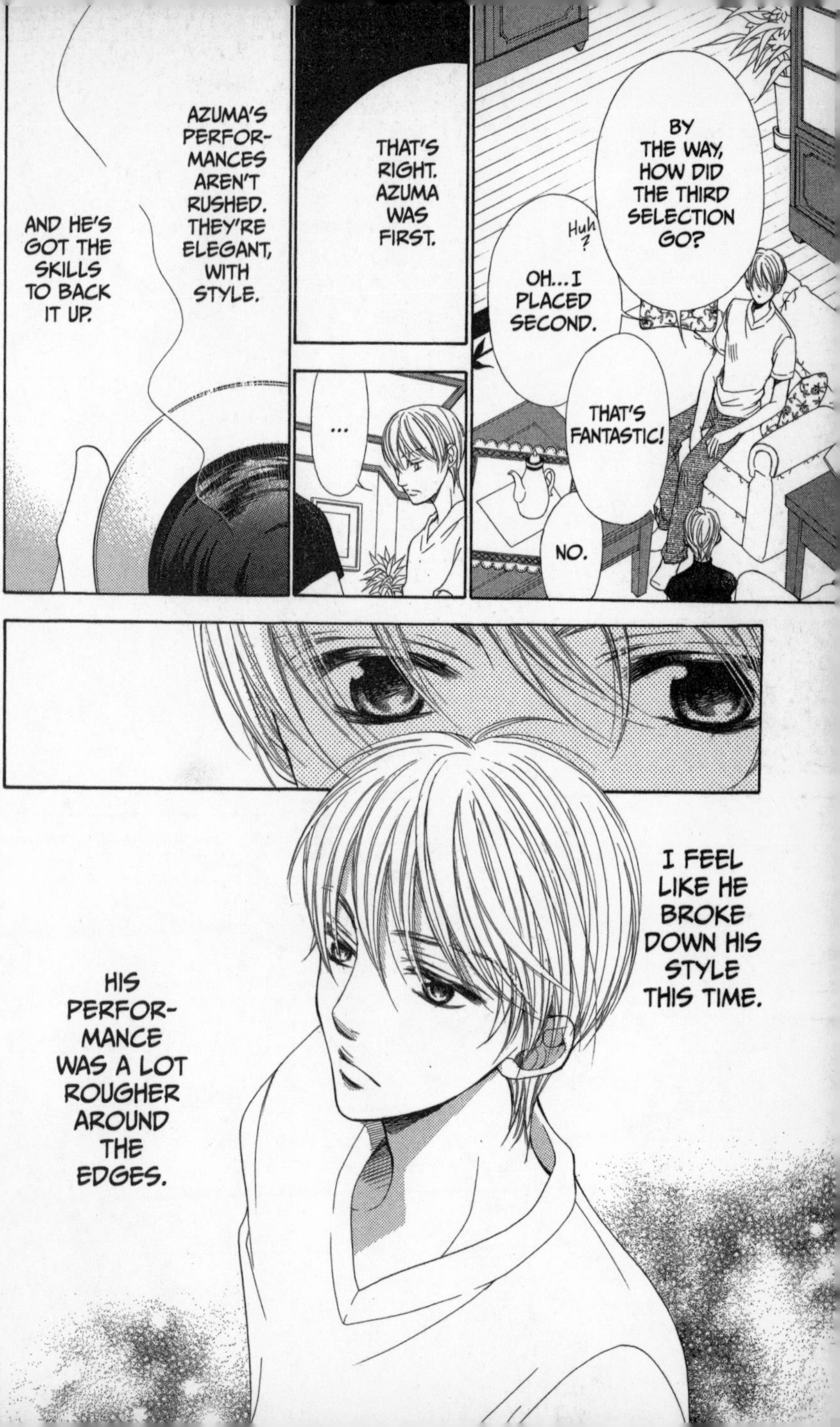
BY THE WAY, HOW DID THE THIRD SELECTION GO?
Huh?
OH...I PLACED SECOND.
THAT'S FANTASTIC!
NO.
THAT'S RIGHT. AZUMA WAS FIRST.
...
AZUMA'S PERFORMANCES AREN'T RUSHED. THEY'RE ELEGANT, WITH STYLE.
AND HE'S GOT THE SKILLS TO BACK IT UP.
I FEEL LIKE HE BROKE DOWN HIS STYLE THIS TIME.
HIS PERFORMANCE WAS A LOT ROUGHER AROUND THE EDGES.

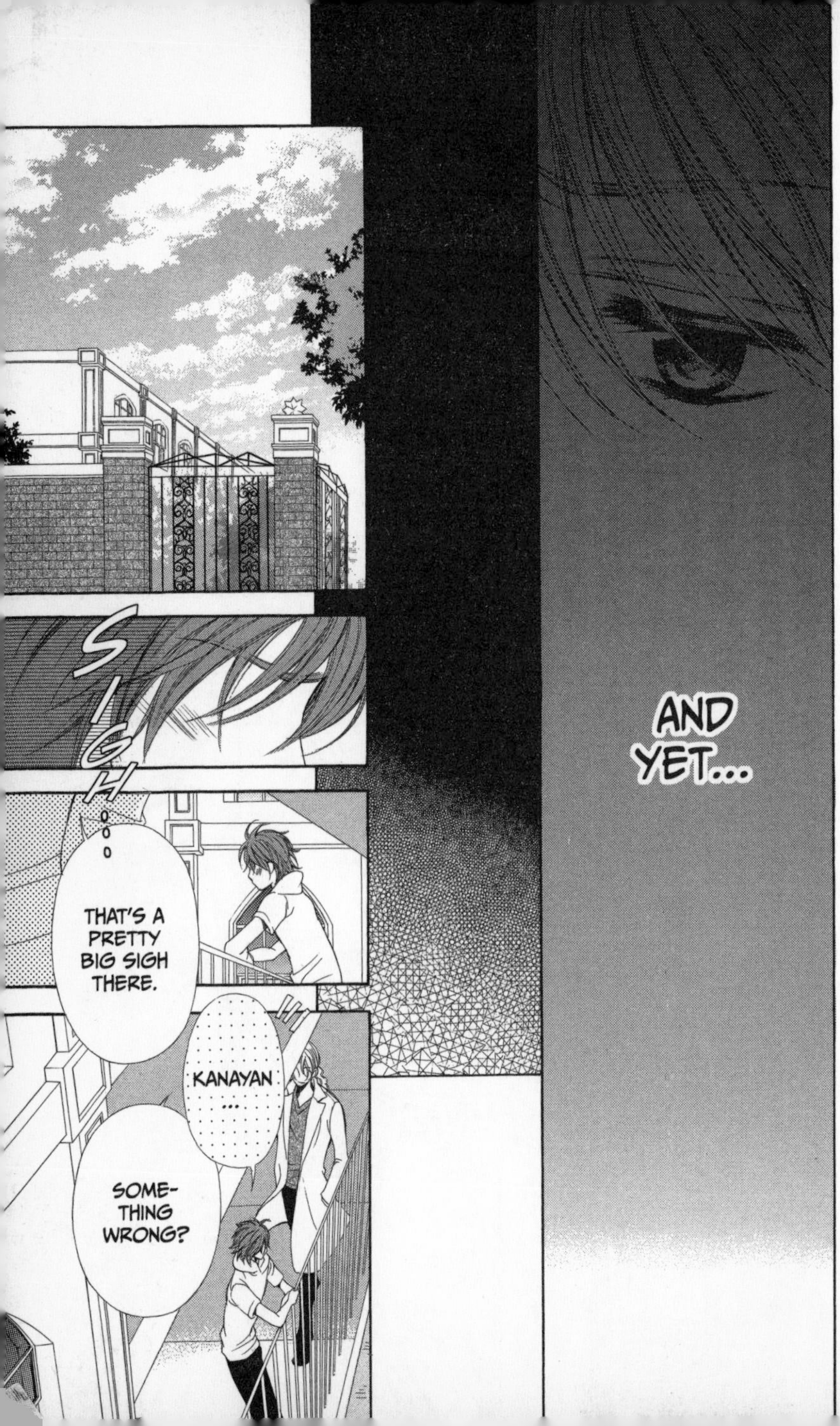
AND YET...
SIGH...
THAT'S A PRETTY BIG SIGH THERE.
KANAYAN...
SOME-THING WRONG?

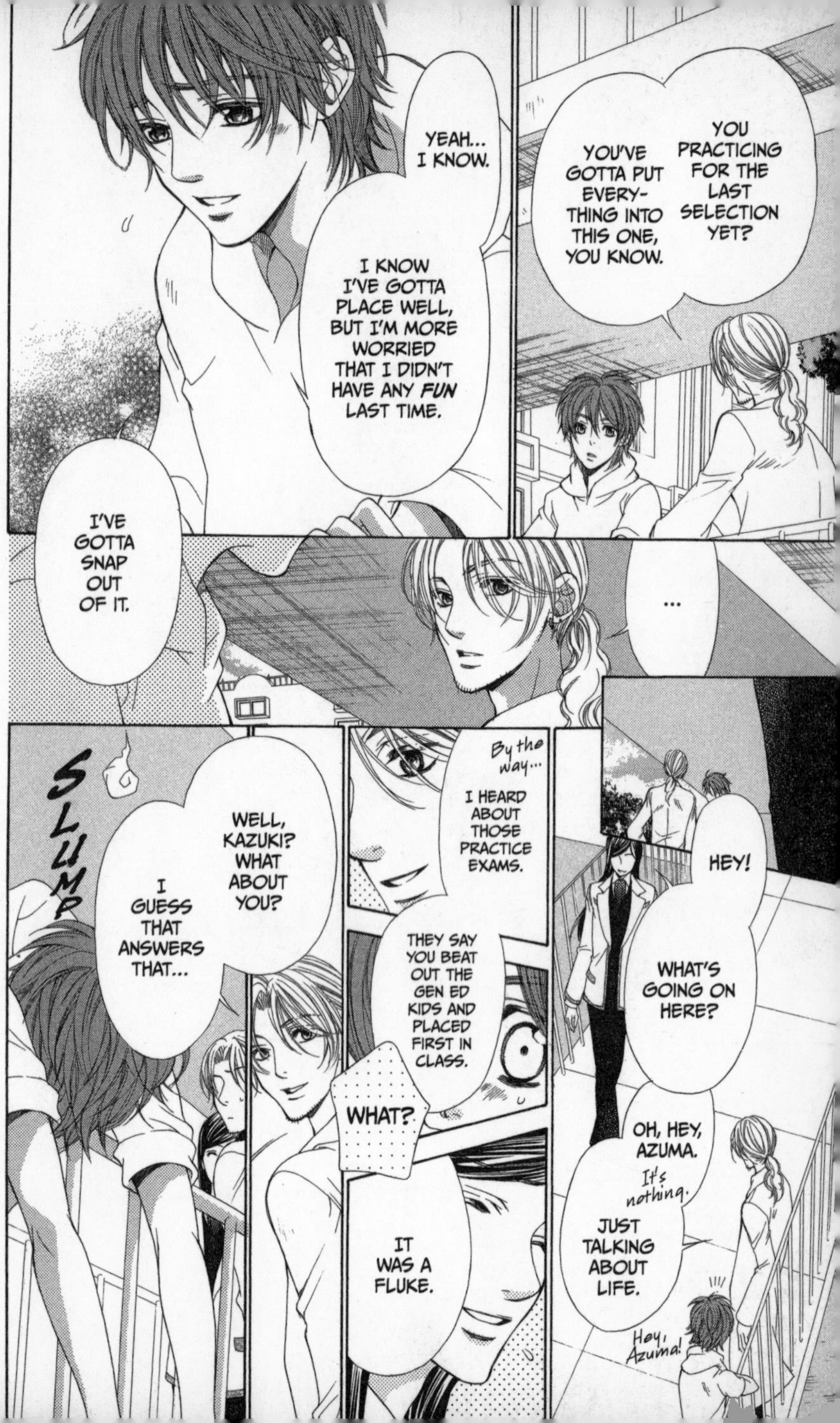
YOU PRACTICING FOR THE LAST SELECTION YET?
YOU'VE GOTTA PUT EVERY-THING INTO THIS ONE, YOU KNOW.
YEAH... I KNOW.
I KNOW I'VE GOTTA PLACE WELL, BUT I'M MORE WORRIED THAT I DIDN'T HAVE ANY *FUN* LAST TIME.
I'VE GOTTA SNAP OUT OF IT.
...
HEY!
WHAT'S GOING ON HERE?
OH, HEY, AZUMA.
It's nothing.
JUST TALKING ABOUT LIFE.
Hey, Azuma!
By the way...
I HEARD ABOUT THOSE PRACTICE EXAMS.
THEY SAY YOU BEAT OUT THE GEN ED KIDS AND PLACED FIRST IN CLASS.
WHAT?
IT WAS A FLUKE.
WELL, KAZUKI? WHAT ABOUT YOU?
SLUMP
I GUESS THAT ANSWERS THAT...

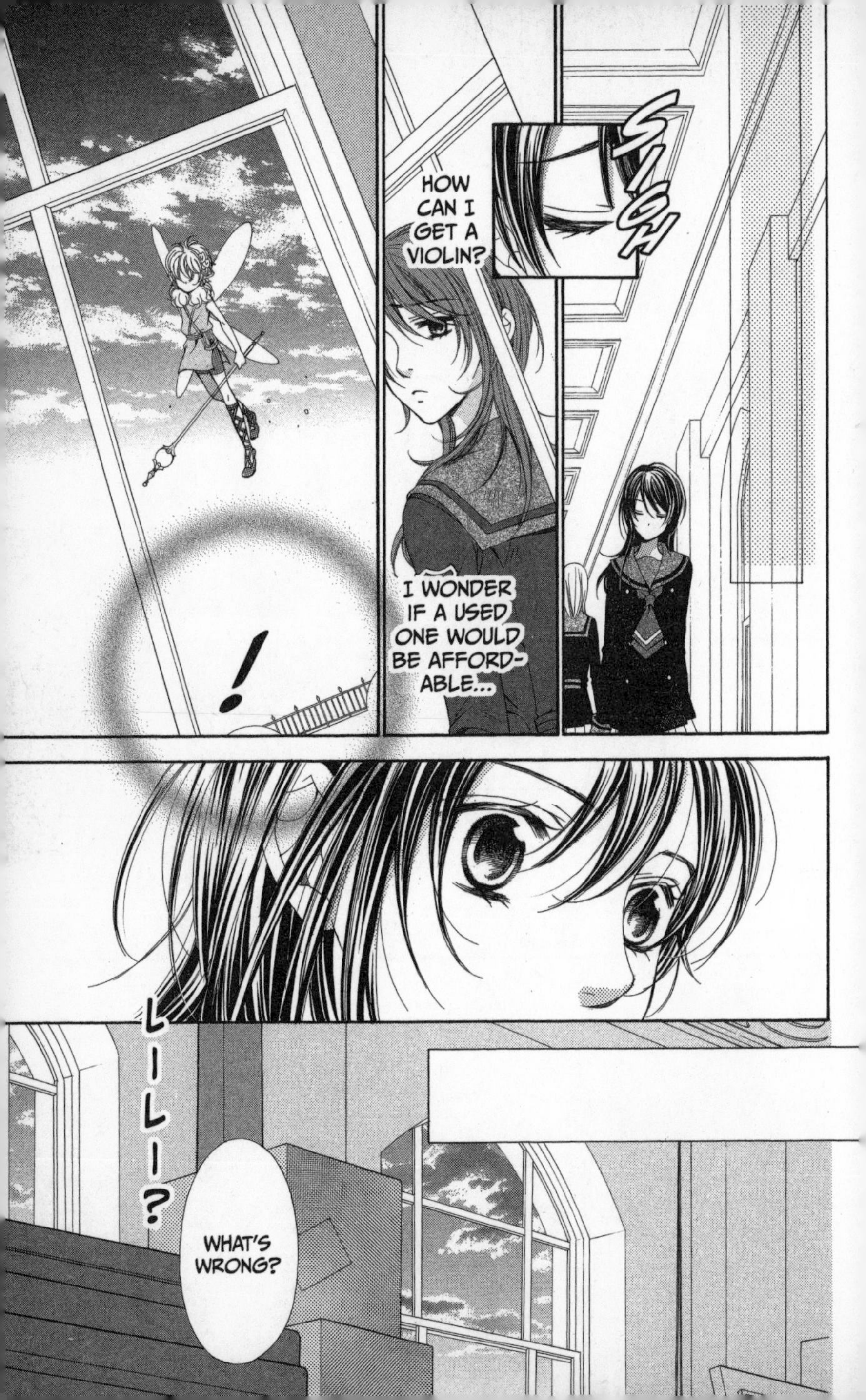
SIGH
HOW CAN I GET A VIOLIN?
I WONDER IF A USED ONE WOULD BE AFFORD-ABLE...
!
LILI?
WHAT'S WRONG?

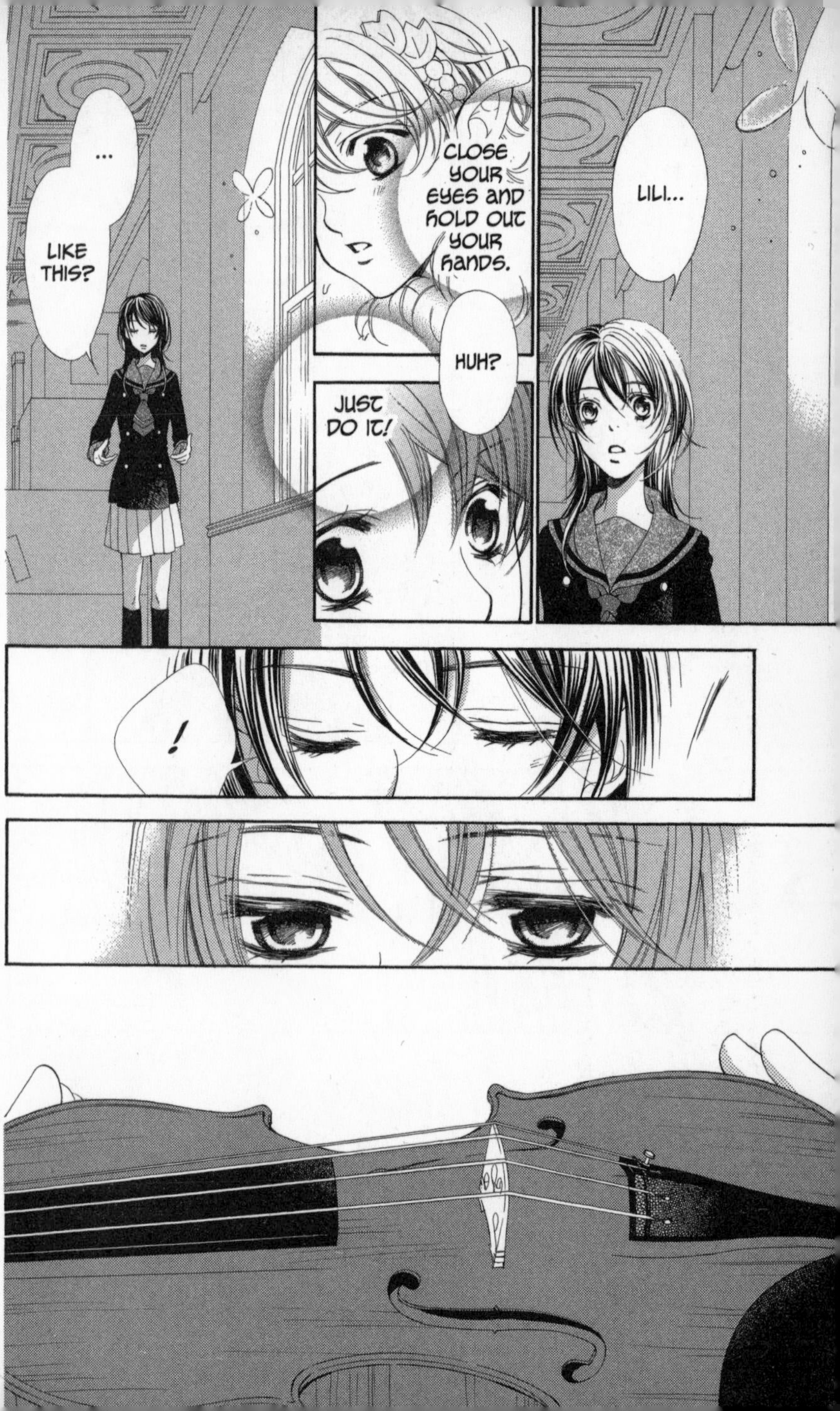
LILI...
CLOSE YOUR EYES AND HOLD OUT YOUR HANDS.
HUH?
JUST DO IT!
...
LIKE THIS?
!

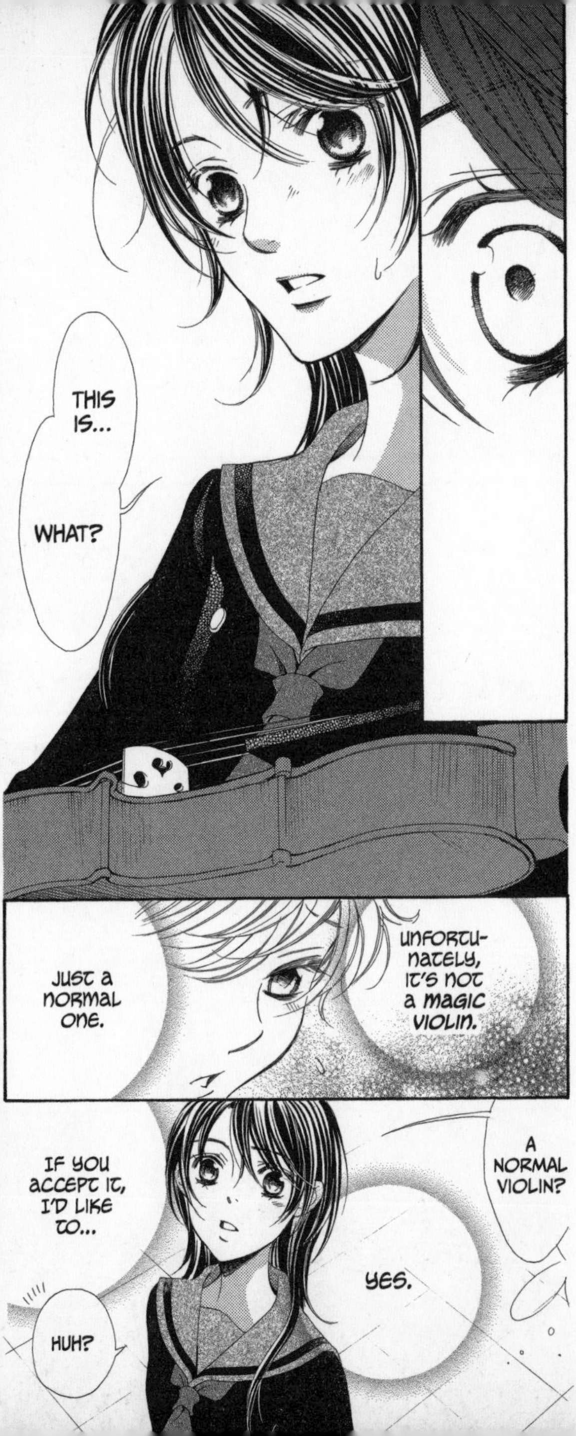
THIS IS...
WHAT?
UNFORTUNATELY, IT'S NOT A MAGIC VIOLIN.
JUST A NORMAL ONE.
A NORMAL VIOLIN?
YES.
IF YOU ACCEPT IT, I'D LIKE TO...
HUH?

**THREE**

We finally got to the scene where the violin breaks. It went by quickly... but in a way, it didn't...

I gave Len his first fast-food experience in Measure 33. He doesn't seem the type to go with friends... Or be caught dead going alone. I think it's safe to say that it's not the type of place he frequents. And it seems natural that Ryotaro and Kazuki are regulars. I remember going all the time when I was a student. (I guess I still do now.) I actually had a part time job at McXXX... The good ol' days... It really doesn't matter, I guess.

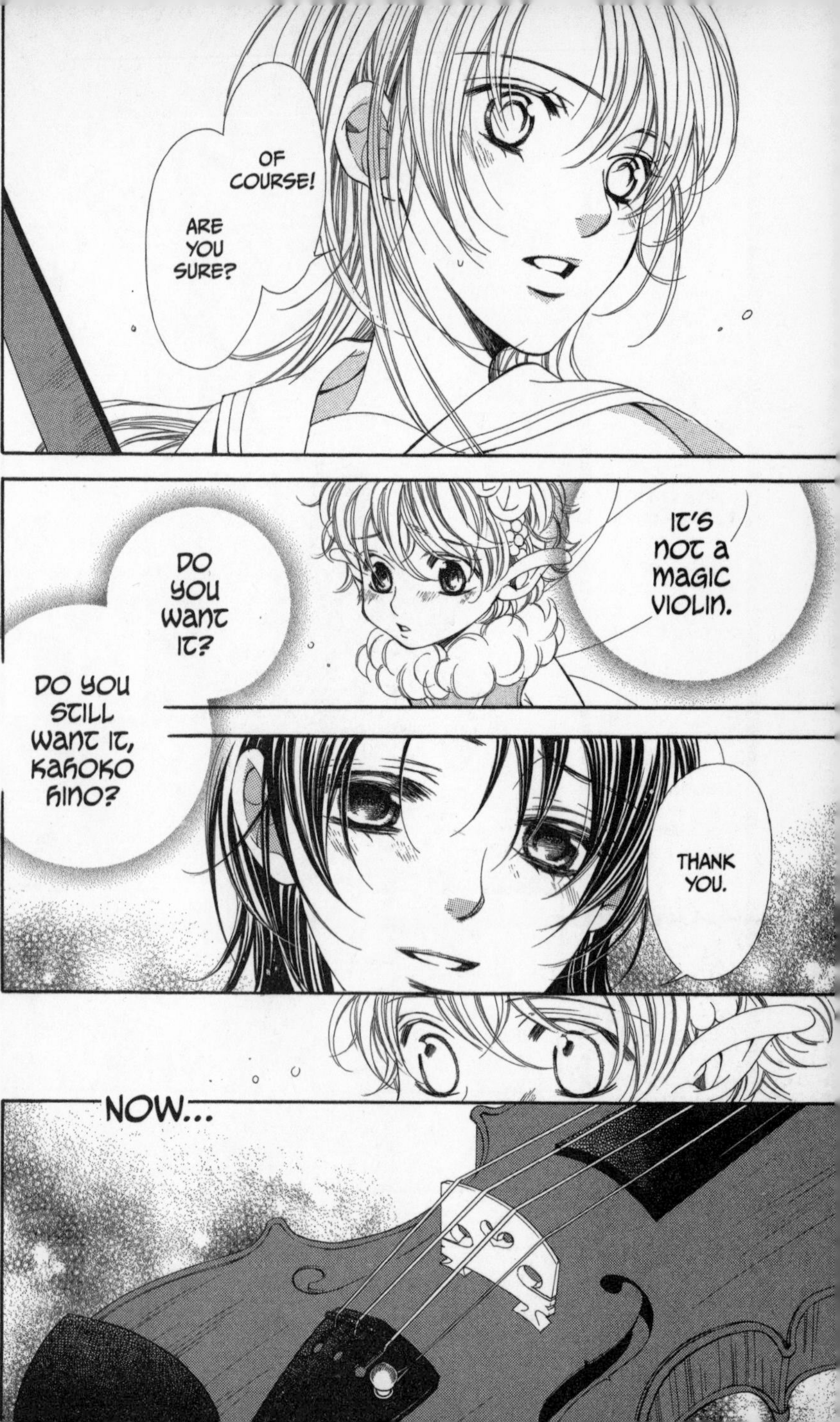

OF COURSE!
ARE YOU SURE?
IT'S NOT A MAGIC VIOLIN.
DO YOU WANT IT?
DO YOU STILL WANT IT, KAHOKO HINO?
THANK YOU.
NOW...

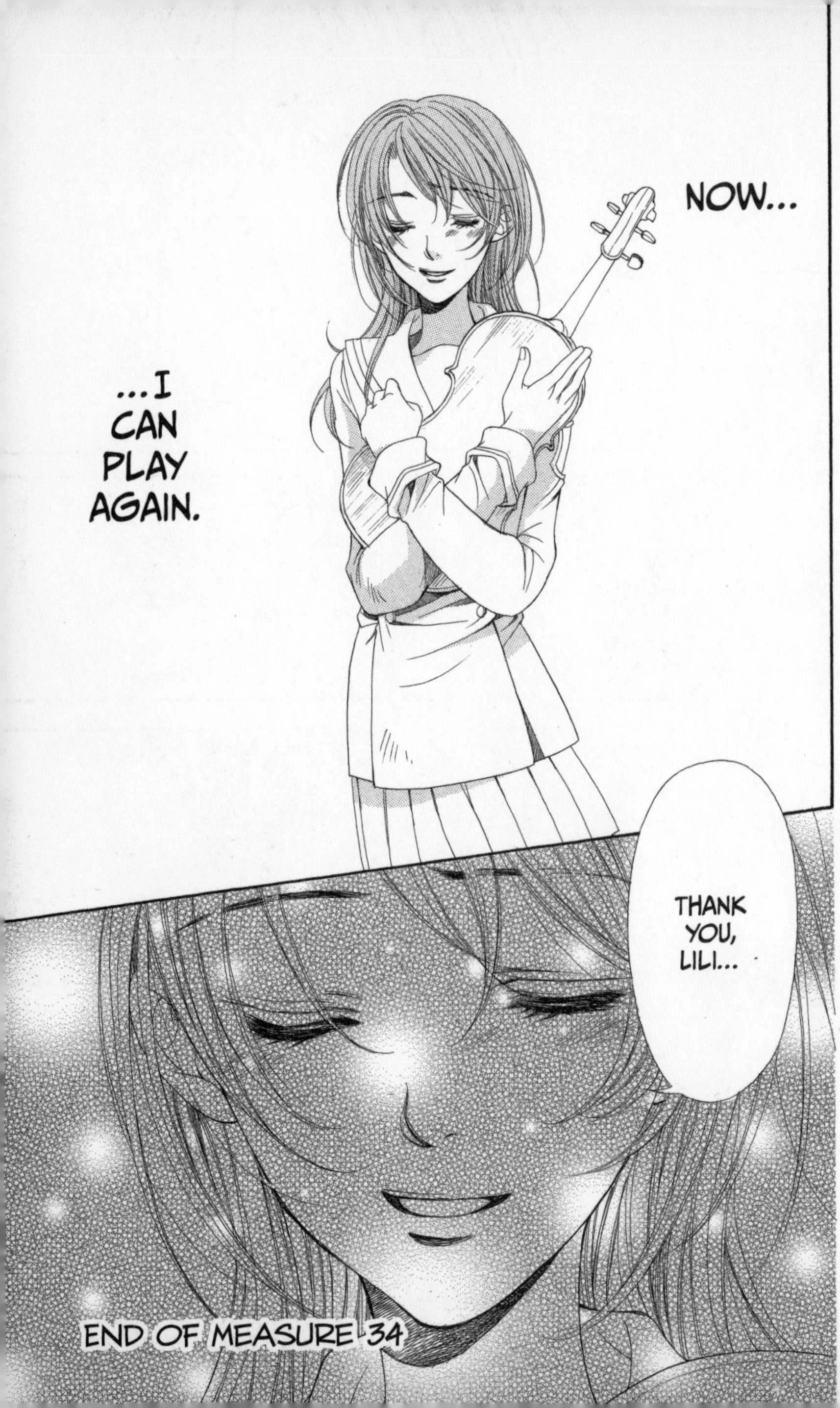
NOW...
...I CAN PLAY AGAIN.
THANK YOU, LILI...
END OF MEASURE 34

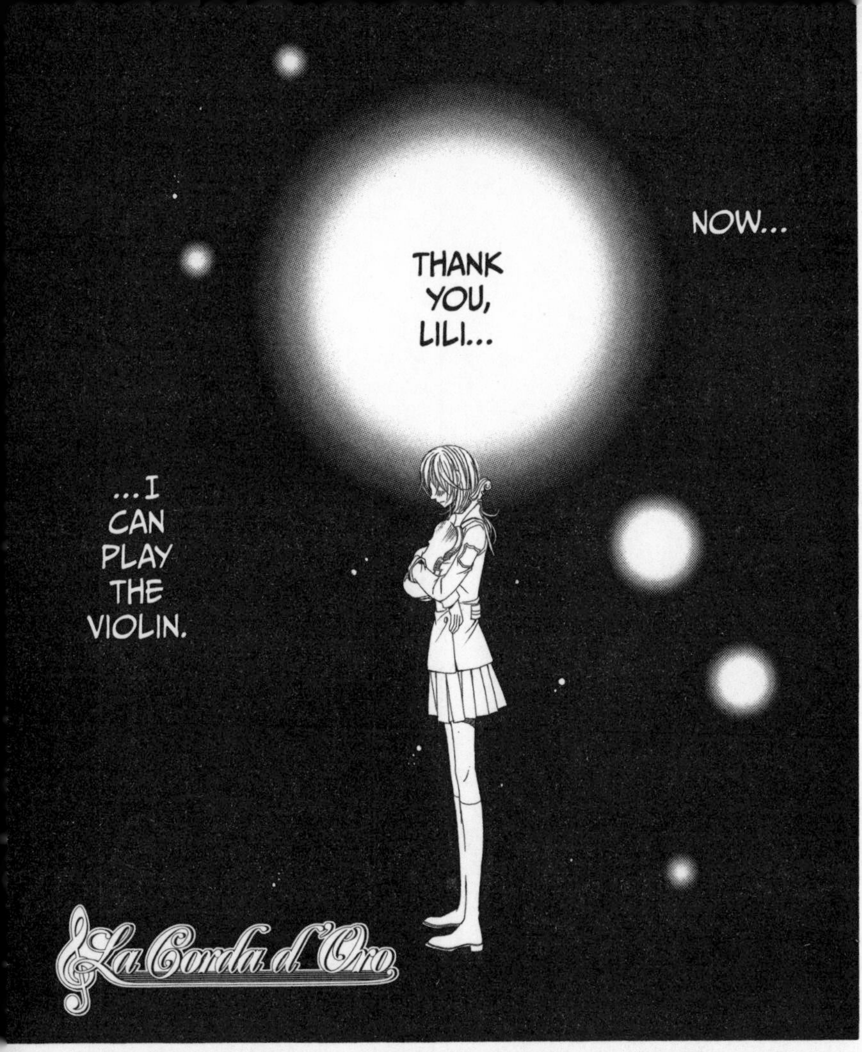
NOW...
THANK YOU, LILI...
...I CAN PLAY THE VIOLIN.
La Corda d'Oro

**Daily Happenings 27**
*...local souvenirs...*

For the most part, I'm not interested in cell phone straps and the other common collectibles that a lot of souvenir shops carry, but recently...

...I've really gotten into buying local sweets. (lol)

My favorites are tart cups from Ehime. They're so cute. I also like things like uiro, views of Mount Fuji and portraits of Shingen.

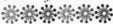

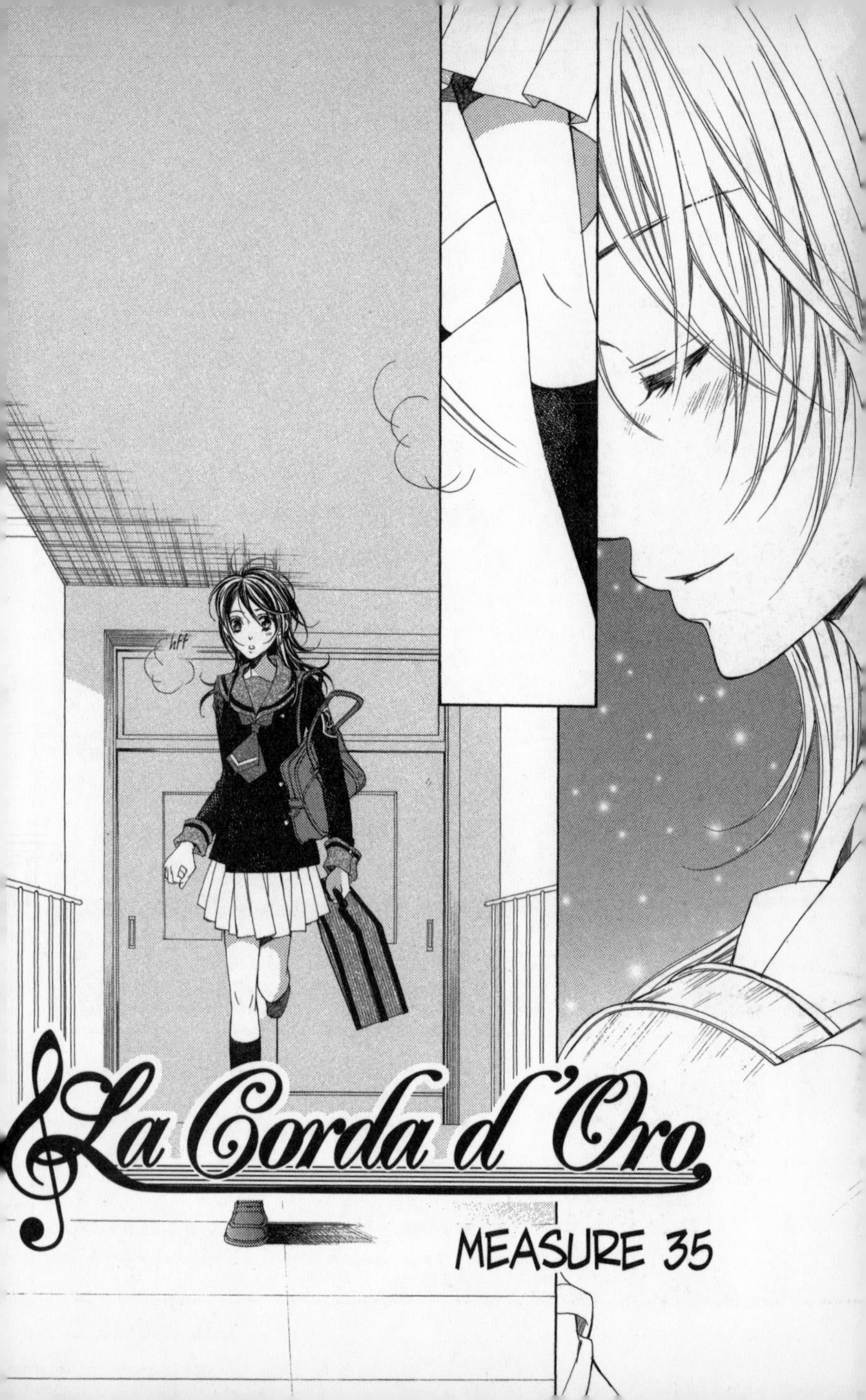
hff
La Corda d'Oro
MEASURE 35

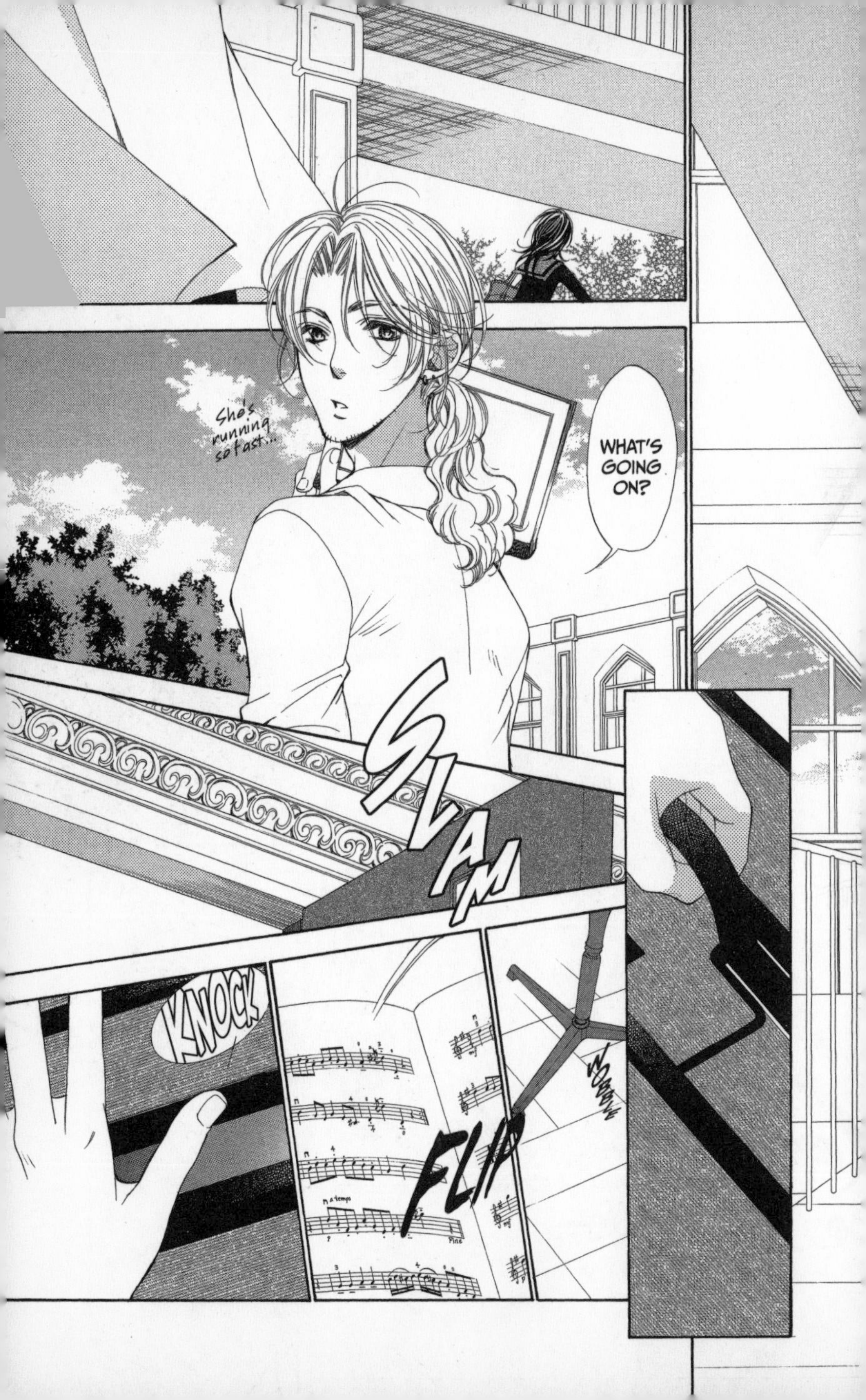

WHAT'S GOING ON?
She's running so fast...
SLAM
WOBBLE
FLIP
KNOCK

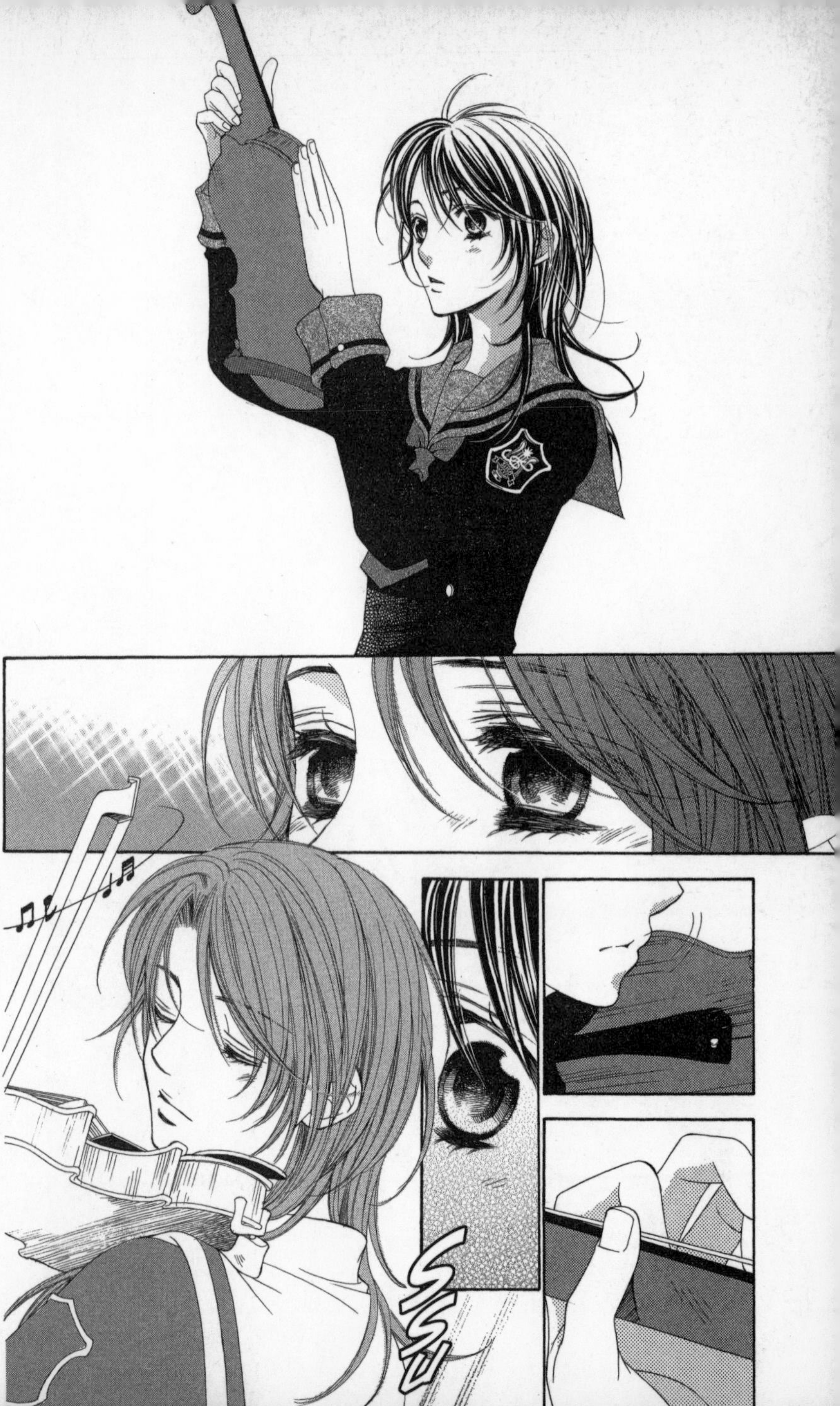
SSU

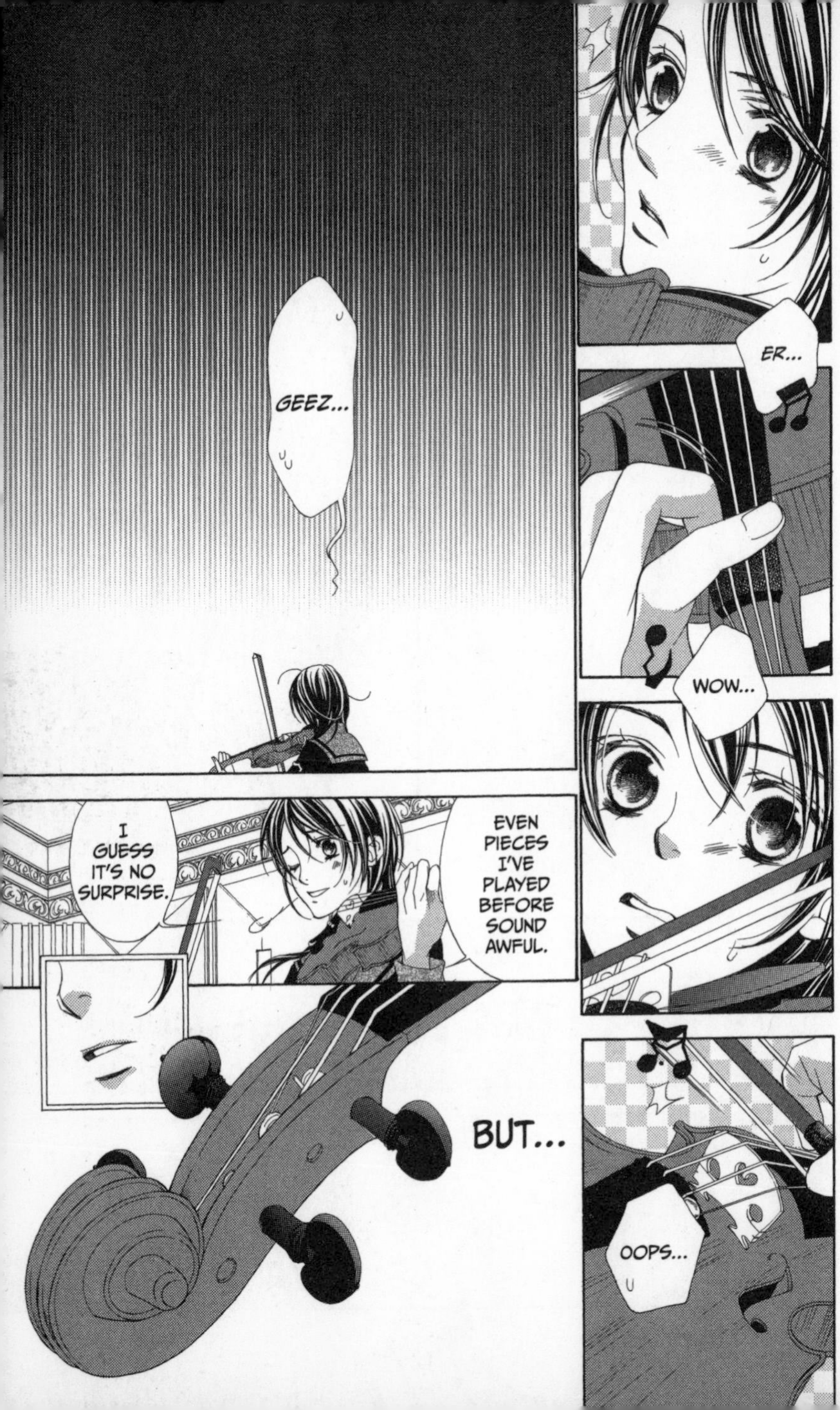
ER...
WOW...
OOPS...
GEEZ...
EVEN PIECES I'VE PLAYED BEFORE SOUND AWFUL.
I GUESS IT'S NO SURPRISE.
BUT...

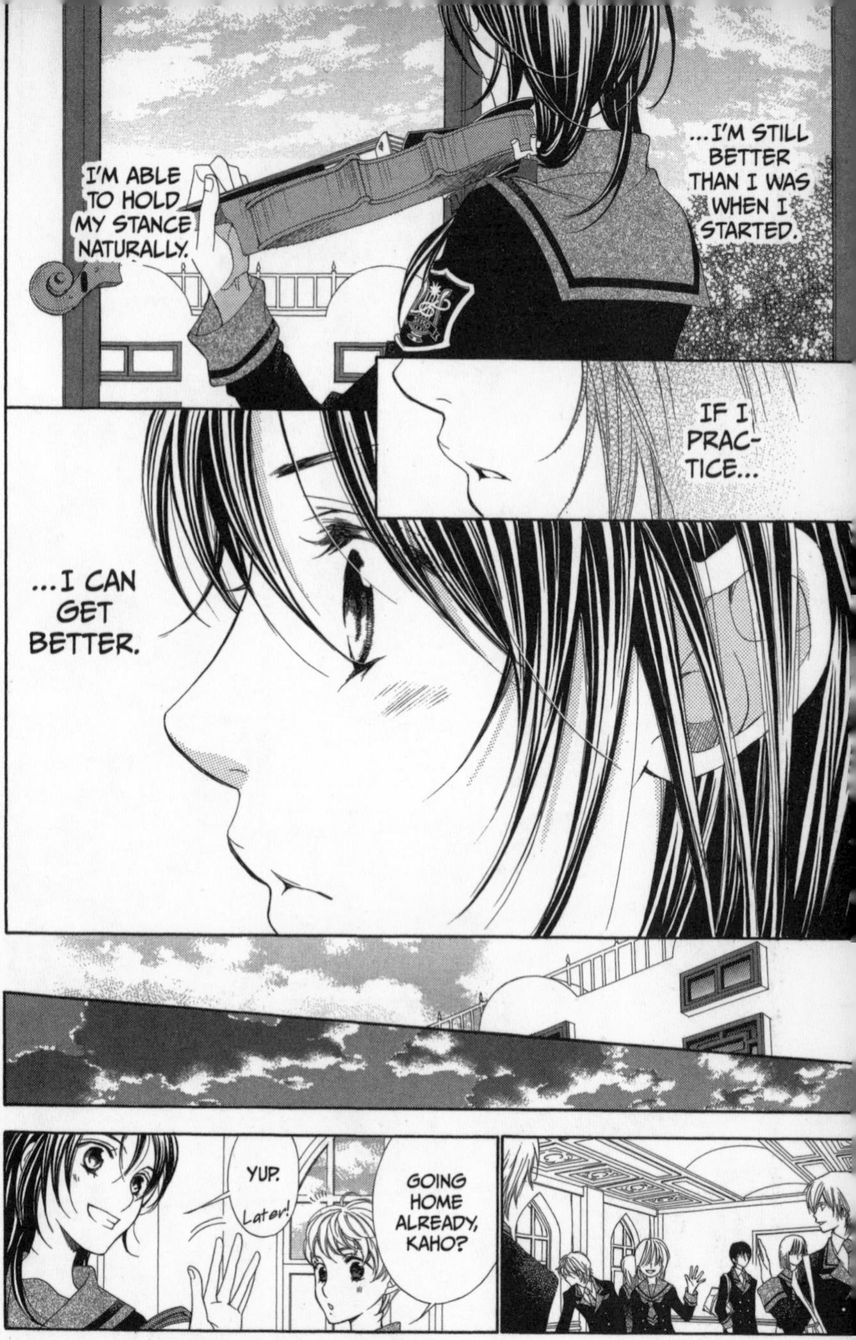
...I'M STILL BETTER THAN I WAS WHEN I STARTED.
I'M ABLE TO HOLD MY STANCE NATURALLY.
IF I PRAC-TICE...
...I CAN GET BETTER.
GOING HOME ALREADY, KAHO?
YUP.
Later!

## FOUR

The girl who appears at the very end of Measure 33 is in the *La Corda* game as well. Yes, it's that girl. I hadn't really put any thought into her character design until I realized that she appears in the anime too. Then I drew her in a frenzy.

It's very refreshing to draw a uniform other than Seiso Academy's. She's going to appear regularly from Measure 34 on, so please welcome her to the story.

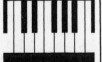

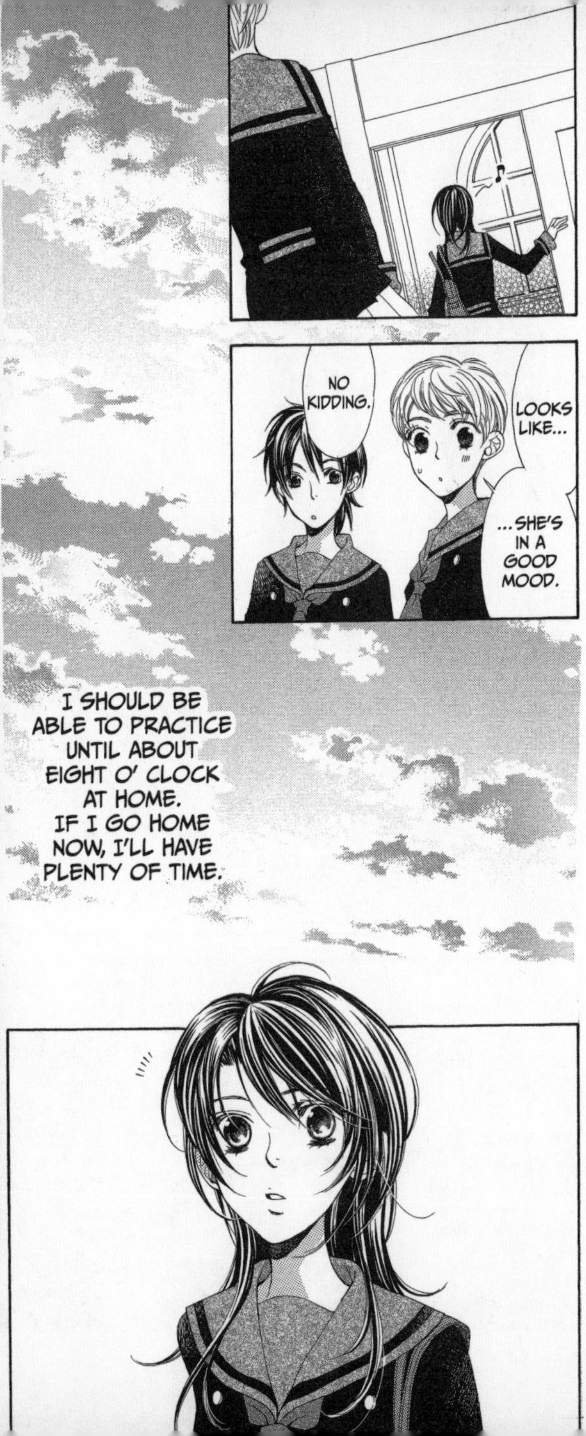
LOOKS LIKE...
...SHE'S IN A GOOD MOOD.
NO KIDDING.
I SHOULD BE ABLE TO PRACTICE UNTIL ABOUT EIGHT O' CLOCK AT HOME. IF I GO HOME NOW, I'LL HAVE PLENTY OF TIME.

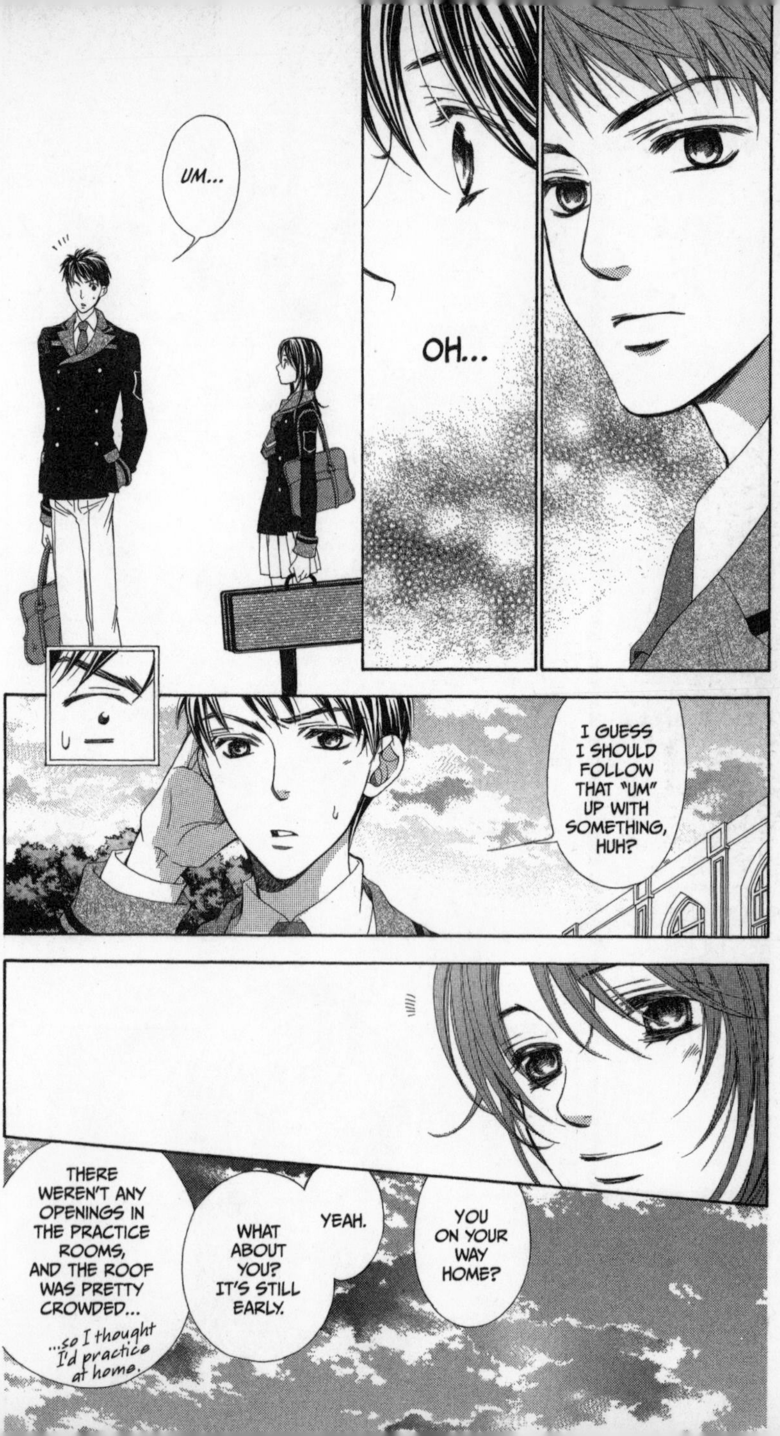
OH...
UM...
I GUESS I SHOULD FOLLOW THAT "UM" UP WITH SOMETHING, HUH?
YOU ON YOUR WAY HOME?
YEAH.
WHAT ABOUT YOU? IT'S STILL EARLY.
THERE WEREN'T ANY OPENINGS IN THE PRACTICE ROOMS, AND THE ROOF WAS PRETTY CROWDED...
...so I thought I'd practice at home.

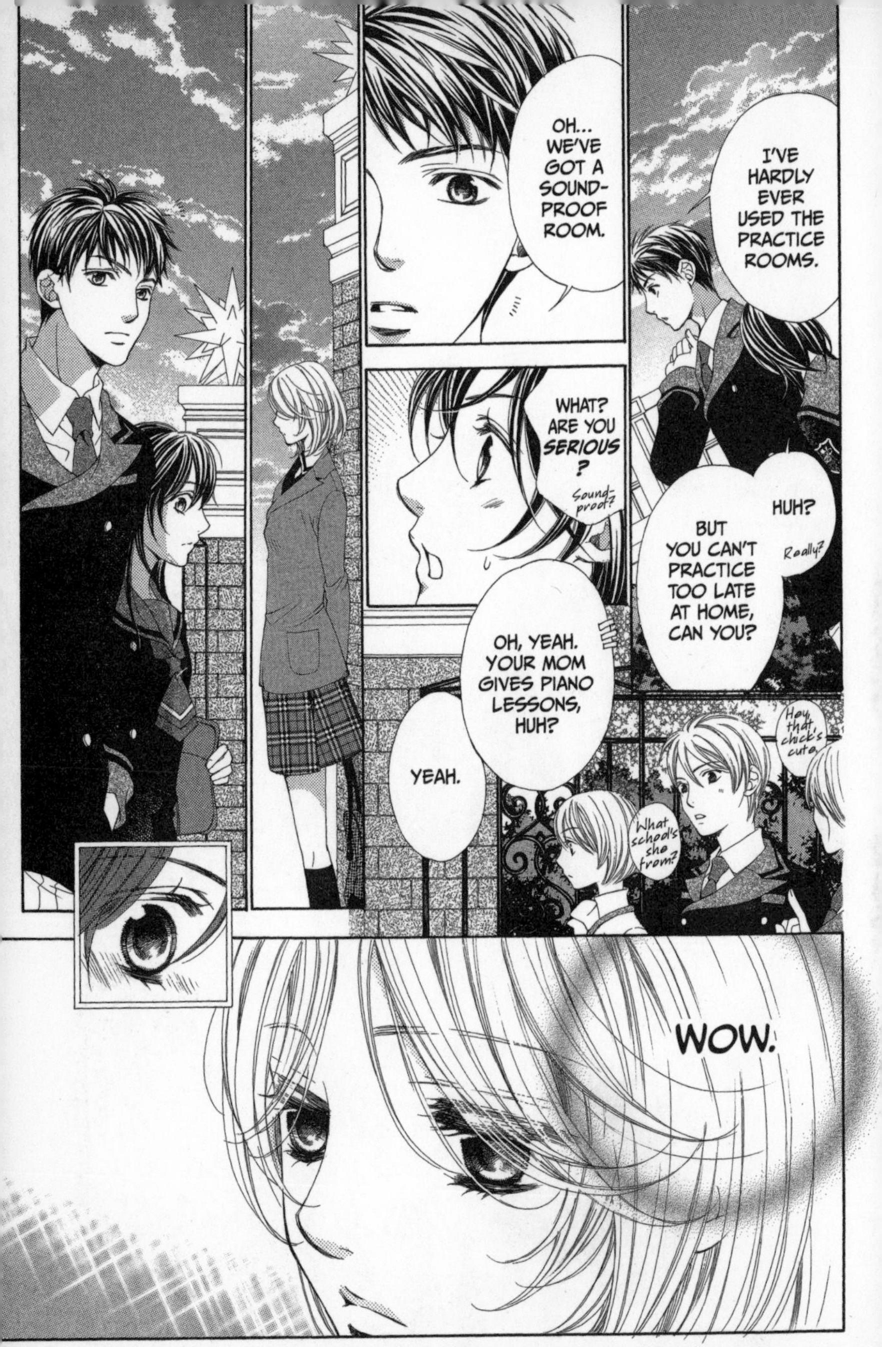
I'VE HARDLY EVER USED THE PRACTICE ROOMS.
HUH?
Really?
BUT YOU CAN'T PRACTICE TOO LATE AT HOME, CAN YOU?
OH... WE'VE GOT A SOUND-PROOF ROOM.
WHAT? ARE YOU *SERIOUS* ?
Sound-proof?
OH, YEAH. YOUR MOM GIVES PIANO LESSONS, HUH?
YEAH.
Hey, that chick's cute
What school's she from?
WOW.

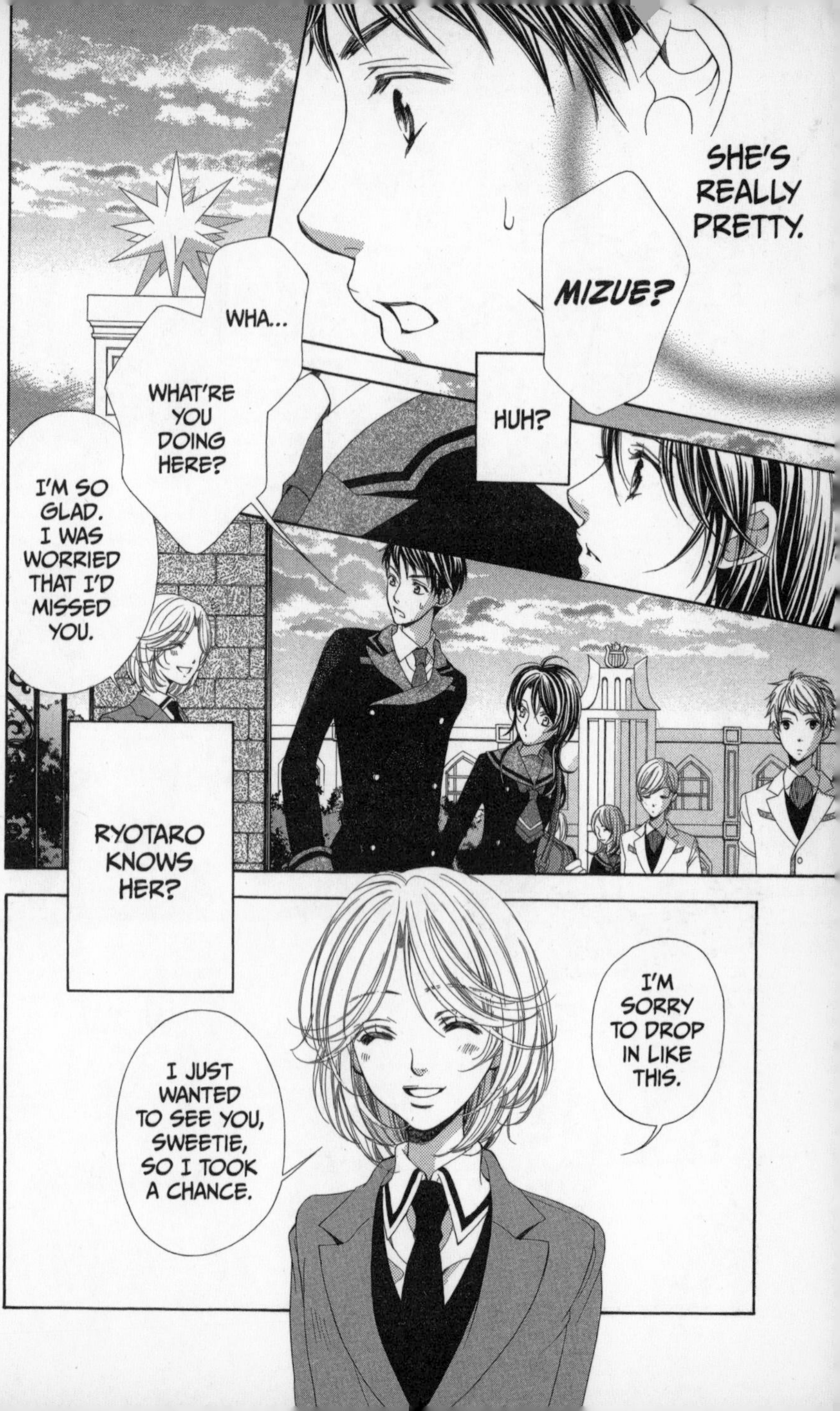
SHE'S REALLY PRETTY.
MIZUE?
HUH?
WHA...
WHAT'RE YOU DOING HERE?
I'M SO GLAD. I WAS WORRIED THAT I'D MISSED YOU.
RYOTARO KNOWS HER?
I'M SORRY TO DROP IN LIKE THIS.
I JUST WANTED TO SEE YOU, SWEETIE, SO I TOOK A CHANCE.

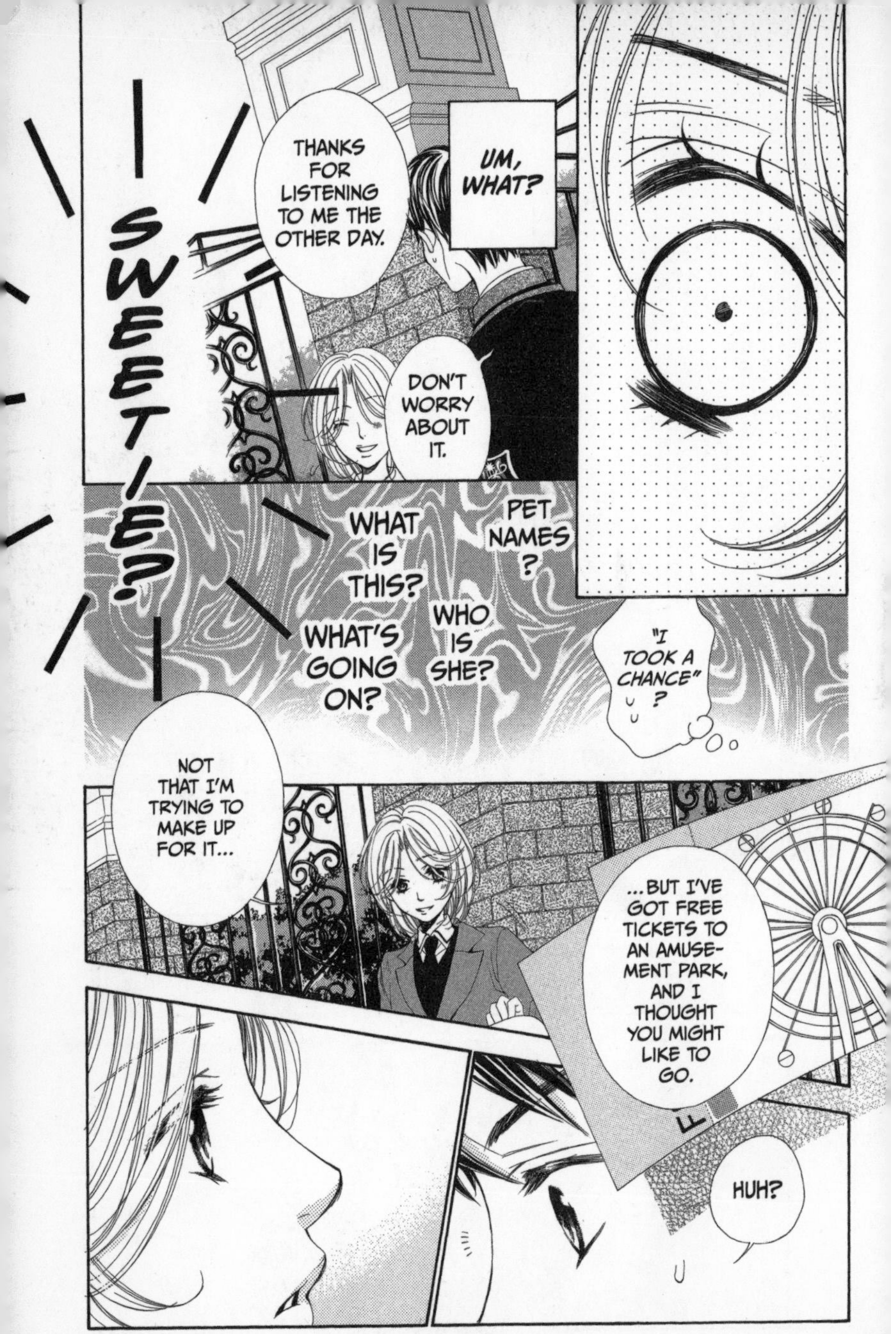
UM, WHAT?
THANKS FOR LISTENING TO ME THE OTHER DAY.
SWEETIE?!
DON'T WORRY ABOUT IT.
PET NAMES?
WHAT IS THIS?
WHO IS SHE?
WHAT'S GOING ON?
"I TOOK A CHANCE"?
NOT THAT I'M TRYING TO MAKE UP FOR IT...
...BUT I'VE GOT FREE TICKETS TO AN AMUSEMENT PARK, AND I THOUGHT YOU MIGHT LIKE TO GO.
HUH?

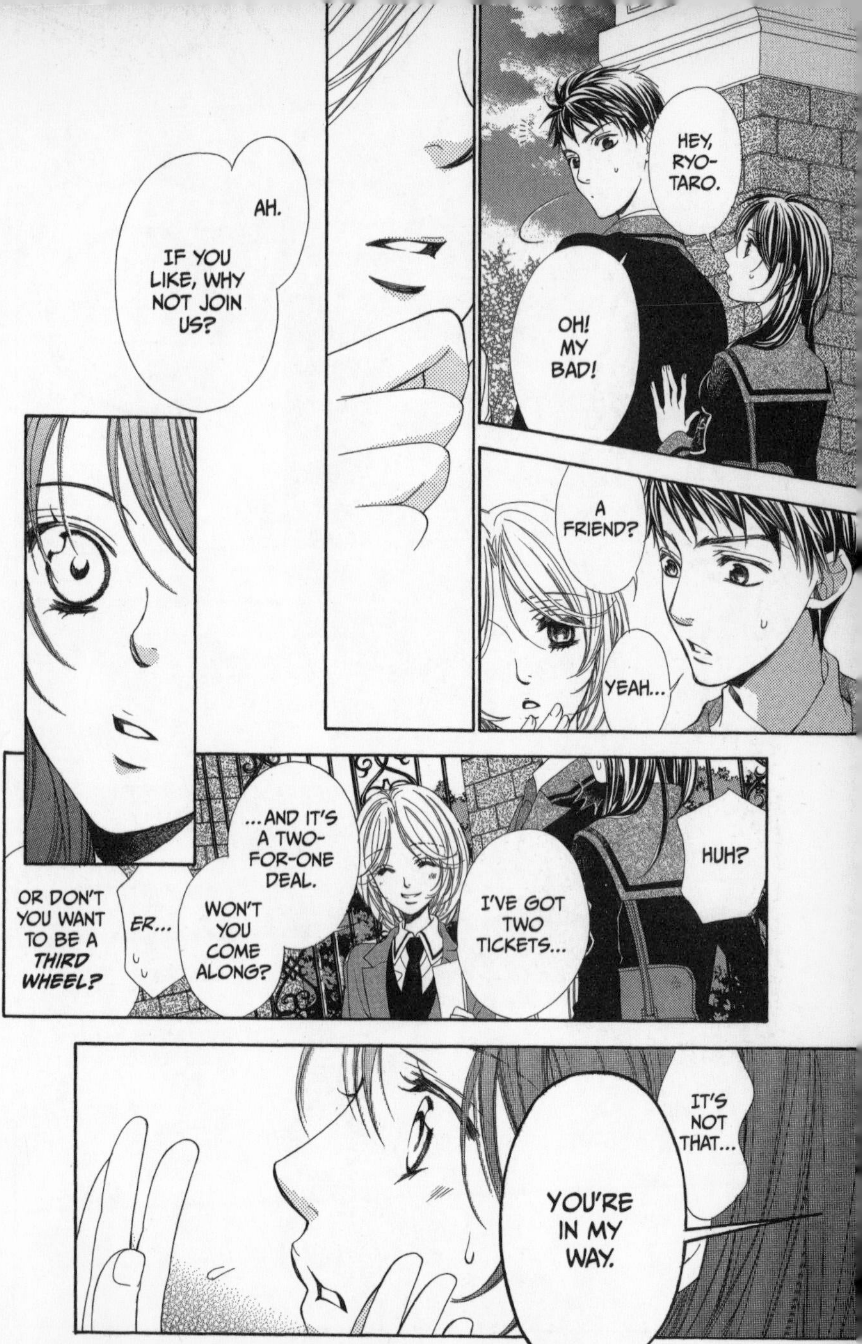
HEY, RYOTARO.
OH! MY BAD!
A FRIEND?
YEAH...
AH.
IF YOU LIKE, WHY NOT JOIN US?
HUH?
I'VE GOT TWO TICKETS...
...AND IT'S A TWO-FOR-ONE DEAL.
WON'T YOU COME ALONG?
ER...
OR DON'T YOU WANT TO BE A *THIRD WHEEL?*
IT'S NOT THAT...
YOU'RE IN MY WAY.

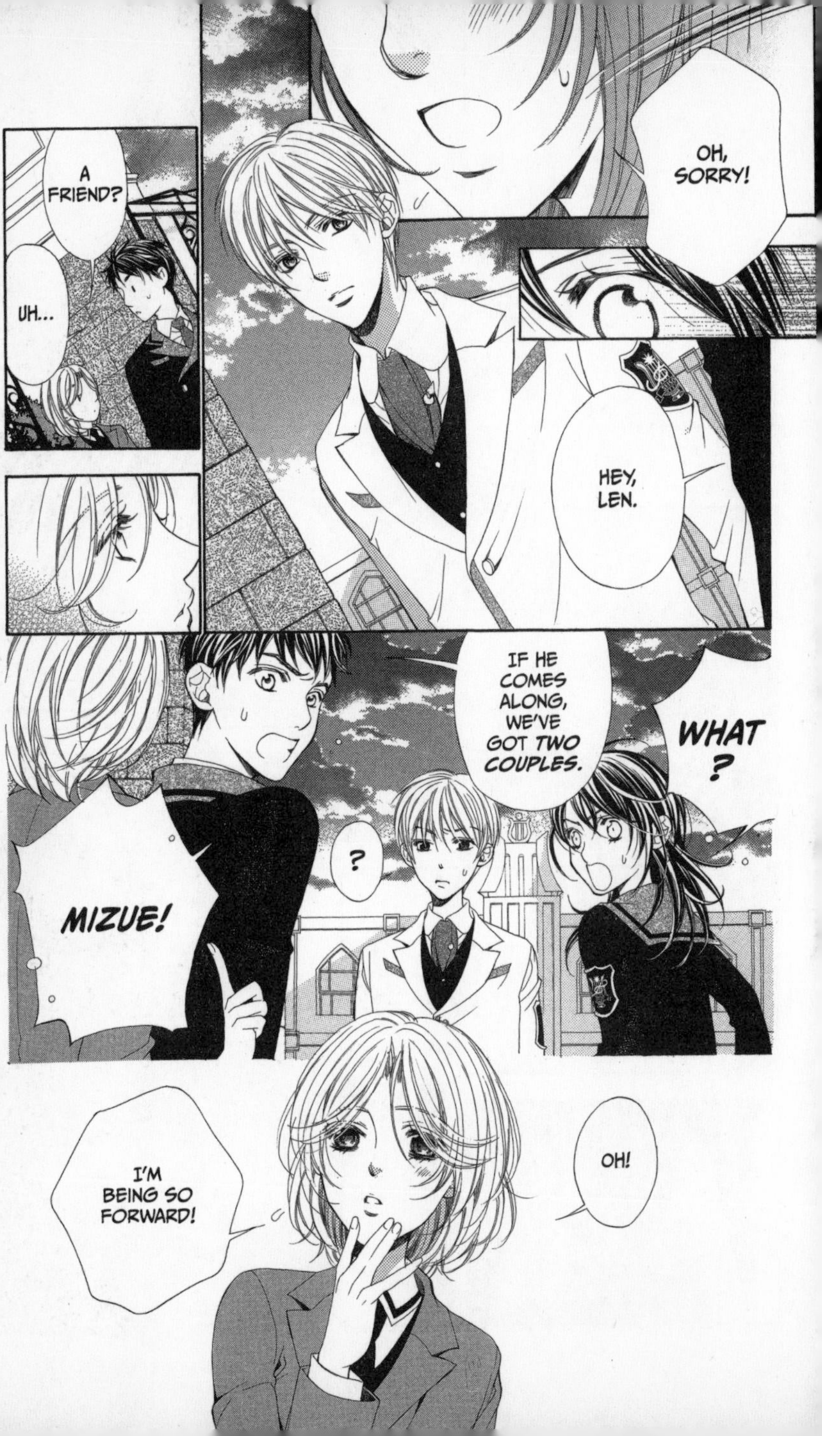
OH, SORRY!
HEY, LEN.
A FRIEND?
UH...
IF HE COMES ALONG, WE'VE GOT TWO COUPLES.
WHAT ?
?
MIZUE!
OH!
I'M BEING SO FORWARD!

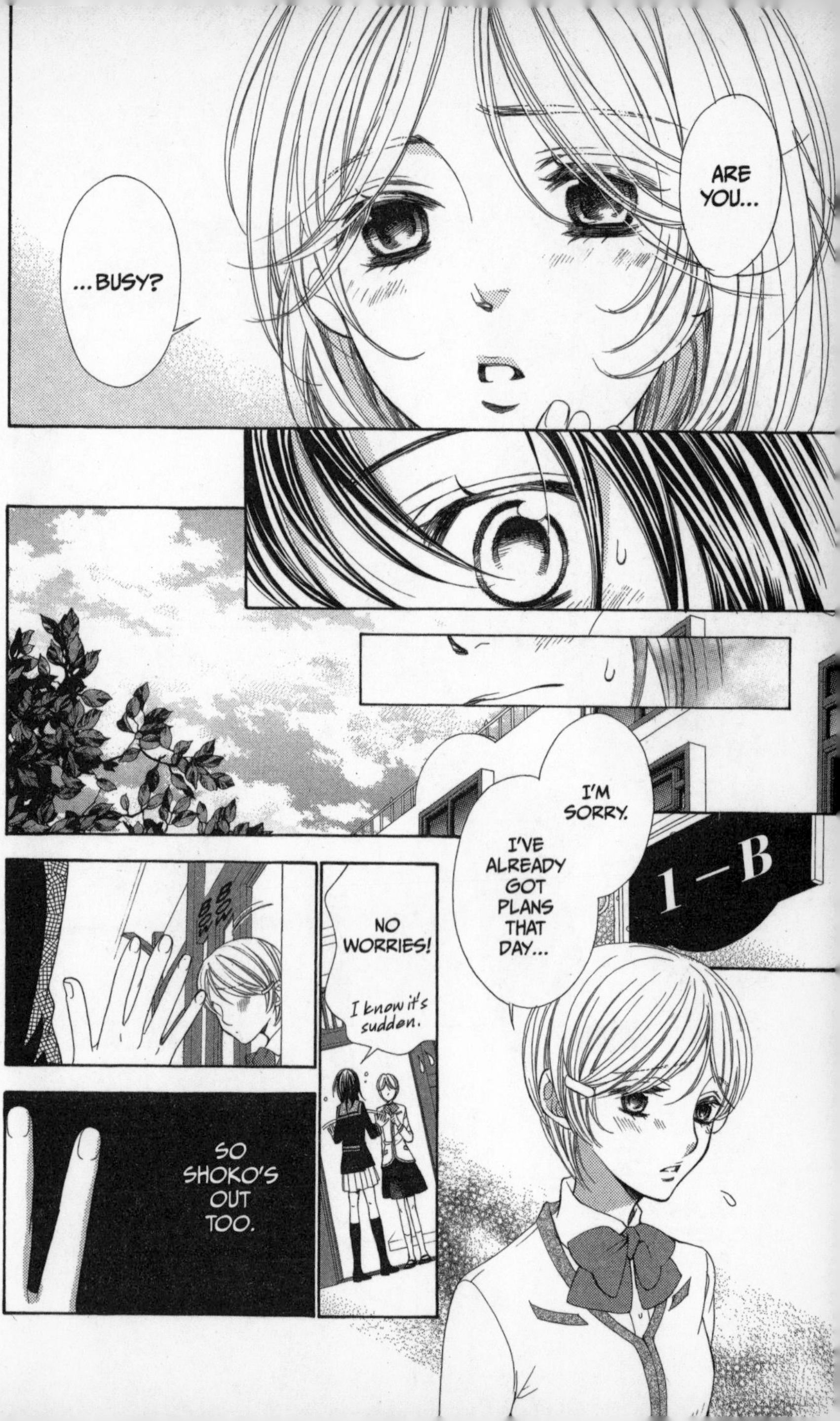
ARE YOU...
...BUSY?
1—B
I'M SORRY.
I'VE ALREADY GOT PLANS THAT DAY...
NO WORRIES!
I know it's sudden.
BOW BOW
SO SHOKO'S OUT TOO.

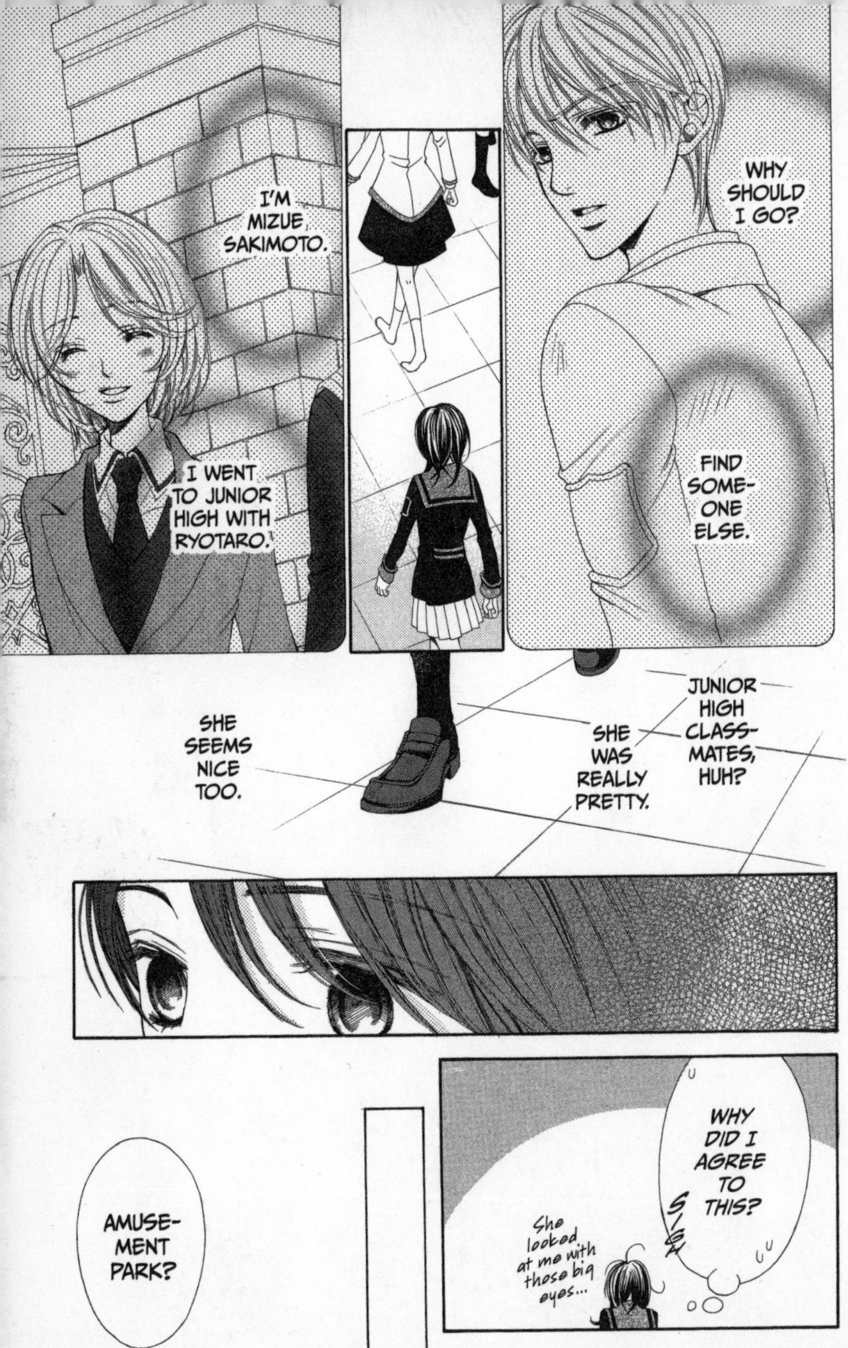
WHY SHOULD I GO?
FIND SOME-ONE ELSE.
I'M MIZUE SAKIMOTO.
I WENT TO JUNIOR HIGH WITH RYOTARO.
JUNIOR HIGH CLASS-MATES, HUH?
SHE WAS REALLY PRETTY.
SHE SEEMS NICE TOO.
WHY DID I AGREE TO THIS?
SIGH
She looked at me with those big eyes...
AMUSE-MENT PARK?

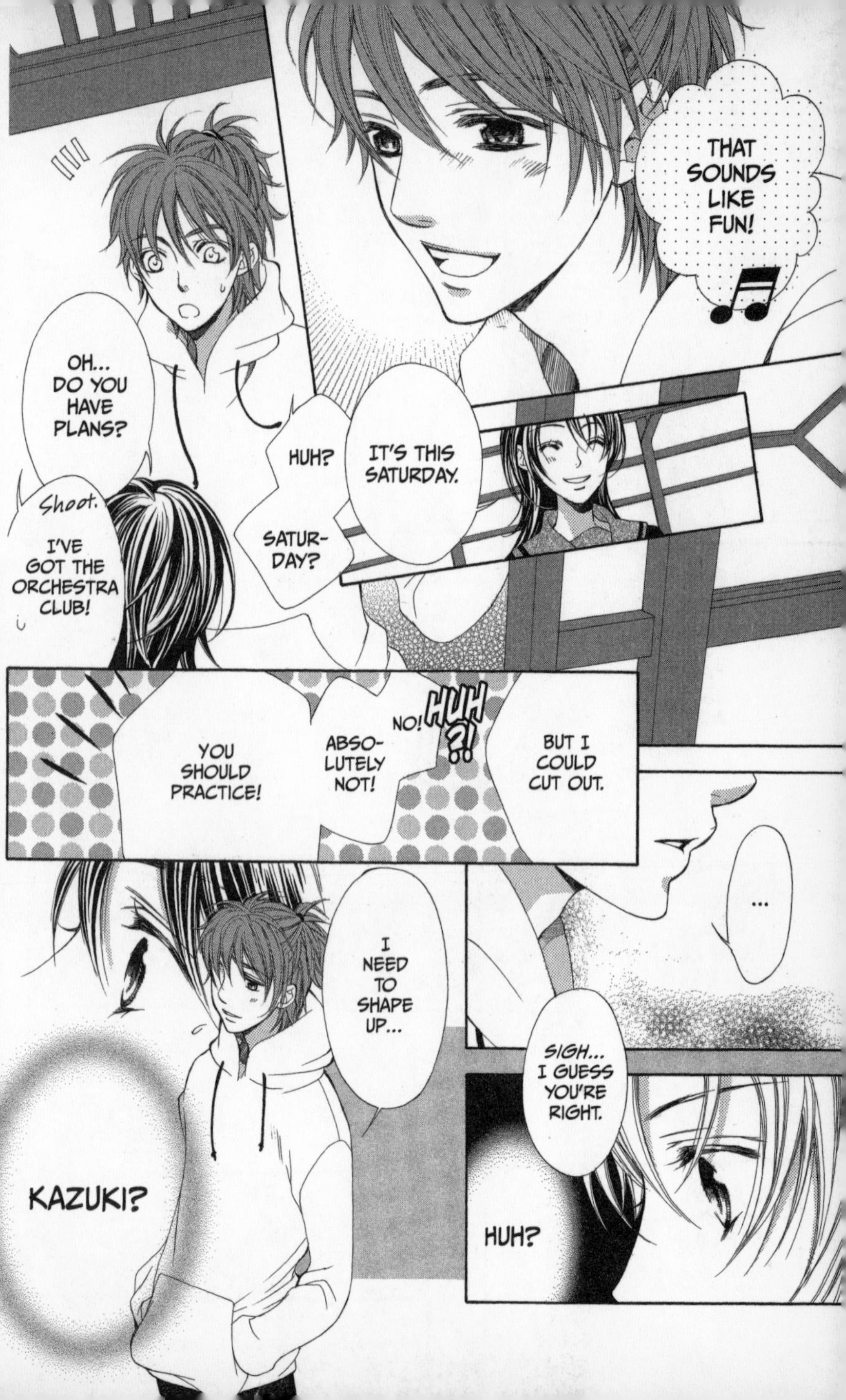
THAT SOUNDS LIKE FUN!
IT'S THIS SATURDAY.
HUH?
SATURDAY?
!!!
OH... DO YOU HAVE PLANS?
Shoot.
I'VE GOT THE ORCHESTRA CLUB!
BUT I COULD CUT OUT.
HUH ?!
NO!
ABSOLUTELY NOT!
YOU SHOULD PRACTICE!
...
SIGH... I GUESS YOU'RE RIGHT.
HUH?
I NEED TO SHAPE UP...
KAZUKI?

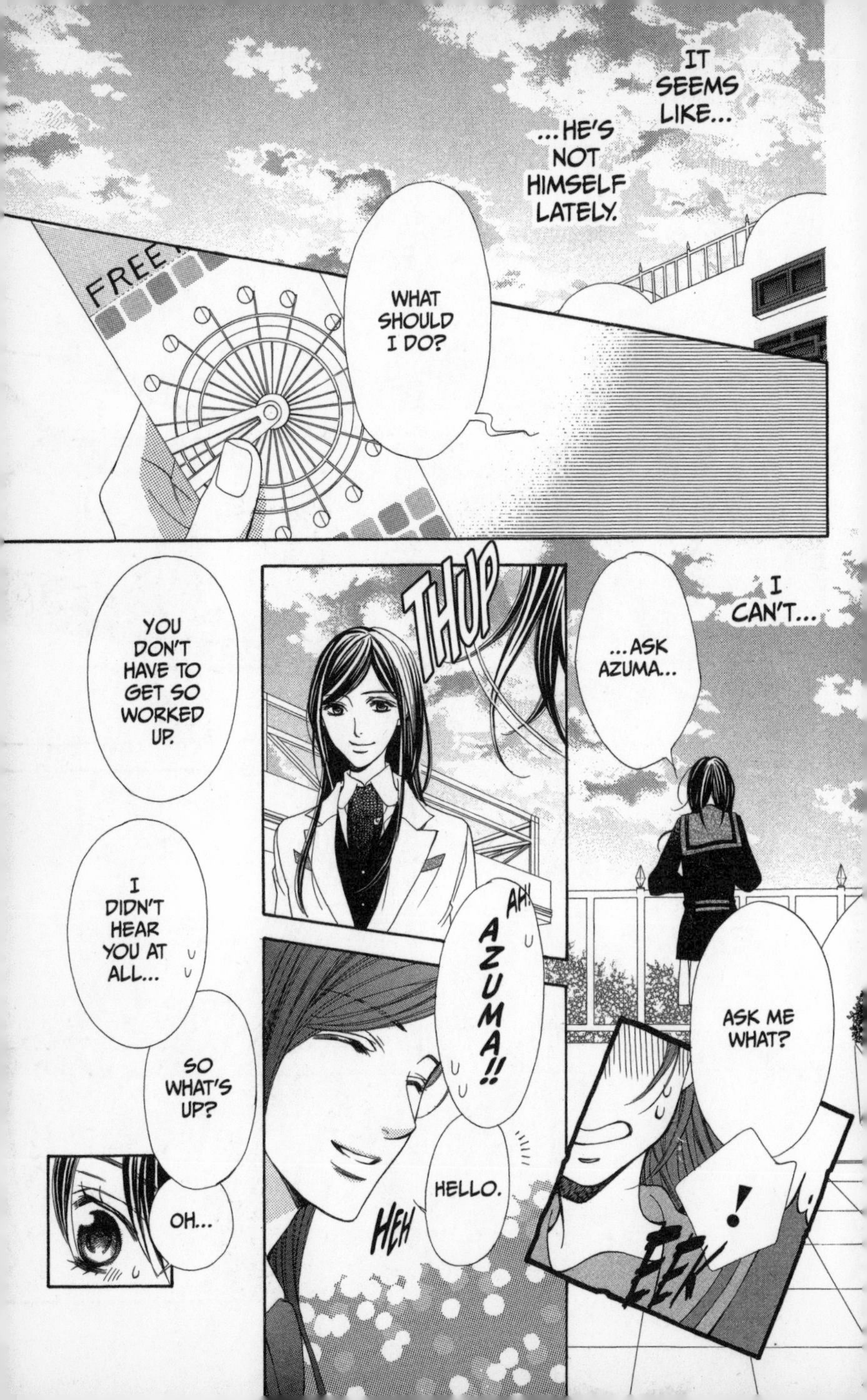
IT SEEMS LIKE...
...HE'S NOT HIMSELF LATELY.
FREE
WHAT SHOULD I DO?
I CAN'T...
...ASK AZUMA...
THUP
ASK ME WHAT?
!
EEK
AH! AZUMA!!
YOU DON'T HAVE TO GET SO WORKED UP.
I DIDN'T HEAR YOU AT ALL...
HELLO.
HEH
SO WHAT'S UP?
OH...

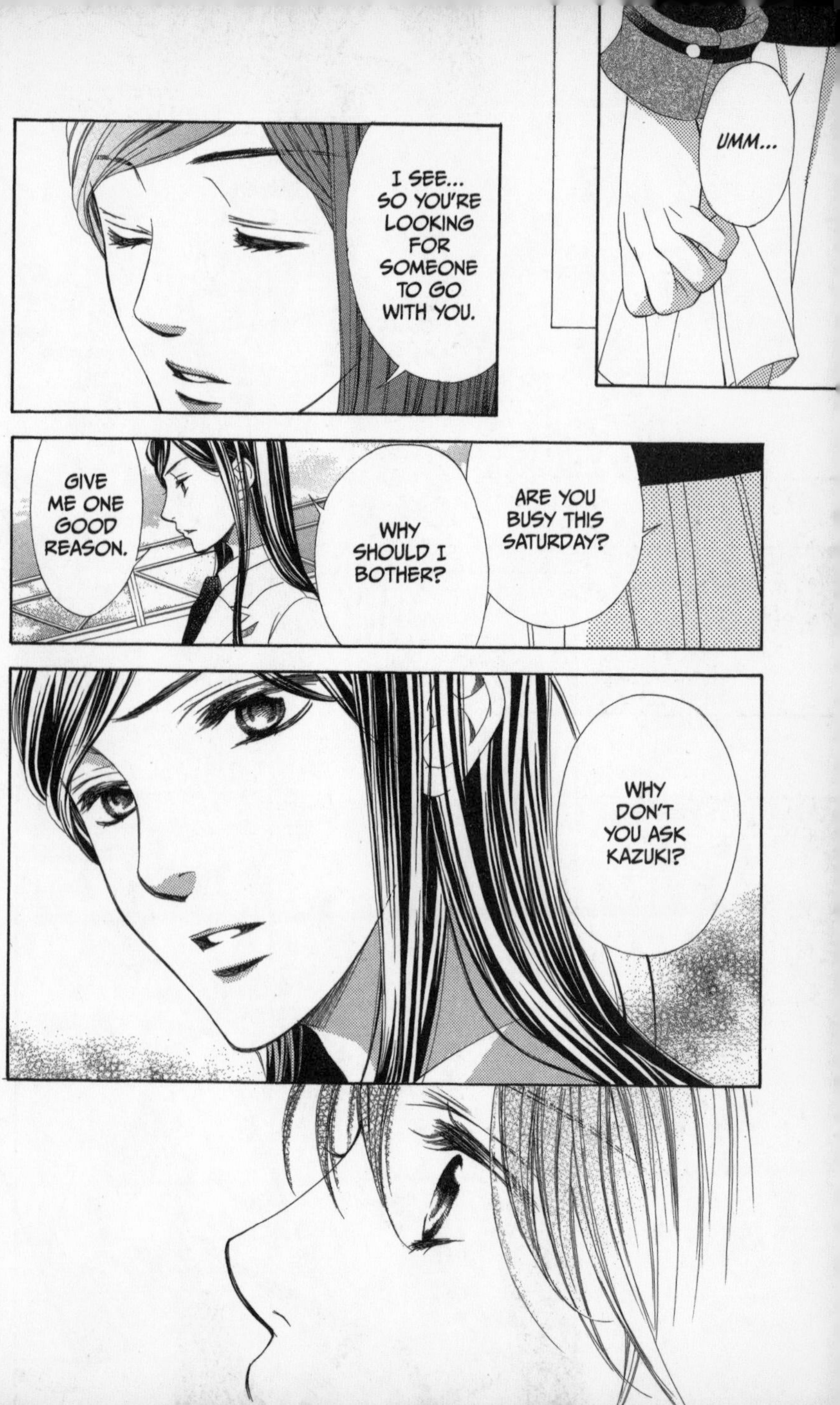
UMM...
I SEE... SO YOU'RE LOOKING FOR SOMEONE TO GO WITH YOU.
ARE YOU BUSY THIS SATURDAY?
WHY SHOULD I BOTHER?
GIVE ME ONE GOOD REASON.
WHY DON'T YOU ASK KAZUKI?

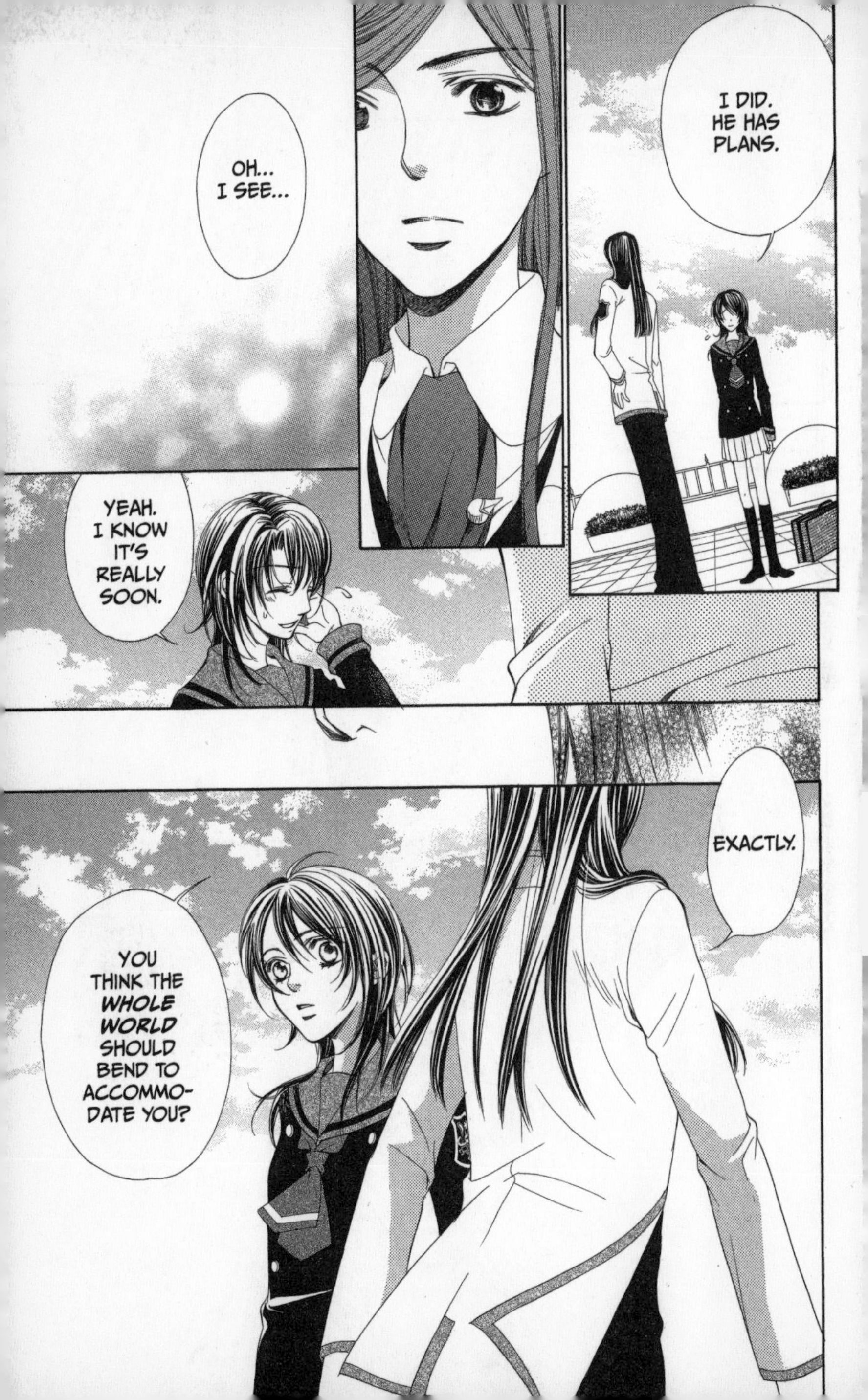
I DID. HE HAS PLANS.
OH... I SEE...
YEAH. I KNOW IT'S REALLY SOON.
EXACTLY.
YOU THINK THE *WHOLE WORLD* SHOULD BEND TO ACCOMMO-DATE YOU?

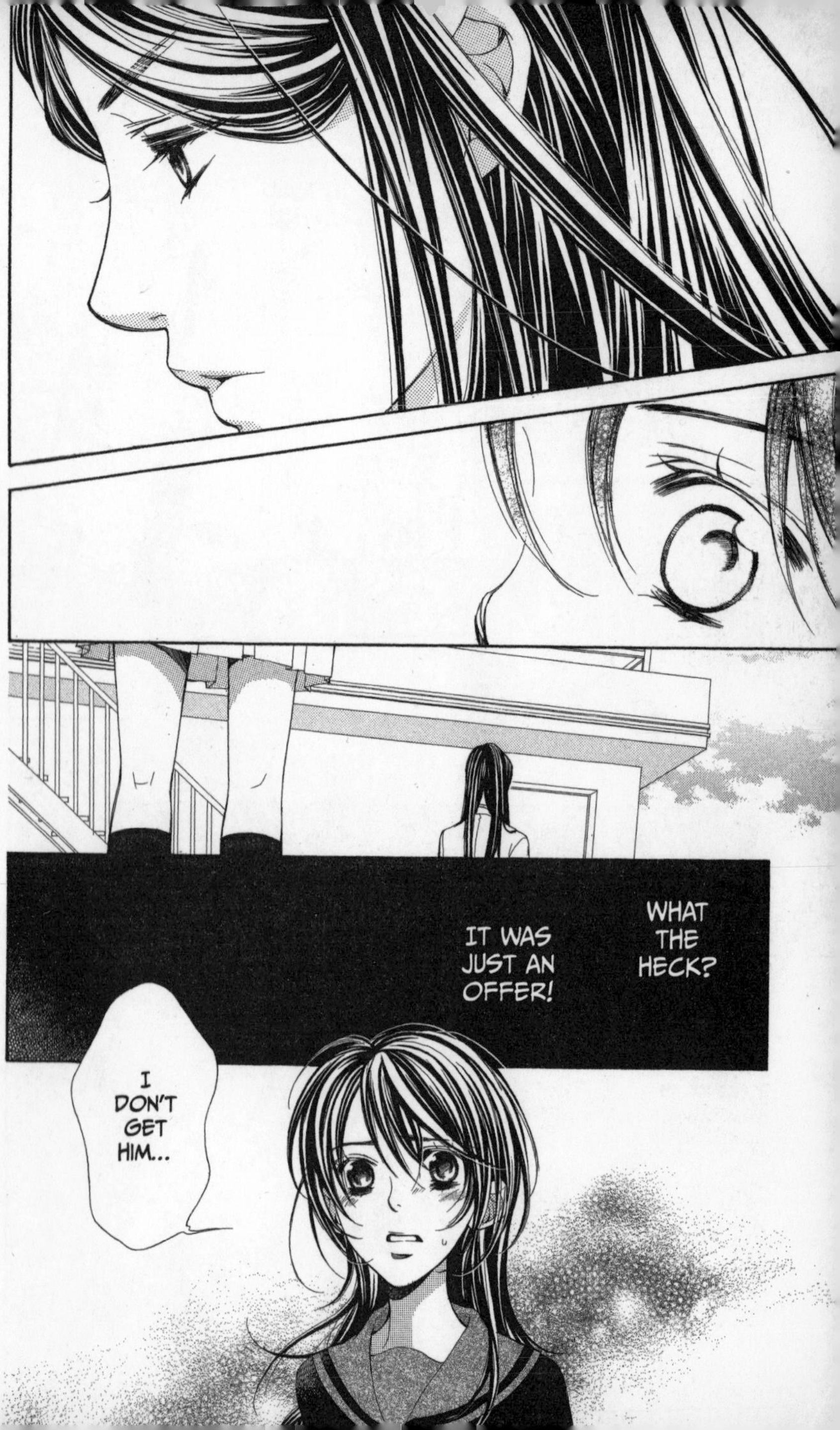
WHAT THE HECK?
IT WAS JUST AN OFFER!
I DON'T GET HIM...

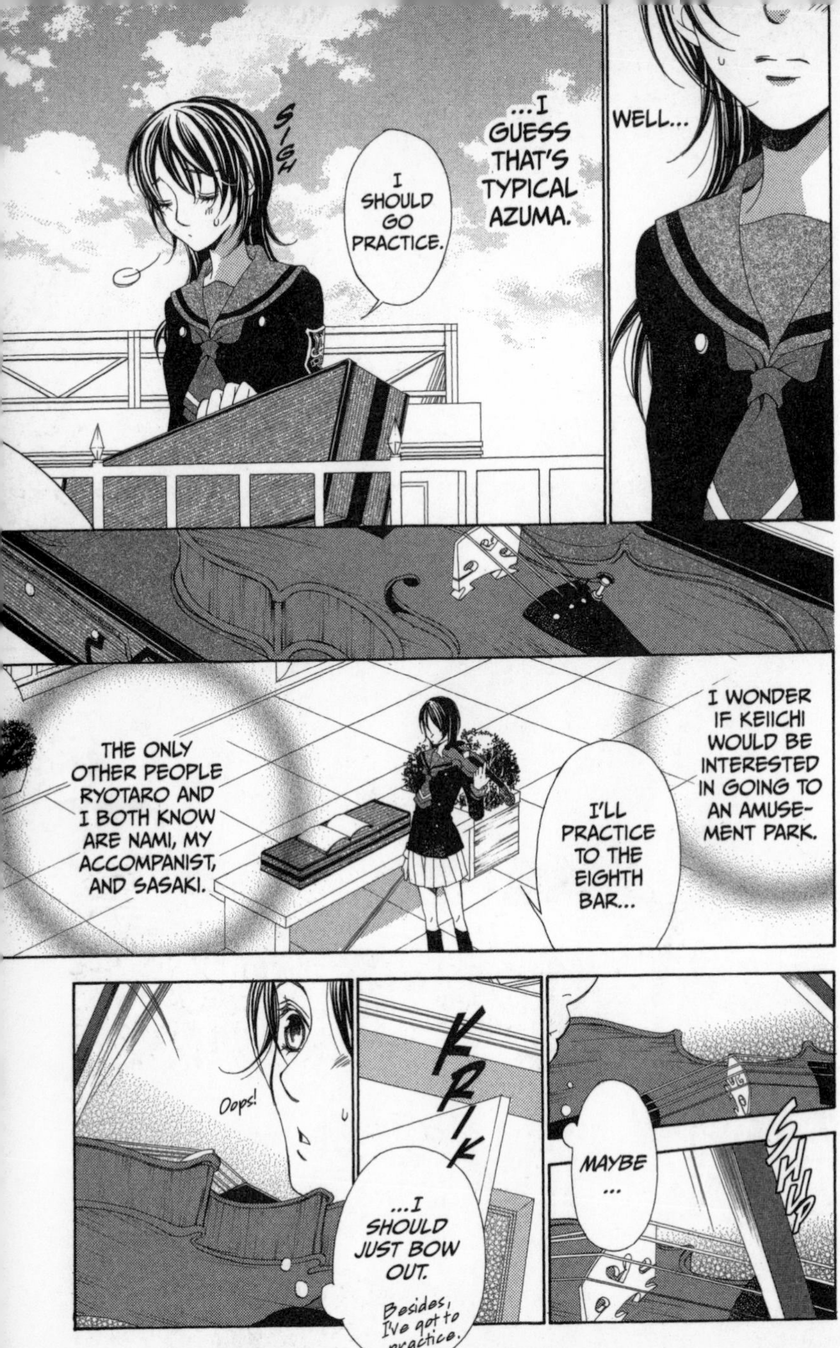
WELL...
...I GUESS THAT'S TYPICAL AZUMA.
I SHOULD GO PRACTICE.
SIGH
I WONDER IF KEIICHI WOULD BE INTERESTED IN GOING TO AN AMUSEMENT PARK.
I'LL PRACTICE TO THE EIGHTH BAR...
THE ONLY OTHER PEOPLE RYOTARO AND I BOTH KNOW ARE NAMI, MY ACCOMPANIST, AND SASAKI.
SHHA
MAYBE...
KRIK
...I SHOULD JUST BOW OUT.
Besides, I've got to practice.
Oops!

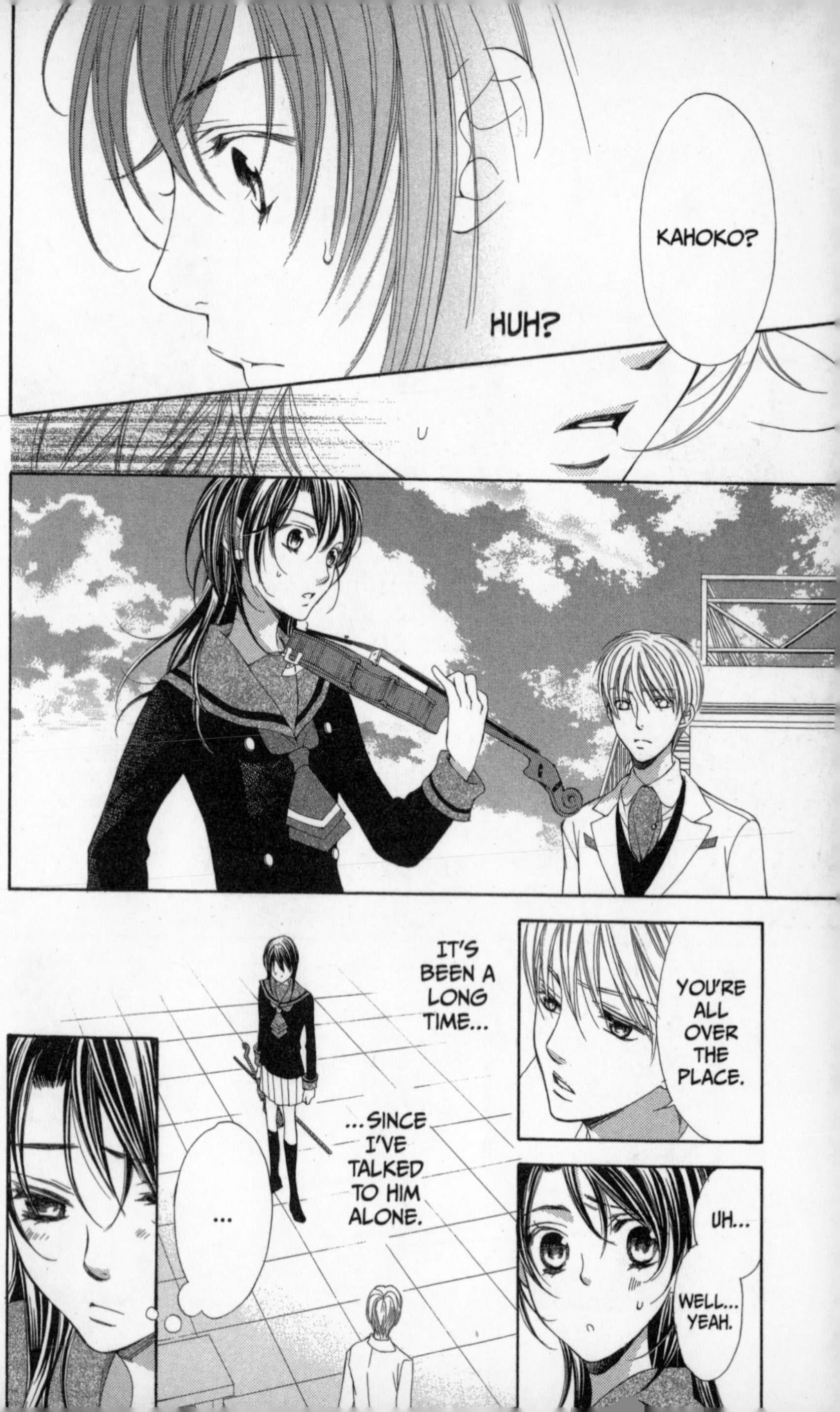
KAHOKO?
HUH?
YOU'RE ALL OVER THE PLACE.
UH...
WELL... YEAH.
IT'S BEEN A LONG TIME...
...SINCE I'VE TALKED TO HIM ALONE.
...

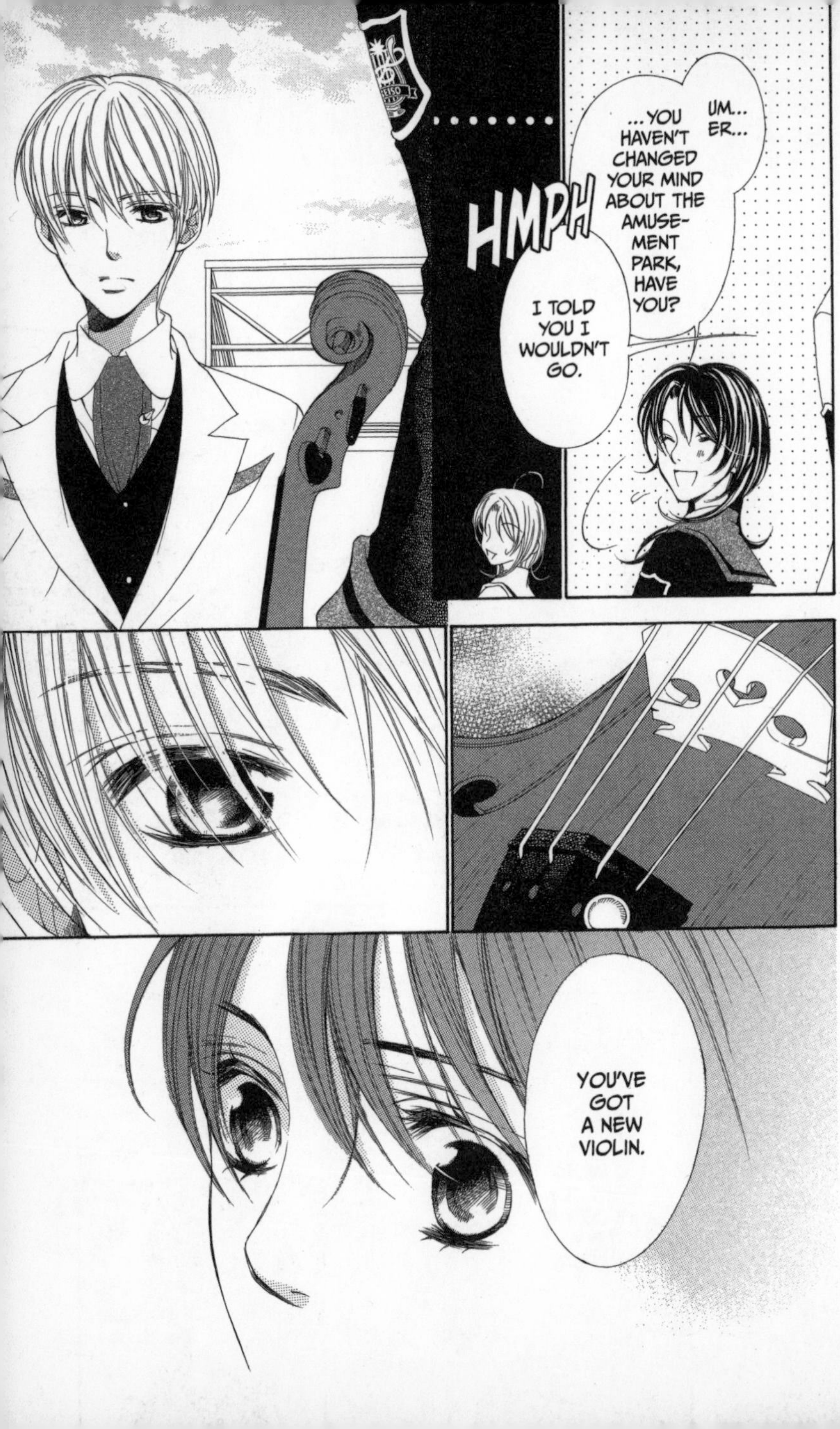
UM... ER...
...YOU HAVEN'T CHANGED YOUR MIND ABOUT THE AMUSE-MENT PARK, HAVE YOU?
HMPH
I TOLD YOU I WOULDN'T GO.
YOU'VE GOT A NEW VIOLIN.

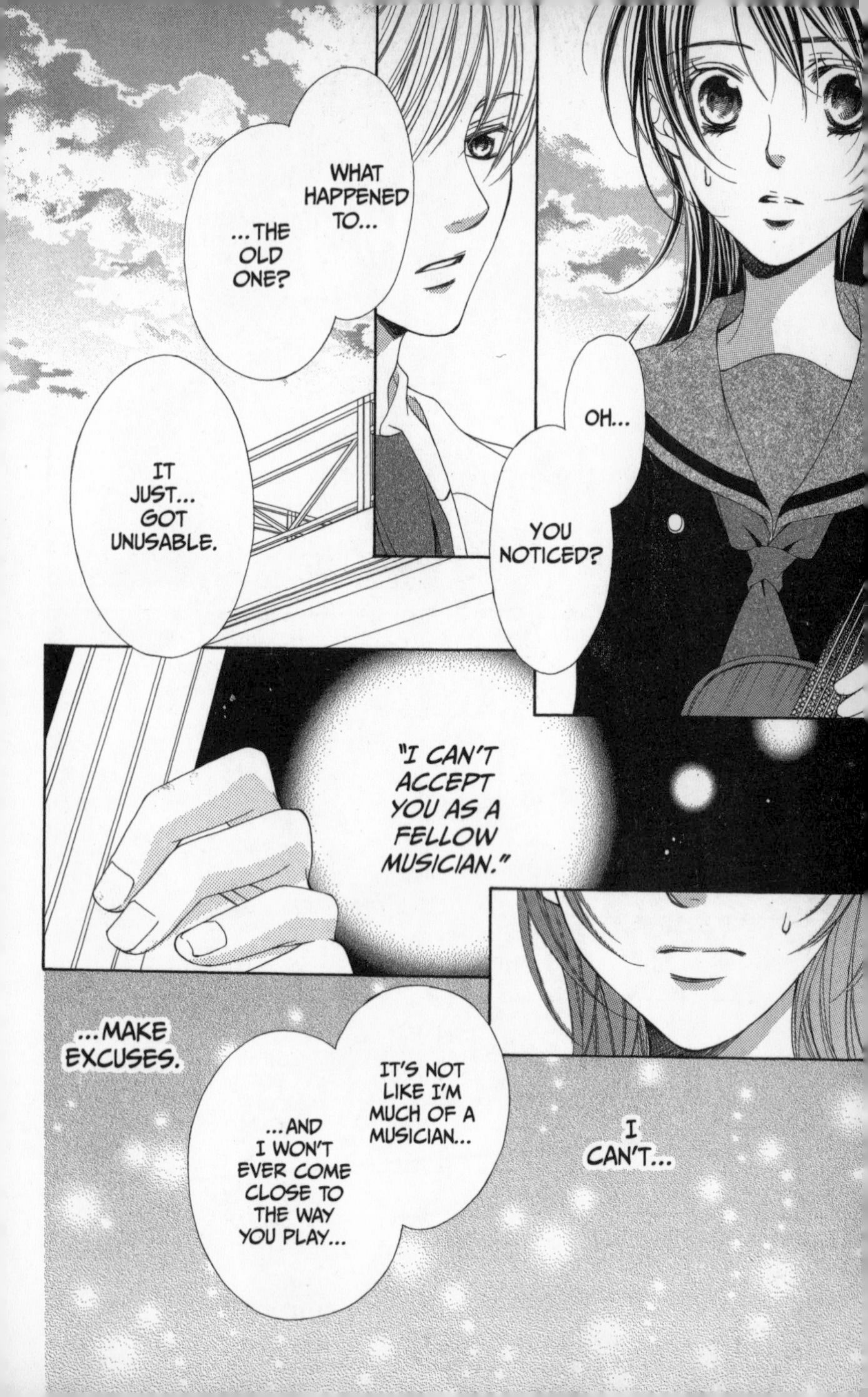
OH... YOU NOTICED?
WHAT HAPPENED TO...
...THE OLD ONE?
IT JUST... GOT UNUSABLE.
"I CAN'T ACCEPT YOU AS A FELLOW MUSICIAN."
I CAN'T...
IT'S NOT LIKE I'M MUCH OF A MUSICIAN...
...AND I WON'T EVER COME CLOSE TO THE WAY YOU PLAY...
...MAKE EXCUSES.

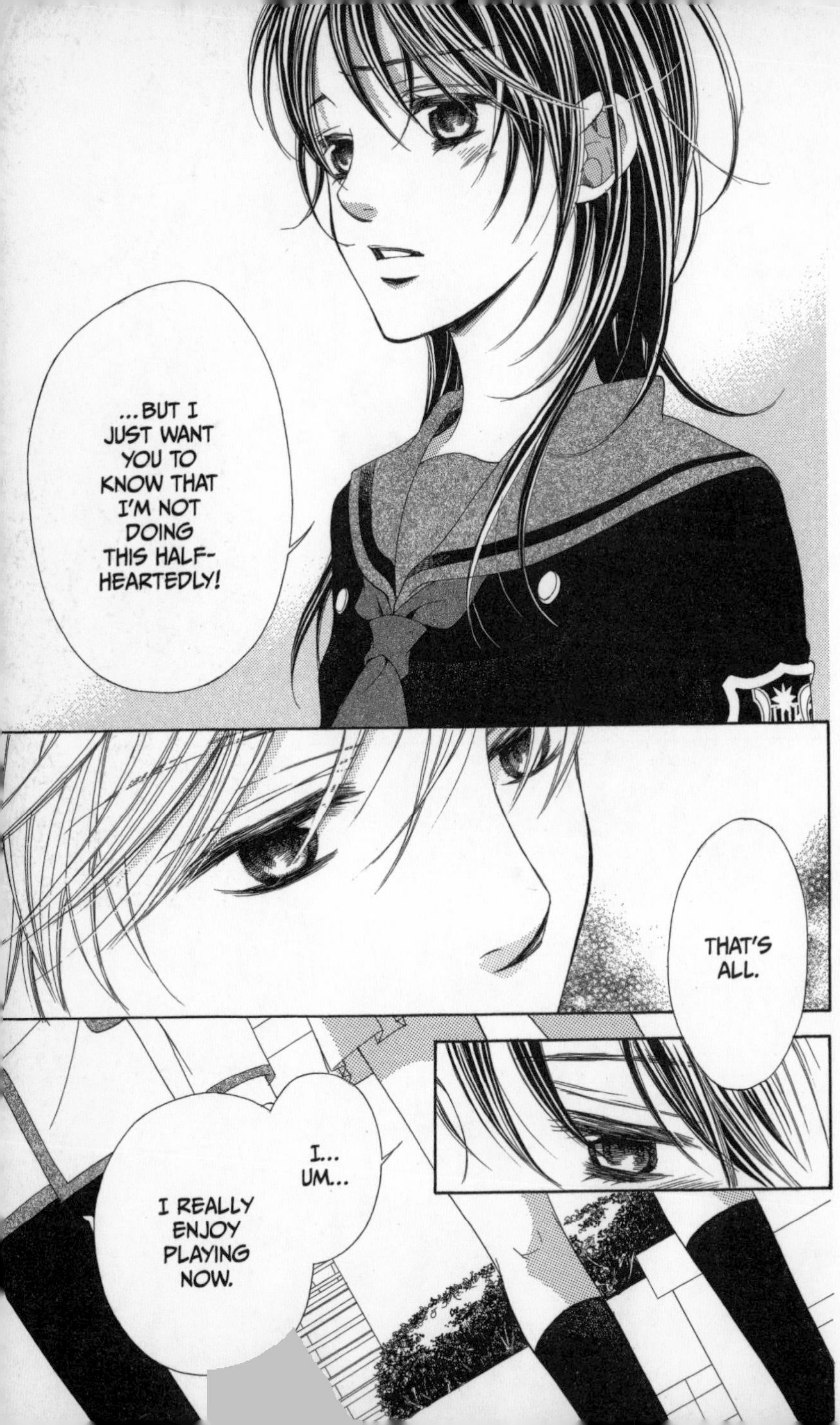
...BUT I JUST WANT YOU TO KNOW THAT I'M NOT DOING THIS HALF-HEARTEDLY!
THAT'S ALL.
I... UM...
I REALLY ENJOY PLAYING NOW.

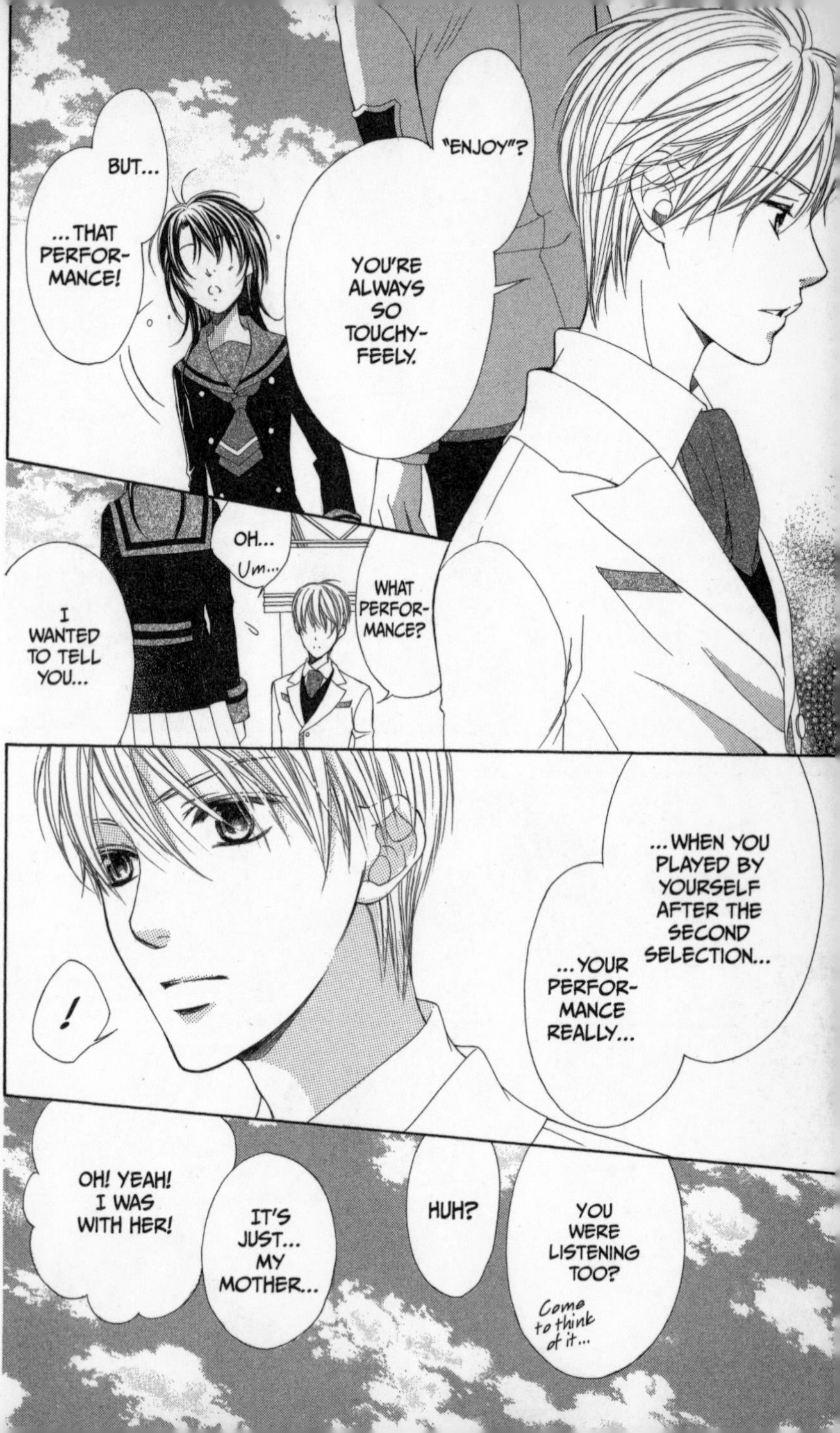
"ENJOY"?
YOU'RE ALWAYS SO TOUCHY-FEELY.
BUT...
...THAT PERFORMANCE!
WHAT PERFORMANCE?
OH... Um...
I WANTED TO TELL YOU...
...WHEN YOU PLAYED BY YOURSELF AFTER THE SECOND SELECTION...
...YOUR PERFORMANCE REALLY...
!
YOU WERE LISTENING TOO?
Come to think of it...
HUH?
IT'S JUST... MY MOTHER...
OH! YEAH! I WAS WITH HER!

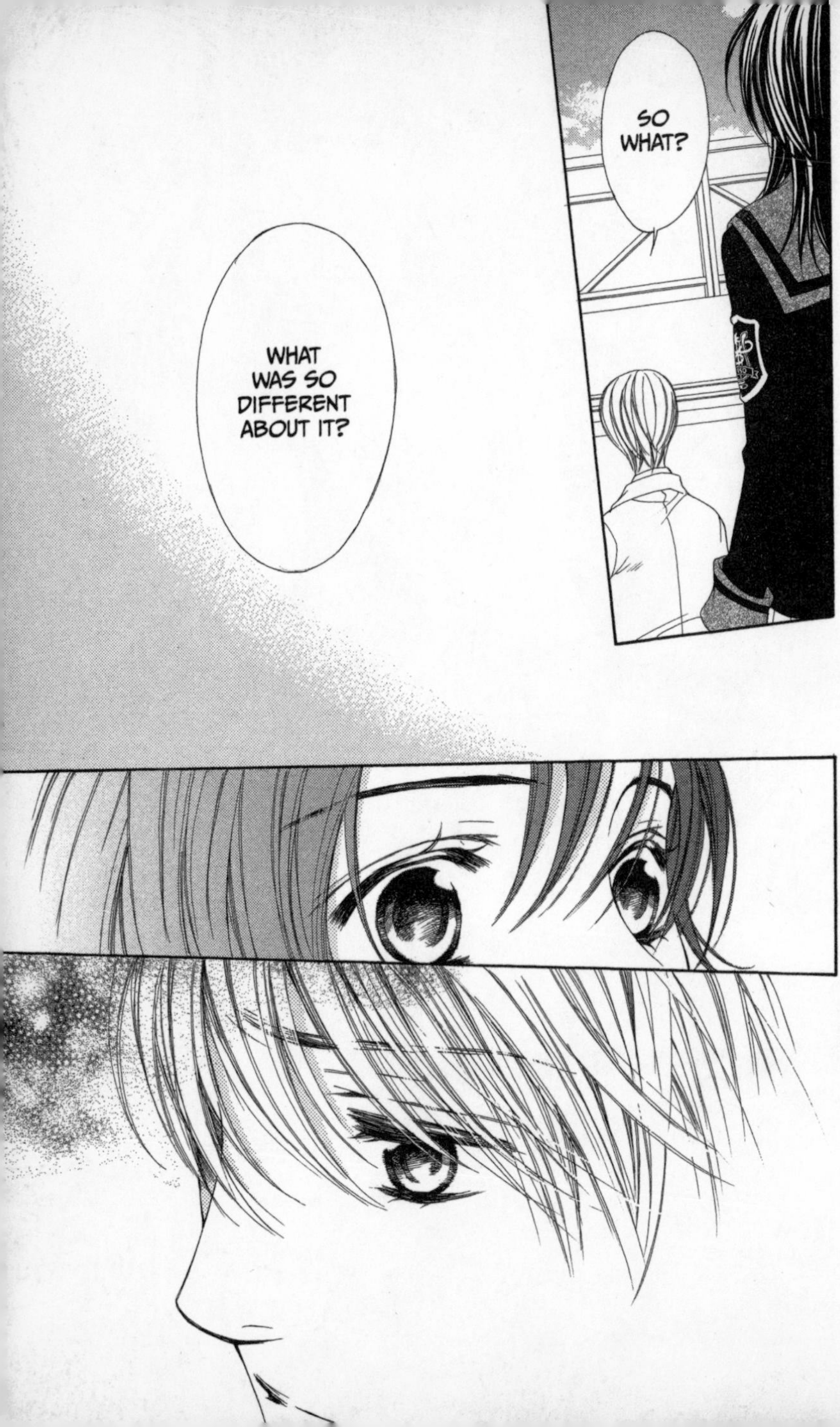
SO WHAT?
WHAT WAS SO DIFFERENT ABOUT IT?

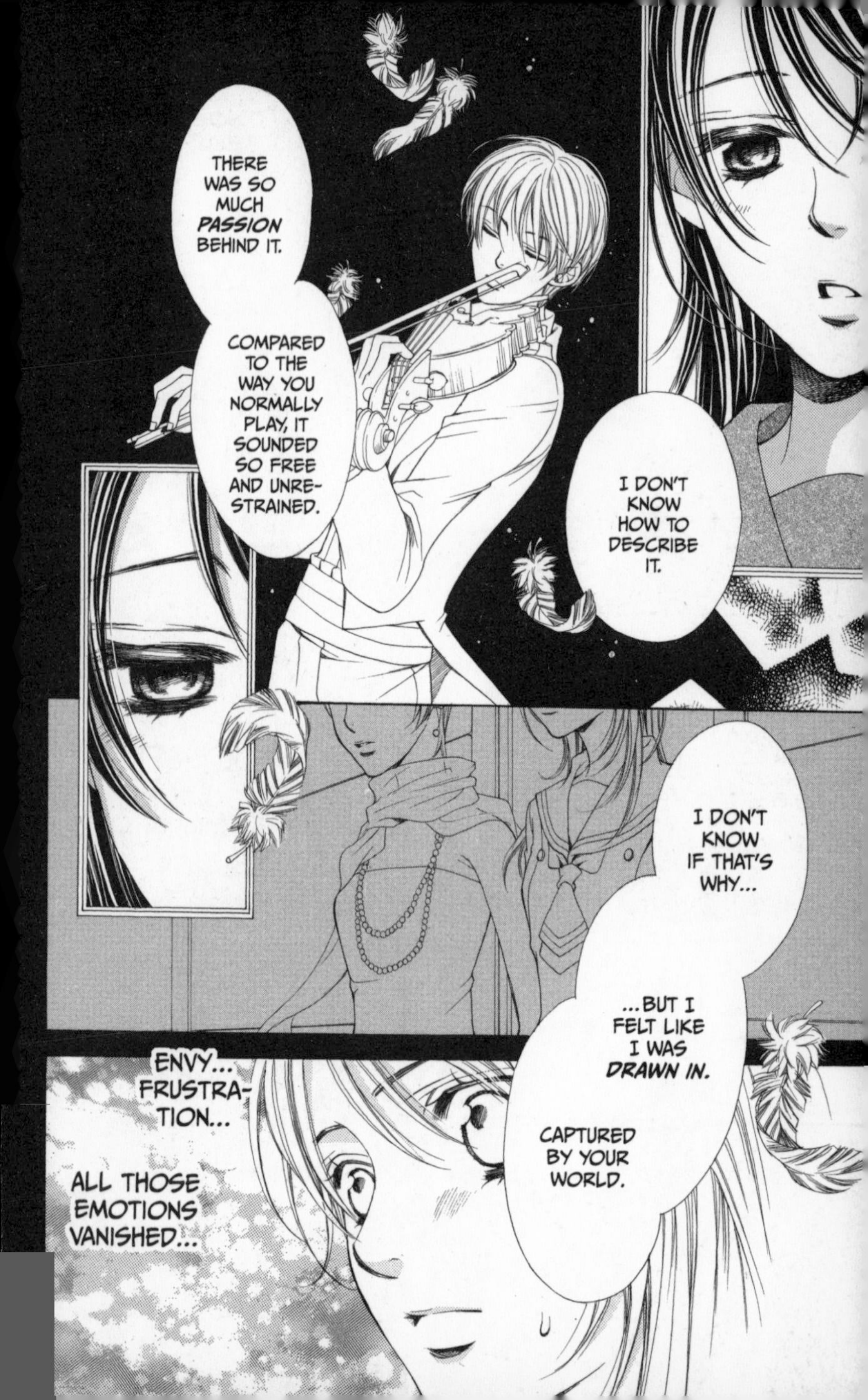
THERE WAS SO MUCH *PASSION* BEHIND IT.
COMPARED TO THE WAY YOU NORMALLY PLAY, IT SOUNDED SO FREE AND UNRE-STRAINED.
I DON'T KNOW HOW TO DESCRIBE IT.
I DON'T KNOW IF THAT'S WHY...
...BUT I FELT LIKE I WAS *DRAWN IN.*
CAPTURED BY YOUR WORLD.
ENVY... FRUSTRA-TION...
ALL THOSE EMOTIONS VANISHED...

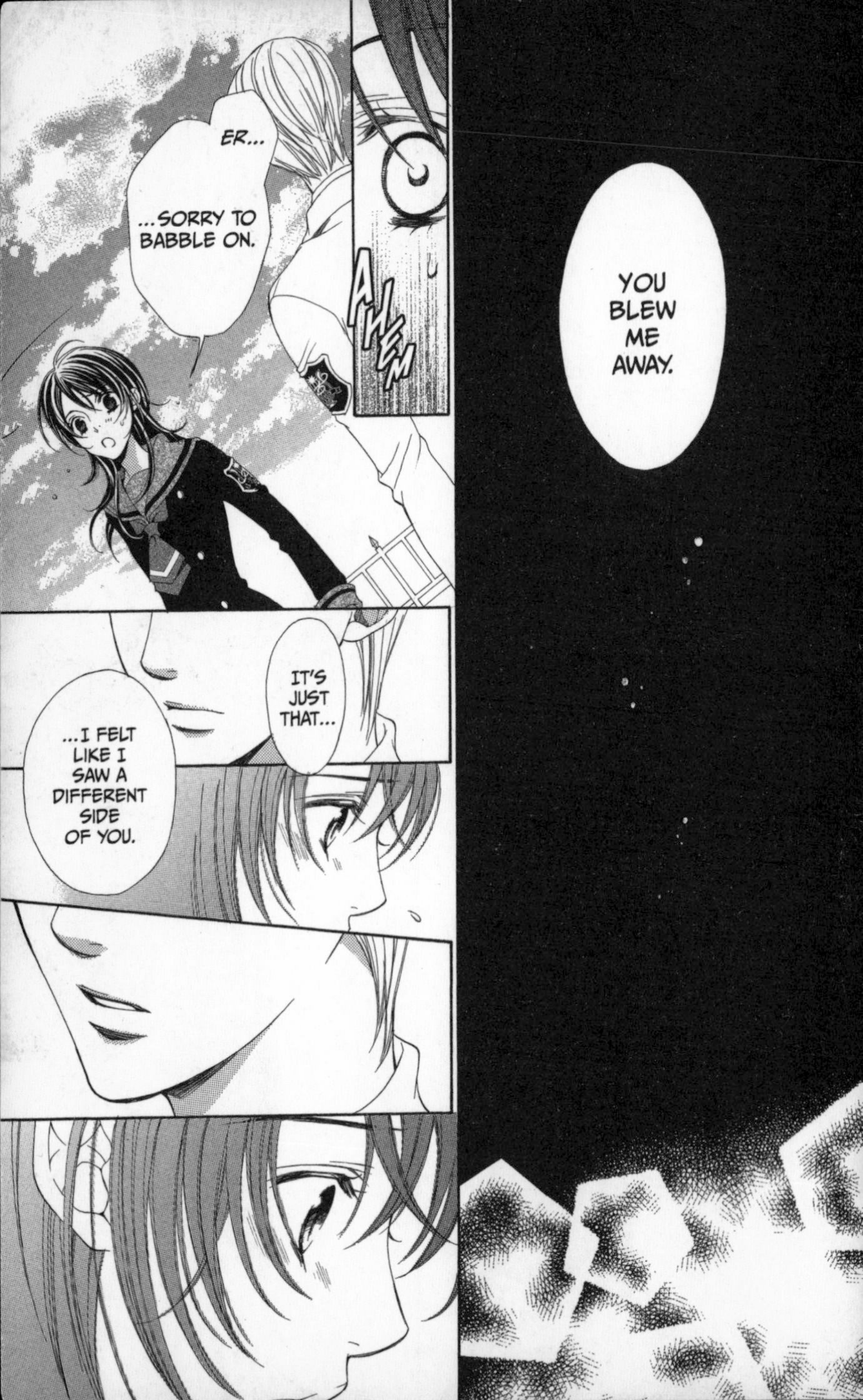
YOU BLEW ME AWAY.
ER...
...SORRY TO BABBLE ON.
AHEM
IT'S JUST THAT...
...I FELT LIKE I SAW A DIFFERENT SIDE OF YOU.

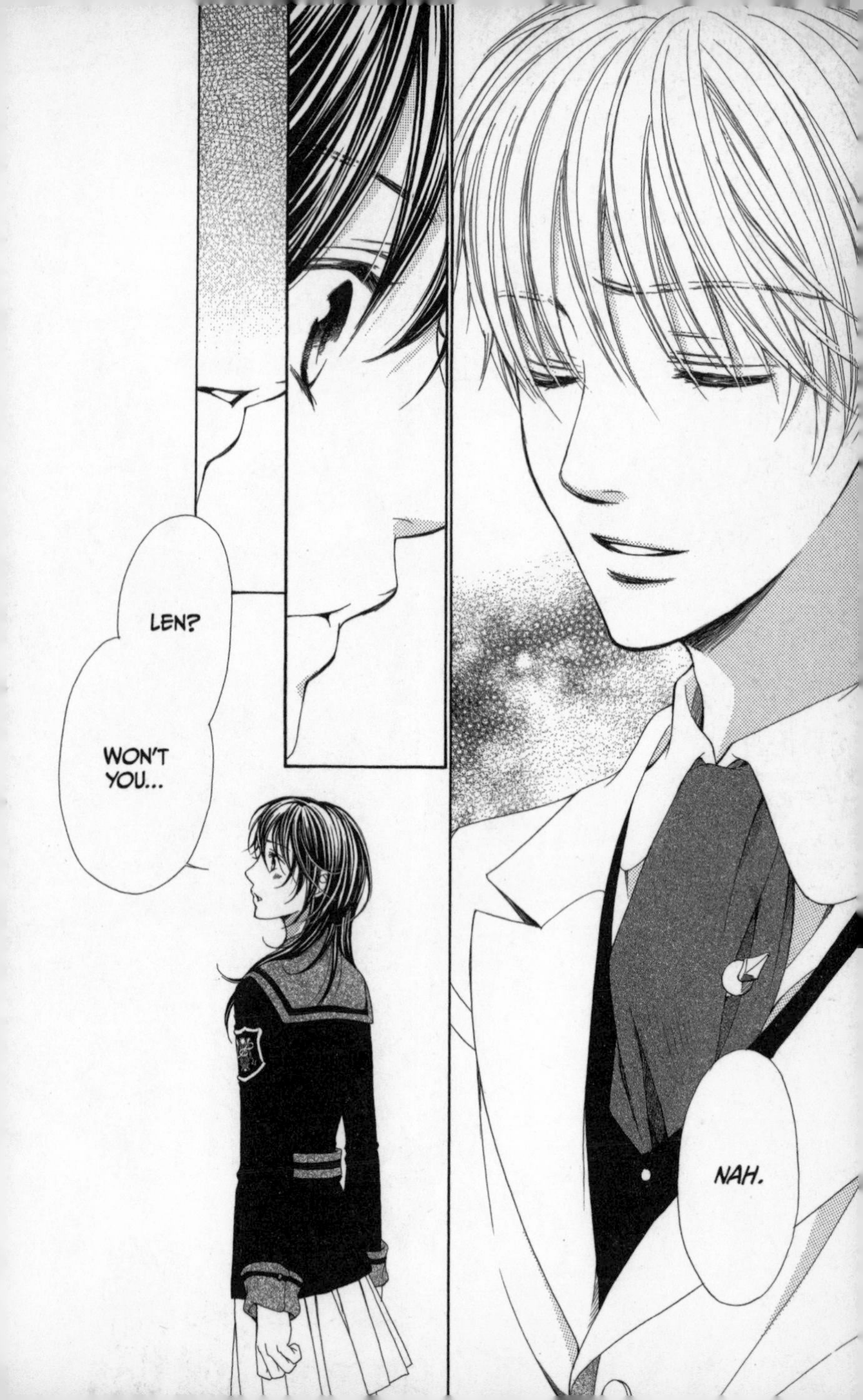
LEN?
WON'T YOU...
NAH.

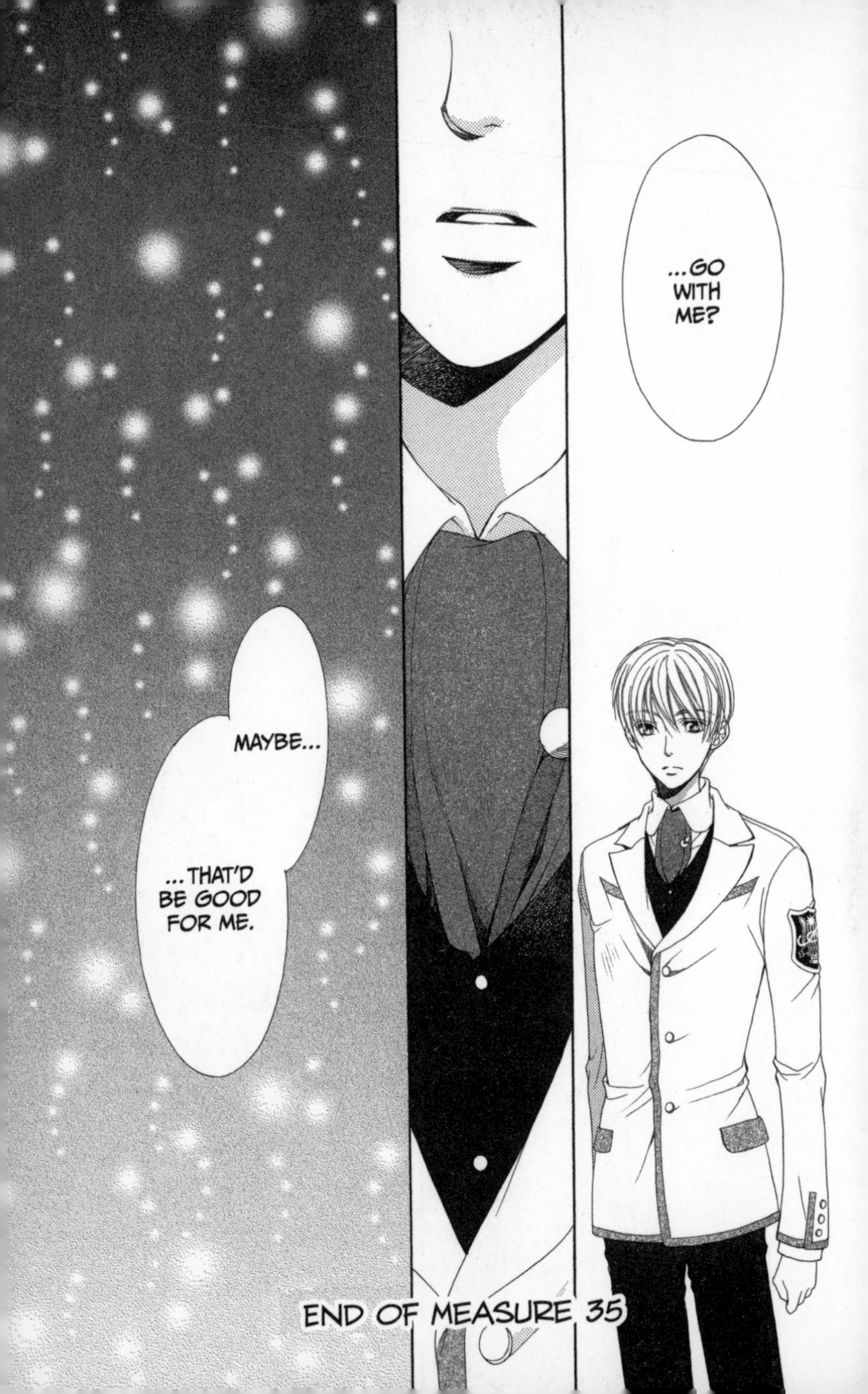
...GO WITH ME?
MAYBE...
...THAT'D BE GOOD FOR ME.
END OF MEASURE 35

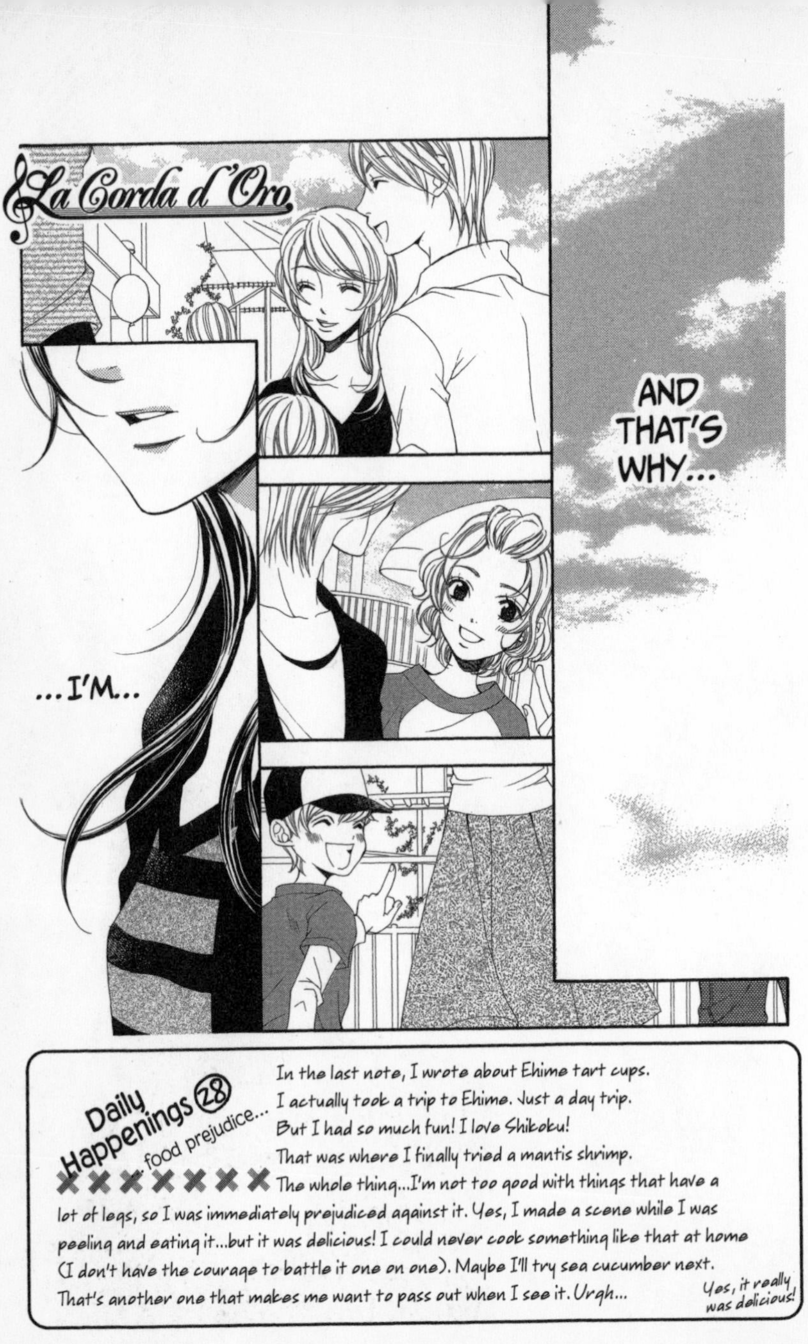
La Corda d'Oro
AND THAT'S WHY...
...I'M...

**Daily Happenings 28** ...food prejudice...

In the last note, I wrote about Ehime tart cups. I actually took a trip to Ehime. Just a day trip. But I had so much fun! I love Shikoku! That was where I finally tried a mantis shrimp. The whole thing...I'm not too good with things that have a lot of legs, so I was immediately prejudiced against it. Yes, I made a scene while I was peeling and eating it...but it was delicious! I could never cook something like that at home (I don't have the courage to battle it one on one). Maybe I'll try sea cucumber next. That's another one that makes me want to pass out when I see it. Urgh...

Yes, it really was delicious!

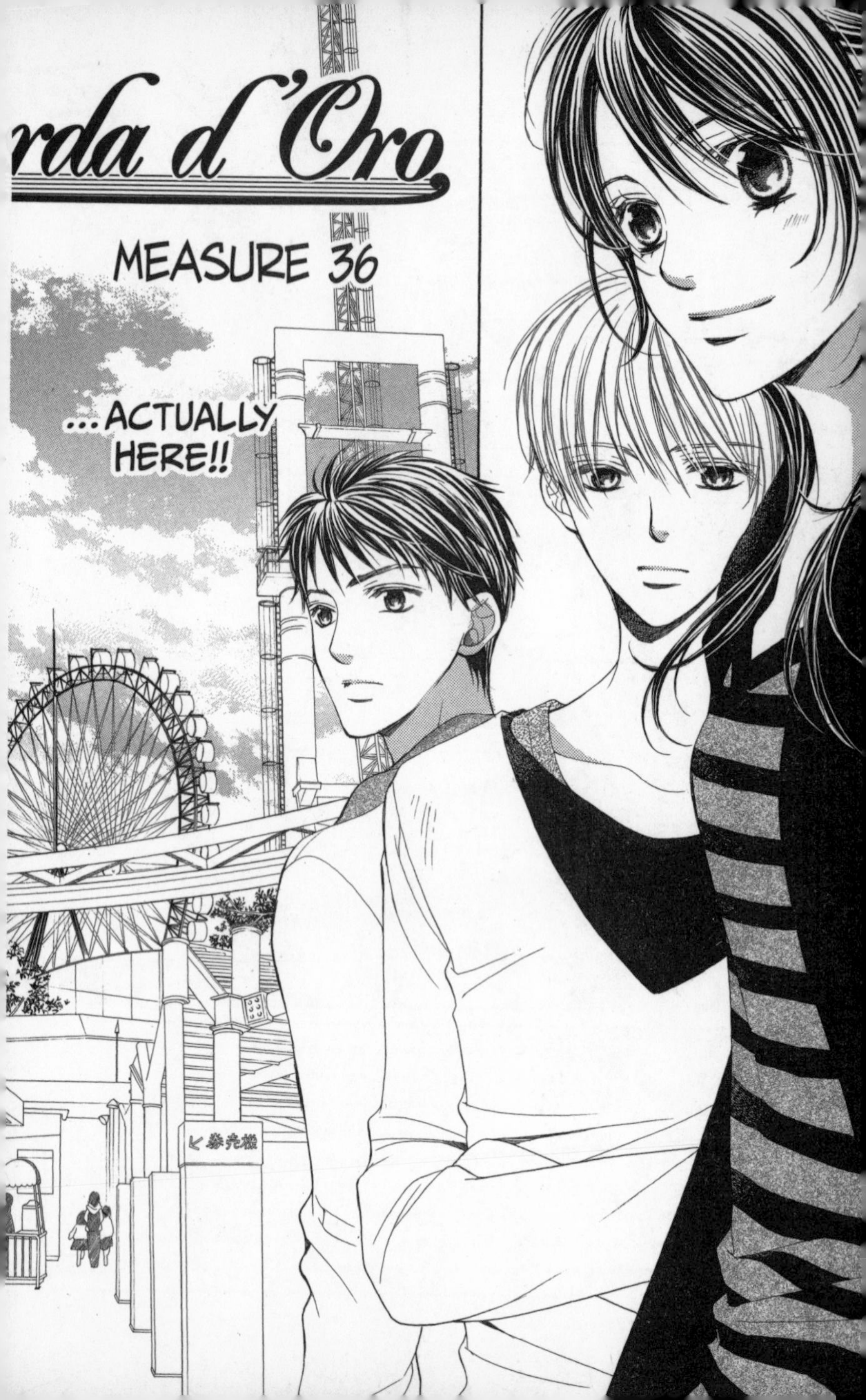
rda d'Oro
MEASURE 36
...ACTUALLY HERE!!

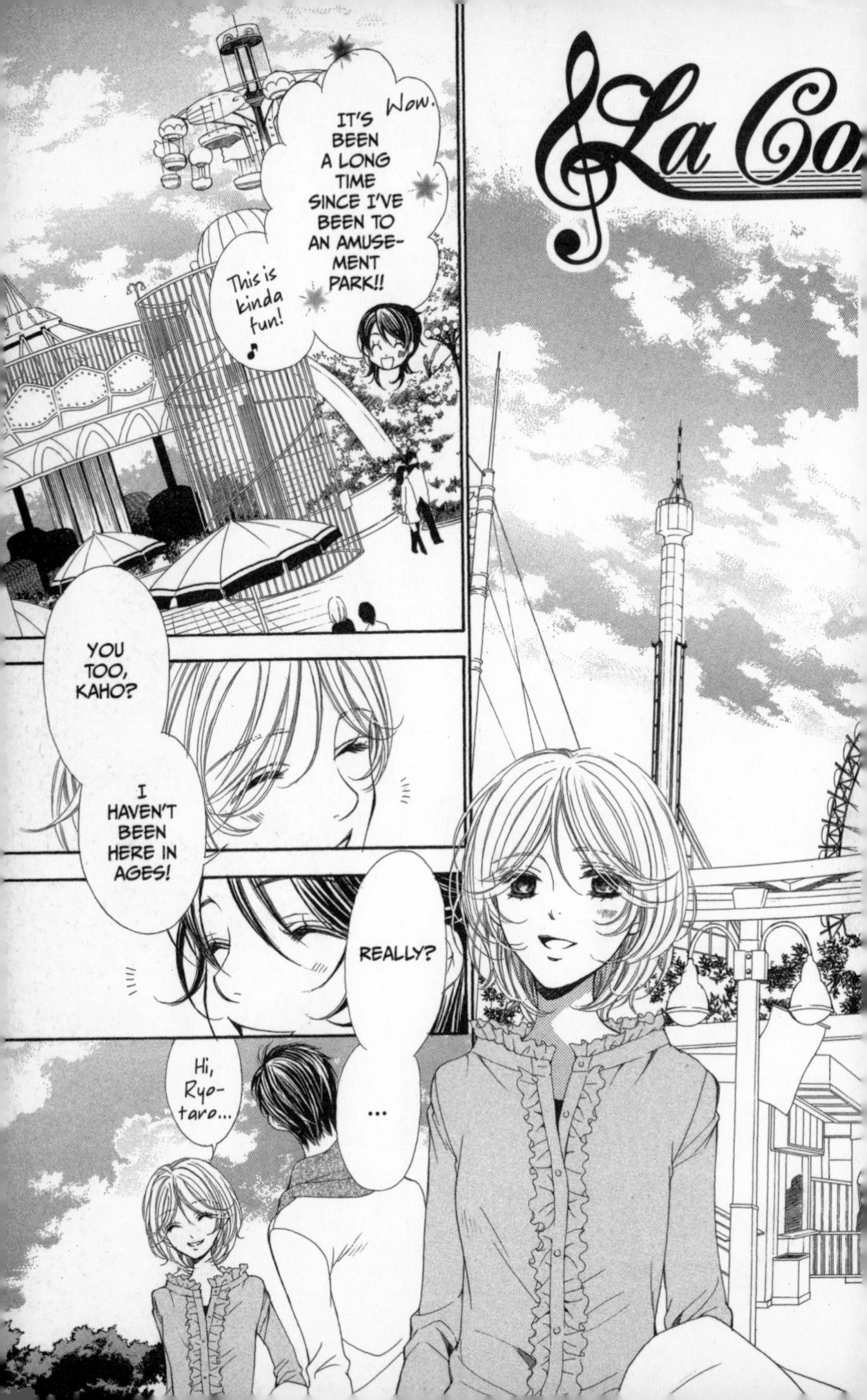
La Co
Wow.
IT'S BEEN A LONG TIME SINCE I'VE BEEN TO AN AMUSEMENT PARK!!
This is kinda fun! ♪
YOU TOO, KAHO?
I HAVEN'T BEEN HERE IN AGES!
REALLY?
Hi, Ryotaro...
...

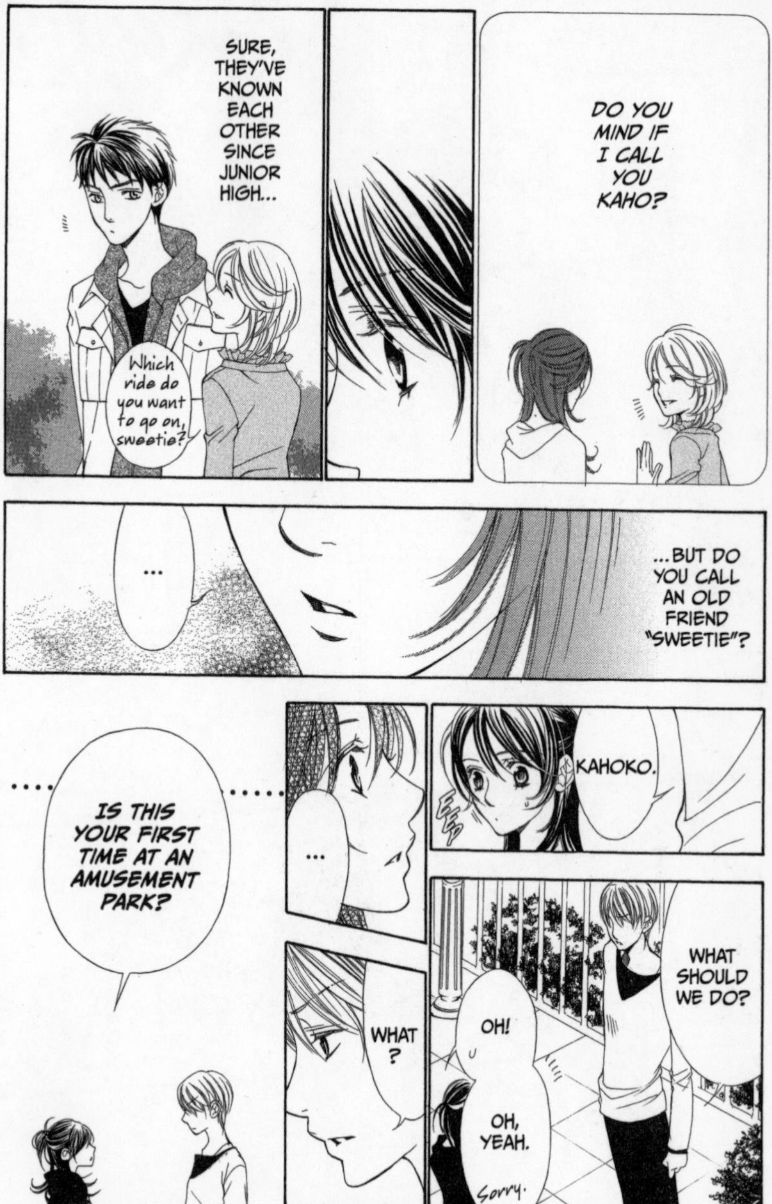
DO YOU MIND IF I CALL YOU KAHO?
SURE, THEY'VE KNOWN EACH OTHER SINCE JUNIOR HIGH...
Which ride do you want to go on, sweetie?
...BUT DO YOU CALL AN OLD FRIEND "SWEETIE"?
...
KAHOKO.
WHAT SHOULD WE DO?
OH!
OH, YEAH.
Sorry.
...
WHAT?
IS THIS YOUR FIRST TIME AT AN AMUSEMENT PARK?

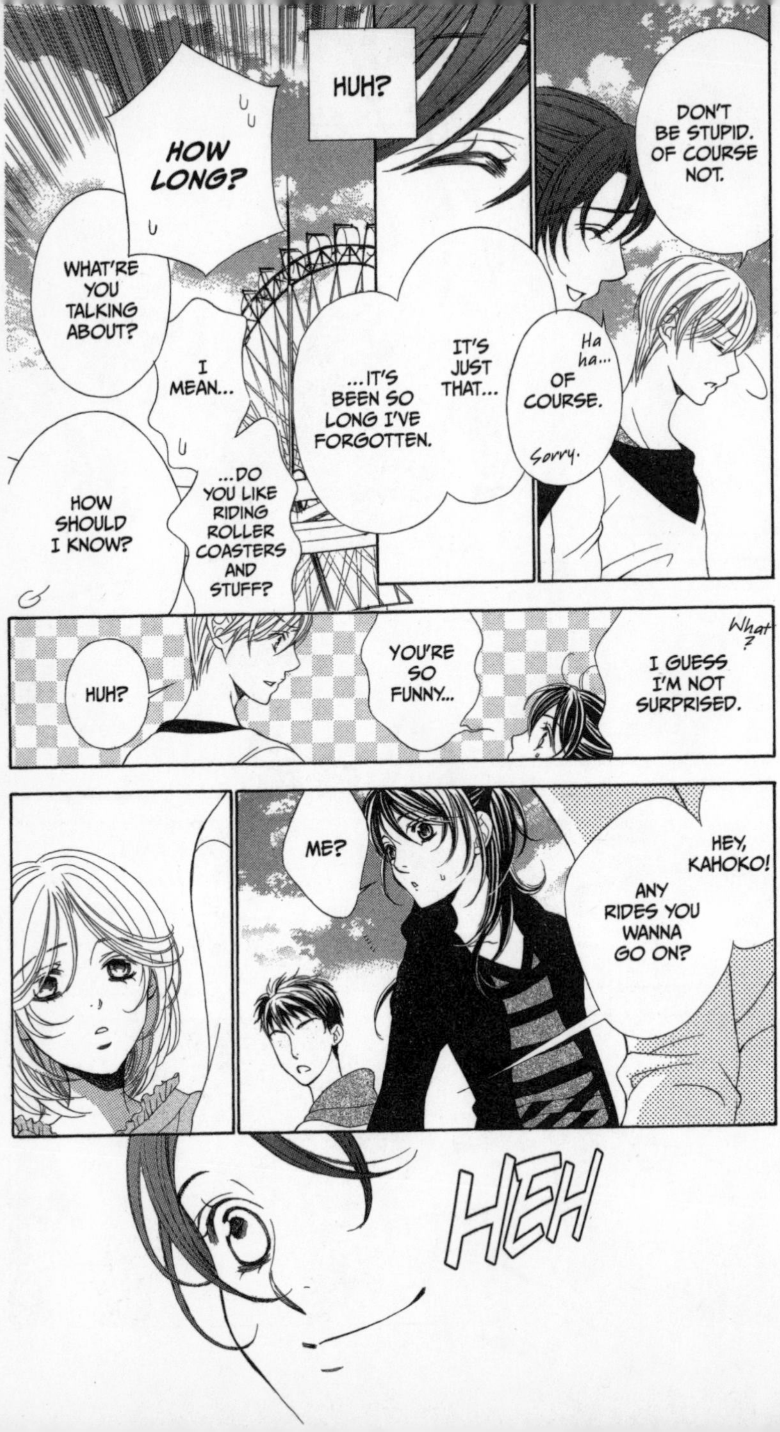
DON'T BE STUPID. OF COURSE NOT.
Ha ha... OF COURSE.
Sorry.
IT'S JUST THAT...
...IT'S BEEN SO LONG I'VE FORGOTTEN.
HUH?
HOW LONG?
WHAT'RE YOU TALKING ABOUT?
I MEAN...
...DO YOU LIKE RIDING ROLLER COASTERS AND STUFF?
HOW SHOULD I KNOW?
What?
I GUESS I'M NOT SURPRISED.
YOU'RE SO FUNNY...
HUH?
HEY, KAHOKO!
ANY RIDES YOU WANNA GO ON?
ME?
HEH

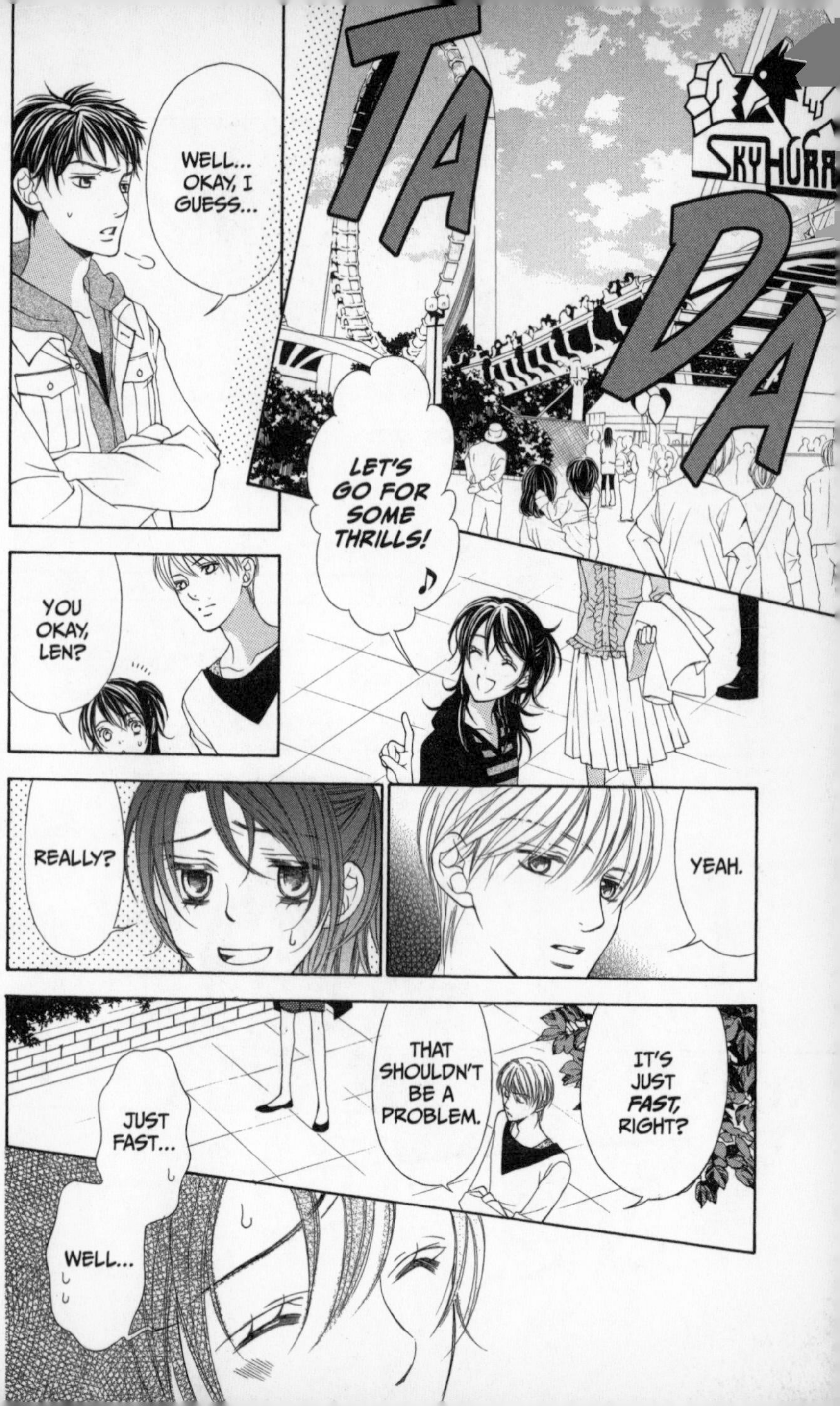
SKY HURR
TA
DA
LET'S GO FOR SOME THRILLS! ♪
WELL... OKAY, I GUESS...
YOU OKAY, LEN?
YEAH.
REALLY?
IT'S JUST *FAST*, RIGHT?
THAT SHOULDN'T BE A PROBLEM.
JUST FAST...
WELL...

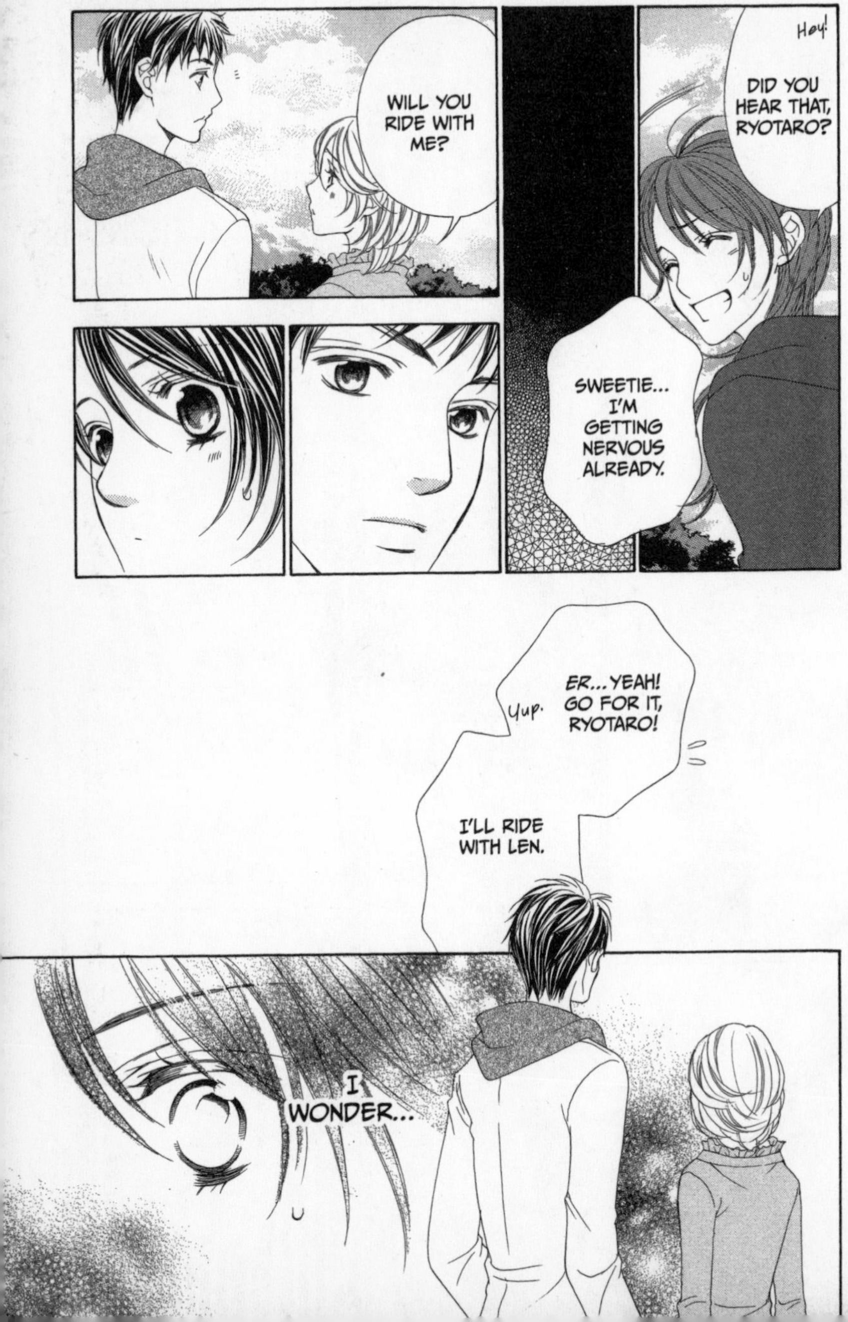
Hey!
DID YOU HEAR THAT, RYOTARO?
SWEETIE... I'M GETTING NERVOUS ALREADY.
WILL YOU RIDE WITH ME?
ER...YEAH! GO FOR IT, RYOTARO!
Yup.
I'LL RIDE WITH LEN.
I WONDER...

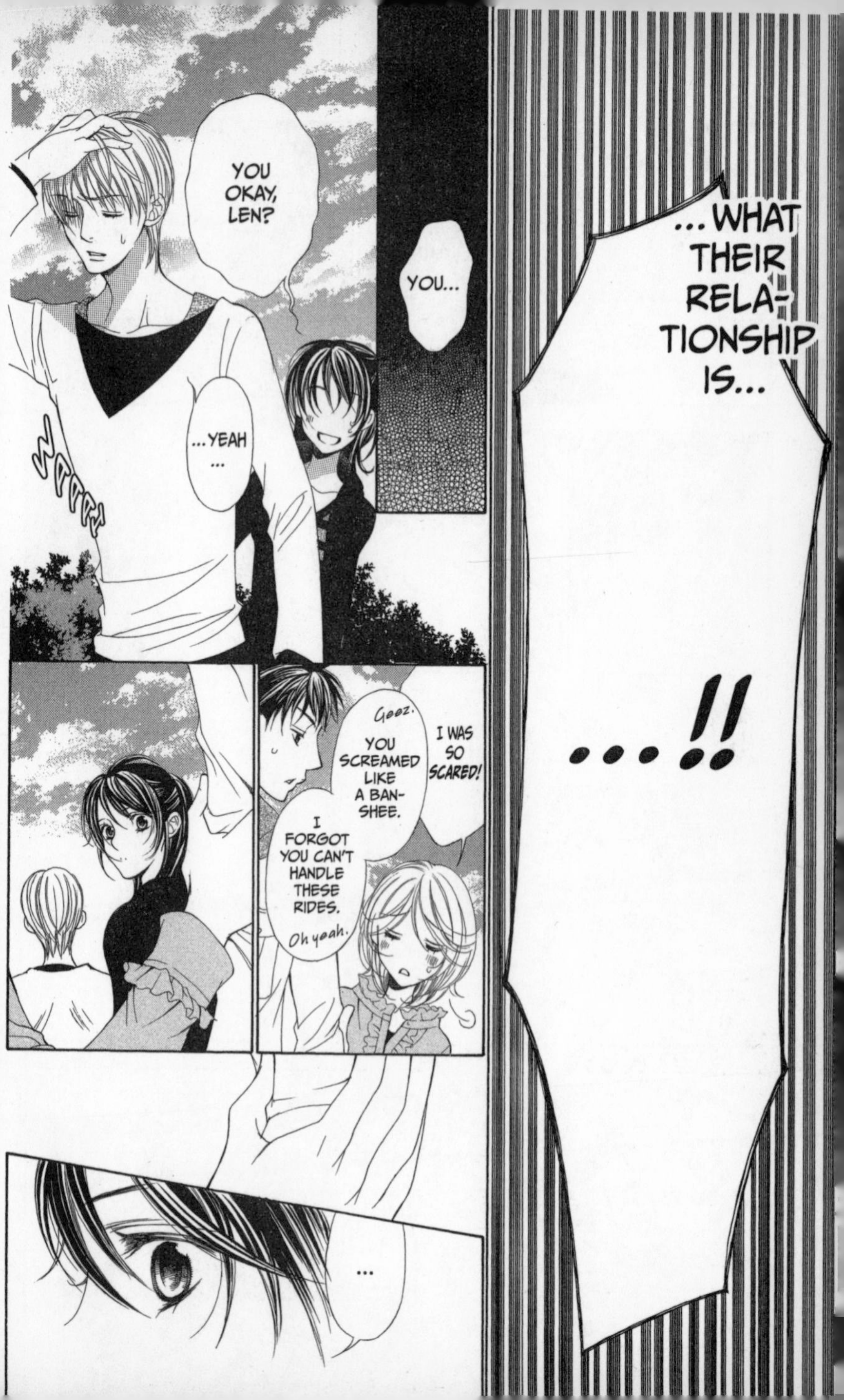
...WHAT THEIR RELA-TIONSHIP IS...
...!!
YOU...
YOU OKAY, LEN?
...YEAH ...
I WAS SO SCARED!
Geez. YOU SCREAMED LIKE A BAN-SHEE.
I FORGOT YOU CAN'T HANDLE THESE RIDES.
Oh yeah.
...

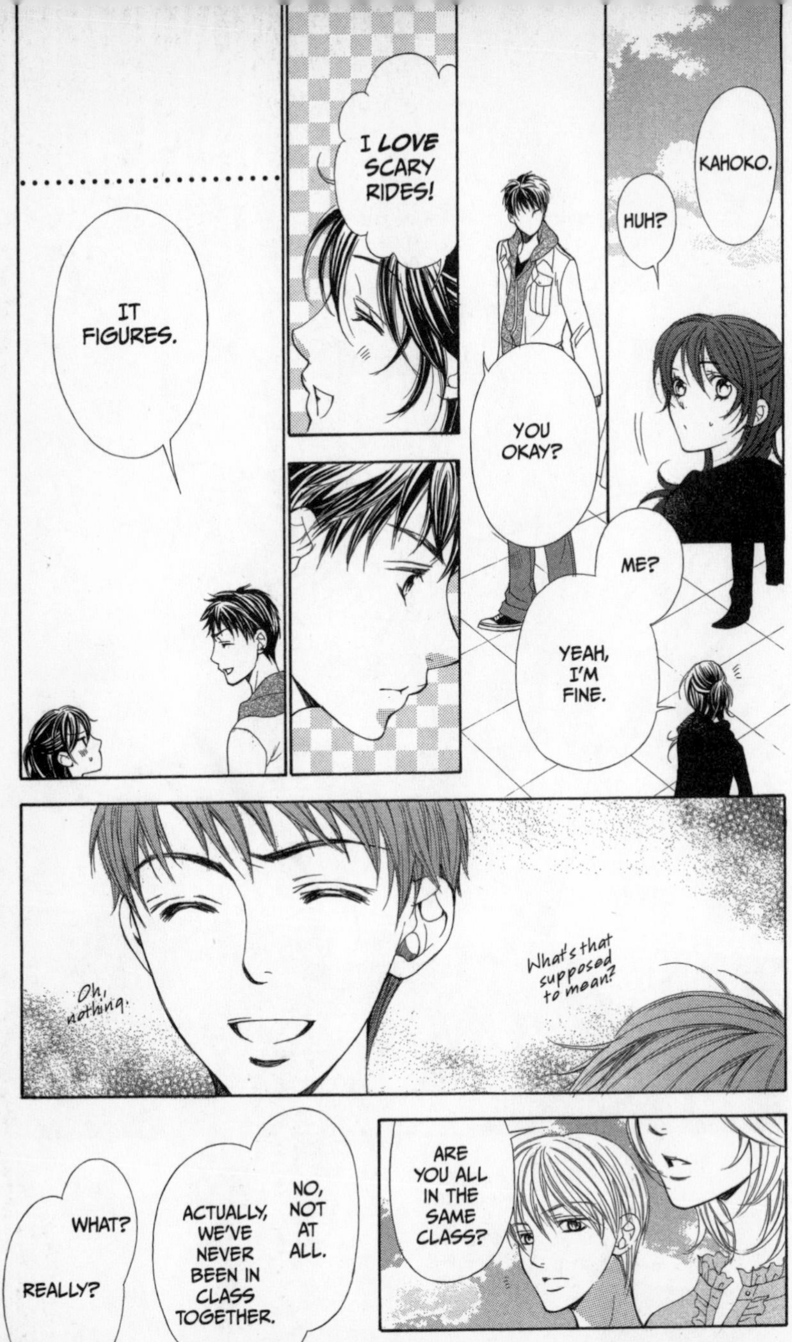

KAHOKO.
HUH?
YOU OKAY?
ME?
YEAH, I'M FINE.
I LOVE SCARY RIDES!
IT FIGURES.
What's that supposed to mean?
Oh, nothing.
ARE YOU ALL IN THE SAME CLASS?
NO, NOT AT ALL.
ACTUALLY, WE'VE NEVER BEEN IN CLASS TOGETHER.
WHAT?
REALLY?

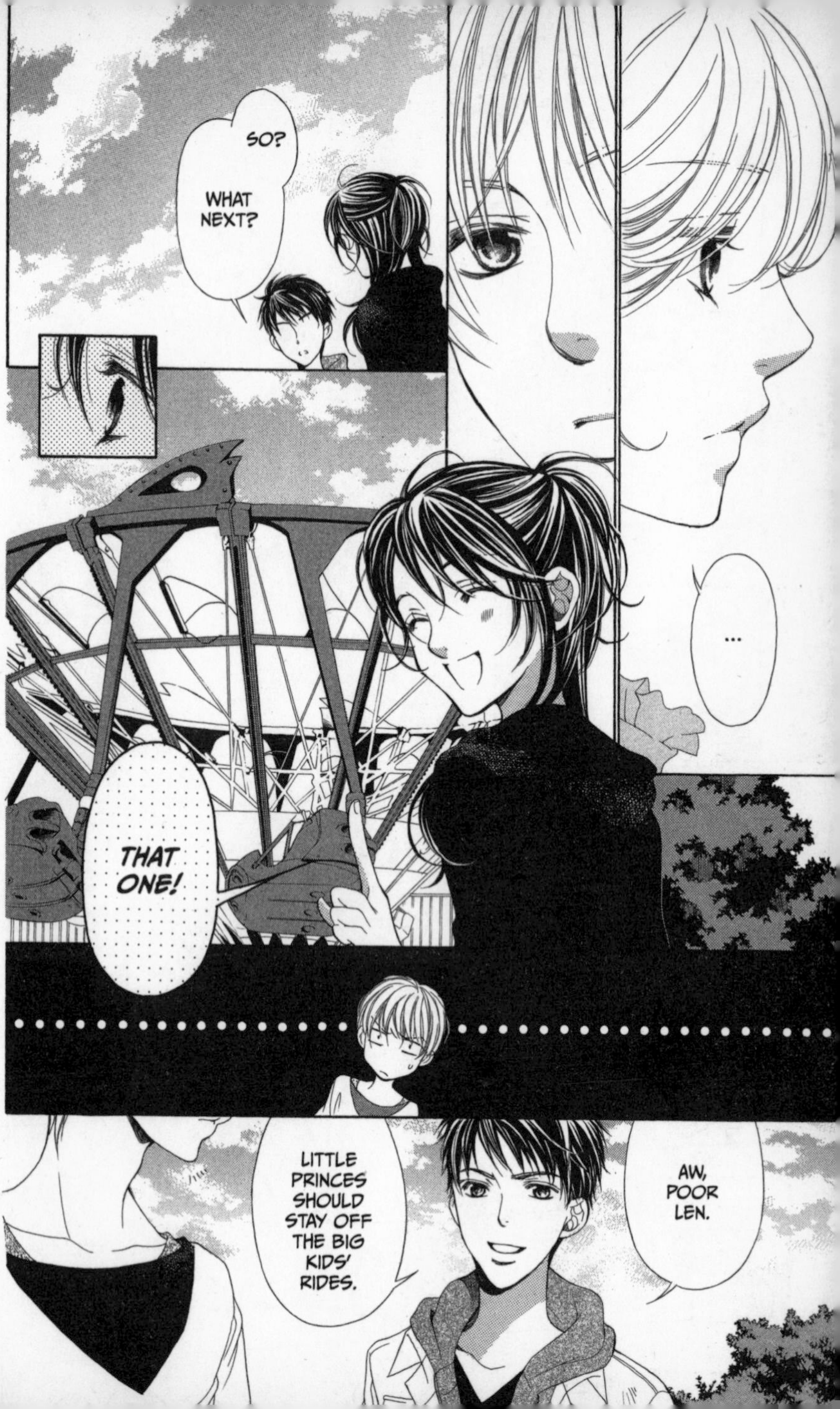
...
SO? WHAT NEXT?
THAT ONE!
AW, POOR LEN.
LITTLE PRINCES SHOULD STAY OFF THE BIG KIDS' RIDES.

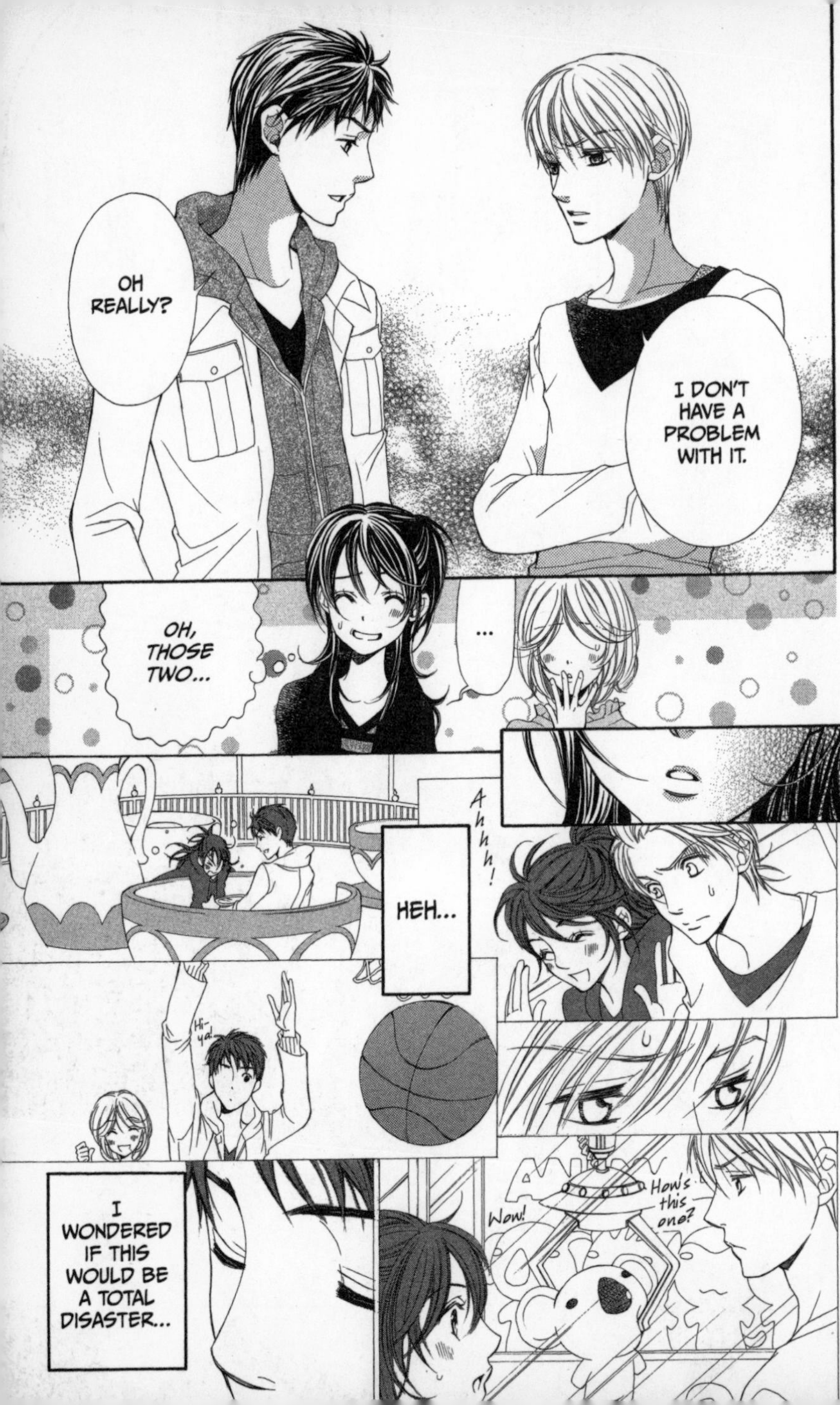
I DON'T HAVE A PROBLEM WITH IT.
OH REALLY?
...
OH, THOSE TWO...
Ahhh!
HEH...
Hi-ya!
How's this one?
Wow!
I WONDERED IF THIS WOULD BE A TOTAL DISASTER...

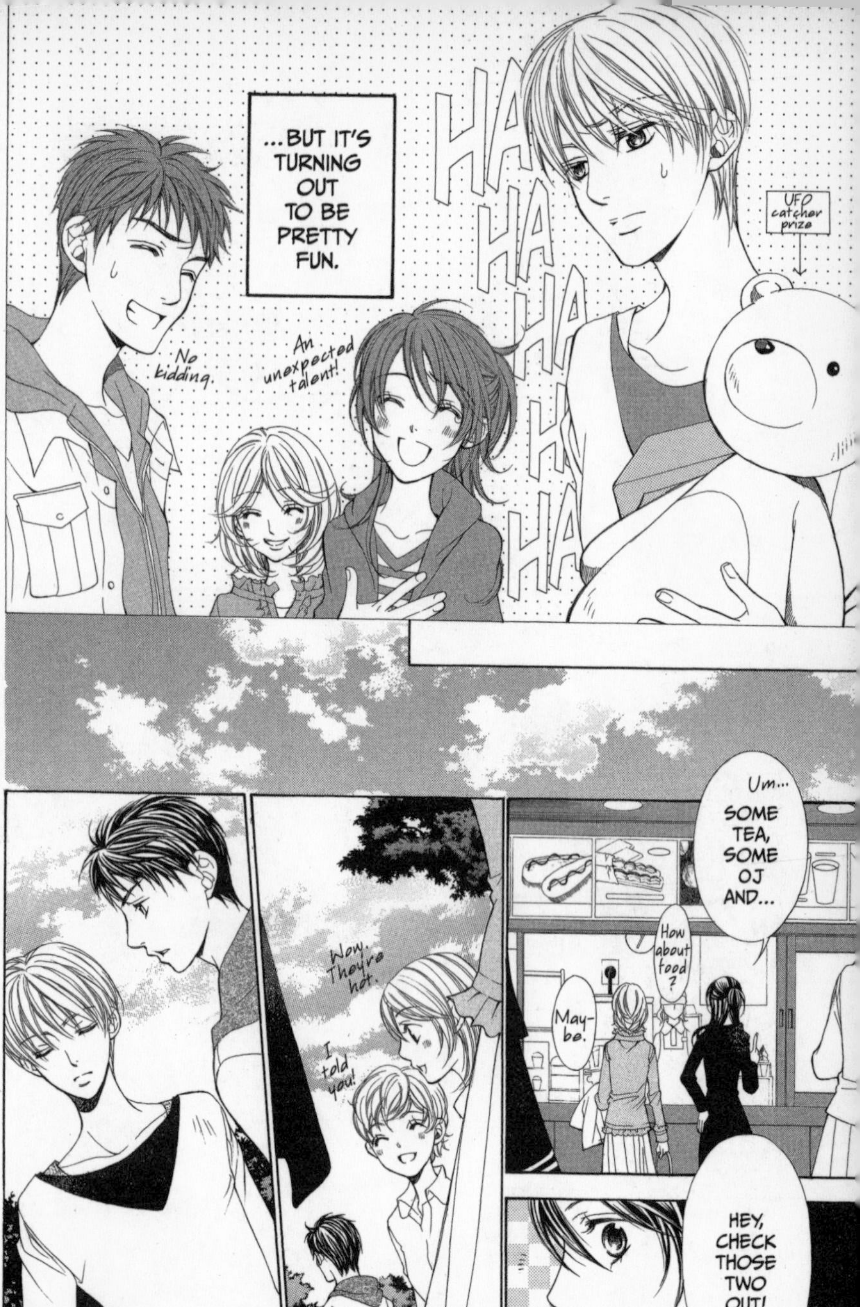

UFO catcher prize
HA HA HA HA HA HA
...BUT IT'S TURNING OUT TO BE PRETTY FUN.
An unexpected talent!
No kidding.
Um... SOME TEA, SOME OJ AND...
How about food?
May-be.
HEY, CHECK THOSE TWO OUT!
Wow. They're hot.
I told you!

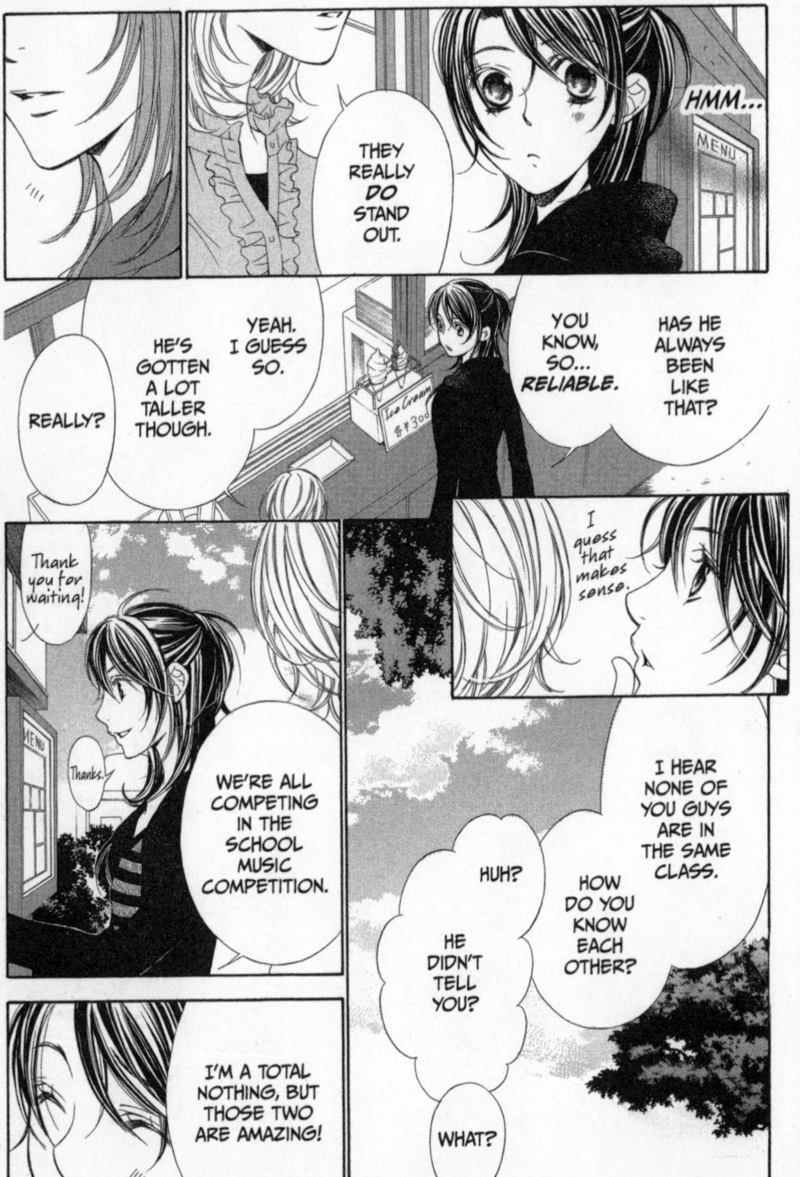
HMM...
THEY REALLY DO STAND OUT.
HAS HE ALWAYS BEEN LIKE THAT?
YOU KNOW, SO... RELIABLE.
YEAH. I GUESS SO.
HE'S GOTTEN A LOT TALLER THOUGH.
REALLY?
MENU
I guess that makes sense.
I HEAR NONE OF YOU GUYS ARE IN THE SAME CLASS.
HOW DO YOU KNOW EACH OTHER?
HUH?
HE DIDN'T TELL YOU?
WHAT?
Thank you for waiting!
Thanks.
WE'RE ALL COMPETING IN THE SCHOOL MUSIC COMPETITION.
I'M A TOTAL NOTHING, BUT THOSE TWO ARE AMAZING!

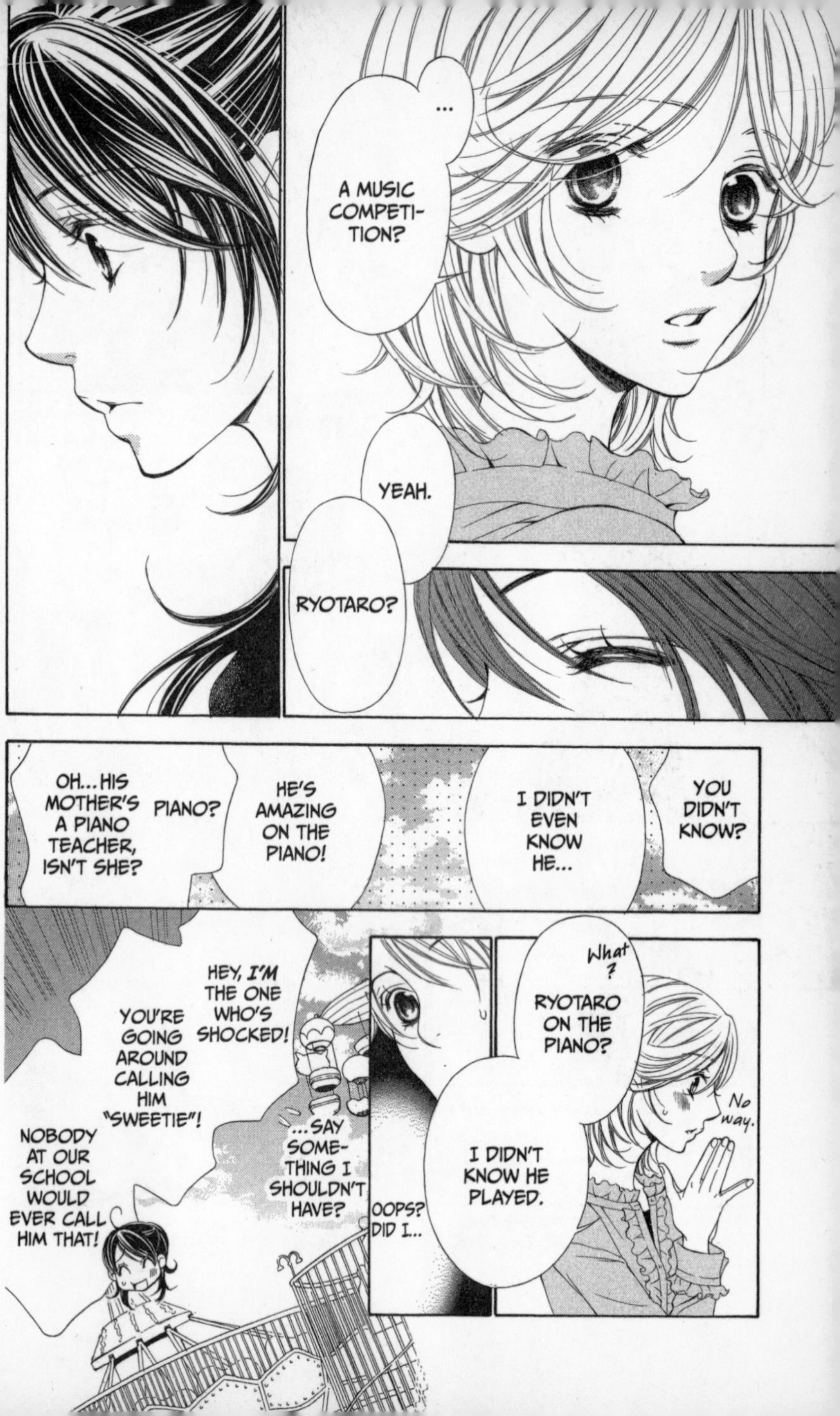
...
A MUSIC COMPETITION?
YEAH.
RYOTARO?
YOU DIDN'T KNOW?
I DIDN'T EVEN KNOW HE...
HE'S AMAZING ON THE PIANO!
PIANO?
OH... HIS MOTHER'S A PIANO TEACHER, ISN'T SHE?
What?
RYOTARO ON THE PIANO?
No way.
I DIDN'T KNOW HE PLAYED.
OOPS? DID I...
...SAY SOMETHING I SHOULDN'T HAVE?
HEY, I'M THE ONE WHO'S SHOCKED!
YOU'RE GOING AROUND CALLING HIM "SWEETIE"!
NOBODY AT OUR SCHOOL WOULD EVER CALL HIM THAT!

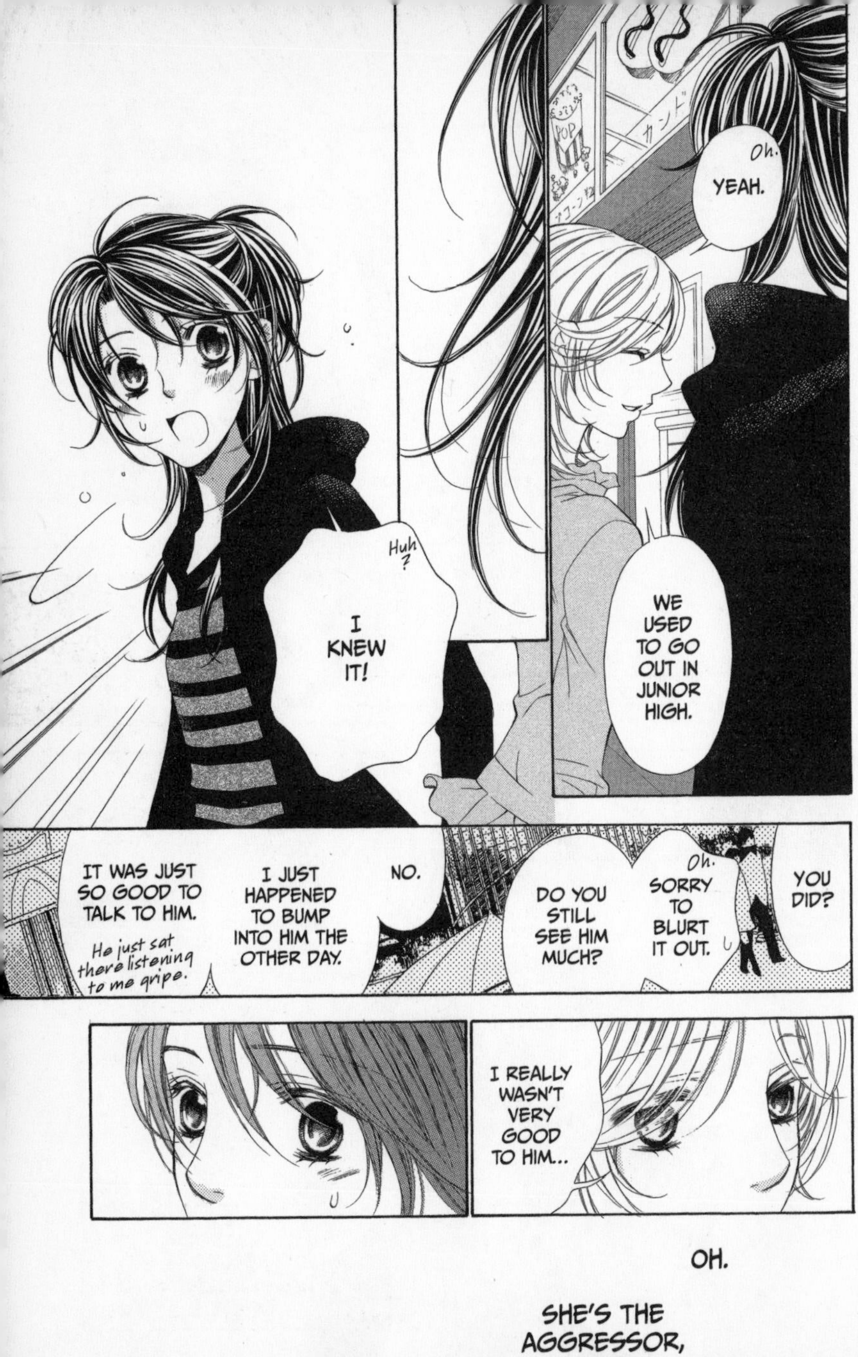
Oh.
YEAH.
WE USED TO GO OUT IN JUNIOR HIGH.
Huh?
I KNEW IT!
YOU DID?
Oh.
SORRY TO BLURT IT OUT.
DO YOU STILL SEE HIM MUCH?
NO.
I JUST HAPPENED TO BUMP INTO HIM THE OTHER DAY.
IT WAS JUST SO GOOD TO TALK TO HIM.
He just sat there listening to me gripe.
I REALLY WASN'T VERY GOOD TO HIM...
OH.
SHE'S THE AGGRESSOR, HUH?

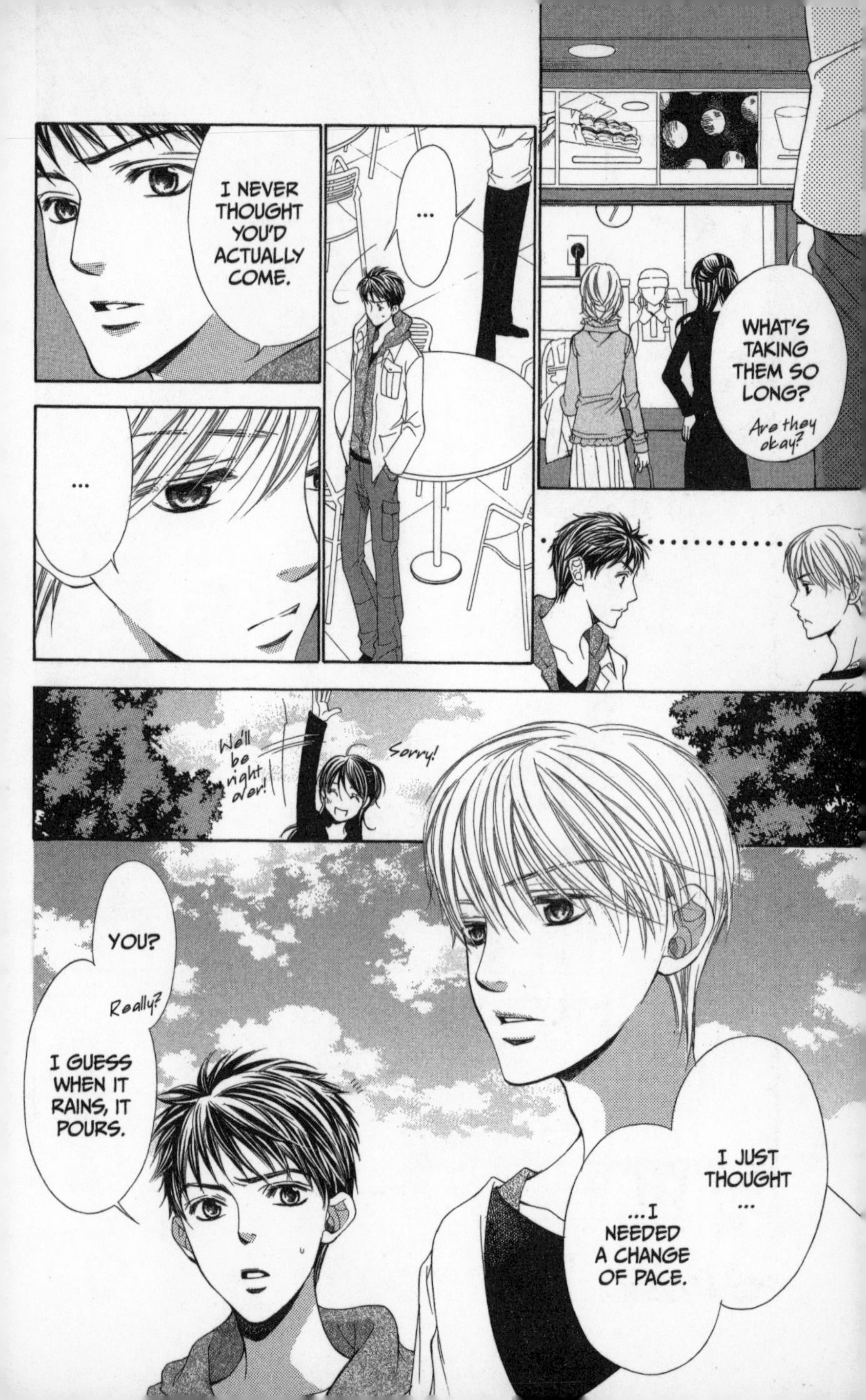
WHAT'S TAKING THEM SO LONG?
Are they okay?
........
...
I NEVER THOUGHT YOU'D ACTUALLY COME.
...
Sorry!
We'll be right over!
I JUST THOUGHT ...
...I NEEDED A CHANGE OF PACE.
YOU?
Really?
I GUESS WHEN IT RAINS, IT POURS.

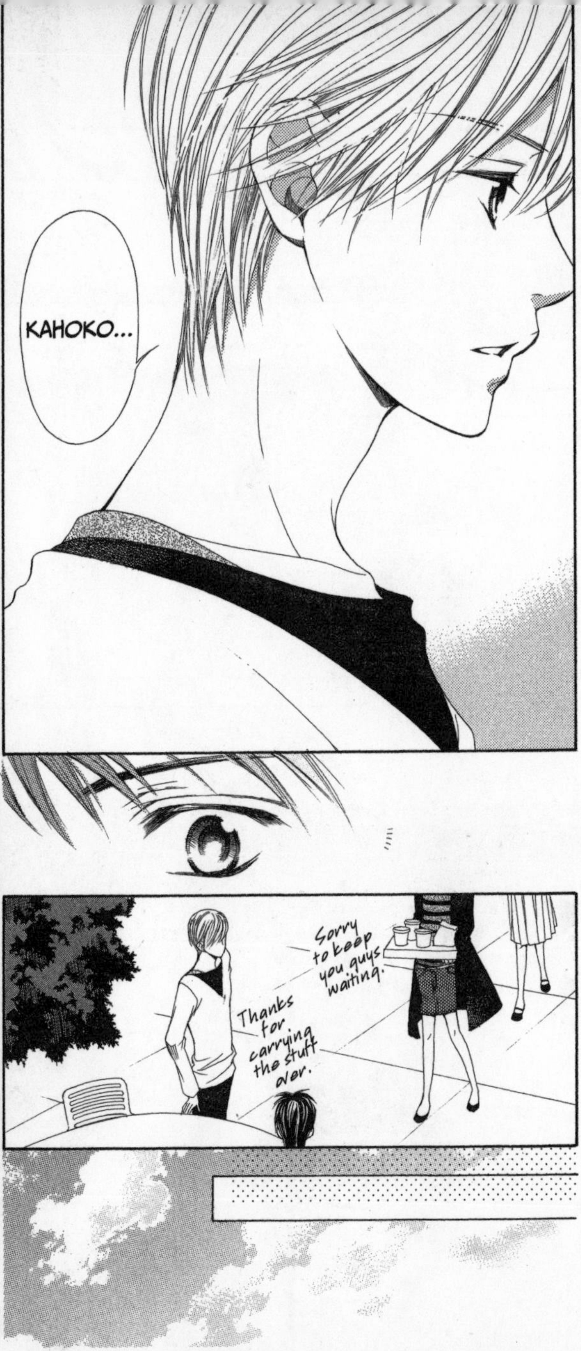
KAHOKO...
Sorry to keep you guys waiting.
Thanks for carrying the stuff over.

### FIVE

Measure 36 is set at an amusement park. When I announced that we were doing an amusement park story while we were working on Measure 35, my staff was shocked. They couldn't believe they were about to be subjected to drawing Ferris wheels... (lol)

We went to an amusement park to take pictures! I rode a Ferris wheel with a friend on New Year's Eve! I hadn't gone in like three years... We were only able to check out the Ferris wheel though, One of these days, I'd like to spend more time at the park and have fun.

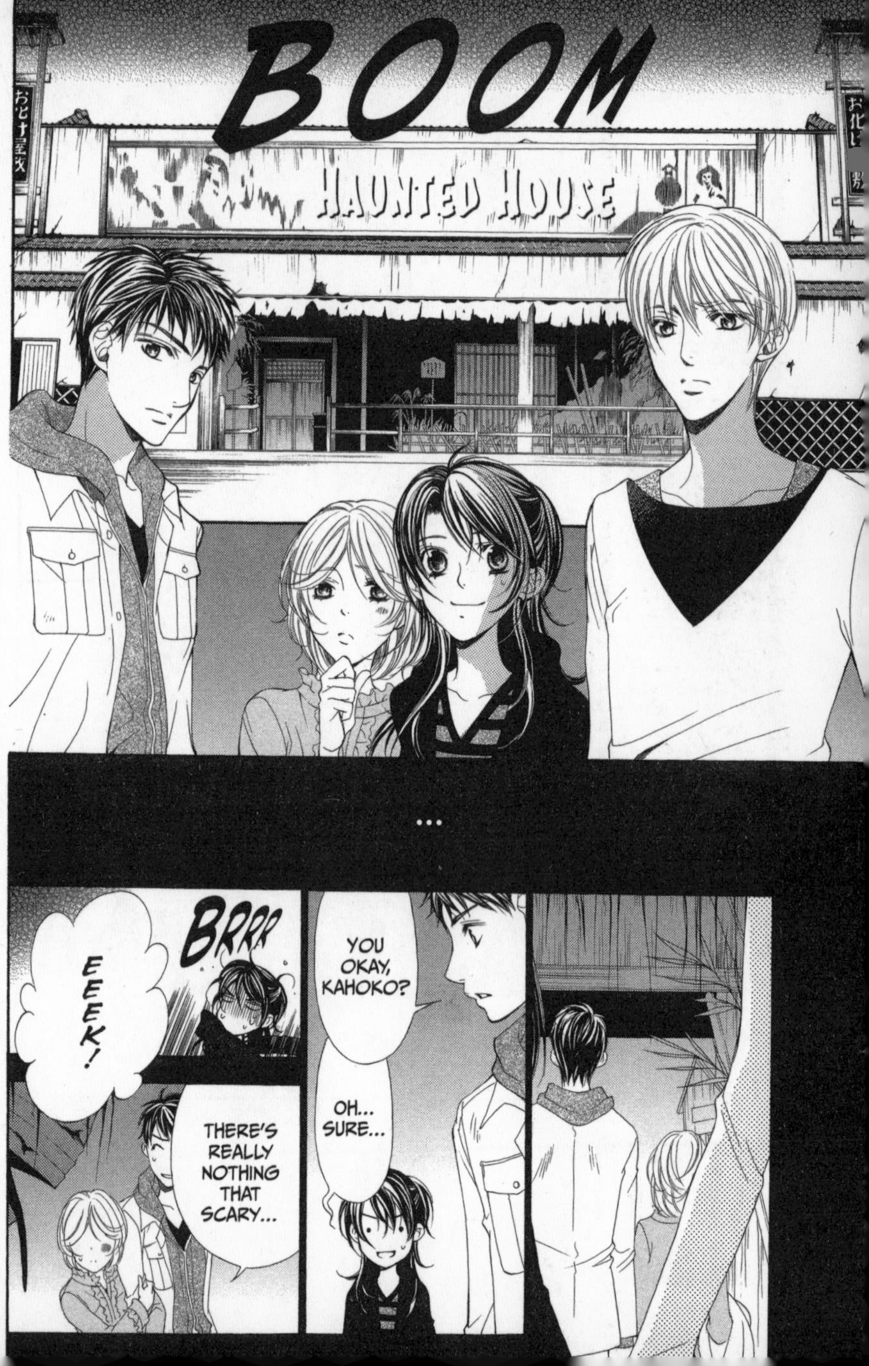
BOOM
HAUNTED HOUSE
...
YOU OKAY, KAHOKO?
OH... SURE...
BRRR
EEEK!
THERE'S REALLY NOTHING THAT SCARY...

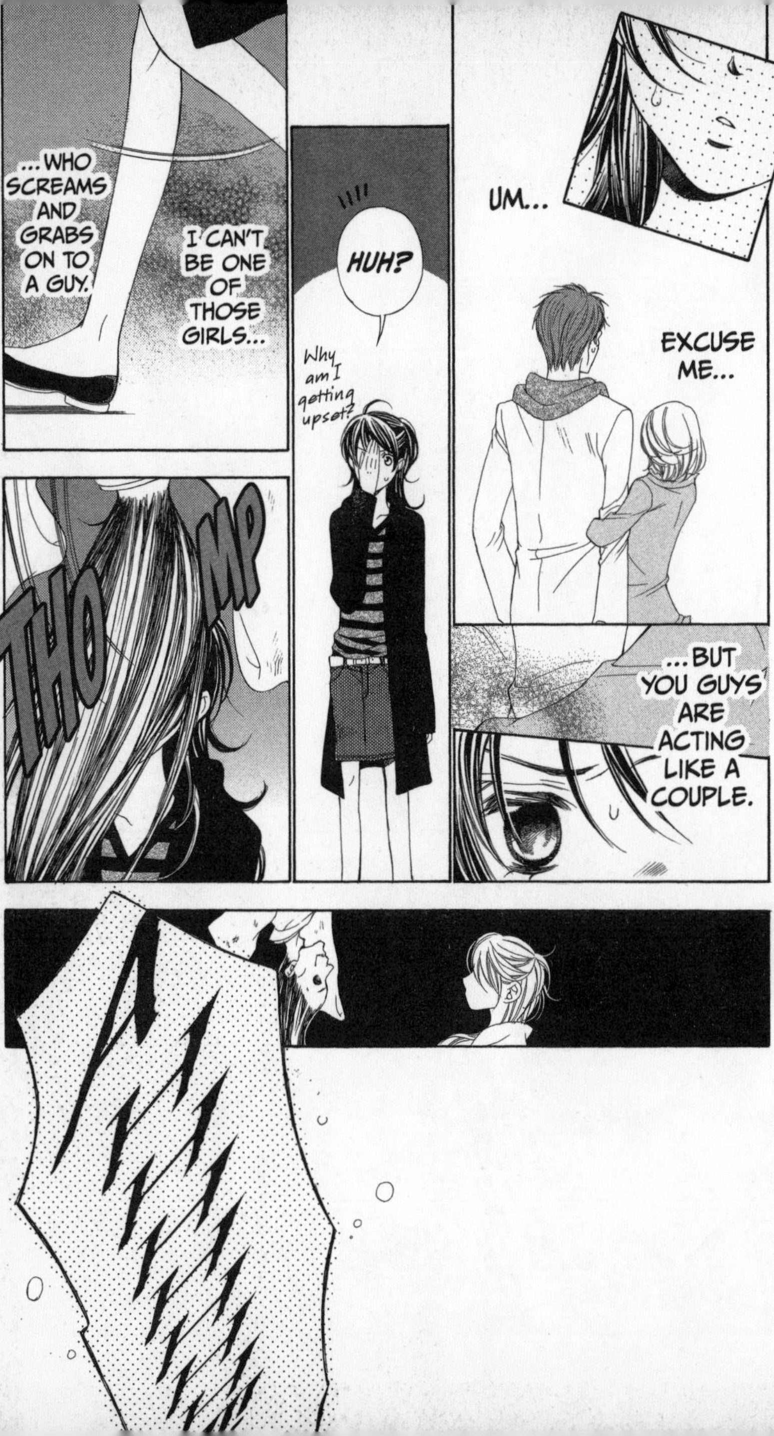
UM...
EXCUSE ME...
...BUT YOU GUYS ARE ACTING LIKE A COUPLE.
HUH?
Why am I getting upset?
I CAN'T BE ONE OF THOSE GIRLS...
...WHO SCREAMS AND GRABS ON TO A GUY.
THOMP

ER...

SORRY!!

IT'S OKAY...

SNAP

HUPP

GEEEK

HA

BOOM

BOOM

BDM BDM BDM

BDM BDM

AHHHHH!!

AHHHHH!!

O.M.G.

152

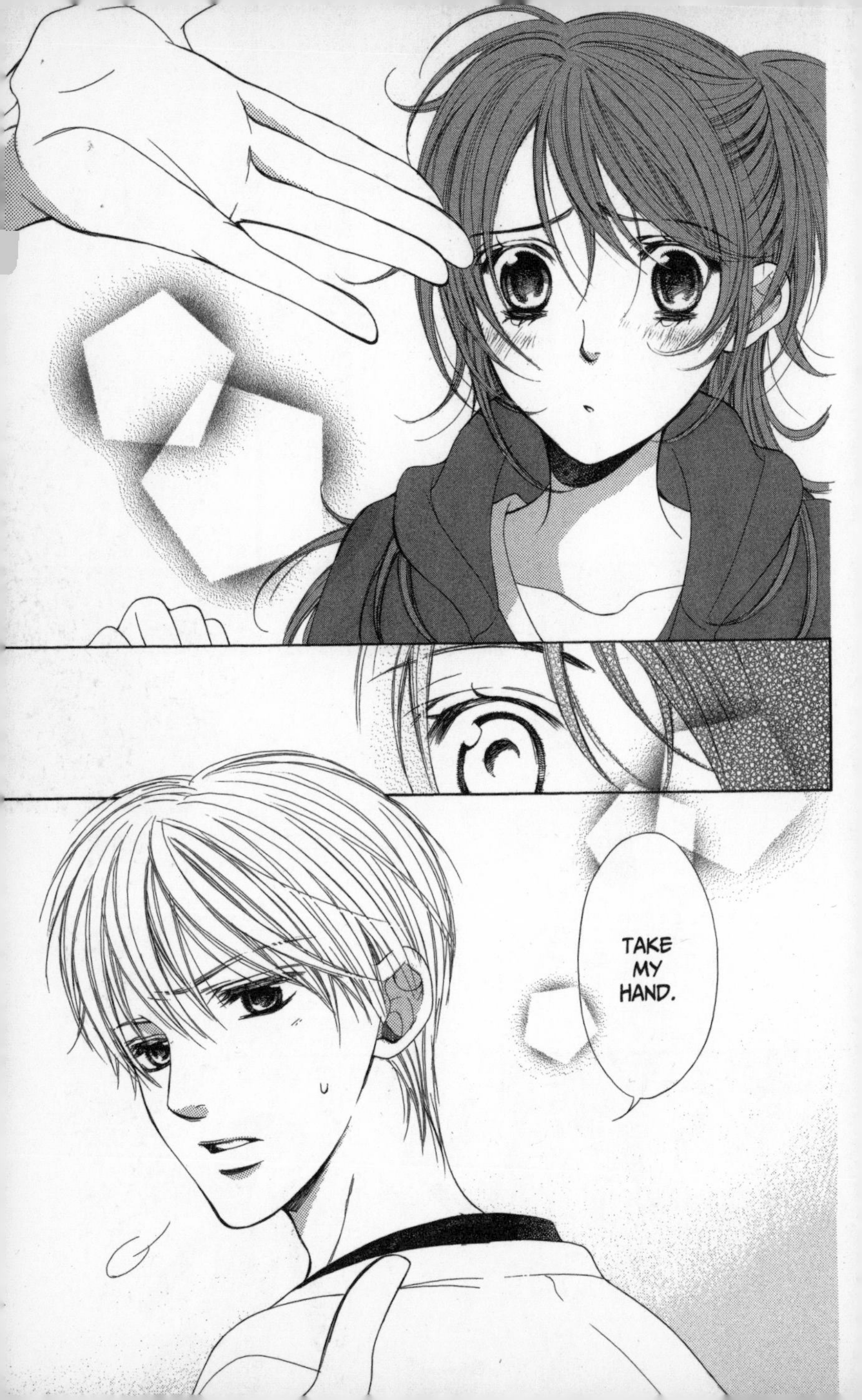
TAKE MY HAND.

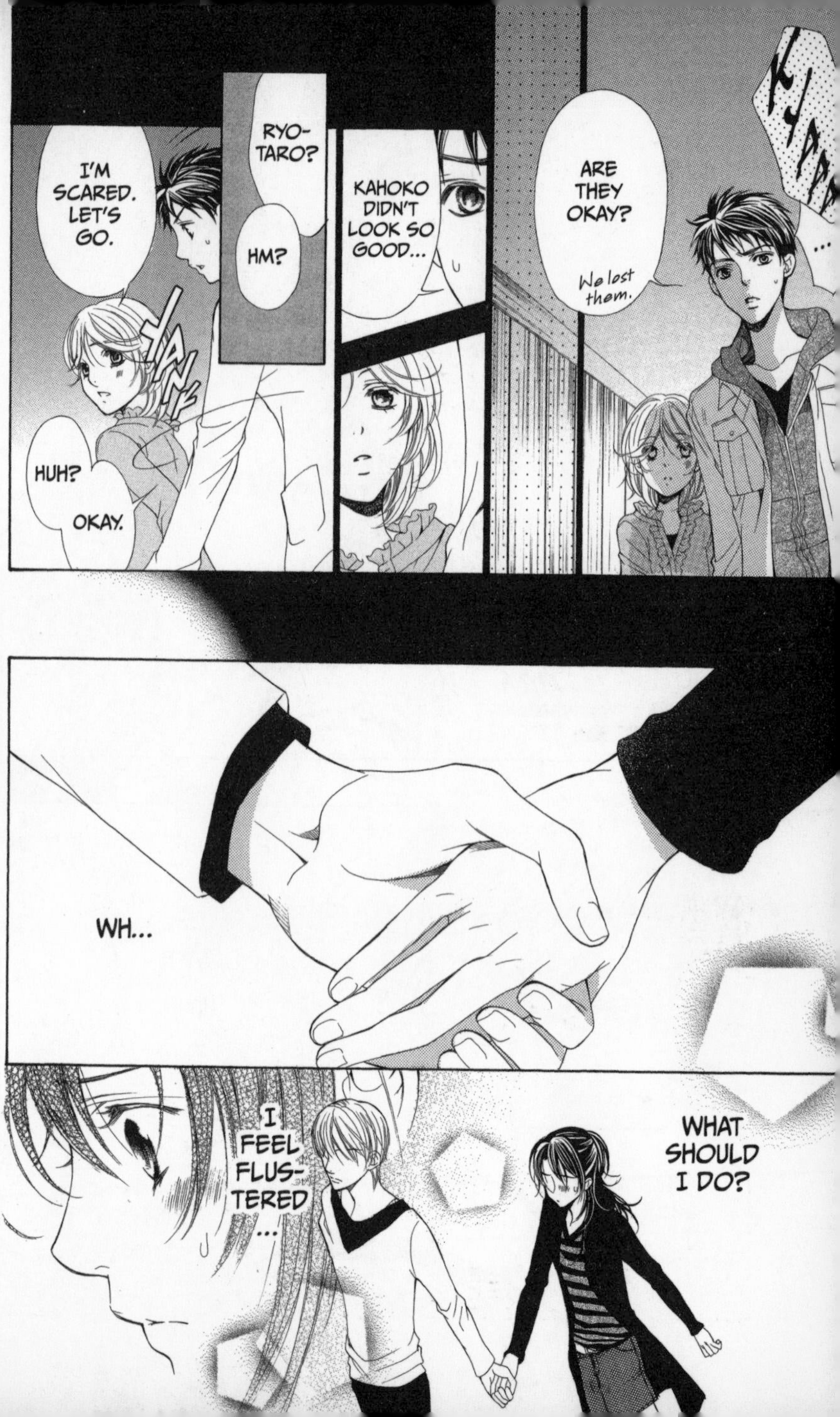
...
ARE THEY OKAY?
We lost them.
KAHOKO DIDN'T LOOK SO GOOD...
RYO-TARO?
HM?
I'M SCARED. LET'S GO.
HUH?
OKAY.
WH...
WHAT SHOULD I DO?
I FEEL FLUS-TERED...

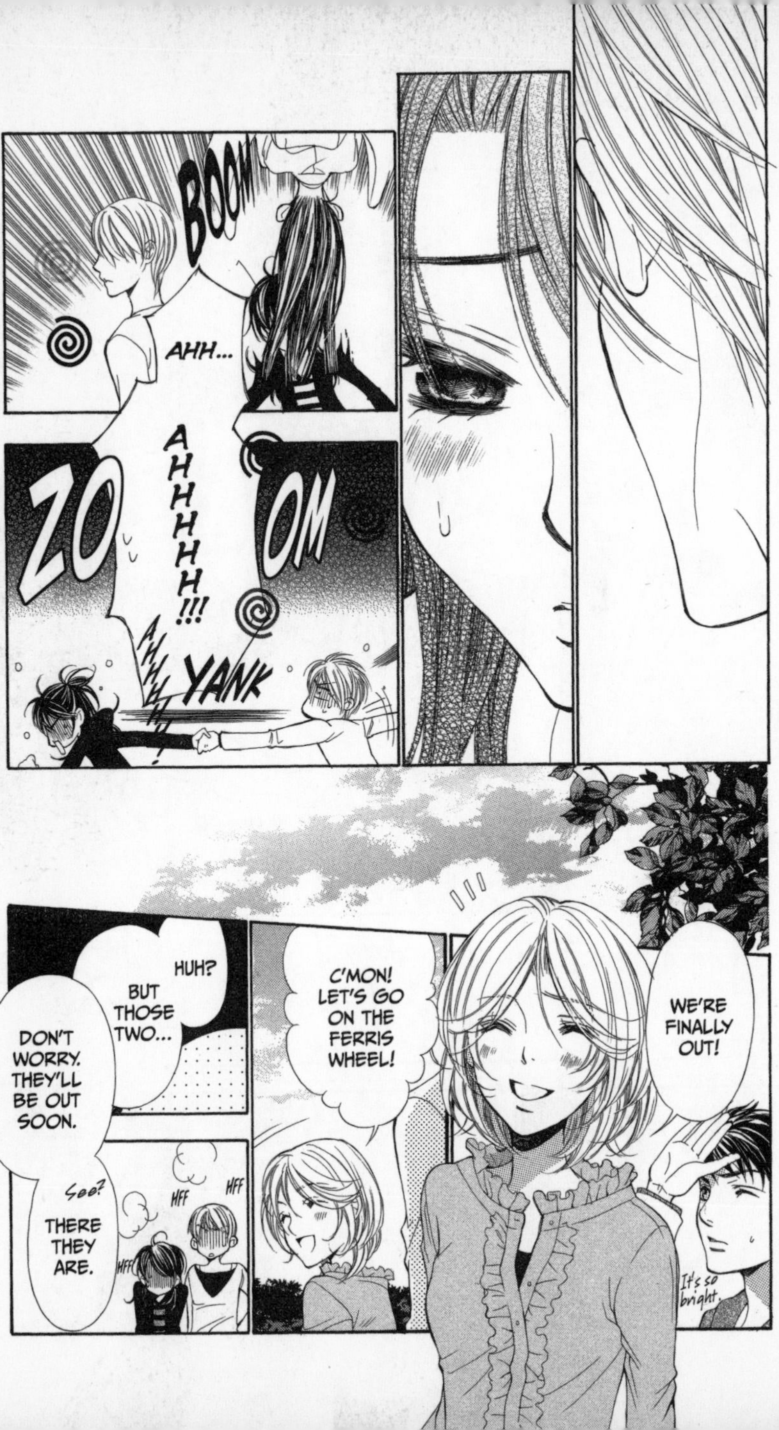
BOOM
AHH...
ZO OM
AHHHHH!!!
YANK
WE'RE FINALLY OUT!
It's so bright.
C'MON! LET'S GO ON THE FERRIS WHEEL!
HUH?
BUT THOSE TWO...
DON'T WORRY. THEY'LL BE OUT SOON.
See?
THERE THEY ARE.
HFF
HFF
HFF

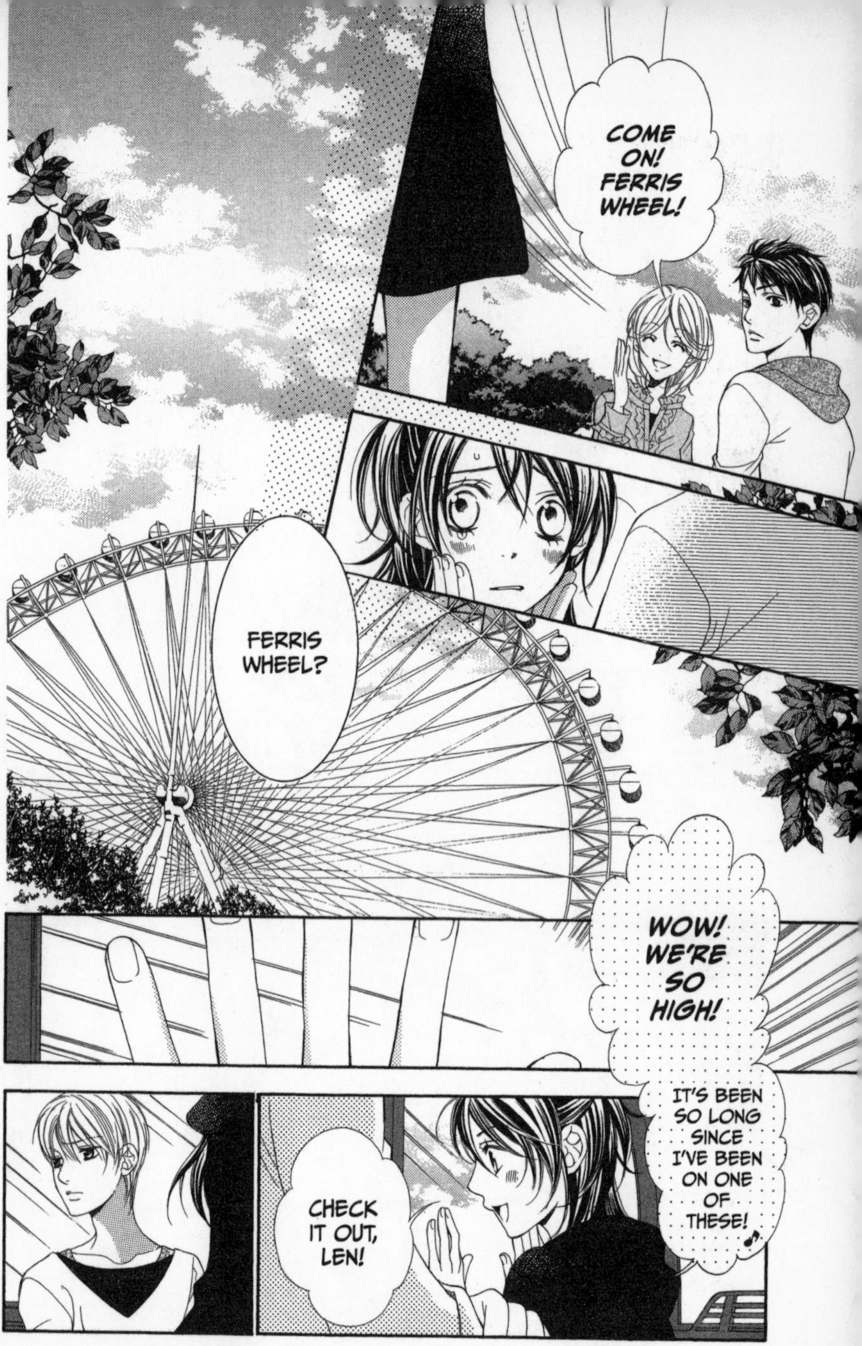
COME ON! FERRIS WHEEL!
FERRIS WHEEL?
WOW! WE'RE SO HIGH!
IT'S BEEN SO LONG SINCE I'VE BEEN ON ONE OF THESE!
CHECK IT OUT, LEN!

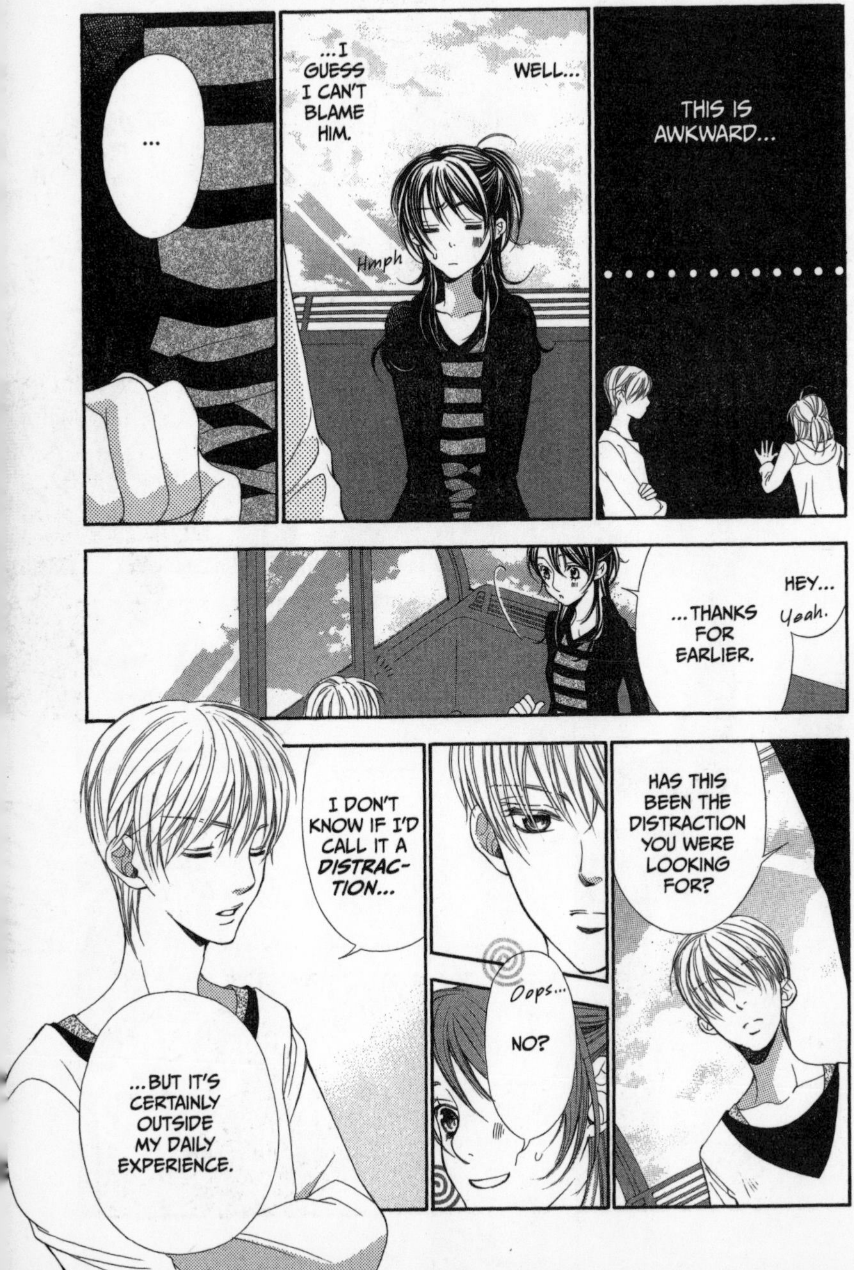
THIS IS AWKWARD...
............
WELL...
...I GUESS I CAN'T BLAME HIM.
Hmph
...
HEY...
Yeah.
...THANKS FOR EARLIER.
HAS THIS BEEN THE DISTRACTION YOU WERE LOOKING FOR?
Oops...
NO?
I DON'T KNOW IF I'D CALL IT A DISTRACTION...
...BUT IT'S CERTAINLY OUTSIDE MY DAILY EXPERIENCE.

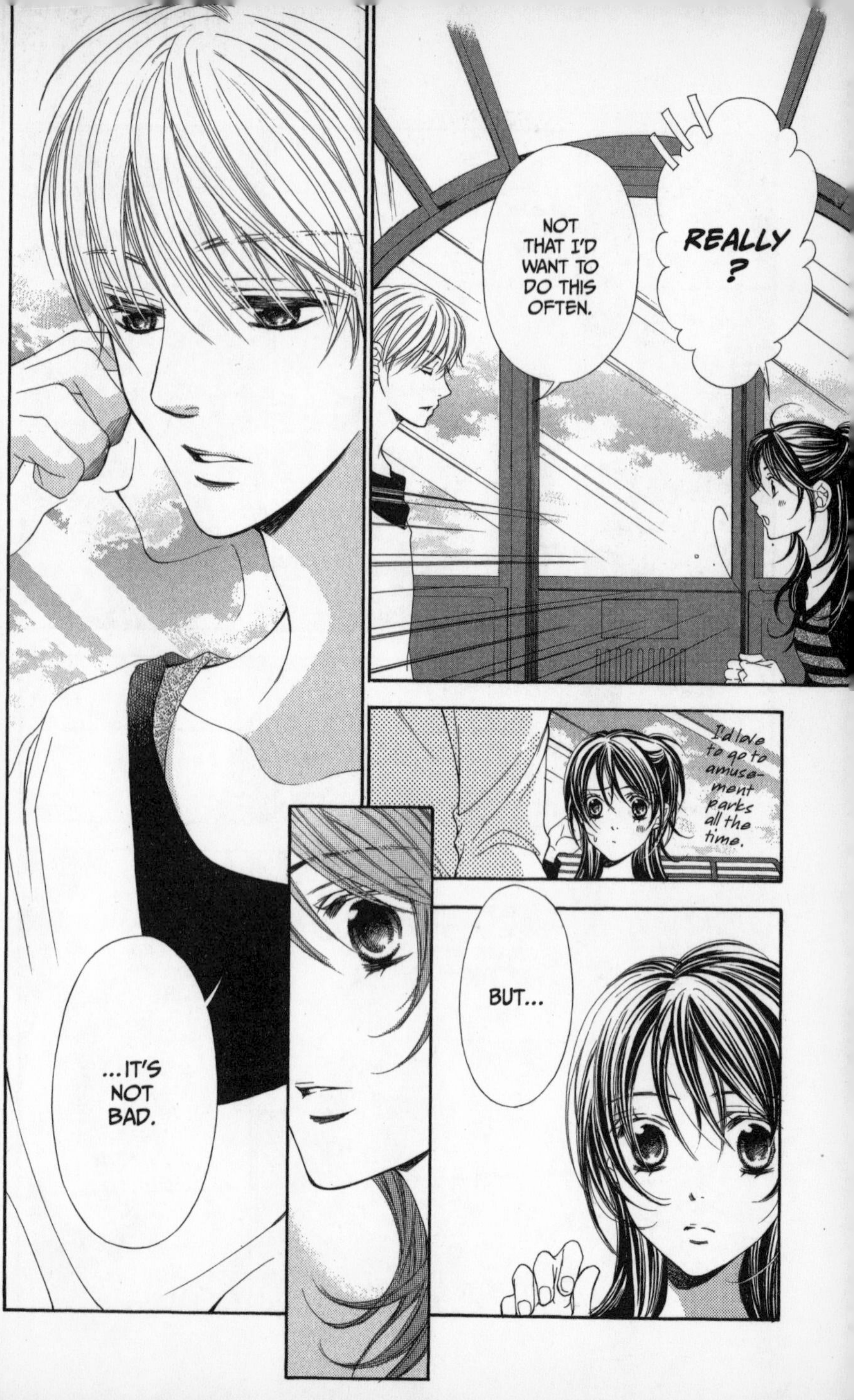
REALLY ?
NOT THAT I'D WANT TO DO THIS OFTEN.
I'd love to go to amusement parks all the time.
BUT...
...IT'S NOT BAD.

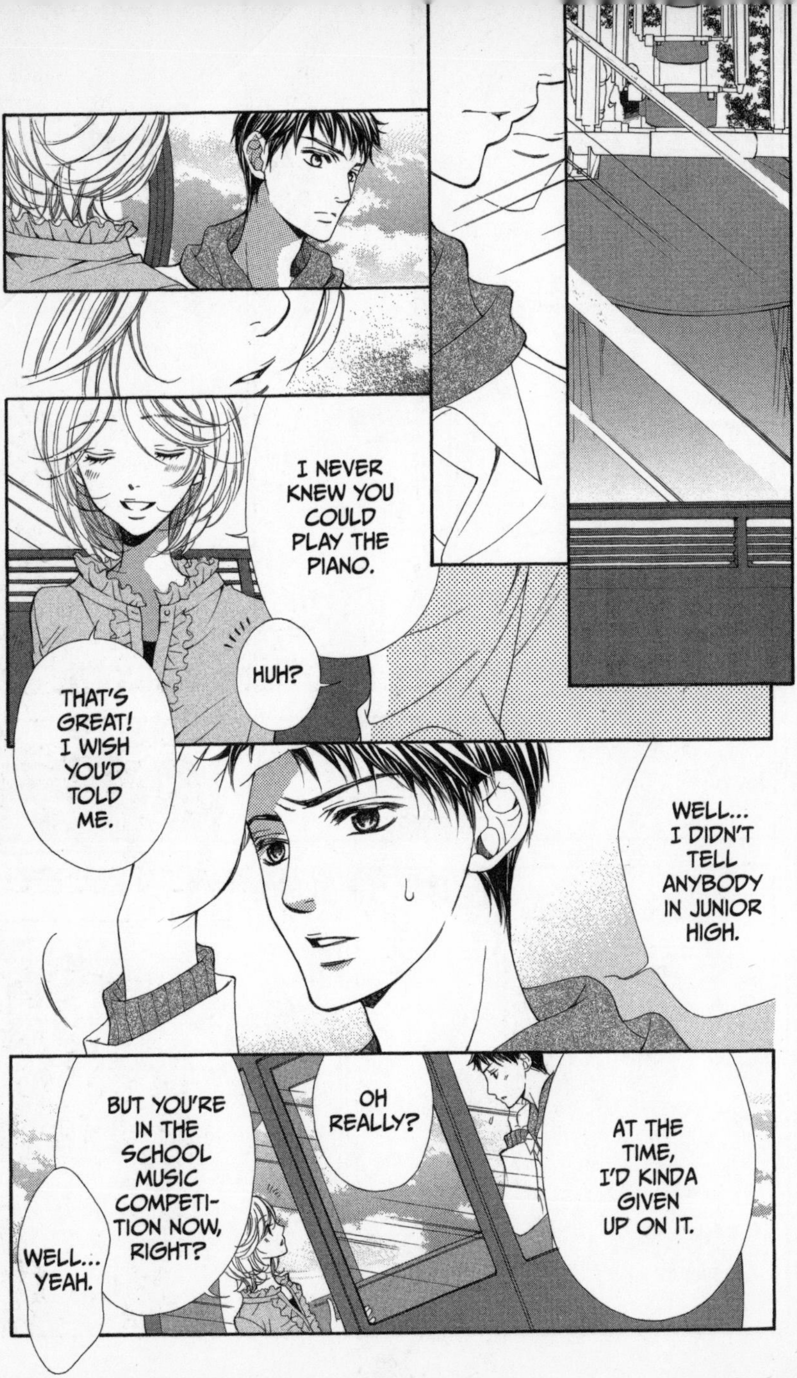
I NEVER KNEW YOU COULD PLAY THE PIANO.
HUH?
THAT'S GREAT! I WISH YOU'D TOLD ME.
WELL... I DIDN'T TELL ANYBODY IN JUNIOR HIGH.
AT THE TIME, I'D KINDA GIVEN UP ON IT.
OH REALLY?
BUT YOU'RE IN THE SCHOOL MUSIC COMPETITION NOW, RIGHT?
WELL... YEAH.

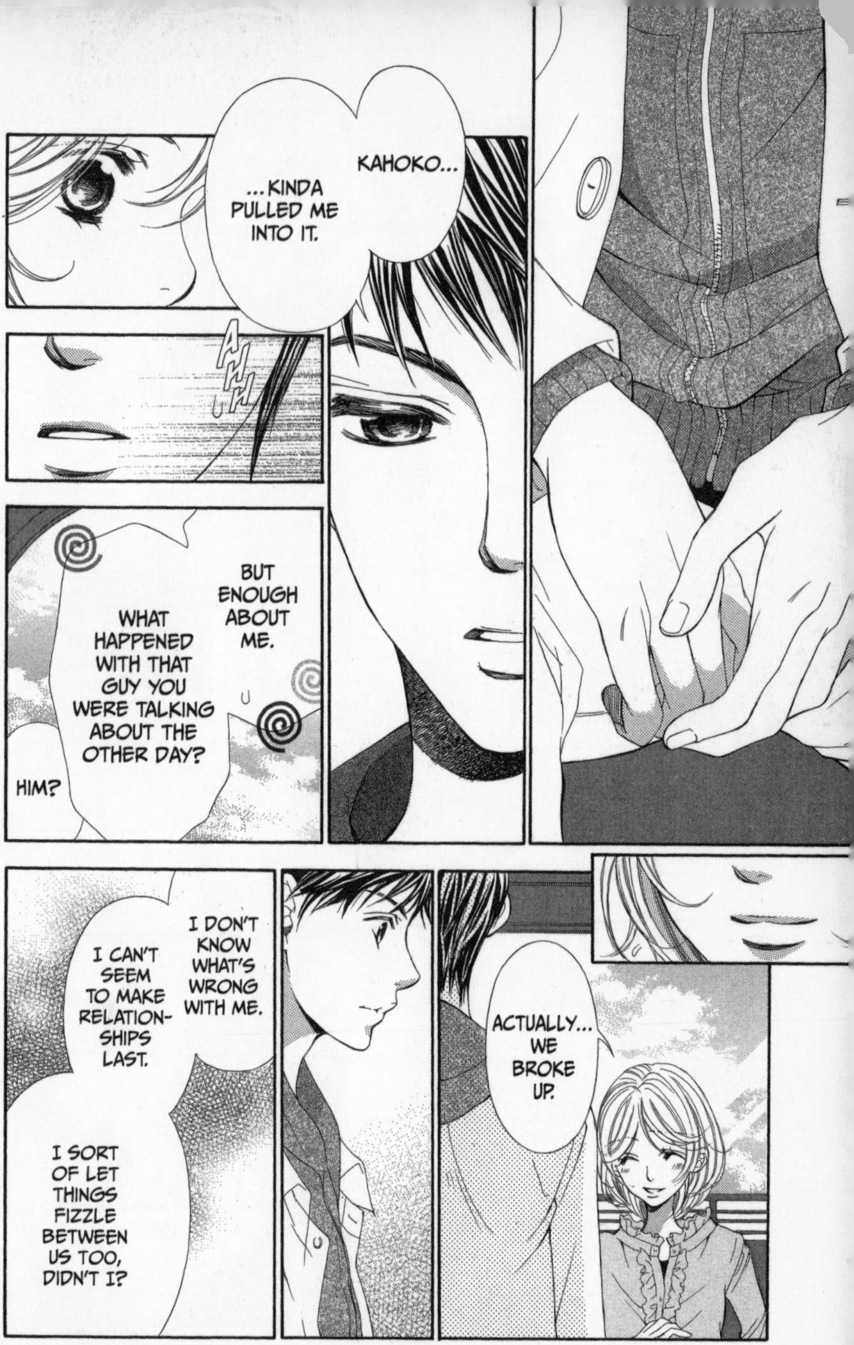
KAHOKO...
...KINDA PULLED ME INTO IT.
AHH
BUT ENOUGH ABOUT ME.
WHAT HAPPENED WITH THAT GUY YOU WERE TALKING ABOUT THE OTHER DAY?
HIM?
ACTUALLY... WE BROKE UP.
I DON'T KNOW WHAT'S WRONG WITH ME.
I CAN'T SEEM TO MAKE RELATION-SHIPS LAST.
I SORT OF LET THINGS FIZZLE BETWEEN US TOO, DIDN'T I?

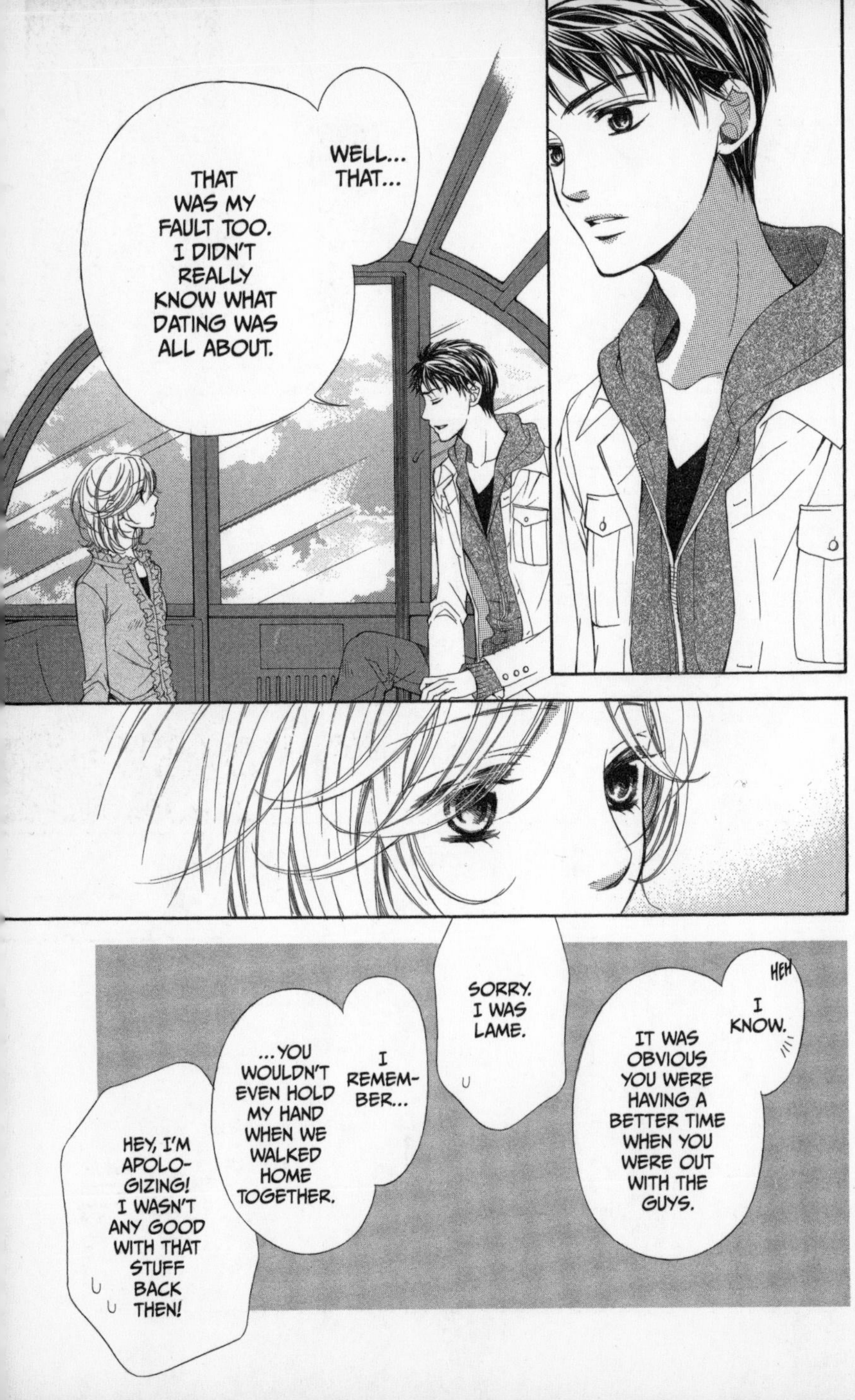
WELL... THAT...
THAT WAS MY FAULT TOO. I DIDN'T REALLY KNOW WHAT DATING WAS ALL ABOUT.
HEH
I KNOW.
IT WAS OBVIOUS YOU WERE HAVING A BETTER TIME WHEN YOU WERE OUT WITH THE GUYS.
SORRY. I WAS LAME.
I REMEMBER...
...YOU WOULDN'T EVEN HOLD MY HAND WHEN WE WALKED HOME TOGETHER.
HEY, I'M APOLOGIZING! I WASN'T ANY GOOD WITH THAT STUFF BACK THEN!

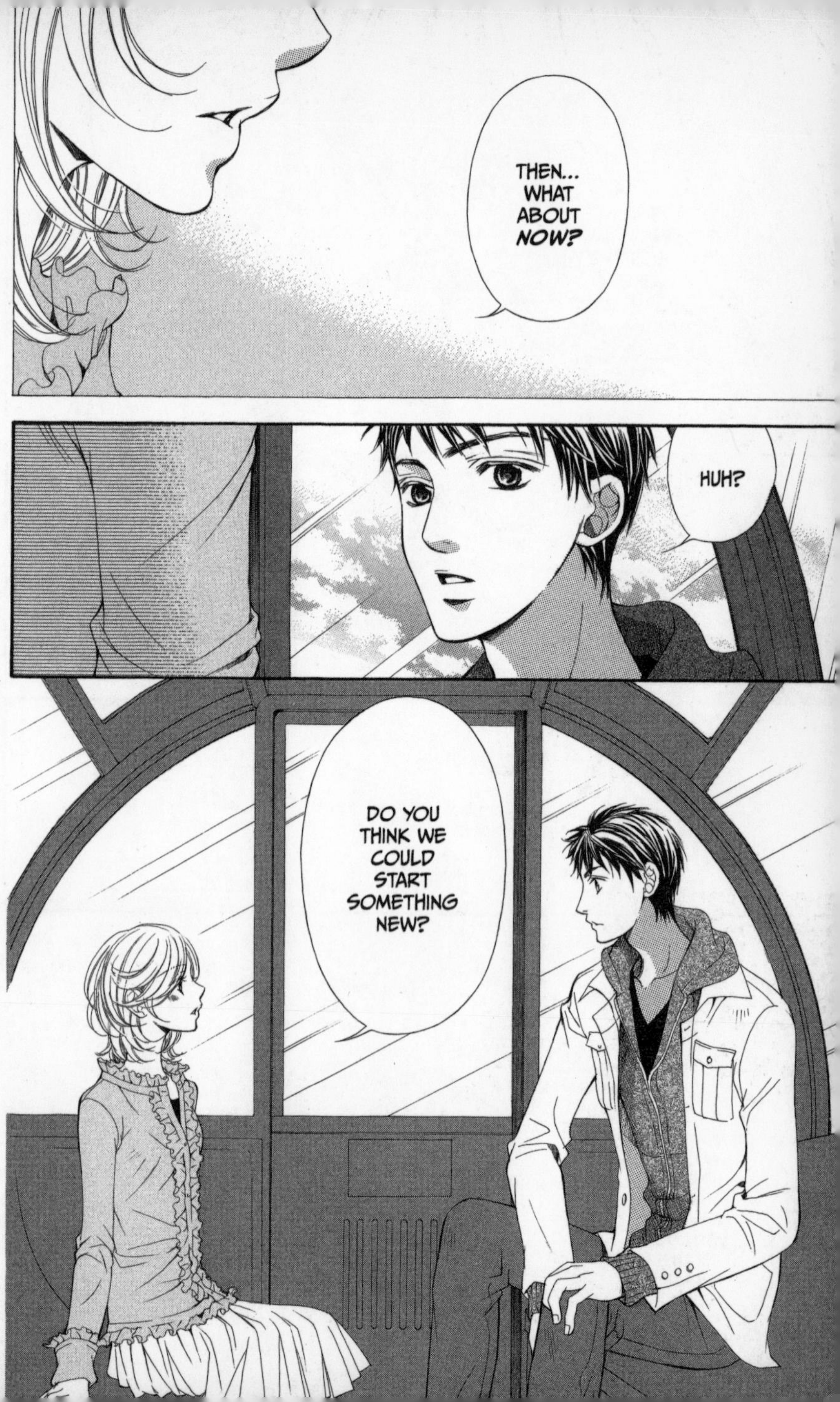
THEN... WHAT ABOUT NOW?
HUH?
DO YOU THINK WE COULD START SOMETHING NEW?

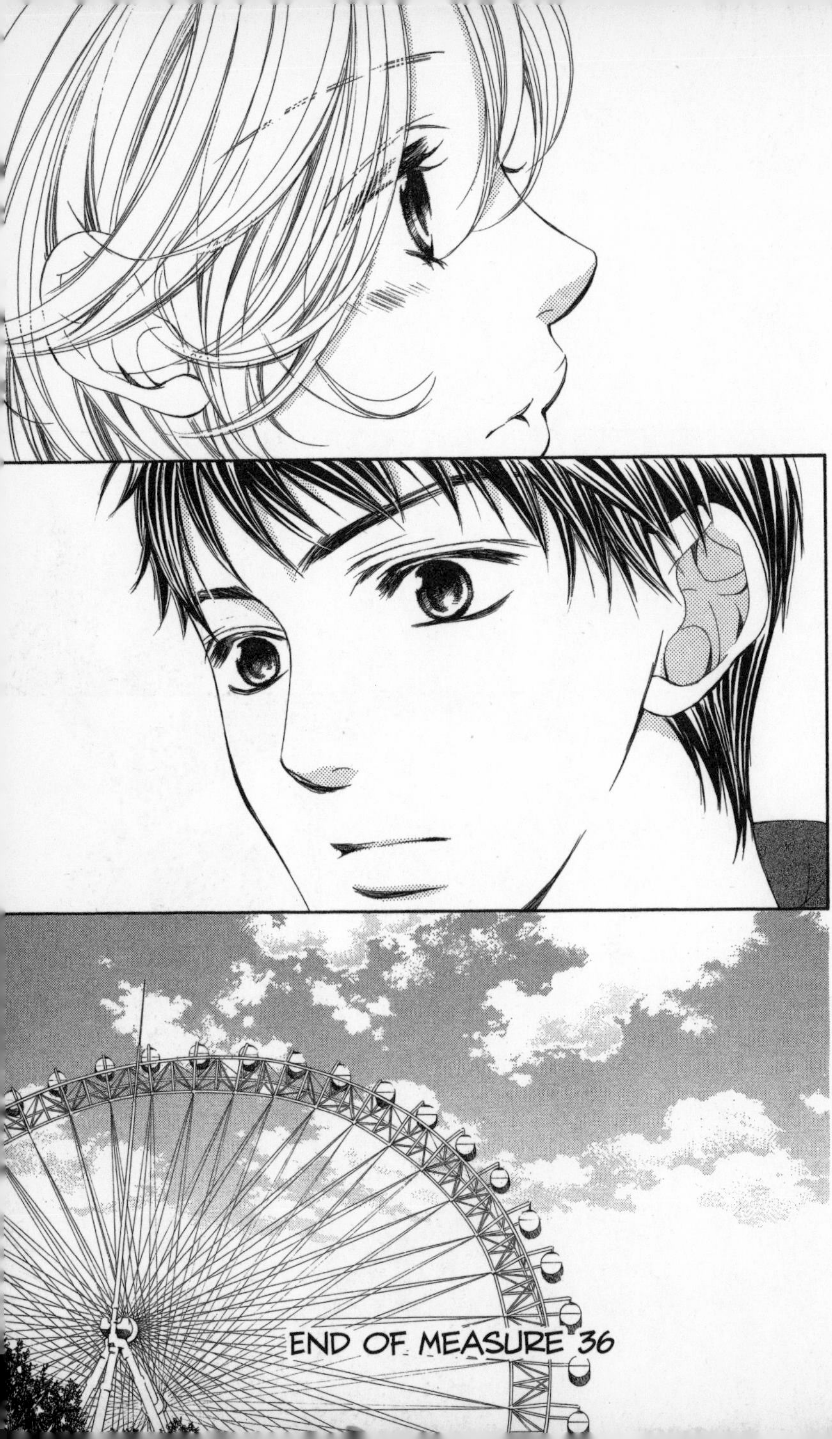
END OF MEASURE 36

# FIRST STEP?

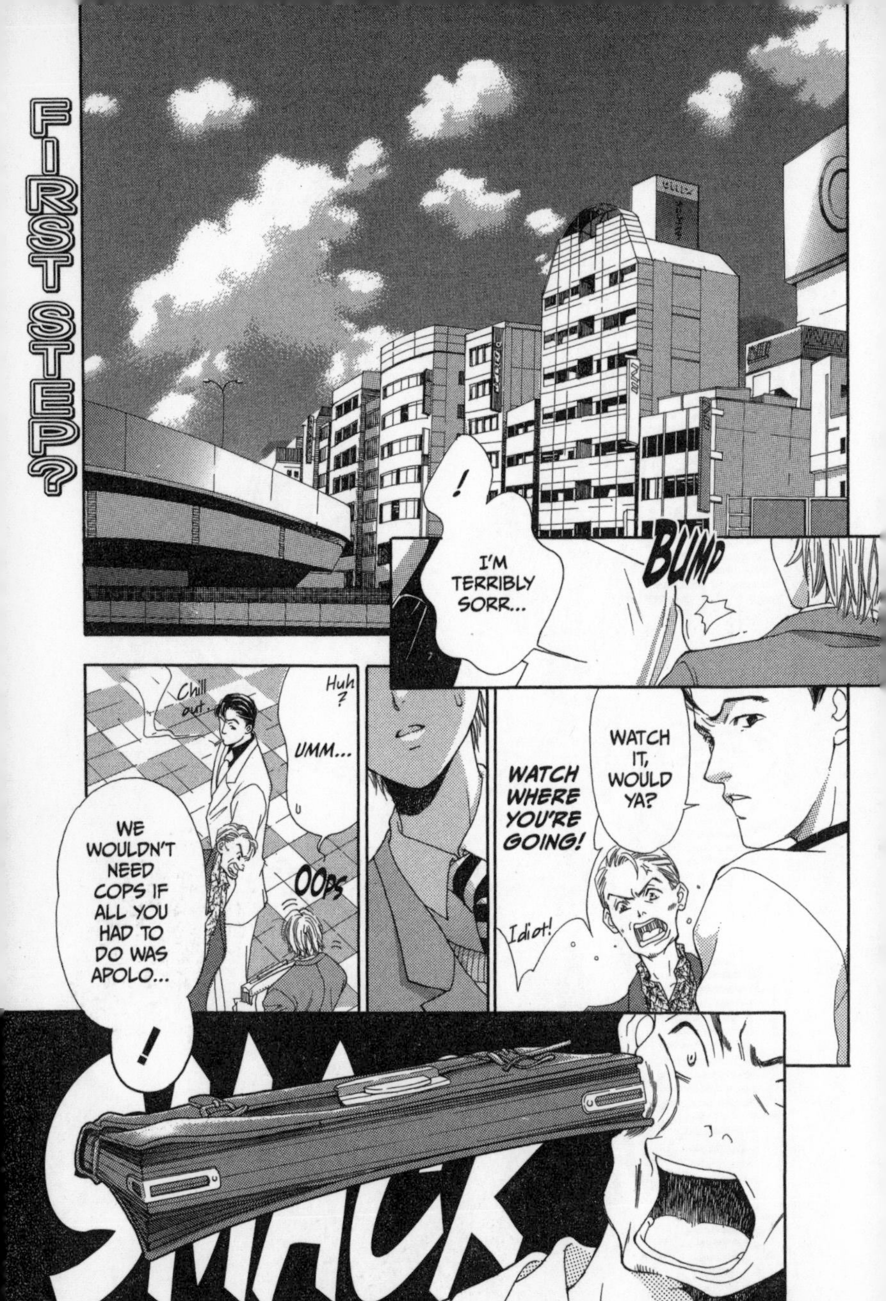
!
I'M TERRIBLY SORR...
BUMP
WATCH IT, WOULD YA?
WATCH WHERE YOU'RE GOING!
Idiot!
Huh?
UMM...
OOPS
Chill out.
WE WOULDN'T NEED COPS IF ALL YOU HAD TO DO WAS APOLO...
!
SMACK

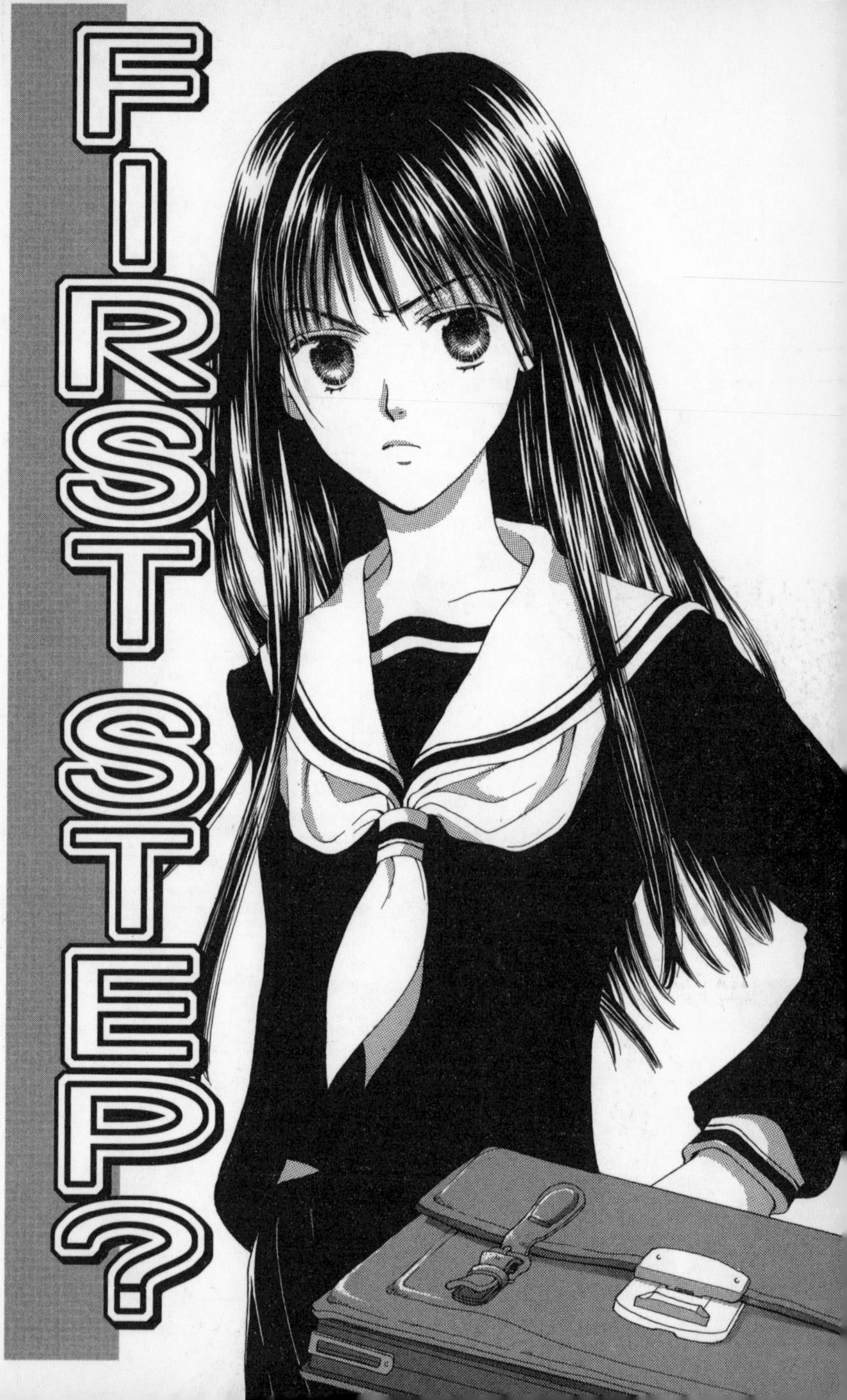
FIRST STEP?

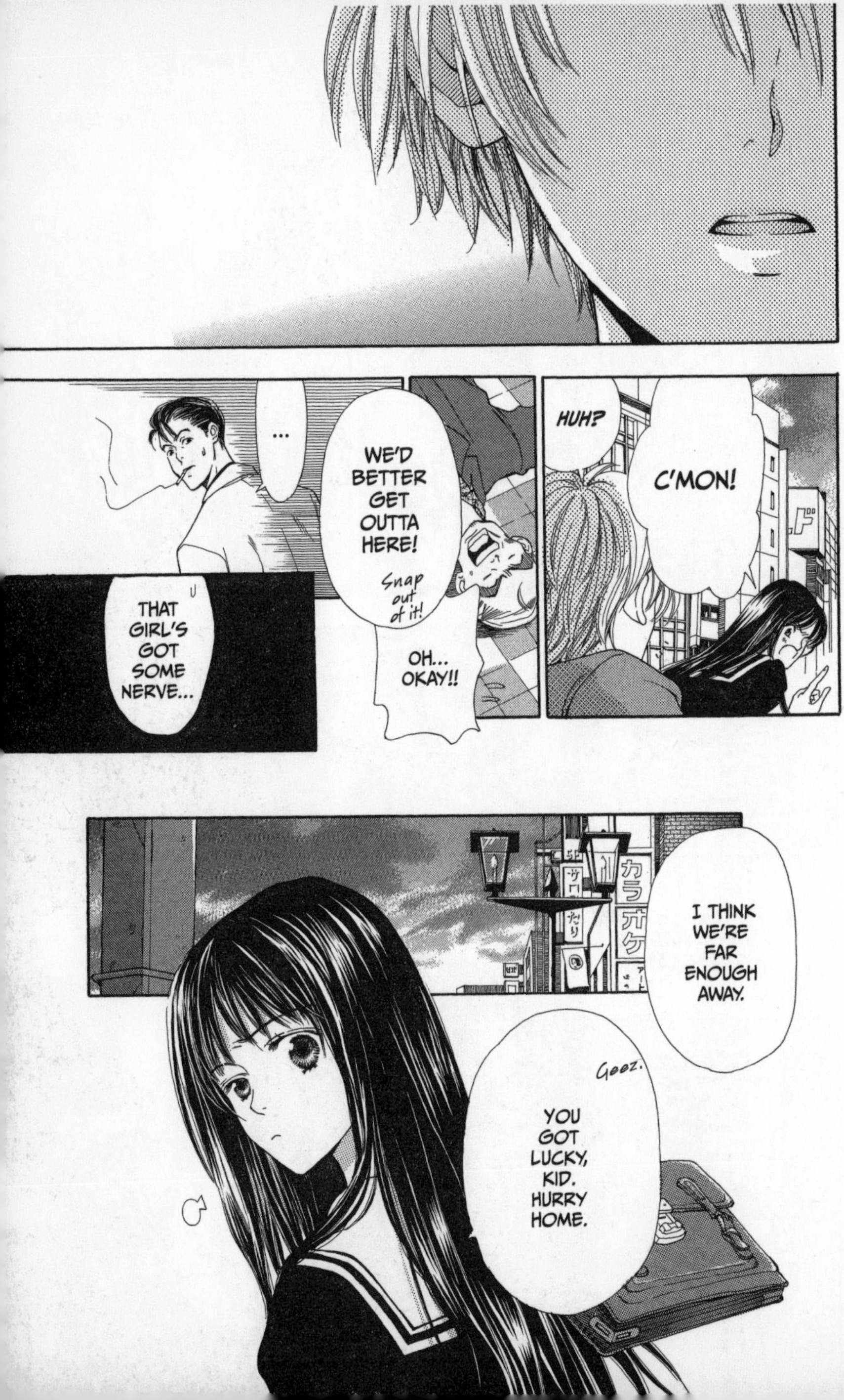
C'MON!
HUH?
WE'D BETTER GET OUTTA HERE!
Snap out of it!
OH... OKAY!!
...
THAT GIRL'S GOT SOME NERVE...
I THINK WE'RE FAR ENOUGH AWAY.
カラオケ
Geez.
YOU GOT LUCKY, KID. HURRY HOME.

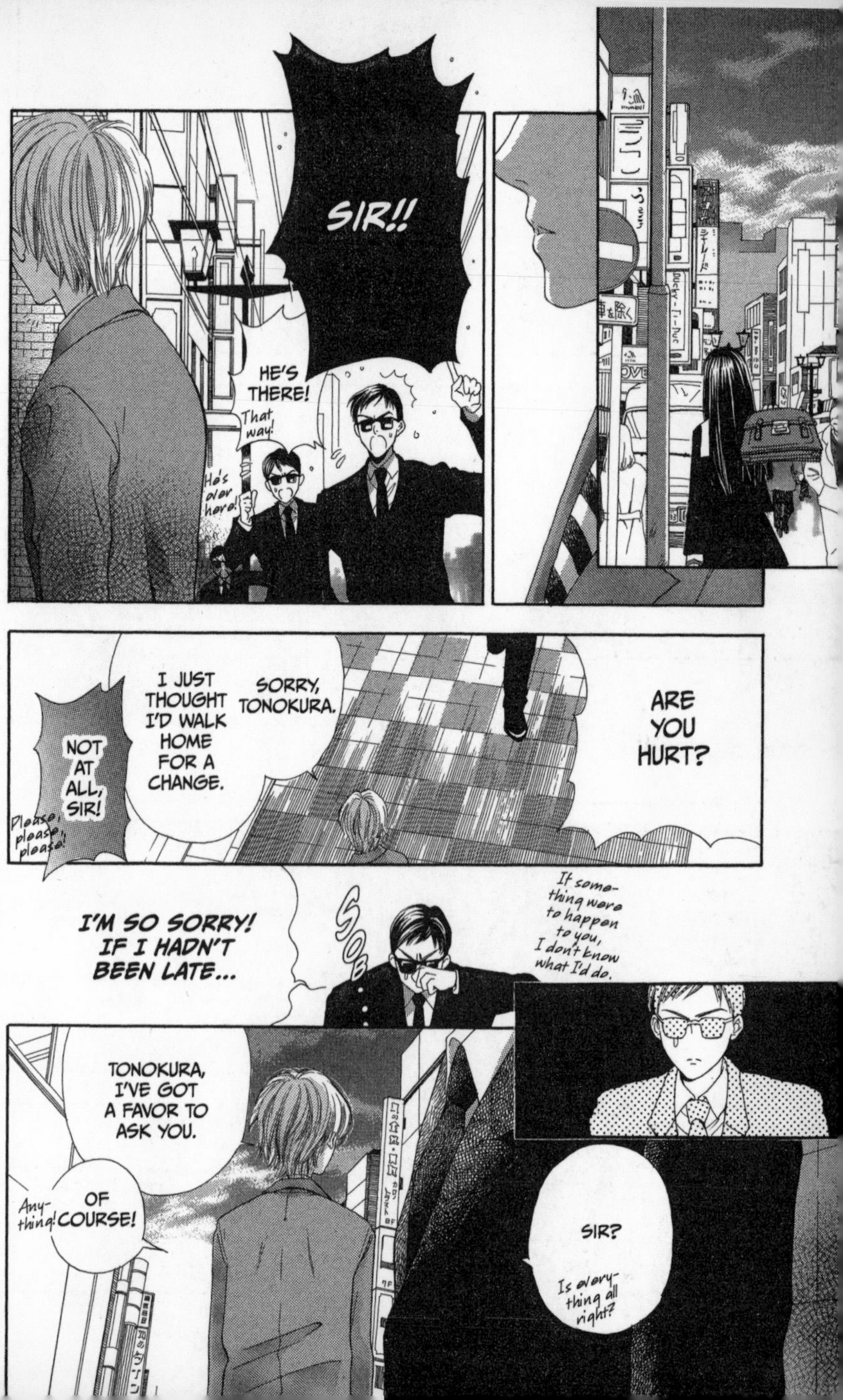
SIR!!
HE'S THERE!
That way!
He's over here!
ARE YOU HURT?
SORRY, TONOKURA.
I JUST THOUGHT I'D WALK HOME FOR A CHANGE.
NOT AT ALL, SIR!
Please, please, please!
If something were to happen to you, I don't know what I'd do.
SOB
I'M SO SORRY! IF I HADN'T BEEN LATE...
SIR?
Is everything all right?
TONOKURA, I'VE GOT A FAVOR TO ASK YOU.
OF COURSE!
Anything!

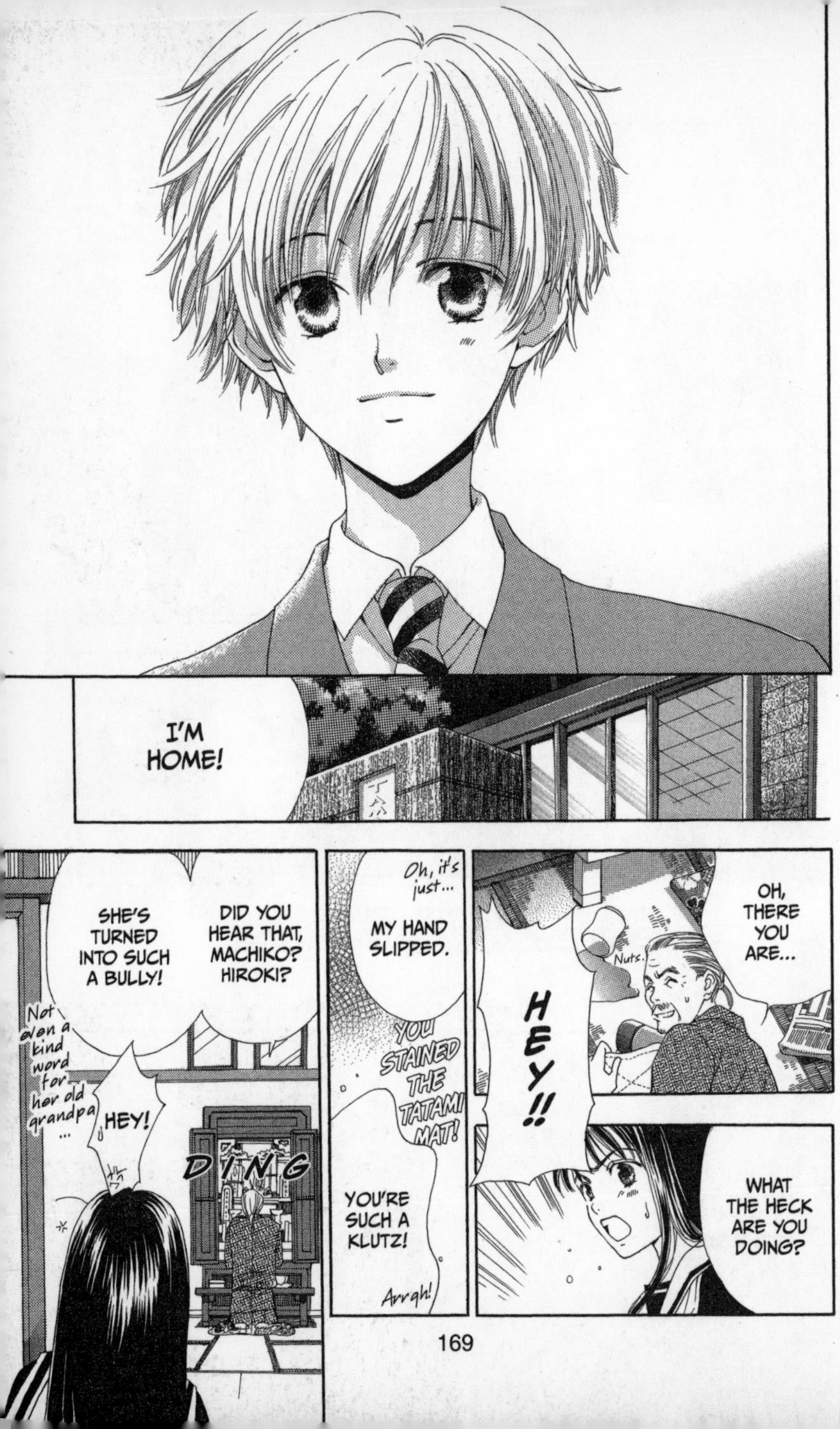
I'M HOME!
OH, THERE YOU ARE...
Nuts.
HEY!!
WHAT THE HECK ARE YOU DOING?
Oh, it's just...
MY HAND SLIPPED.
YOU STAINED THE TATAMI MAT!
YOU'RE SUCH A KLUTZ!
Arrgh!
DID YOU HEAR THAT, MACHIKO? HIROKI?
SHE'S TURNED INTO SUCH A BULLY!
Not even a kind word for her old grandpa...
HEY!
DING

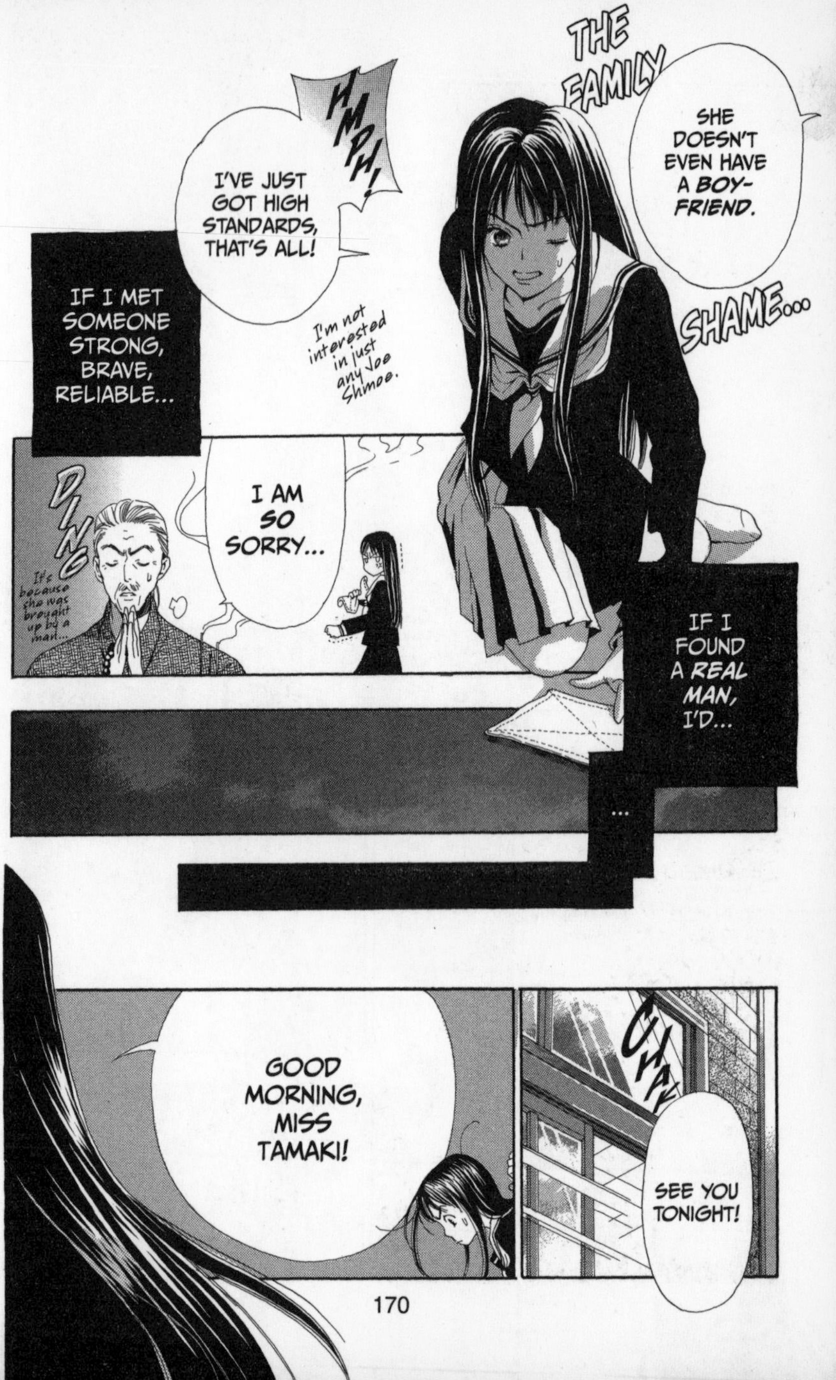
THE FAMILY SHAME...
SHE DOESN'T EVEN HAVE A BOY-FRIEND.
HMPH!
I'VE JUST GOT HIGH STANDARDS, THAT'S ALL!
I'm not interested in just any Joe Shmoe.
IF I MET SOMEONE STRONG, BRAVE, RELIABLE...
I AM SO SORRY...
DING
It's because she was brought up by a man...
IF I FOUND A REAL MAN, I'D...
...
CHAK
SEE YOU TONIGHT!
GOOD MORNING, MISS TAMAKI!

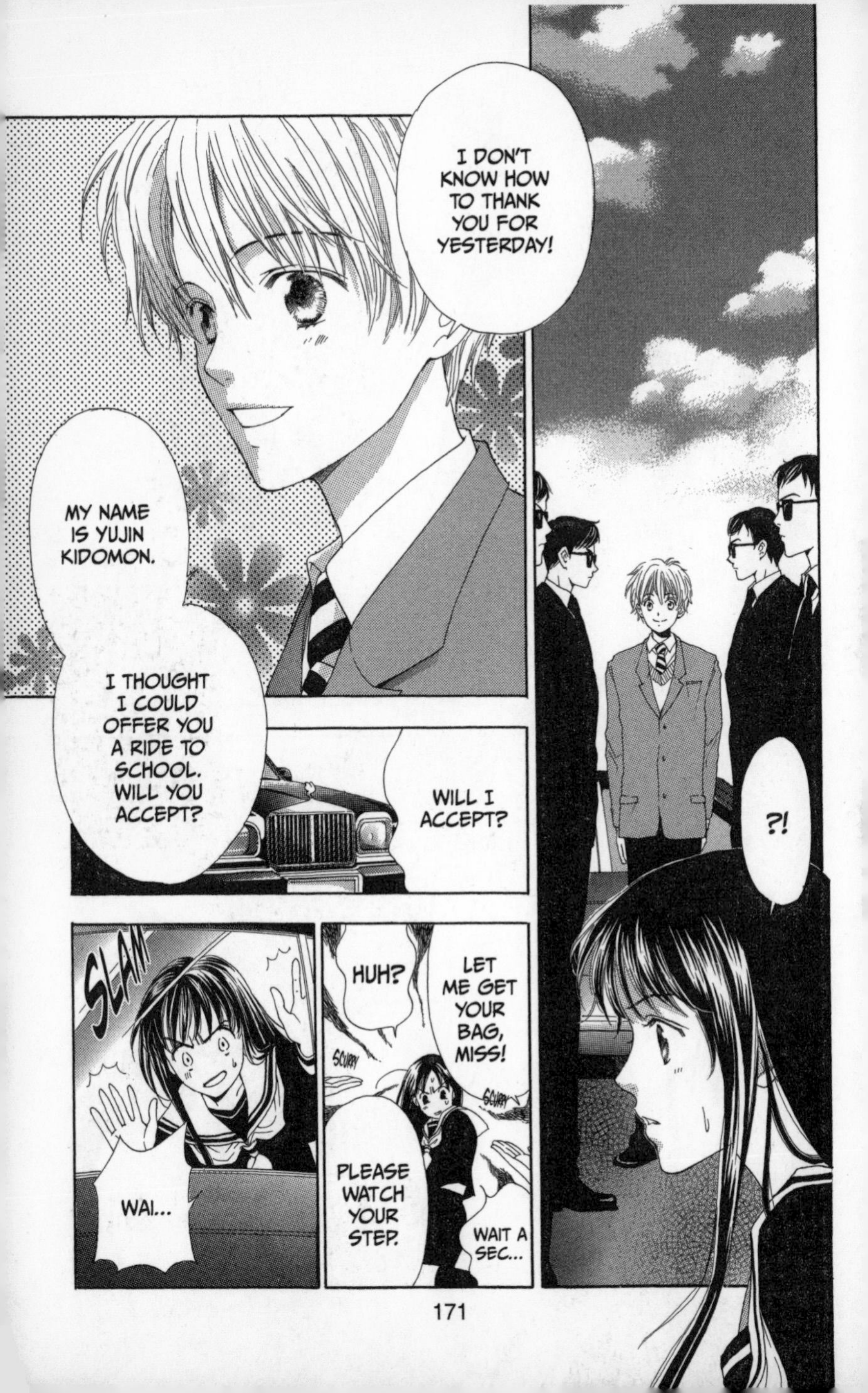
I DON'T KNOW HOW TO THANK YOU FOR YESTERDAY!
?!
MY NAME IS YUJIN KIDOMON.
I THOUGHT I COULD OFFER YOU A RIDE TO SCHOOL. WILL YOU ACCEPT?
WILL I ACCEPT?
LET ME GET YOUR BAG, MISS!
HUH?
SCURRY
SCURRY
PLEASE WATCH YOUR STEP.
WAIT A SEC...
SLAM
WAI...

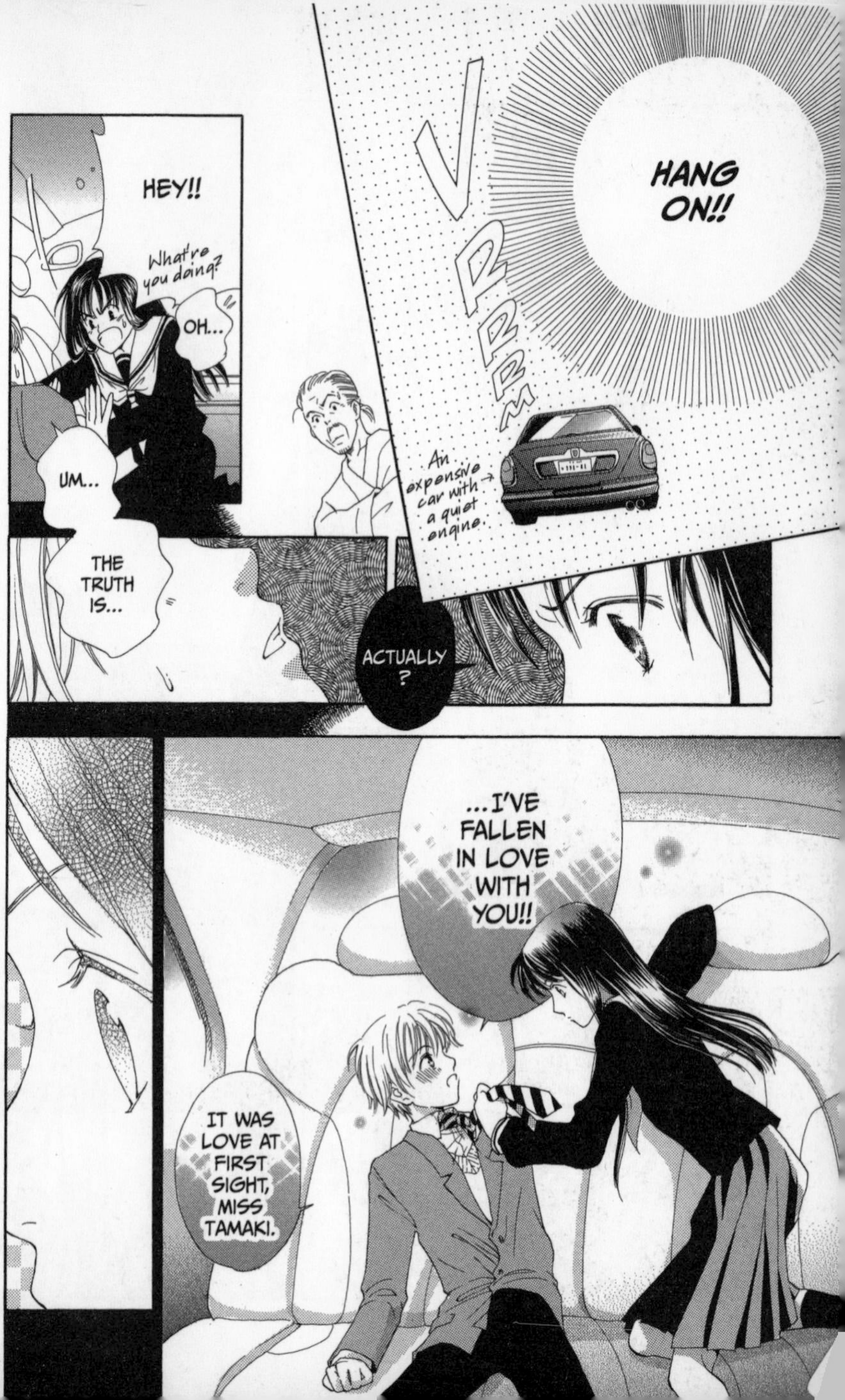
HANG ON!!
VRRRM
An expensive car with a quiet engine.
HEY!!
What're you doing?
OH...
UM...
THE TRUTH IS...
ACTUALLY?
...I'VE FALLEN IN LOVE WITH YOU!!
IT WAS LOVE AT FIRST SIGHT, MISS TAMAKI.

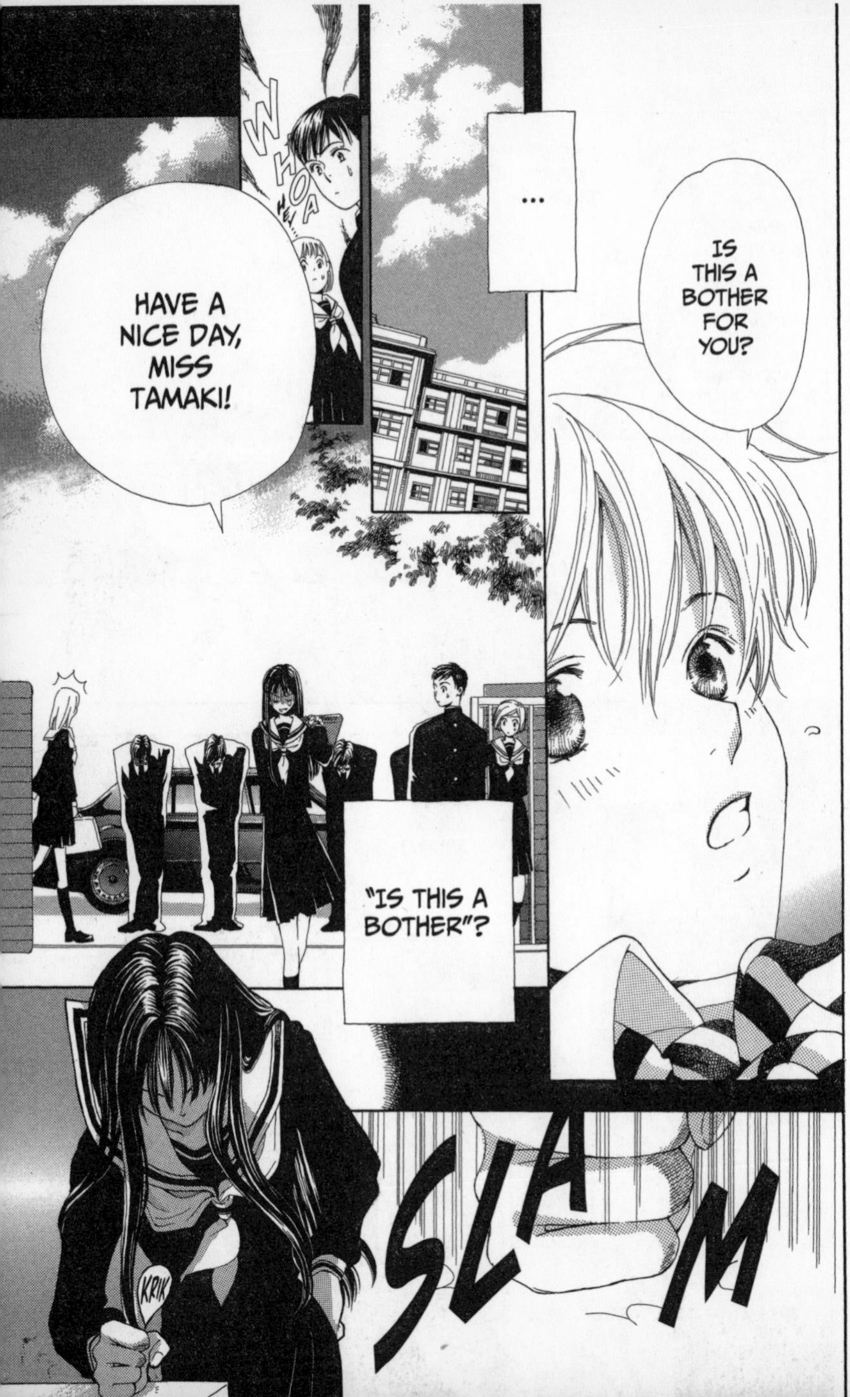
IS THIS A BOTHER FOR YOU?
...
WHOA
HEY...
HAVE A NICE DAY, MISS TAMAKI!
"IS THIS A BOTHER"?
SLAM
KRIK

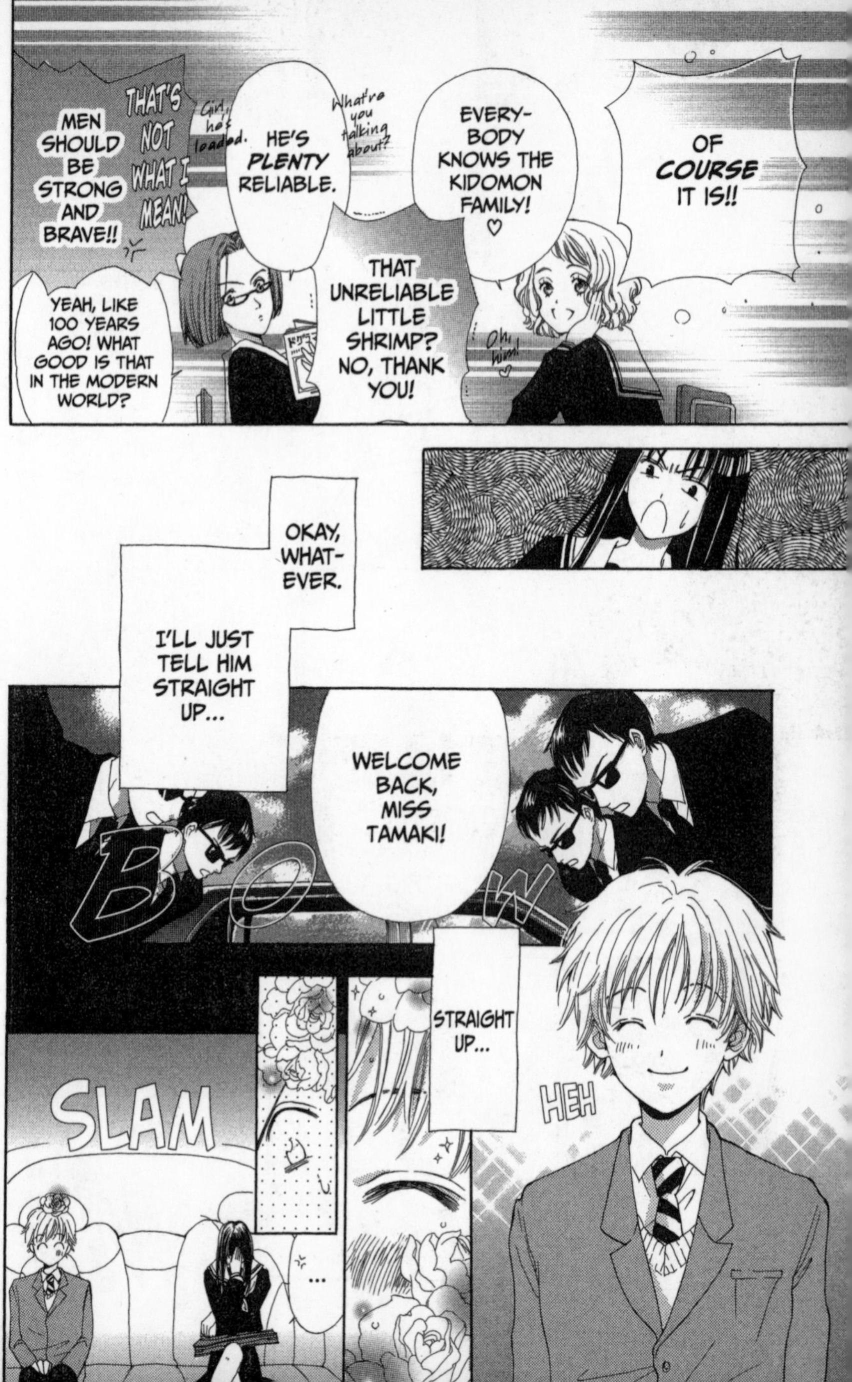
OF COURSE IT IS!!
EVERY-BODY KNOWS THE KIDOMON FAMILY! ♡
Oh, him! ♡
What're you talking about?
HE'S PLENTY RELIABLE.
Girl, he's loaded.
THAT UNRELIABLE LITTLE SHRIMP? NO, THANK YOU!
THAT'S NOT WHAT I MEAN!
MEN SHOULD BE STRONG AND BRAVE!!
YEAH, LIKE 100 YEARS AGO! WHAT GOOD IS THAT IN THE MODERN WORLD?
OKAY, WHAT-EVER.
I'LL JUST TELL HIM STRAIGHT UP...
WELCOME BACK, MISS TAMAKI!
BOW
STRAIGHT UP...
HEH
...
SLAM

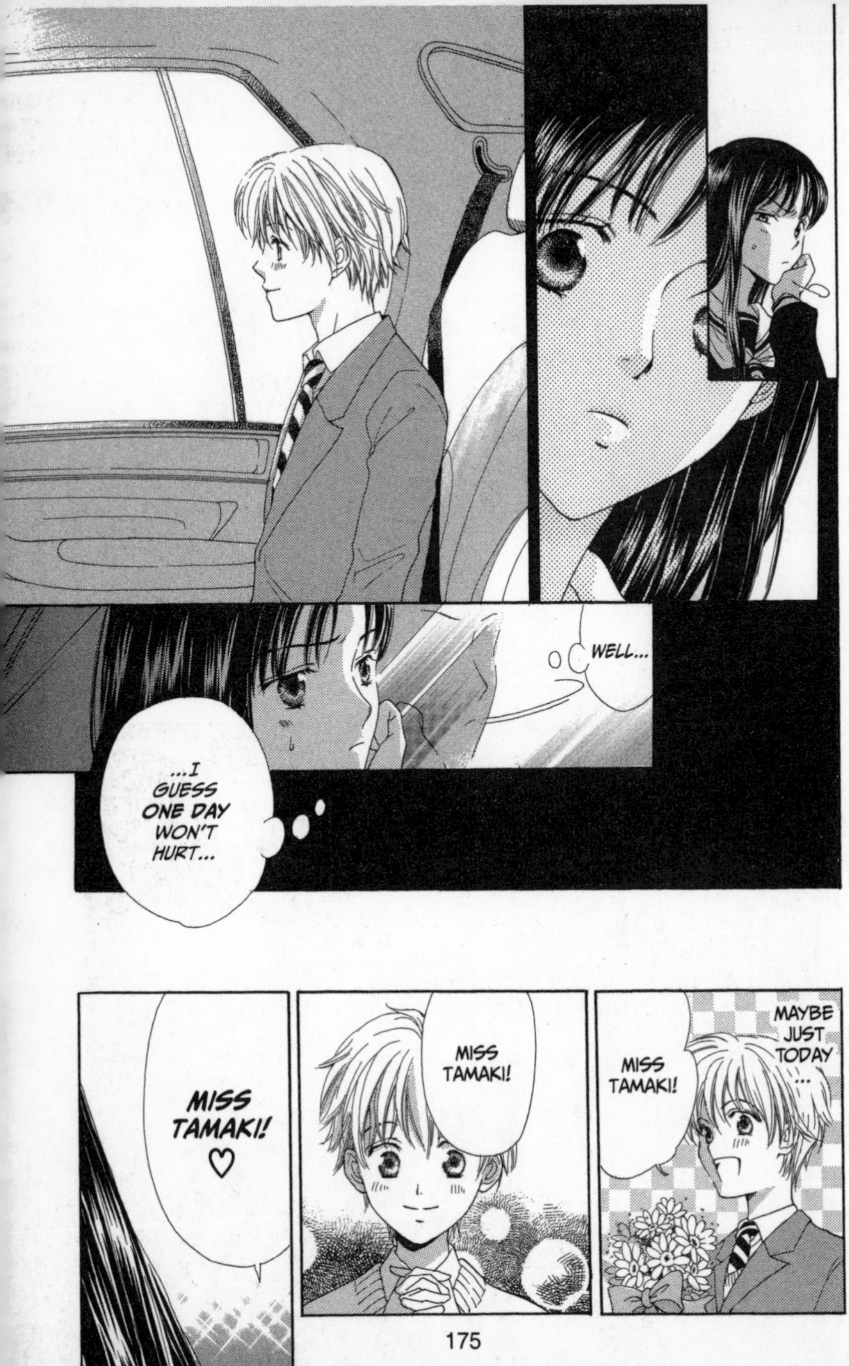
WELL...
...I GUESS ONE DAY WON'T HURT...
MAYBE JUST TODAY...
MISS TAMAKI!
MISS TAMAKI!
MISS TAMAKI! ♡

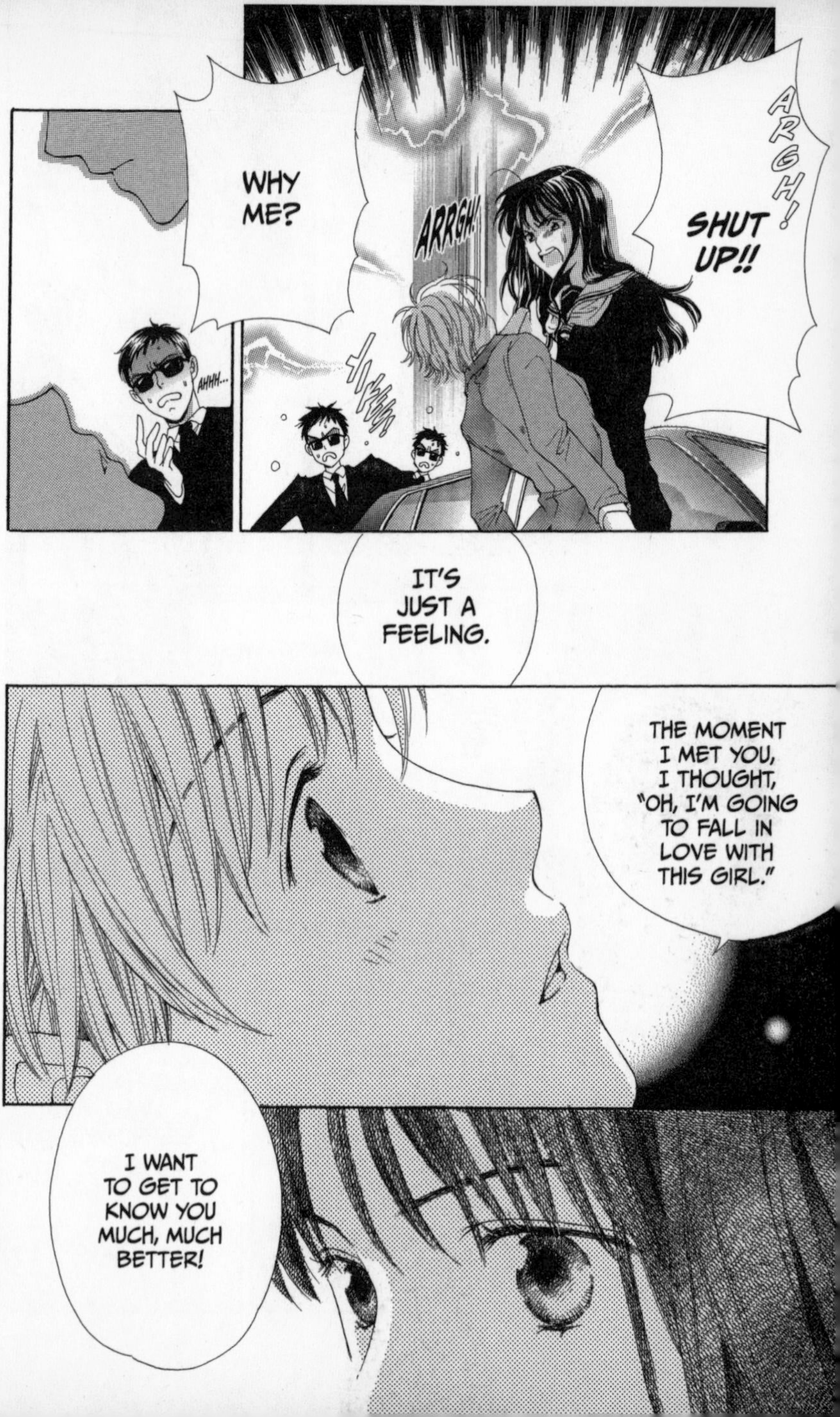
ARGH!
SHUT UP!!
ARRGH!
WHY ME?
AHHH...
IT'S JUST A FEELING.
THE MOMENT I MET YOU, I THOUGHT, "OH, I'M GOING TO FALL IN LOVE WITH THIS GIRL."
I WANT TO GET TO KNOW YOU MUCH, MUCH BETTER!

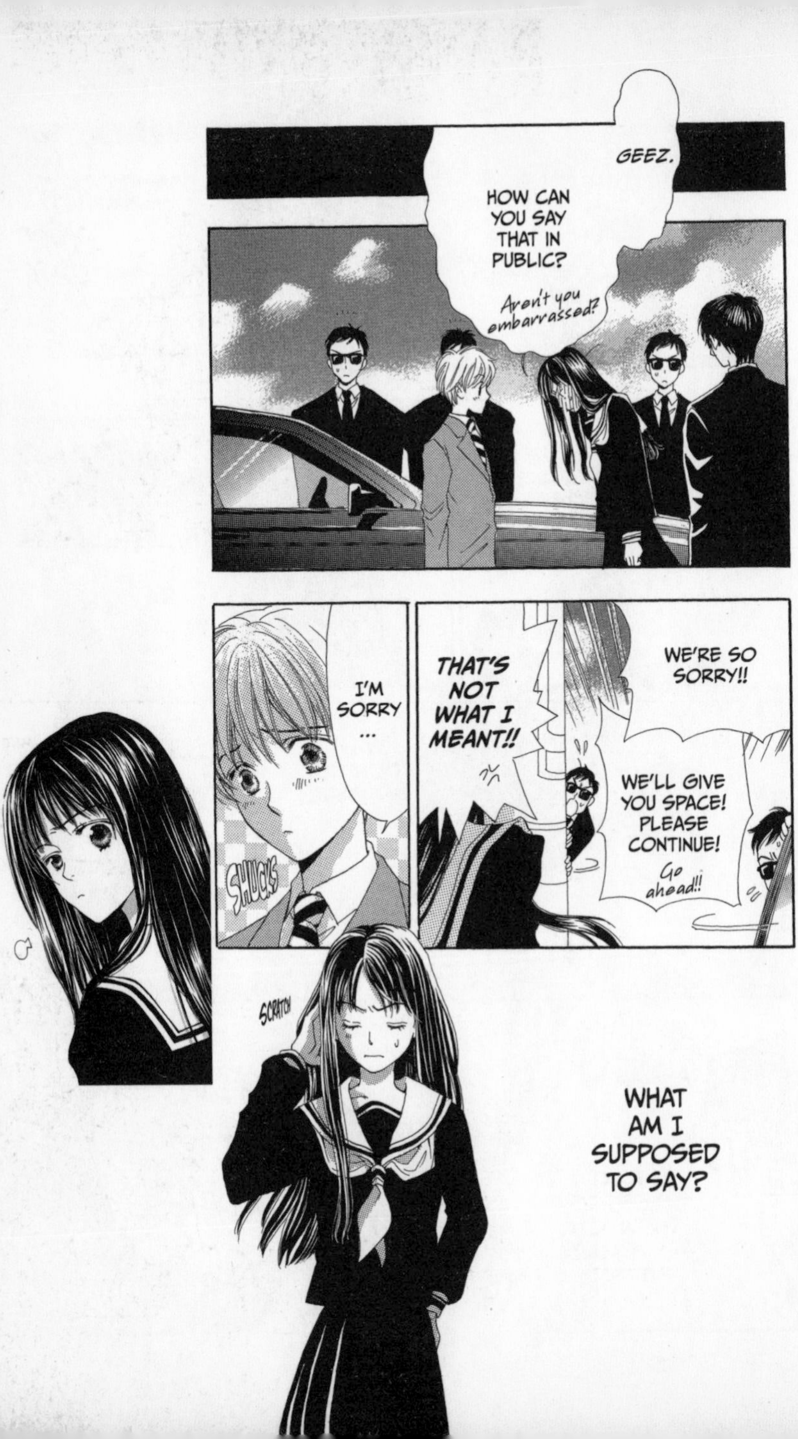
GEEZ.
HOW CAN YOU SAY THAT IN PUBLIC?
Aren't you embarrassed?
WE'RE SO SORRY!!
WE'LL GIVE YOU SPACE! PLEASE CONTINUE!
Go ahead!!
THAT'S NOT WHAT I MEANT!!
I'M SORRY...
SHUCKS
WHAT AM I SUPPOSED TO SAY?
SCRATCH

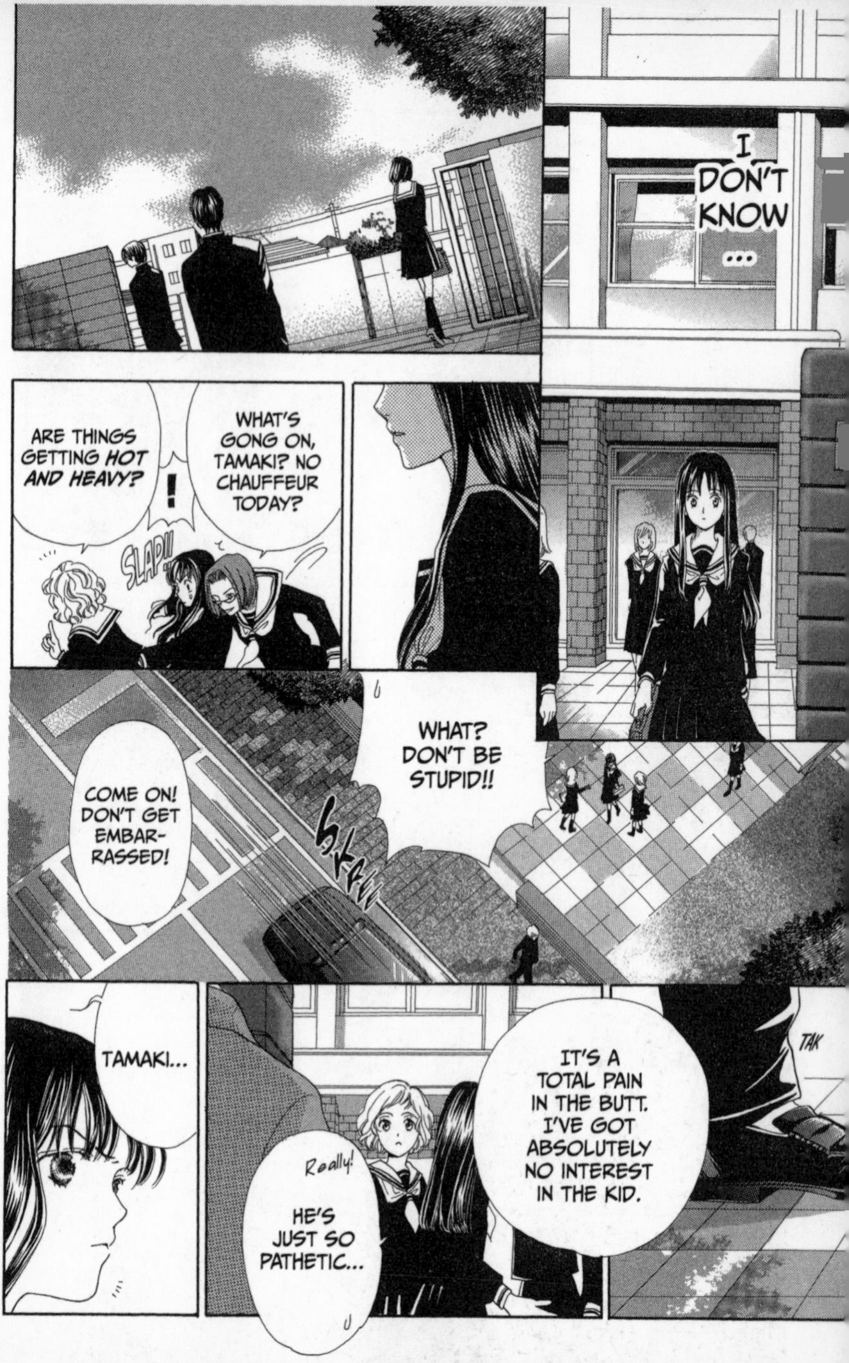
I DON'T KNOW ...
WHAT'S GONG ON, TAMAKI? NO CHAUFFEUR TODAY?
!
ARE THINGS GETTING *HOT AND HEAVY?*
SLAP!!
WHAT? DON'T BE STUPID!!
SKREEE
COME ON! DON'T GET EMBAR-RASSED!
TAK
IT'S A TOTAL PAIN IN THE BUTT. I'VE GOT ABSOLUTELY NO INTEREST IN THE KID.
Really!
HE'S JUST SO PATHETIC...
TAMAKI...

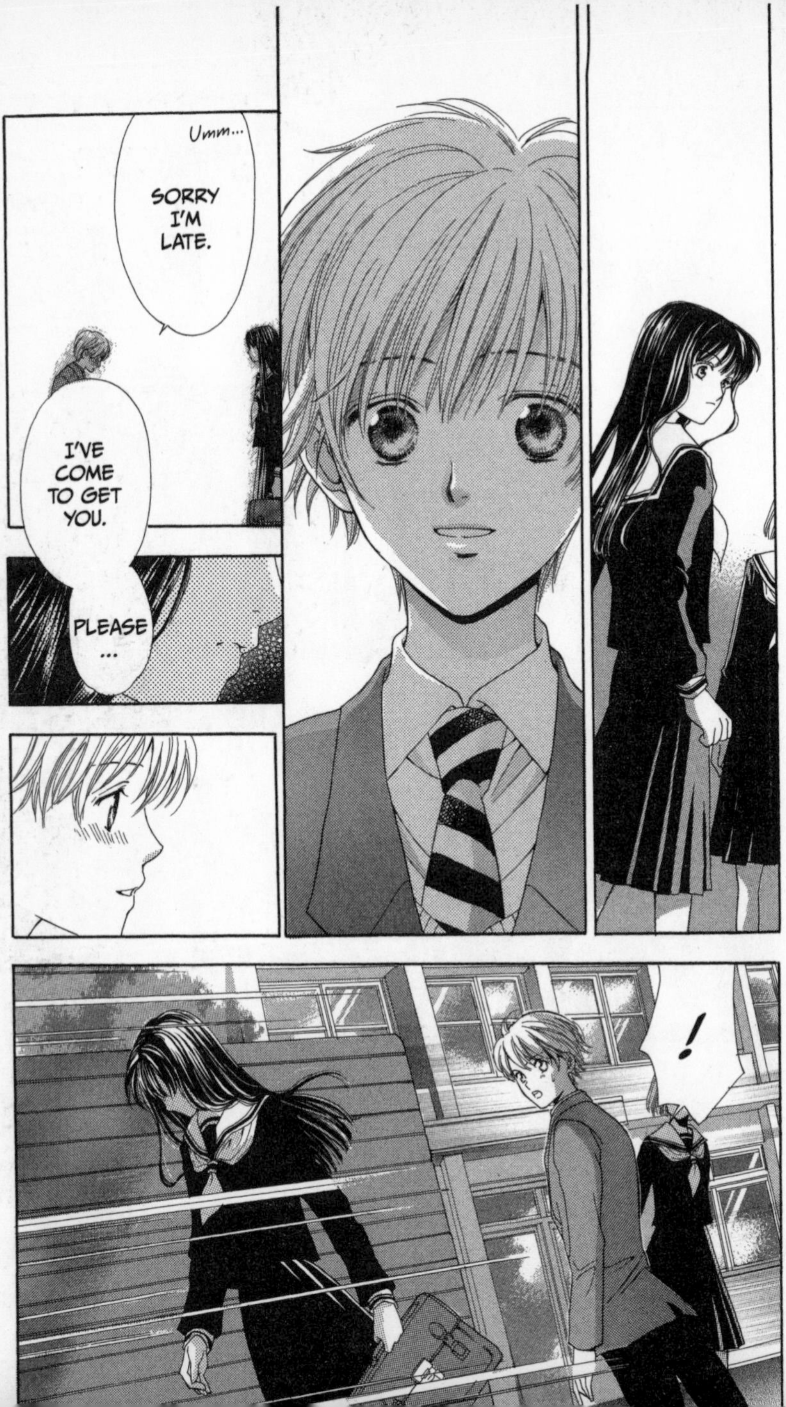
Umm...
SORRY I'M LATE.
I'VE COME TO GET YOU.
PLEASE ...
!

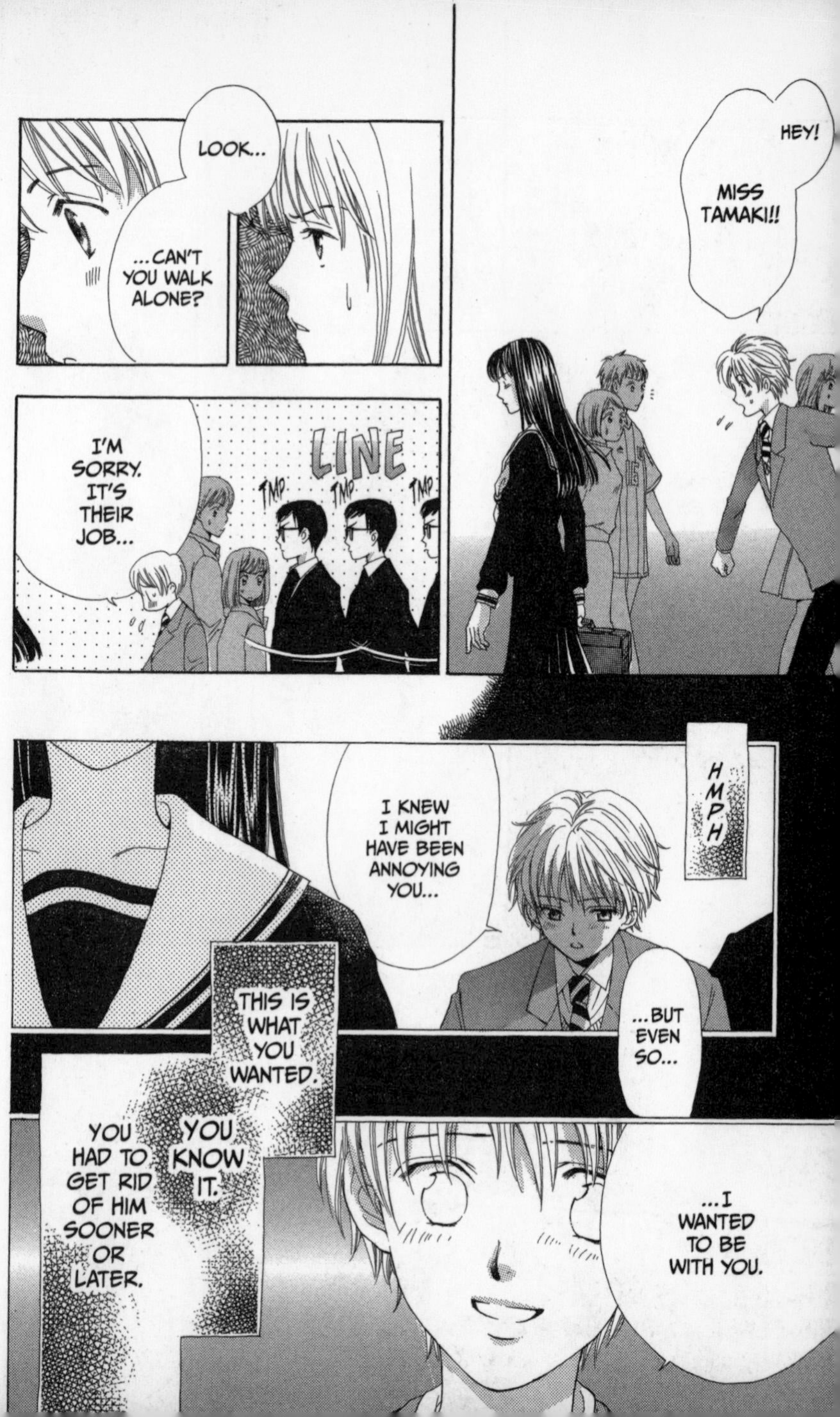
HEY!
MISS TAMAKI!!
LOOK...
...CAN'T YOU WALK ALONE?
I'M SORRY. IT'S THEIR JOB...
LINE
TMP
TMP
TMP
HMPH
I KNEW I MIGHT HAVE BEEN ANNOYING YOU...
...BUT EVEN SO...
...I WANTED TO BE WITH YOU.
THIS IS WHAT YOU WANTED.
YOU KNOW IT.
YOU HAD TO GET RID OF HIM SOONER OR LATER.

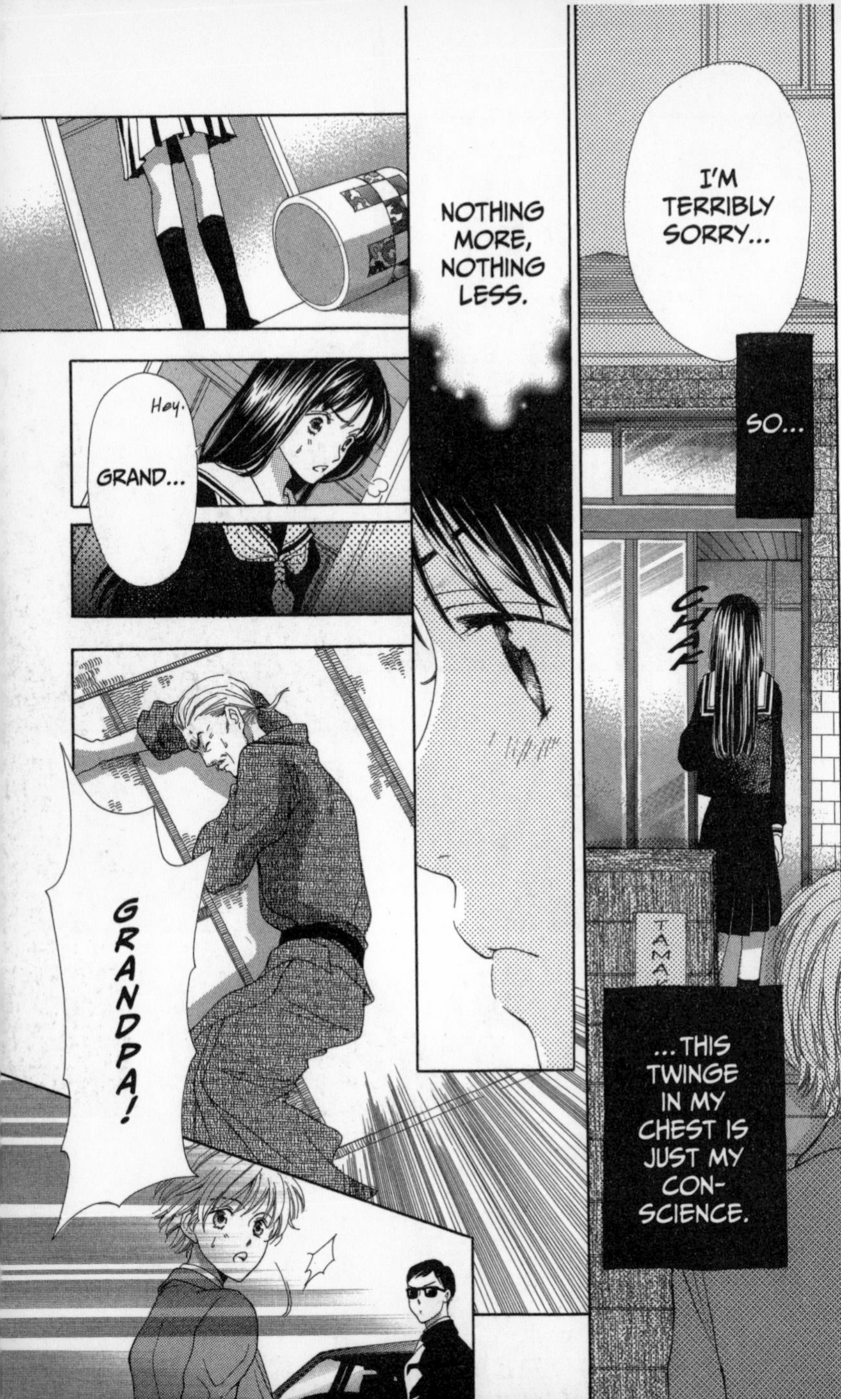
I'M TERRIBLY SORRY...
SO...
...THIS TWINGE IN MY CHEST IS JUST MY CON-SCIENCE.
NOTHING MORE, NOTHING LESS.
Hey.
GRAND...
GRANDPA!

GRA... GRAND- PA'S...

MISS TAMAKI ?

HE'S HAD A STROKE!

HAS HE HAD ANY HISTORY ?

WHAT DO I DO?

MISS TAMAKI!!

*SLAP*

WHAT DO I DO?

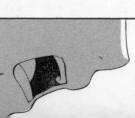

PULL YOURSELF TOGETHER!

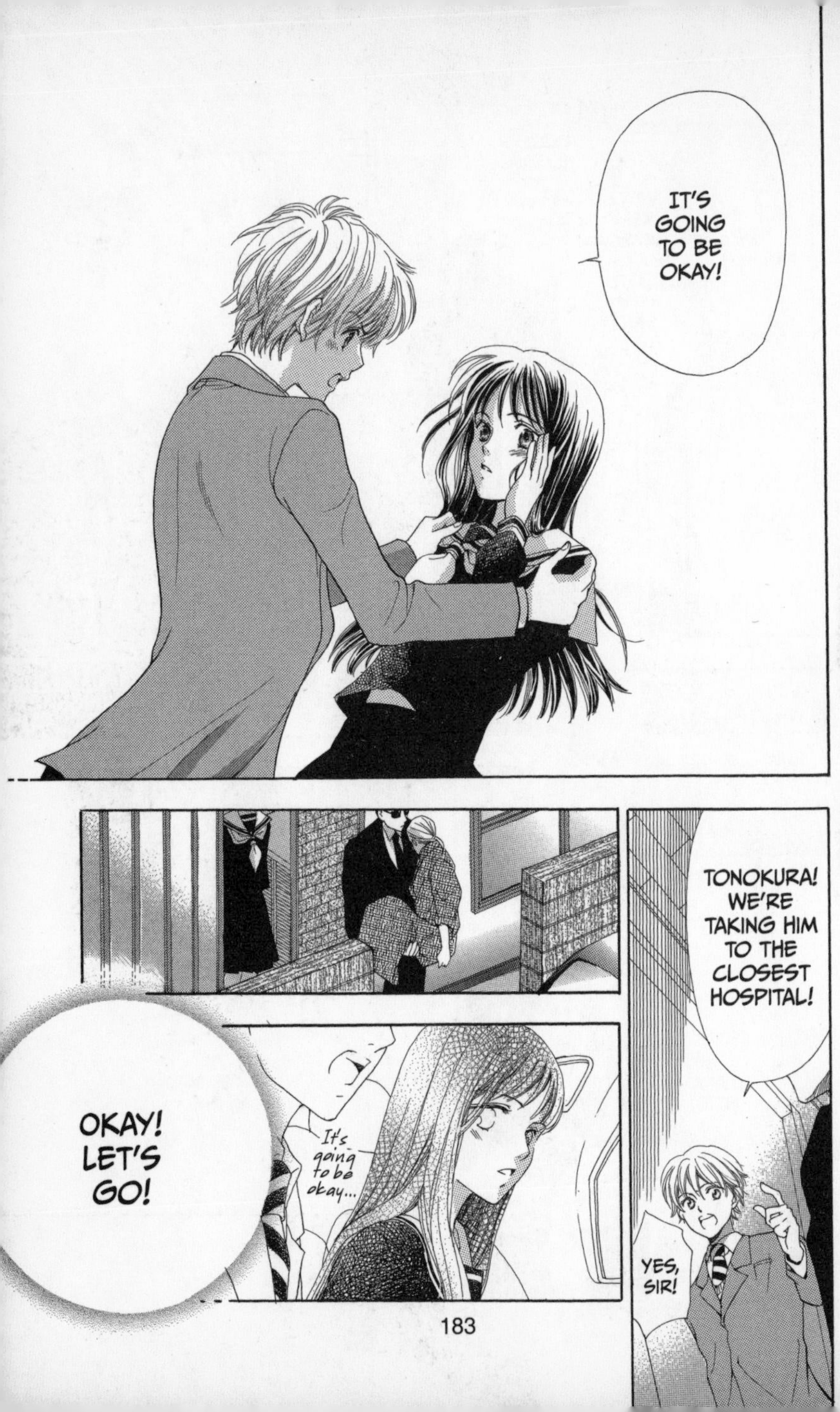
IT'S GOING TO BE OKAY!
TONOKURA! WE'RE TAKING HIM TO THE CLOSEST HOSPITAL!
YES, SIR!
OKAY! LET'S GO!
It's going to be okay...

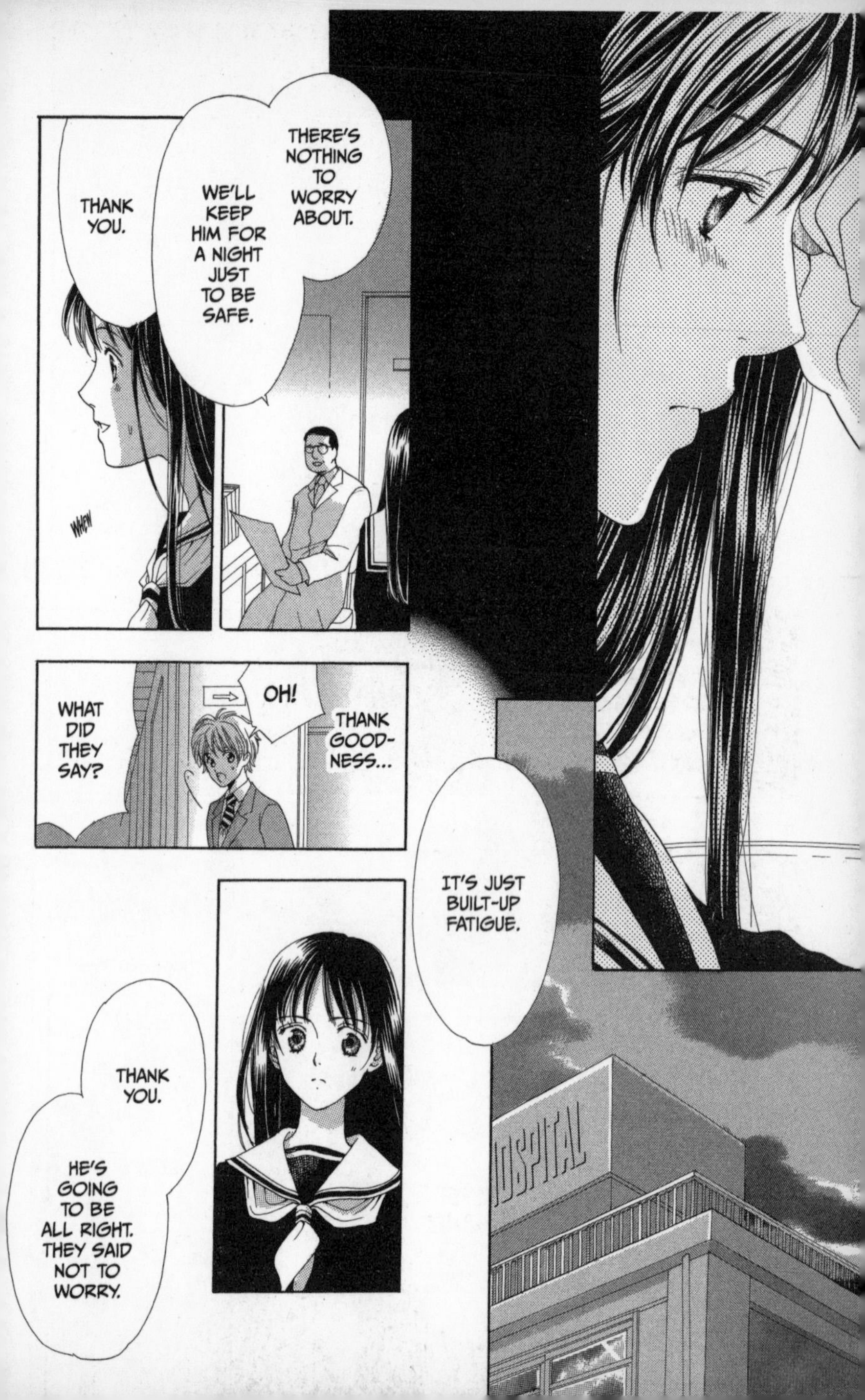
IT'S JUST BUILT-UP FATIGUE.
HOSPITAL
THERE'S NOTHING TO WORRY ABOUT.
WE'LL KEEP HIM FOR A NIGHT JUST TO BE SAFE.
THANK YOU.
WHEW
OH!
THANK GOODNESS...
WHAT DID THEY SAY?
THANK YOU.
HE'S GOING TO BE ALL RIGHT. THEY SAID NOT TO WORRY.

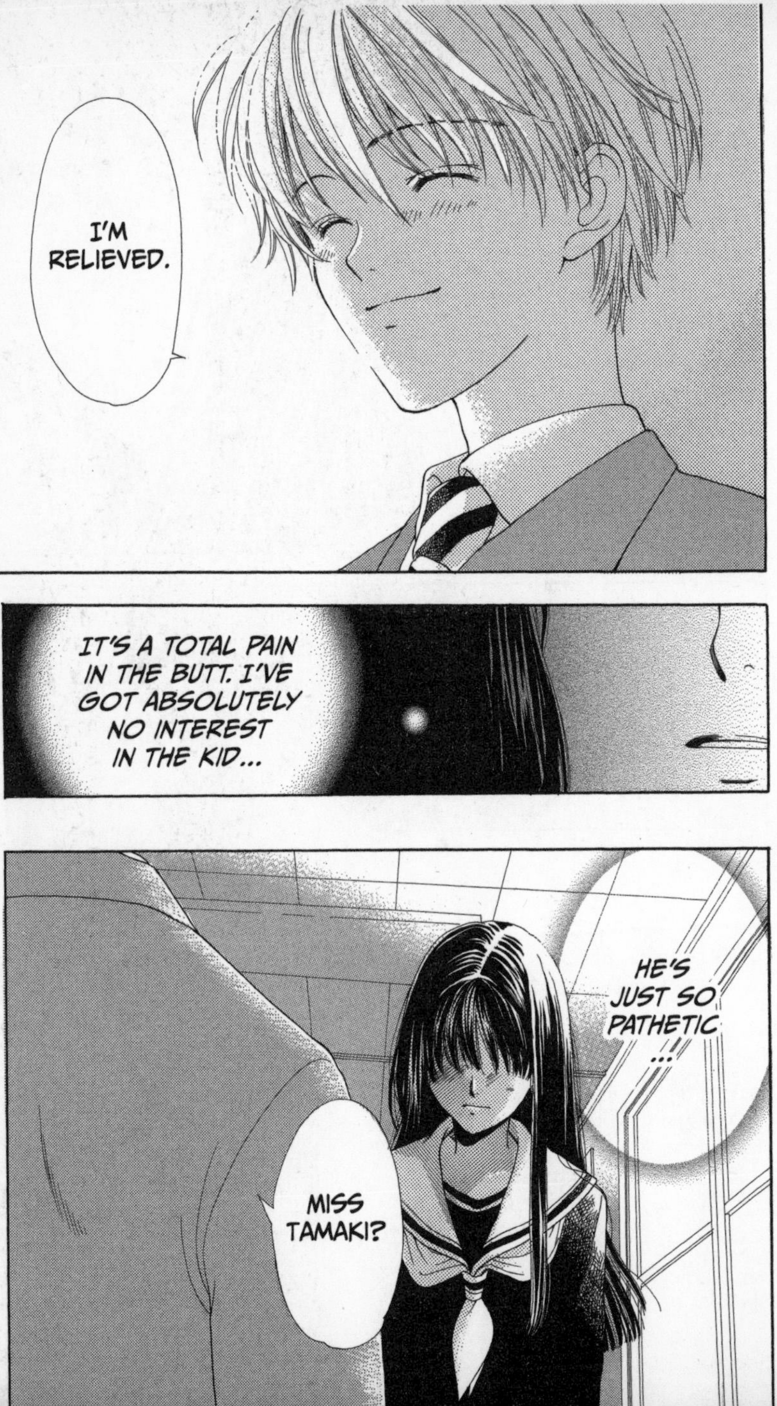
I'M RELIEVED.
IT'S A TOTAL PAIN IN THE BUTT. I'VE GOT ABSOLUTELY NO INTEREST IN THE KID...
HE'S JUST SO PATHETIC...
MISS TAMAKI?

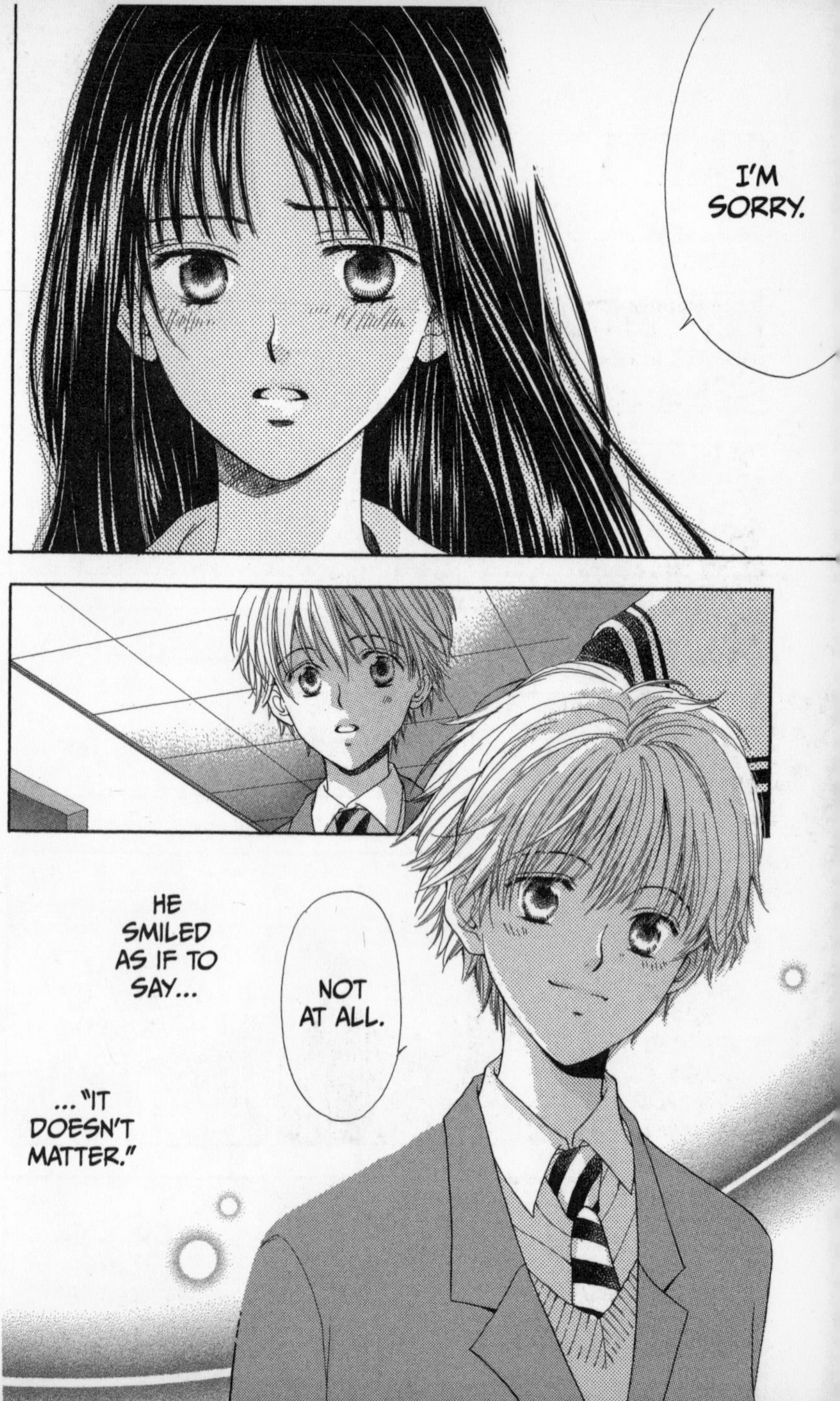
I'M SORRY.
NOT AT ALL.
HE SMILED AS IF TO SAY...
..."IT DOESN'T MATTER."

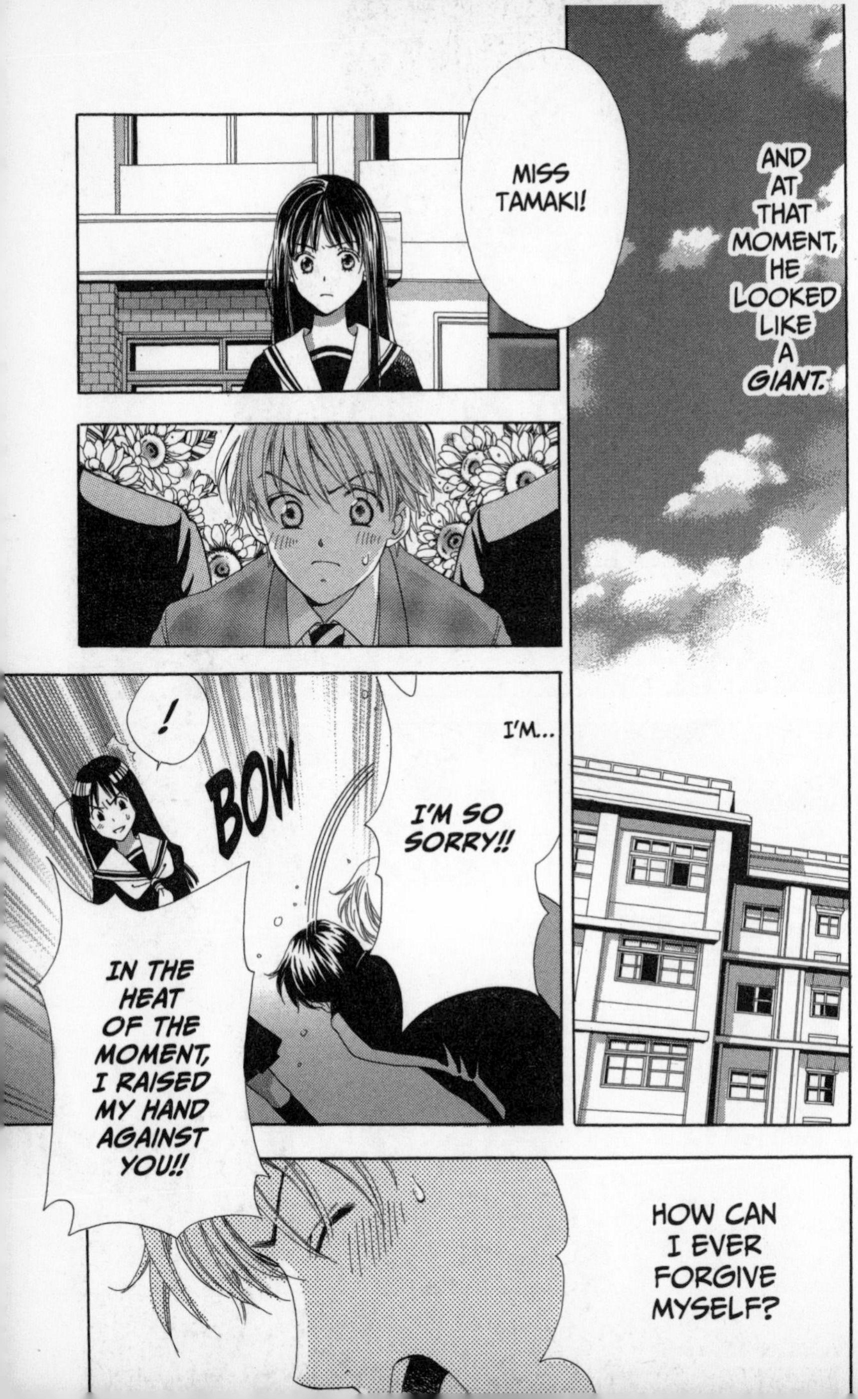
AND AT THAT MOMENT, HE LOOKED LIKE A GIANT.
MISS TAMAKI!
I'M...
!
BOW
I'M SO SORRY!!
IN THE HEAT OF THE MOMENT, I RAISED MY HAND AGAINST YOU!!
HOW CAN I EVER FORGIVE MYSELF?

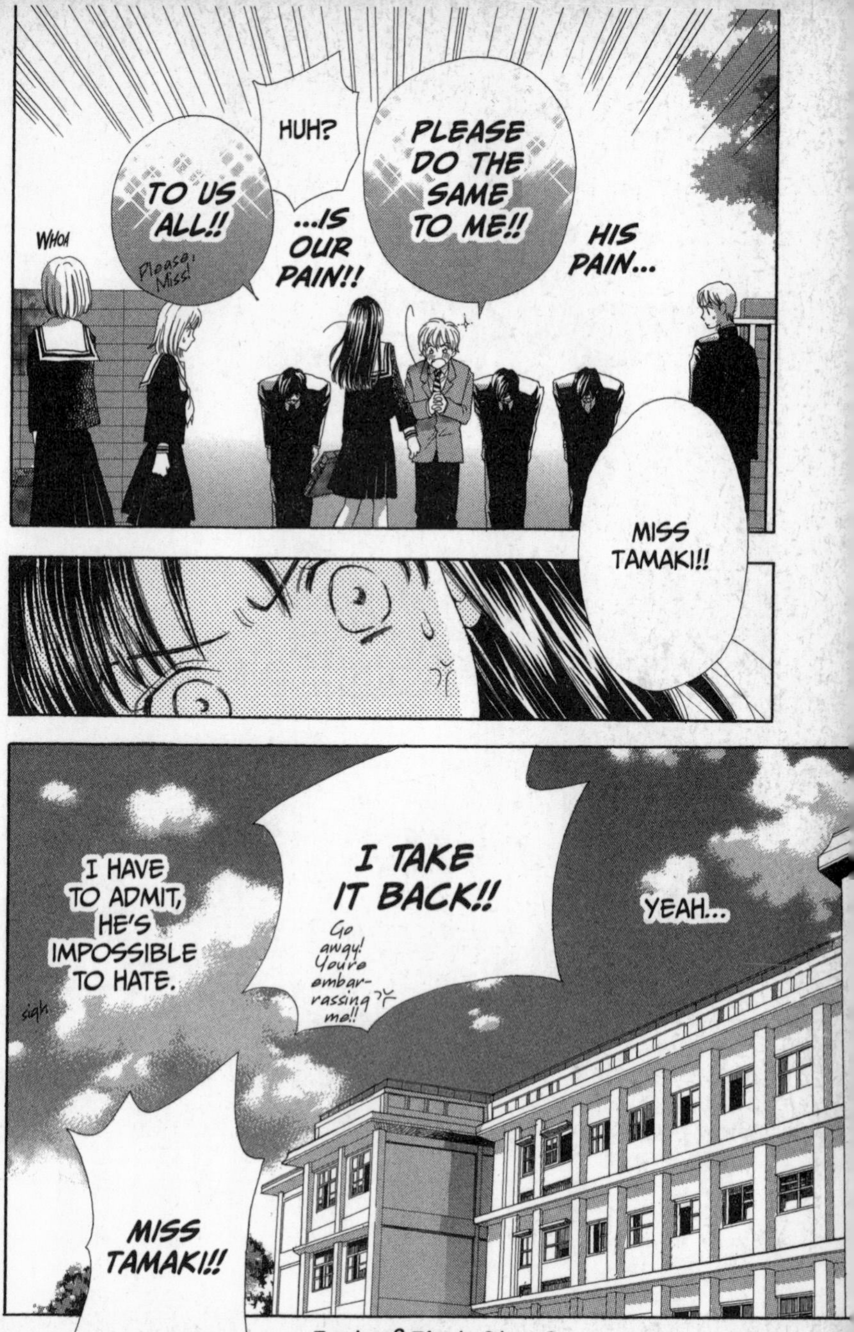
HIS PAIN...
PLEASE DO THE SAME TO ME!!
HUH?
...IS OUR PAIN!!
TO US ALL!!
Please, Miss!
WHOA
MISS TAMAKI!!
YEAH...
I TAKE IT BACK!!
Go away! You're embarrassing me!!
I HAVE TO ADMIT, HE'S IMPOSSIBLE TO HATE.
sigh
MISS TAMAKI!!

End of First Step?

## SPECIAL  THANKS

A.Kashima
A.Ogura
M.Shiino
M.Hiyama
N.Sato
W.Hibiki
Y.Uruno

One day in June, they were recording a scene from the La Corda anime at a studio in Ichigaya, so I went with my editor and publisher.

# LA CORDA
Notes on a Trip
Classical recording

Illustrations and script: Yuki Kure

Hee Hee

A sun umbrella, although it can be sort of embarrassing.

I think it looked like this...

The studio had a bunch of equipment. I had no idea what any of it did, but I liked that the producer's chair was a piano stool. ♡ The piano was a Steinway!

It's a treacherous schedule...

| Time | Character |
|------|-----------|
| 11 : 30 | Ryotaro |
| 12 : 0 | Ryotaro |
| 23 : 15 | Keiichi |
| 23 : 55 | Keiichi |

It's always permed.

I TRIED STRAIGHTENING MY HAIR TODAY.

Kahoko was played by an actual teenager.

Tee Hee

Kahoko's just filling in here. The real actress was much cuter!

WHENEVER I TRY TO PLAY WELL, I FUMBLE...

...AND WHEN I TRY TO FUMBLE, I PLAY EVERY NOTE.

All the performers were students and recent graduates from a music school. An impressive group!!! They even sort of looked like their characters! My first reaction was, "Can high school students really play this well?" (lol) My second reaction was that they were all BEA UTIFUL!!

Ouch...

So... So bright!!

Recording Kaho's not-so-good performances was extra difficult.

The muscle the pianist had right here was impressive! I wanted to touch it... (←What?)

Big hands and long fingers!

It was so much fun to see and hear. I had a wonderful time. Thank you so much for the precious memories! (The recording went past midnight, and the editing went to dawn...) The staff did such a great job!!

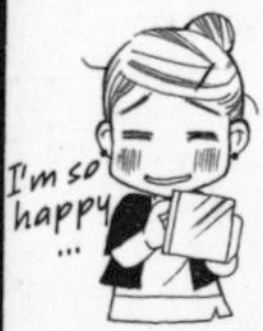
I'm so happy...

Mr. Muroya, who played Len, gave me a CD. The whole day was just wonderful. I got to chat with so many talented people! I can't wait to hear them in the anime!

Hello again. This is Yuki Kure.

I drew this when I visited a recording studio last summer, so it's a little out of date. It's the same thing that happened with one of the side notes in Volume Seven...

I don't think the anime series will be out by the time this volume is published, but I'd like to extend my gratitude to everybody who worked on it! There were so many experts from different fields working together, and it was truly a magical experience. I was even able to sit in on a rough recording! Thank you so much!

Again, I cut it close with the deadline and caused all kinds of people to run around like crazy! When I'd hear someone say, "This is my limit! I can't stay up any longer!" the stress of the business really hit home. (Sorry.) I'll change my ways, I swear...

To my publisher and everybody who showed up to help, to my family and my readers... Thank you so much. I'm very grateful.

Well, hope to see you in Volume 9!
Until then...

Yuki Kurie

# La Corda d'Oro End Notes

You can appreciate music just by listening to it, but knowing the story behind a piece can help enhance your enjoyment. In that spirit, here is background information about some of the topics mentioned in *La Corda d'Oro*. Enjoy!

**Page 25, panel 3: *Revolution* by Chopin**
Chopin's *Étude in C Minor*, Op. 10, No. 12, or the *Revolutionary Étude*, was written around the time of the November Uprising, a rebellion in Poland and Lithuania against Russian rule. Chopin supported the Polish rebellion but was too frail to fight; instead, he poured his revolutionary feelings into many of his compositions.

**Page 43, Author's Note: Meiji/Taisho era**
Traditionally, Japanese eras are divided by an emperor's reign. The Meiji era ran from 1868 to 1912; the Taisho era ran from 1912 to 1926. These eras were marked by a merging of traditional Japanese culture with modernization and Western ideas.

**Page 79, panel 6: Boccherini**
Luigi Boccherini (1743-1805) was an Italian cellist and composer with a genteel, classical style. He composed a massive amount of music but is best known for two pieces, his String Quintet in E and Cello Concerto in B Flat Major.

**Page 101, Author's Note: local sweets**
Sampling local delicacies is a big part of tourism in Japan, and many areas are associated with particular sweets. Ehime Prefecture, on the island of Shikoku, is known for its tarts, originally borrowed from Europe but now commonly made with Japanese ingredients like red bean paste or chestnut. *Uiro* are traditional sweets made from steamed rice flour and sugar. Takeda Shingen (1521-1573) is a famous medieval samurai.

**Page 133, Author's Note: mantis shrimp and sea cucumber**
Mantis shrimp are not true shrimp, but marine crustaceans of the order *Stomatopoda*. They can grow up to a foot long. In Japan, they're usually eaten boiled as sushi or sashimi. The sea cucumber, a marine echinoderm that resembles a spiky, leathery cucumber, is another intimidating Japanese delicacy.

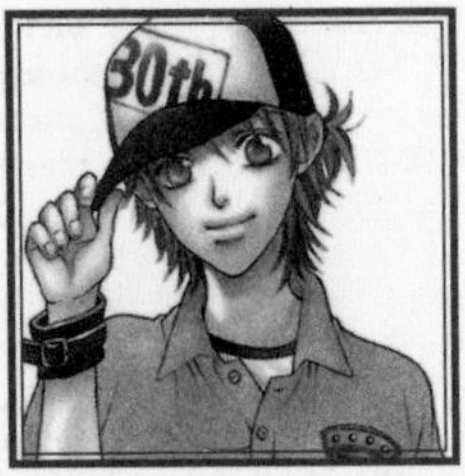
30th

Yuki Kure made her debut in 2000 with the story *Chijo yori Eien ni* (Forever from the Earth), published in monthly *LaLa* magazine. *La Corda d'Oro* is her first manga series published. Her hobbies are watching soccer games and collecting small goodies.

# LA CORDA D'ORO
## Vol. 8
### The Shojo Beat Manga Edition

## STORY AND ART BY
## YUKI KURE
### ORIGINAL CONCEPT BY
### RUBY PARTY

English Translation & Adaptation/Mai Ihara
Touch-up Art & Lettering/Gia Cam Luc
Cover Design/Yukiko Whitley
Interior Design/Izumi Evers
Editor/Shaenon K. Garrity

Editor in Chief, Books/Alvin Lu
Editor in Chief, Magazines/Marc Weidenbaum
VP of Publishing Licensing/Rika Inouye
VP of Sales/Gonzalo Ferreyra
Sr. VP of Marketing/Liza Coppola
Publisher/Hyoe Narita

Printed in Canada

Published by VIZ Media, LLC
P.O. Box 77010
San Francisco, CA 94107

Shojo Beat Manga Edition
10 9 8 7 6 5 4 3 2 1
First printing, July 2008

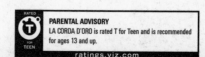

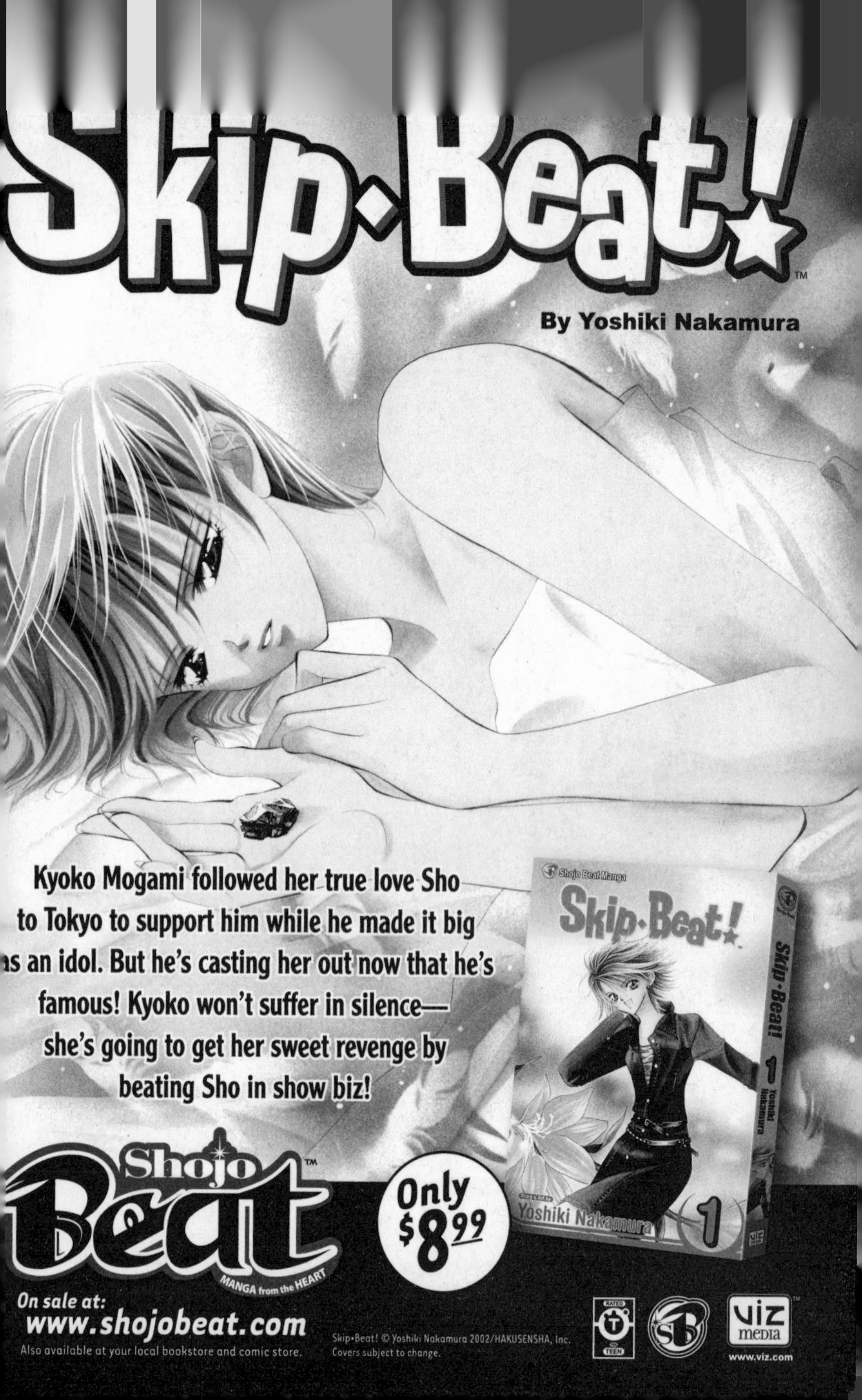
Skip·Beat!™
By Yoshiki Nakamura
Kyoko Mogami followed her true love Sho to Tokyo to support him while he made it big as an idol. But he's casting her out now that he's famous! Kyoko won't suffer in silence— she's going to get her sweet revenge by beating Sho in show biz!
Shojo Beat Manga
Skip·Beat!
Yoshiki Nakamura
1
Shojo Beat™
MANGA from the HEART
Only $8.99
On sale at:
www.shojobeat.com
Also available at your local bookstore and comic store.
Skip•Beat! © Yoshiki Nakamura 2002/HAKUSENSHA, Inc.
Covers subject to change.
RATED T TEEN
VIZ media
www.viz.com

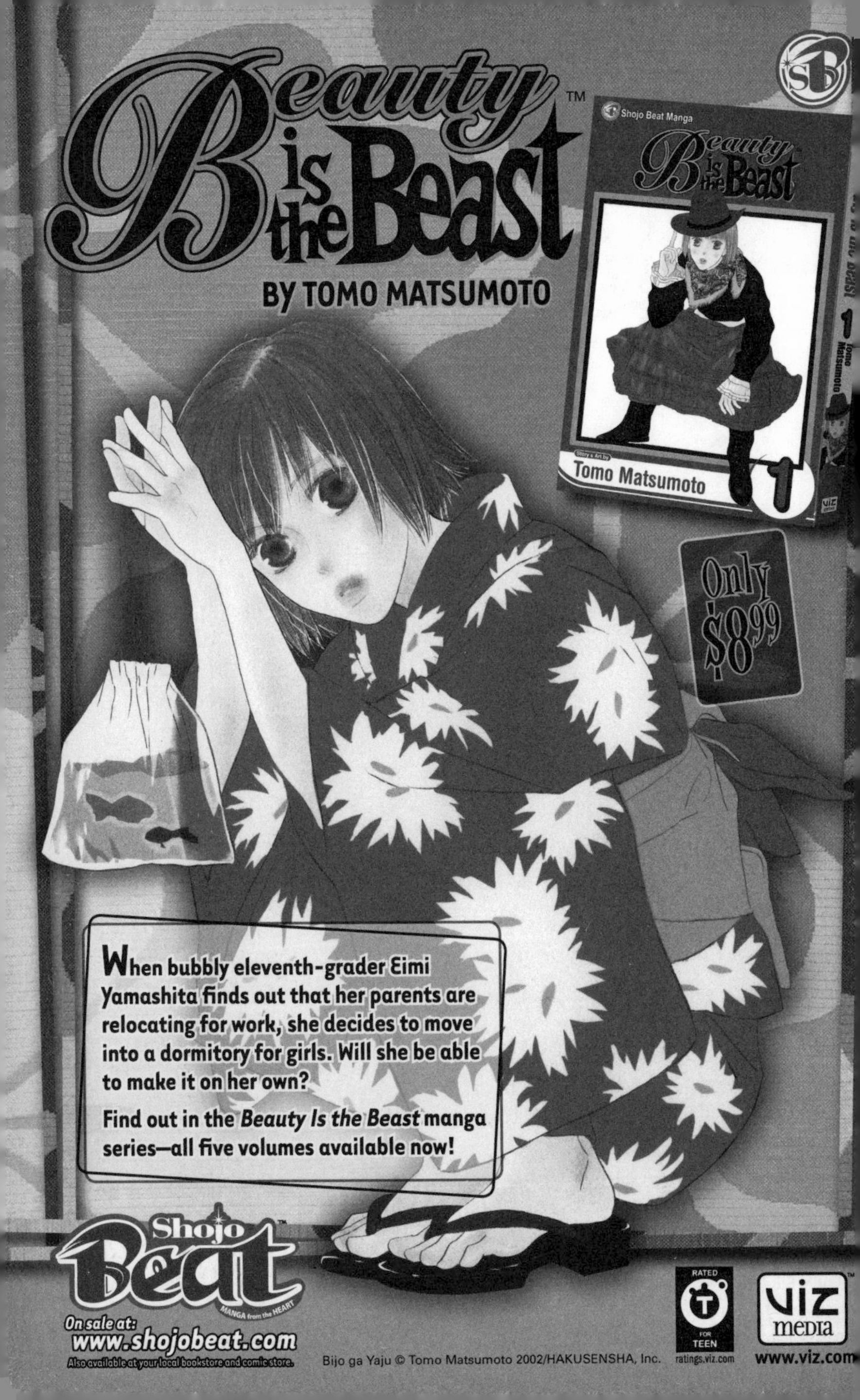
Beauty is the Beast™
BY TOMO MATSUMOTO
Shojo Beat Manga
Beauty is the Beast
Tomo Matsumoto
1
Only $8.99
When bubbly eleventh-grader Eimi Yamashita finds out that her parents are relocating for work, she decides to move into a dormitory for girls. Will she be able to make it on her own?
Find out in the *Beauty Is the Beast* manga series—all five volumes available now!
Shojo Beat™
MANGA from the HEART
On sale at:
www.shojobeat.com
Also available at your local bookstore and comic store.
Bijo ga Yaju © Tomo Matsumoto 2002/HAKUSENSHA, Inc.
RATED T FOR TEEN
ratings.viz.com
VIZ media
www.viz.com

## The Shojo Manga Authority

This monthly magazine is injected with the most **ADDICTIVE** shojo manga stories from Japan. PLUS, unique editorial coverage on the arts, music, culture, fashion, and much more!

Over **300 pages** per issue!

☑ **YES!** Please enter my one-year subscription (12 GIANT issues) to *Shojo Beat* at the LOW SUBSCRIPTION RATE of **$34.99!**

NAME

ADDRESS

CITY                          STATE      ZIP

E-MAIL ADDRESS                                          P7GNC1

☐ MY CHECK IS ENCLOSED (PAYABLE TO *Shojo Beat*)   ☐ BILL ME LATER

CREDIT CARD:    ☐ VISA   ☐ MASTERCARD

ACCOUNT #                              EXP. DATE

SIGNATURE

CLIP AND MAIL TO →

SHOJO BEAT
Subscriptions Service Dept.
P.O. Box 438
Mount Morris, IL 61054-0438

Canada price for 12 issues: $46.99 USD, including GST, HST and QST. US/CAN orders only. Allow 6-8 weeks for delivery. Must be 16 or older to redeem offer. By redeeming this offer I represent that I am 16 or older.

RATED
T+
FOR OLDER TEEN
ratings.viz.com

Vampire Knight © Matsuri Hino 2004/HAKUSENSHA, Inc. Nana Kitade © Sony Music Entertainment (Japan), Inc.
CRIMSON HERO © 2002 by Mitsuba Takanashi/SHUEISHA Inc.